# the
# Superintendent's
# FIELDBOOK
## second edition

# *the* Superintendent's FIELDBOOK

## *second edition*

*A Guide
for Leaders
of Learning*

**James Harvey**

**Nelda Cambron-McCabe**

**Luvern L. Cunningham**

**Robert H. Koff**

A Joint Publication

## CORWIN
A SAGE Company

FOR INFORMATION:

Corwin

A SAGE Company

2455 Teller Road

Thousand Oaks, California 91320

(800) 233-9936

www.corwin.com

SAGE Publications Ltd.

1 Oliver's Yard

55 City Road

London EC1Y 1SP

United Kingdom

SAGE Publications India Pvt. Ltd.

B 1/I 1 Mohan Cooperative Industrial Area

Mathura Road, New Delhi 110 044

India

SAGE Publications Asia-Pacific Pte. Ltd.

3 Church Street

#10-04 Samsung Hub

Singapore 049483

Acquisitions Editor:   Arnis Burvikovs

Associate Editor:   Desirée A. Bartlett

Editorial Assistants:   Lauren Schroeder and
Mayan White

Permissions Editor:   Jennifer Barron

Project Editor:   Veronica Stapleton Hooper

Copy Editor:   Pam Schroeder

Typesetter:   C&M Digitals (P) Ltd.

Proofreader:   Scott Oney

Indexer:   Molly Hall

Cover Designer:   Scott Van Atta

Copyright © 2013 by Corwin

Printed in the United States of America.

A catalog record of this book is available from the Library of Congress.

ISBN: 9781452217499

This book is printed on acid-free paper.

SFI
Certified Sourcing
www.sfiprogram.org
SFI-00453

16 17 10 9 8 7 6 5 4 3

# Contents

# *Preface to the Second Edition*

As a school leader, you have a lot to do and little time to spare. There's the governor's demand that you close the achievement gap. There's pressure to join Race to the Top (RTTT). And, of course, your board members often fall out among themselves or with you, while parents request expensive new programs that your taxpayers are often reluctant to support. You have a lot on your plate. Why should you spend any of your time on another book about school leadership? Because the world is changing. You won't be able to get by with yesterday's ideas. Many of the lessons in this book can make a difference in children's lives . . . and some of them may save your career. This orientation introduces you to how that world is changing and what it means for you and the schools you lead.

So, you're sitting at the school superintendent's desk, or you aspire to be behind it. Congratulations. It's a wonderful profession. Your career choice is a sign of your commitment to young people and your community. It's a good feeling, isn't it? Your family is proud of you. Your neighbors look up to you. But what are you going to do if any of the following scenarios unfolds?

- Directed by your board to bring student achievement up to national norms, you've created a national profile for your leadership. But the price has been high. Contention with principals and the teachers' union has alarmed and divided the board. And this morning, your finance director drops a bombshell. The district is facing an immediate $40 million budget hole, a consequence, apparently, of the new computer system's inability to work with the old financial program. Your job is on the line.

- Asked to make a presentation to the local business community about student achievement, you turn to your research director for data. What you learn is alarming. As you work through the numbers with her, it becomes apparent that respectable districtwide averages disguise an alarming achievement gap. The correlation between student performance and family income is almost perfect. You can bury this information in your presentation, but can you live with yourself?

• At a public meeting, a local activist stands up to harangue you. Research says the public is paying more for education and getting less, he reports. American standing on international assessments has fallen off the cliff. You and your buddies are putting the nation at risk. How do you respond?

• Your worst nightmare as an educator comes to life. In the middle of routine meetings one morning, you learn of a shooting at one of your elementary schools. Soon, it emerges that a deranged gunman with an assault rifle has murdered 20 six- and seven-year-olds, six staff members, and his mother before killing himself. How do you help heal this shattered community?

• The telephone rings as you return from lunch with the union president. It's the local reporter who's been questioning district spending on technology. Today, he has a new issue. Parents at one of your elementary schools are picketing the school about a library exhibit on the family. It seems the exhibit includes pictures of gay couples and their children. What do you say?

• Newly elected board members realize that an oversight on the previous board's part coupled with a new court ruling offers the board the opportunity to terminate your contract. Unceremoniously, you are deprived of your title and your office and find yourself assigned to an empty desk without a telephone, a computer, or any work. Several months later, you are informed that your services are no longer required in the district in any capacity. How do you protect yourself from that?

There's nothing theoretical about any of these scenarios. Working with more than 300 superintendents in the past 20 years, the authors of this volume have encountered each of them. And many of these developments cost someone a job. We could cite dozens of similar examples. The truth is that the high-minded pursuit of what's best for children often runs into the rough realities of budget catastrophes, interest-group politics, human folly, and the residue and by-products of the nation's racial past. School superintendents have to be prepared to confront and deal with these challenges.

That's why this book is important. As a potential or current superintendent, you must understand that what you do not know can kill you professionally. The world is changing. Your world as an educator is changing with it. Where once school superintendents could be content to define themselves as managers, today, they must understand that they are leaders of learning who are simultaneously public figures. This *Fieldbook* can help you cope with these challenges. It is called a *fieldbook* because it draws on the stories and accumulated wisdom and experience of more than 300 school leaders—members of either the National Superintendents Roundtable or the Danforth Foundation's Forum for the American School

Superintendent—as they struggled with the problems of leading today's schools. (See Appendices B and C for list of these leaders.)

## WHAT'S DIFFERENT ABOUT THE SECOND EDITION?

Whenever authors ask readers to deal with a second edition of a book, they have an obligation to explain what's different in the new volume. We want to point to several things. First, the school policy and political environment has changed with warp speed since our first edition went to press in 2004. Even then, it was clear that accountability and assessment were becoming new hallmarks of American education, but these developments have since accelerated at a jaw-dropping rate. Today, in addition to a transformed policy environment, you face new pressures for privatization and the challenges of dealing with the wild card of technology.

Second, this volume adds the experience of 100 school leaders active in the superintendency in the last five years to the lessons learned from 200 superintendents who contributed to the first volume.

Readers familiar with the first volume will also find that the book has been dramatically changed to reflect the latest thinking in learning and assessment, including the emerging debate about performance-based teacher compensation.

All told, readers will find more than 100 pages of new and reshaped material in this second edition of the *Fieldbook,* most developed by members of the National Superintendents Roundtable, and the elimination or reduction of a comparable amount of other material from the original.

Over some 20 years, the 300 superintendents who helped us develop this *Fieldbook* and its predecessor worked extremely hard. They examined the latest research on brain development and tried to understand how it applies to early learning and school programs. They worried about how to respond to public demands for higher standards and new assessments. They fretted about how to defend a system in which they believed while the broader environment criticized it. They explored district governance with their boards and unions. And they wrestled with the challenges of race and class in the United States, the great fault lines in our national life. Although four of us developed this book, in a very real sense, these superintendents wrote it. You'll find their stories and the lessons of their experience here.

## WHO THIS BOOK IS FOR

We developed *The Superintendent's Fieldbook: A Guide for Leaders of Learning* with several audiences in mind:

- School superintendents in districts of all kinds (urban, rural, and suburban) who want to ratchet up their effectiveness will find this text a valuable resource. If you're a superintendent, this is the book you need as you struggle with the demanding leadership responsibilities of your position. Here, you'll learn how to work with your board, deal with your union, and engage with your public in your high-profile job. We've also got advice on how to craft a newsworthy statement, tackle the media interview, and respond to critics of American public schools.

• Teachers, administrators, and deputy superintendents who are interested in moving into the superintendent's chair will gain a sense of the job's challenges. Experience is a great teacher. One definition of experience is *learning by making mistakes*. Most of the school leadership mistakes that can be made have been made by the authors and contributors to this volume. Learn from them without the pain. Among other things, here you'll learn how to land that first job, craft an entry plan, and work with principals and teachers to advance student learning.

• Principals interested in enhancing their own leadership will find a lot to use in this *Fieldbook*. Here, you can explore school-level issues of leadership, public engagement, collaboration, and how to create better learning environments.

• School board members, union leaders, and superintendents worried about the sheer amount of public criticism schools absorb can use this volume to move beyond today's sterile dialogue about governance. Some of what you find here may call into question how your district functions, but the exercises will offer positive ways to move forward. You'll also find in this book the data you need to respond to attacks on public education.

• Schools and colleges of education preparing potential administrators will find this a useful text. We were encouraged by the many adoptions of the first edition of this book for graduate courses and programs. Each of the authors of this volume is or has been affiliated with a major university, and we understand the importance of improving professional preparation. This *Superintendent's Fieldbook* can support preparation programs by buttressing theory with practical insights and hands-on experience.

• Government officials and philanthropists interested in improving pre- and in-service professional administrator development can use this book as a guide. Too frequently, government and private funders find themselves trying to improve professional development without knowing exactly what to do. This volume provides some insights.

• We would hope too that the *Fieldbook* can offer philanthropists and federal and state government leaders keener insights into the challenges of managing large-scale change at the local level. There are many ways to try to improve school performance. Based on our investigations at home and overseas, it seems that, although accountability and competition are the tools of choice in the United States and England, the Chinese and French rely more on directives from on high, while Finns describe their approach as "gentle steering based on the principle of trust." While the Finnish model cannot be imported wholesale to the United States, there seems to be little doubt it has produced better results and attracted very talented people into the profession.

Although developed, in brief, for current and aspiring school superintendents, this *Fieldbook* has much to offer a variety of school and public leaders and institutions of higher education.

## OVERVIEW

So, what is essential in a school leader? What should a fieldbook addressed to leaders incorporate? Do you need to be able to teach everything from the alphabet to calculus, trigonometry, and quantum physics? What about the budget? Perhaps you need to know how to design the spreadsheet that develops it. How about technology? Surely, that's important in a new century. Should you be double-checking building wiring schematics?

Of course, you shouldn't be doing any of those things. There aren't enough hours in the day, and you probably couldn't do most of them anyway. You don't have to actually do them, but you do have to see that each is done with a degree of excellence. Those tasks, however difficult, define the superintendency of the previous century; this *Fieldbook* helps you look ahead to the challenges of the new millennium.

*The Superintendent's Fieldbook* is divided into 10 major parts. These parts are laid out as follows:

**Part I. *Orientation*.** This section is made up of an overview of how demands on school leaders are changing today and an introduction to what we call the *commonplaces* of leadership.

The overview of emerging demands touches on the changing political environment, choice, and competition in Pre-K–12 education and the challenges and promise of technology. It includes two thoughtful essays from national leaders on their decades of work shaping national policy for schools. It also features a provocative essay by a Roundtable superintendent on what changes in the larger world mean for school superintendents.

The *Fieldbook* itself is organized around seven "commonplaces" outlined in brief here and discussed more fully below. The "commonplaces" begin with the major elements that you need to worry about in terms of leading your organization: leadership, governance, learning and assessment, race and class in our schools, the imperative to develop school principals, collaboration with other agencies of government, and engaging your community and its citizens. The remaining parts of the *Fieldbook* develop each of these "commonplaces" in turn. The final section asks what all of this means, responds to public education's critics, and draws some lessons from education abroad.

**Part II.** *Leading Your Schools.* Here, you'll learn how to think about your organization and how to distinguish between merely technical problems and adaptive challenges requiring deep-rooted institutional change. It's in this part that we introduce you to one of the central framing ideas of this *Fieldbook,* the idea of *images of organization.* We have also added new material from leadership experts that rounds out our understanding of what organizational leadership means and what defines an effective leader in any organizational context.

**Part III.** *Coping With Governance Challenges.* Do the ins-and-outs and headaches of dealing with school boards and unions bedevil you? Here, you can find some answers. This part suggests that you need to understand not only how you think about your organization but also how your board and union members think about it as well. After all, you have your images; they have theirs. And in two highly personal essays, two Roundtable superintendents reflect on the importance of developing an entry-level plan when approaching a new position and on the challenges and rewards of leading a small district with a small staff.

**Part IV.** *Learning and Assessment.* With new demands for accountability and legislation such as No Child Left Behind (NCLB) and RTTT, it's a brave new world out there for school leaders. This part helps you make sense out of accountability, value-added assessment, and performance-based compensation.

**Part V.** *Addressing Race and Class.* These are the great fault lines in American life. They can also be a "third rail" that school leaders touch at their peril. Part V provides some ideas about how to approach this third rail, how to begin to close the achievement gap, and how to think about what is often a difficult set of challenges: the combination of race, class, and poverty.

**Part VI.** *Developing Your Principals.* It's a truism that schools are only as good as their principals. Here, you'll find some exciting ideas about how to turn principals from building managers into leaders of learning. This section draws heavily on 10 years of recent research from the Wallace Foundation about developing effective school leaders.

**Part VII.** *Collaborating With Your Allies.* Think you can do it all by yourself? Think again. Who are your allies? What about the child protective services system? The employment security and public assistance offices? Medicaid and well-baby screening? This section touches on the many agencies concerned with child welfare in the United States and suggests some ways you can partner with them, particularly around early child care and learning.

Part VIII. *Engaging Your Community*. You don't want to be the leader who turns around and finds no one behind her. Nor do you want to be the poor guy scurrying to get in front of the parade. School leaders, like most public officials, once thought of public engagement as public relations. It was enough to persuade the public to go along with the established policy. That no longer works. Today's public insists on helping develop that policy. This part suggests a new concept of *public engagement*, one that encourages citizens to help create a shared vision of the future.

Part IX. *So, What Does All This Mean?* Here, the *Fieldbook* pulls it all together, linking the "commonplaces" to theories of organizational leadership to show how the combination can encourage certain kinds of behavior within your district. Are you curious about why your last district insisted on the party line while your new district promotes a lot of open discussion? Did your last district empower teachers and encourage a thousand flowers to bloom, while your new one specifies curriculum and assessment techniques in exquisite detail? The explanation probably lies in the different images that these districts hold of themselves. No matter what kind of school system you lead, or aspire to lead, you'll find it here. This section also helps you deal with the widespread criticism of American public education and adds relevant new research from the University of Chicago based on 30 years of examining school reform in the Windy City. One of the central findings of this research emphasizes the importance of social capital and community support.

*Appendices*. The final part is made up of appendices, primarily brief descriptions of the contributors to this volume and descriptions of the Danforth Forum and the National Superintendents Roundtable.

Within each of these major sections, you will find discussions of what these issues involve along with vignettes describing what they look like on the ground. The districts discussed cover densely populated urban areas on the East and West Coasts, sparsely populated local education agencies in the Southern and Plains states, and everything in between. You'll also find something else here in each major section: tools you can use in your district to get a better handle on these challenges. Finally, each part concludes with questions for reflective practice, a series of provocative questions designed to encourage you and your colleagues to think deeply about what you are doing.

## HOW TO USE THE *FIELDBOOK*

If you're like most of us in education, you will be inclined to think you should start *The Superintendent's Fieldbook* on page one and continue until you reach the end. If you want to do that, by all means, be our guest, but that's not how most people use it. A fieldbook is more like a reference manual than a textbook. Our inspiration came from Peter Senge's pioneering "fifth discipline" work and the fieldbooks associated with it. A fieldbook is something you should use as you need it. You will probably find that dipping in and out of the material as your needs change is the most profitable use of this *Fieldbook.*

Some morning, your challenge may be explaining student test results at a local community forum. You're likely to want to look at Part IV: Learning and Assessment while ignoring the rest. The following week, you may find yourself with a major public relations crisis on your hands. Here, you're likely to find Parts II: Leading Your Schools and VIII: Engaging Your Community more immediately useful.

You may find the *Fieldbook* useful as a guide to a series of seminars you might want to offer in your district. It benefits you little to possess a fine theoretical understanding of governance and organizational images if your board, administrators, or teachers don't know what you're talking about. The *Fieldbook* and the exercises incorporated into it can help you develop the leadership team with which you work.

# *Acknowledgments*

The four of us have many people we want to thank. Of course, we appreciate Corwin for its foresight in agreeing to publish this fieldbook when it was little more than a concept in our minds and then reissuing this second edition with new material. We are especially grateful to Arnis Burvikovs, acquisitions editor, for leading us through the process, to Lauren Schroeder for her great care with administrative matters, to Pam Schroeder for her tireless editing, and to Scott Van Atta for his very handsome cover design. And we owe a great debt of gratitude to Veronica Stapleton Hooper, books project editor for SAGE Publications, for leading us patiently through the intricacies of turning a cumbersome manuscript into a beautiful book.

We also want to acknowledge the many individuals who developed papers and vignettes for the *Fieldbook*. Authors are identified at the beginning of their contributions and are listed with their affiliations in Appendix D. Throughout the text, you will find artwork that illustrates our ideas, including a dynamic jigsaw triangle outlining the seven "commonplaces" of school reform and how they fit together. The triangle recurs as an icon throughout the text to help orient you to where we are in discussing the "commonplaces." We thank illustrator Greg LaFever of Oxford, Ohio, for this artwork. His talent and skill helped bring our ideas to life.

Above all, we want to thank the 300+ superintendents with whom we have worked for the past 20 years as members of either the Forum for the American School Superintendent or the National Superintendents Roundtable. They improved our understanding of life on the front lines in many, many ways. Some succeeded in what they were trying to do; some did not. We learned from them all. These superintendents were tireless public servants working year after year, often thanklessly, to improve the quality of life for the children and families in their communities. This *Fieldbook* is dedicated to them.

# *About the Authors*

 **James Harvey**, Executive Director of the National Superintendents Roundtable, was a member of the Danforth Forum's advisory board. Earlier in his career, he served in the Carter administration and was on the staff of the Education and Labor Committee of the U.S. House of Representatives. He helped write *A Nation at Risk* (1983) and coauthored *A Legacy of Learning* with David Kearns, former CEO of the Xerox Corporation (2000).

 **Nelda Cambron-McCabe** is a professor in the Department of Educational Leadership, Miami University, Ohio. She was an advisory board member and a coordinator of both the Danforth Foundation's Forum for the American School Superintendent and the National Superintendents Roundtable. The seventh edition of *Public School Law: Teachers' and Students' Rights*, which she coauthored, was published in 2013. She is also a coauthor of Peter Senge's *Schools That Learn* (2nd ed., 2012).

 **Luvern L. Cunningham**, Ed.D. from the University of Oregon, has served in administrative and teaching roles from K–12 through graduate school for more than four decades. A member of the advisory boards of both the Danforth Forum and the Superintendents Roundtable, his specialties are educational leadership, the school superintendency, educational governance, interinstitutional collaboration, and interprofessional education

and practice. He has served in professorships at the University of Chicago, the University of Minnesota, and Ohio State University. For several years, he served as Dean of the College of Education, Ohio State University.

 **Robert H. Koff** directed the Center for Advanced Learning at Washington University, St. Louis, and now serves on the faculty. He previously served as Senior Vice President of the Danforth Foundation, as Dean of the School of Education, State University of New York at Albany, and as a professor of education at Stanford University. He served on a number of state and national advisory bodies at the invitations of New York Governor Mario Cuomo and President Carter and provided editorial advice to journals such as the *Journal of Educational Psychology*.

# PAᴋ

# *Orientatio.*

## A. INTRODUCTION: LEADING LEARNING IN NEW TIMES

*It's been hard to turn anywhere in recent years without hearing about American schools and their problems. Presidents and members of Congress scrutinize them. Governors and legislators develop plans to improve them. Business leaders complain about them. Blue-ribbon commissions issue proclamations about them. And parents and other citizens worry about them. The energy behind school reform in recent decades is unprecedented in its depth, scope, intensity, and duration.*

James Harvey

Nelda Cambron-McCabe

If you get nothing else from this book, understand this: Your world as an educator has changed. It will never again be the same. What does it mean to lead schools in which the majority of students are children of color, while the majority of teachers are white? How do you lead when citizens and local officials insist you do more with less and when national policies encourage private consumption at the expense of public investment?

Parallels to the current ferment in education can be found in few periods of our national history. The late 19th century, when Horace Mann and his colleagues invented the idea of public schools, comes to mind. A few years in the 1960s, as President Lyndon B. Johnson struggled to create the Great Society, might qualify.

For sheer intensity and sustained interest in schools, however, the last three decades are nearly without equal. In 1983, the National Commission on Excellence in Education produced *A Nation at Risk*, with its stern warning of "a rising tide of mediocrity" threatening the American future.

By 1989, President George H. W. Bush had helped develop six National Educational Goals. President Bill Clinton advanced Goals 2000. Throughout the 1990s, states struggled to develop "aligned" educational systems, in which curriculum, assessment, and teacher training would be lined up with state standards. In 2002, the No Child Left Behind (NCLB) legislation advanced by President George W. Bush promised to close the achievement gap by increasing accountability and opening public schools to competition from private tutors and charter schools. The provisions of NCLB became increasingly impractical. And, just as the national economy weakened and 85 percent or more of local school districts faced budget shortfalls in 2010, President Barack Obama and Secretary of Education Arne Duncan promoted a Race to the Top (RTTT) agenda designed around increased accountability and the closing and reopening of schools with new principals and reconfigured teaching staffs.

Meanwhile, by 2011 and 2012, educators (especially those in unions) found themselves criticized and under attack in state capitols in places as diverse as Florida, New Jersey, Indiana, and Wisconsin. They faced new state legislation calling for a redefinition of collective bargaining, the introduction of competition into the educational system via charters and vouchers, and performance-based compensation for teachers. The fact is that you find yourself juggling difficult challenges, while the profession of which you are so proud is asked to justify itself. Recent presidential administrations have put a public priority on education as an issue of national importance in a way that rarely, if ever, has been seen before in the United States. Your daily work has become part of presidential campaigns and international discussions—an exciting if intimidating prospect.

These developments have taken place against a backdrop of dramatic demographic change in American life. Minority enrollment swelled from 35 percent of K–12 students in 1995 (15.7 million students) to 46 percent in 2009 (22.3 million students). In most of the nation's major urban areas, minority students make up a majority of public school enrollment. And the face of minority America is changing. When President Johnson set out to create the Great Society, the term *minority* primarily referred to African Americans. As the nation enters fully into the 21st century, however, Hispanic and Latino Americans make up the largest minority population in the United States. Meanwhile, the number and proportion of Asian Americans is increasing rapidly.

Three decades of demographic change and intense focus on schools promise to transform how Americans define public education. These developments present you, as a school superintendent, with formidable leadership challenges. You can't afford to take them lightly. Troubled? Don't be. As one former superintendent put it, "Leaders make their own good days." Franklin D. Roosevelt, said this superintendent, never "had a good day." Laid low by polio as a young man, President Roosevelt took office during the Great Depression and was then forced to lead the nation in a global war involving unprecedented carnage and loss of life around the world. He died before that war ended. Yet, Roosevelt is universally remembered as the supreme optimist, the Happy Warrior. As a leader, you'll have to make your own good days.

As if the difficulties of dealing with a climate of public skepticism and changing demographics were not sufficient, you may be expected to respond with a financial hand tied behind your back. The 1990s and early years of the 21st century were a bit of an anomaly for public finance. A burgeoning economy and an ebullient stock market promised rivers of cash for public services, including education. Unhappily, that period has ended. The new normal for public services calls for doing more with less for the foreseeable future. Aren't you glad you got into this line of work?

But the effort to improve schools has been dramatically reshaped in recent years. Title I of the Elementary and Secondary Education Act, enacted in 1965 under President Lyndon Johnson, focused on schools in the hope that they could repair the damage low-income children experienced in the larger society. Whether the phrase *compensatory education* was demeaning or justified, the legislation clearly contemplated a benign educational system that could begin to address the educational correlates of poverty.

Its successor, NCLB, and perhaps even more the RTTT program, have reversed that logic. Today, many policy makers consider public schools not as benign engines acting to ameliorate the challenges of childhood poverty but as the transmissions conveying poverty from one generation to the next. The governor of New York, for example, argued that far from being the great equalizer, the "public school system . . . may now be the great discriminator." In this emerging conversation, childhood poverty and its fellow travelers—gangs, neighborhood violence, unstable families, poor health care, and unemployment—instead of being understood as formidable challenges walking through the school door are almost entirely ignored. The emphasis is on technocratic solutions (test-based accountability, scripted learning, competition and choice, and metrics governing the employment of principals and teachers) applied to all schools as though the educational issues facing teachers and administrators in rural, southwest Wisconsin or suburban Scarsdale, New York, differ little from each other or from those facing educators in inner-city New York, Philadelphia, or Oakland.

This first section of the *Fieldbook* orients you around the changing nature of the education discussion in the United States in the last half century, what it means for school superintendents, and what we term the *commonplaces* of school leadership—governance, learning and assessment, race and class, and the like. The remainder of the *Fieldbook* elaborates on these "commonplaces."

# B. FIFTY YEARS OF SCHOOL REFORM

*Readers of the daily newspaper might be forgiven for concluding that the United States just recently realized its schools are in crisis. But, in fact, for at least 50 years, public leaders have worried about American schools and established policies to try to improve them. Here, three authors provide a primer on the history of school reform and what it means for school administrators.*

## 1. Why Have We Fallen Short, and Where Do We Go From Here?

*For 44 years, Jack Jennings helped define national policy in education as chief counsel to an education subcommittee and to the full Committee on Education and Labor in the U.S. House of Representatives and as founder, president, and CEO of the Center on Education Policy (CEP), a highly regarded national think tank helping Americans understand the role of public education in a democracy. On his retirement from CEP, George Washington University published his reflection on the accomplishments and failures of 50 years of school reform. In it, he called for a new commitment that would replace another 50 years of talking about how to improve American schools with the establishment of the right to a high-quality education through high school as an enforceable civil right.*

### Jack Jennings

I believe that American school reform has not been bold enough or comprehensive enough to substantially improve public education. Although our schools are doing a better job than in years past of educating an increasingly diverse student body, we haven't done well enough.

President Obama summed up the situation succinctly in his 2011 State of the Union address:

> Over the next 10 years, nearly half of all new jobs will require education that goes beyond a high school education. And yet, as many as a quarter of our students aren't even finishing high school. The quality of our math and science education lags behind many other nations. America has fallen to ninth in the proportion of young people with a college degree. And so the question is whether all of us—as citizens, and as parents—are willing to do what's necessary to give every child a chance to succeed.

Why have our efforts fallen short? Three major movements aimed at promoting equity, increasing school choice, and using academic standards to leverage improvement have dominated the U.S. school reform movement over the past 50 years. While all three have changed schooling in notable ways, none has brought about the needed level of general improvements because they mostly sought to improve education from the outside rather than the inside.

*Equity-Based Reform*

In the 1960s and 1970s, the federal government enacted a variety of programs and policies to improve educational equity for minority children, poor children, children with disabilities, children with limited English proficiency, and women and girls. The federal government stepped in because local school districts and state governments were not providing these students with equality of opportunity.

This movement took shape in the 1960s when the dominant domestic policy issues were expanding civil rights for African Americans and reducing poverty. The Civil Rights Act in 1964 marked a breakthrough by not only eliminating officially sanctioned race-based discrimination, including separate school systems for white and black students in southern states, but also opening the door to remedies for past discrimination.

The Elementary and Secondary Education Act (ESEA) of 1965 instituted another tool for equity-based education reform—the use of separate, or *categorical*, aid programs to provide extra educational services for specific groups of students at risk of educational problems. Title I of this act introduced a flagship program to improve education for children from low-income families, and this was followed in subsequent years by other smaller programs focusing on the needs of additional groups of students.

Another major law, enacted in 1975 to ensure a free, appropriate public education for children with disabilities, blended civil rights protections for these children with categorical federal aid for their education. Unlike Title I and other categorical programs, this statute, later renamed the Individuals with Disabilities Education Act (IDEA), incorporated strong procedural rights and the authority for parents to sue in court if their children did not receive services guaranteed under the law. Also, unlike other categorical programs, IDEA obligated school districts to pay for the range of services agreed to in a student's individual education plan, regardless of the level of federal and state funding earmarked for the education of children with disabilities.

Title IX of the Education Amendments of 1972 and the U.S. Supreme Court's 1974 *Lau v. Nichols* decision interpreting Title VI of the Civil Rights Act of 1964 also heavily shaped the civil rights component of education law. Title IX forbids recipients of federal aid from discriminating against girls and women. The Supreme Court in the *Lau* decision ruled that children must be given a meaningful education regardless of their language background.

In sum, the equity programs of the 1960s and 1970s improved education for many students, especially when those efforts were backed up by  civil rights guarantees. But they had two major shortcomings. First, their impact was constrained because they became separate, add-on services funded with limited federal aid and placed on top of inequitably distributed state and local funding. Second, by their very nature, categorical funding and individual guarantees of civil rights were not designed to improve the broader educational system.

*School Choice*

The choice movement, the second major school reform, is based on the premise that parents ought to choose, at public expense, the school their child attends. School choice can take many forms, including publicly funded vouchers for private school tuition, charter schools, tax credits to pay for private school tuition, and public school choice programs. The first form is the most controversial.

Educational choice has also expanded through the growth of charter schools, which exhibit aspects of both public and private education. Charter schools are public because they are generally created, or *chartered*, by a governmental agency and rely on public funds for their operation. They must also follow certain legal requirements, such as testing their students under NCLB requirements and not teaching religion. They are similar to private schools in that they may be free from requirements placed on public schools in areas such as choosing their student bodies and employing nonunion teachers. They are also mostly controlled by boards that are not publicly elected and can be managed by profit-making companies as well as nonprofit entities.

For those who favor charters because they believe that these policies will provide a better education for children than regular public schools, the facts are discouraging. Only 17 percent of charter schools produced higher test scores than comparable public schools, according to a comprehensive national review of such schools. Moreover, 37 percent of charters produced lower scores than public schools, and the remainder showed no difference from regular public schools.

> For a critique of charter and privatization proposals, see Fabricant, M., & Fine, M. (2012). *Charter schools and the corporate makeover of public education: What's at stake?* New York: Teachers College Press.

Regarding vouchers, religious proponents are satisfied by just having the right to use public funds to send their children to religious schools. But, for those seeking higher achievement, the results are similar to charters: Test scores for students who attend private schools with vouchers are generally no higher than those for students with similar characteristics who remain in public schools.

*Standards–Based Reform*

The original purpose of the standards-based reform movement was to identify what students should know and be able to do at specific grade levels and to measure whether they were mastering that content. As the movement matured, it took on the additional purpose of applying consequences to schools whose students did not show mastery. In this way, the standards movement morphed into test-driven accountability.

The enactment of NCLB in 2002 was a turning point for the standards movement. Instead of academic standards serving as a focal point to raise the quality of instruction in schools, test-driven accountability became the norm. Teachers understood that, if their students did not pass the annual state accountability tests, their schools would be labeled as *failing* by the news media because of the penalties prescribed by NCLB. In 2011, nearly half of U.S. schools did not meet their state targets for student proficiency.

The standards and testing movement has resulted in clearer expectations for what should be learned in school. The standards movement also has promoted greater equity. The same academic expectations are set for all students in a state, and far greater attention is being directed to narrowing the achievement gap between various groups of students. Results on state tests are generally increasing, although this is not matched with the same level of increase on the National Assessment of Educational Progress.

Despite these benefits, the major problem with standards-based reform is that it has become test-driven reform. The accountability provisions in particular have created a culture in which teachers' actions are motivated by the need to meet annual state targets for the percentage of their students that must score proficient on state tests; if too many students fall short, the school will fail to make adequate yearly progress (AYP).

By 2011, opposition to the law had become so intense that some relief from its provisions had to be provided. Because Congress had not reached agreement on changes, the Obama administration took action to grant waivers from some of the most troublesome provisions of the law.

Clearly, standards-based reform has gone astray. Few would argue that it has broadly raised the quality of American schools.

### Schools and the Three Reform Movements

Each of these three reform movements has left its mark on American education, but each has fallen short of its initial promise. The most noteworthy shortcoming of these movements is that they mostly sought to influence what went on in the classroom—the heart of education—through external means. Greater equity was to be secured by adding on services. Choice was to be a market force sifting out bad schools. Test-driven accountability sought to use test results as a lever for change. The exception to this pattern is the academic standards portion of that last movement, which sought to better define what should be taught.

For half a century, external remedies have been tried and have not been sufficient. If American education is to see major improvement, it is time to concentrate on the core components of what happens in the classroom—who is teaching, what is being taught, and how those key elements are funded. Those are the hard issues, and we have approached them timidly. Now, we must confront them forcefully.

Of these three core components, the greatest progress has been made in influencing what is being taught. The second component of what happens in the classroom, improving the quality of those who are teaching, has been the focus of several reform efforts over the last half century, with some degree of success. For instance, teachers can voluntarily apply for and obtain national certification from the National Board for Professional Teaching Standards through a very demanding process intended to show that they are knowledgeable and effective. According to the board, 3 percent of American educators now have this certification. Other groups, such as the National Commission on Teaching and America's Future, have also sought to improve the quality of the teaching force, but all these efforts have not had the broad effect on America's classrooms that is needed.

Now is the time to treat teachers as true professionals and put a well-prepared and effective teacher in every classroom in America. To achieve this, we should elevate the image of the profession by making transparent the complexities of effective teaching and the skills and conditions necessary for teachers to teach effectively.

This leads to the third factor, how education is funded. It is one thing to say that every child will be taught a challenging curriculum by a well-trained and effective teacher, and it is quite another thing to find the funds to bring that about.

In Illinois, my home state, the Winnetka school district spends about $17,842 a year per student, and only 0.2 percent of its students come from low-income families. The Cicero school district in the same county spends about $8,831 per student, but 90 percent of its students are from low-income families. In light of this reality, how can we pretend that the common standards adopted by Illinois will lead to students in Cicero achieving at the same rate as students in Winnetka?

That is the agenda the United States must pursue to broadly improve our educational system. I would hope that leaders advocate for such a comprehensive reform, but what I see instead is—at best—a piecemeal approach to change. From my experiences, I know that such modest attempts won't succeed in bringing broad improvement. There must be a focal point to attract interest and to direct effort—which leads to the last point.

### A Civil Rights Issue

A key lesson I have learned from nearly half a century of involvement in policy is that big ideas have a much greater impact than small ones. If the three reform movements of the last 50 years have not brought about sufficient improvement, and if we must instead concentrate on the heart of education—curriculum, teaching, and funding—then we must be bold enough to break out of the current ways of dealing with those issues. We must have new big ideas to bring about broad improvement.

Both President George W. Bush and President Barack Obama have suggested an approach along those lines. Each has called education "the civil rights issue of our time."

To make those words a reality, the president should propose, and the Congress should adopt, a law that says that no child in the United States will be denied equal educational opportunity in elementary and secondary education through the lack of a challenging curriculum, well-prepared and effective teachers, and the funding to pay for that education.

In other words, equal educational opportunity for all ought to be declared a federal civil right, as the nation did when it sought to end racial discrimination through the Civil Rights Act of 1964, or eliminate educational barriers to girls and women through Title IX, or guarantee students with disabilities a free and appropriate public education, or assure that the needs of students with limited English proficiency would be addressed. Those areas are where federal action has been most successful because words were backed up by legally enforceable rights.

I know that critics of this proposal will argue that it means federal intervention in the schools, that the terms will be hard to define, and that the costs will be too great. All of those arguments and legislative battles were made against the Civil Rights Act, ESEA, IDEA, Title IX, and the *Lau* remedies. Yet, today we can see that African Americans and Latinos, students with disabilities, English language learners, and girls and women have made progress.

Isn't it time we extended these rights to all students? We will have fights about all this, but bringing about broad improvement to American education is worth the fight.

We have a choice. We can talk for another 50 years about making the schools better and succeed for some. But, if we want broad, major improvement for our nation's schools, we have to act boldly, not just talk or try partial fixes. After all the debate is done, we should recognize that action speaks louder than words and enact legislation to affirm that every American child has a right to a good education.

## 2. A Public Man Looks at Public Education

*During a 22-year career in the United States House of Representatives, Dr. John Brademas was known as Mr. Education for the major role he played in enacting ESEA, the Higher Education Act, P.L. 94-142 (the predecessor to IDEA), and legislation supporting libraries and the arts and humanities in the United States. On leaving Congress, Brademas, who held a doctorate from Oxford University and was the son of a schoolteacher and grandson of a school superintendent, became president of New York University (NYU), raising $1 billion over 10 years to put NYU in the front ranks of research universities internationally. When the National Superintendents Roundtable in 2011 presented him with a special award for a lifetime of contributions to American education and to the American people, he reflected on his public career as an educator. During his remarks, which are excerpted below, he emphasized that* *educators are among the great heroes of American life, insisted that government has a crucial though limited role to play in advancing the national good, and encouraged educators to be confident that today's ugly partisanship will pass, as did much more damaging partisan imbroglios in the 1960s. Schools, colleges, and universities, he said, "are part of the moral arc of American history that have bent this nation toward justice."*

## John Brademas

I am deeply honored to receive this award from the National Superintendents Roundtable. I have long believed that educators are among the great heroes of our country. I am therefore deeply grateful that school leaders would take the time to recognize my labors in the educational vineyard!

### Background

Please allow me some words of background, so you may better understand my deep commitment to education—as a student, a teacher, a legislator, and a university president.

I am the son of a Greek immigrant father and a mother of Scots-Irish-English descent, who was a public school teacher. Her father had been a university professor of history and a high school superintendent. So, I grew up in a family for whom education was central.

In 1958, on my third try, I was elected to the United States House of Representatives and then 10 times reelected. On Capitol Hill, I played an active role in helping write all the legislation enacted during those years, 1959–1981, to assist schools, colleges, and universities and the students who attend them; libraries and museums; the arts and the humanities; and to provide services for children, the elderly, and the disabled. In 1980, I was defeated for reelection to a 12th term and shortly thereafter invited to become president of New York University, a position in which I served from 1981 until 1992, when I became president emeritus, my present position.

### Challenges Facing Education

I'm sure everyone knows that today we face a major struggle if we are to win the resources essential to financing child care, elementary and secondary education, and indeed, the entire spectrum of domestic programs crucial to America's future.

Our country is struggling to maintain our founding commitment to social mobility. We are experiencing unprecedented demographic change. Deregulation of financial institutions and reckless practices on Wall Street produced a Great Recession that has stifled economic growth, hammered the poor and the middle class, and put record numbers of Americans on the list of the long-term unemployed. At a time when government should be working to alleviate the suffering of so many who have been battered by the economy, we have members of Congress and presidential candidates who want to decimate social spending instead of raising any additional revenue from the wealthiest of earners.

All of this, of course, takes place in a political culture that seems to have lost its way as well as the respect of the governed. Where once politicians were fixed on solving problems, they now seem fixed on demonizing whoever disagrees with them.

### Current Political Stalemate

I hope you won't think me parochial if I use as my text for this sermon a recent book by a distinguished faculty member at New York University. I'm referring to the late Tony Judt, whose last book, *Ill Fares the Land*, was published in 2010 just before he passed away. Judt was a scholar of European history and a leading public intellectual. He was also a good friend.

His book was a lament for the decline of progressive ideals. He saw that decline as accompanied by the abandonment of the Keynesian economic consensus and the rise of neoliberal economics under President Ronald Reagan, British Prime Minister Margaret Thatcher, and their successors. He called passionately for a return to the social contract that defined the post–World War II Western consensus—with its emphasis on individual security, fairness, and human dignity. Professor Judt's work reminds us that, within living memory, the words *public servant, educator,* and *government* were not terms of derision.

> For a learned, humane, and accessible examination of changing social mores in the United States, see Judt, Tony. (2010). *Ill fares the land.* New York: Penguin Books. Judt offers a brief commentary on these issues in *The New York Review of Books* (April 29, 2010) at http://tinyurl.com/y7vmunt.

I was defeated in my reelection campaign for Congress during Ronald Reagan's landslide victory over President Carter. I listened, therefore, with great interest to President Reagan's first inaugural address and was dismayed to hear him say, "Government is not the solution to our problem; government is the problem." While that made a politically attractive sound bite, I believe it is a very dangerous attitude. It has led directly to the broken political debate we see everywhere around us today.

Government is far from perfect, but it should be obvious that people who believed not only in restraining government but also in its virtues wrote the Constitution of the United States. We as a nation adopted a Bill of Rights. We ended slavery after the long and bloody Civil War. We ended segregation in schools, housing, and public accommodations. We lifted older Americans out of poverty by the millions through Social Security and Medicare. We created the conditions and the partnerships that spanned the continent in the 19th century with schools, universities, railroads, and telephone lines. Then, in the 20th, we built new systems for interstate commerce involving highways, airports, and the Internet. Twice in my lifetime, government saved Wall Street from itself.

Government did all of this both to promote commerce and industry and to promote the common good. And people committed to public service did it also because they recognized Martin Luther King, Jr.'s prophetic insight: "The arc of the moral universe is long, but it bends toward justice."

### Role of Education

That's the thought I want to leave you with. I know that all of you will agree with me when I say that schools and colleges and universities are part of the moral arc of American history. They have slowly—but steadily and surely—bent this nation toward justice.

I continue to believe that education is the key not only to personal advancement but to a better community and a better country. I believe that, not because education makes us a more competitive nation—although it does—but because it offers individuals a better chance in life and makes our citizens better and more just men and women.

Despite the appeals to selfishness that dominate so much of the national discussion today, I do not consider greed to be a virtue. Nor is government a villain.

I remind you of President Roosevelt's famous 1936 challenge to the citizens of the United States. "This generation of Americans," he said, "has a rendezvous with destiny." Our generation has such a rendezvous, too.

And, as we approach that rendezvous, I want you to be of good cheer. I, for one, am confident that, if we keep faith with the better angels of our natures, our rendezvous with destiny will confirm that America's best days still lie ahead.

What is clear to me is the following: The success of this generation of Americans in meeting the challenges ahead will depend intimately on the quality and strength of our nation's schools—and on the values and sense of decency that the men and women in our classrooms transmit to our children.

> "The success of this generation of Americans in meeting the challenges ahead will depend intimately on the quality and strength of our nation's schools—and on the values and sense of decency that the men and women in our classrooms transmit to our children."
>
> —John Brademas

### 3. Role of the Superintendent in a New Age and a Different World

*In 2010, following 14 years with the New York State Council of School Superintendents (NYSCOSS), Thomas Rogers assumed the role of Superintendent and Chief Executive Officer of the Nassau County Board of Cooperative Education Services (BOCES) on Long Island, working with 56 superintendents responsible for a quarter of a million students. Here, Dr. Rogers reflects on what the changing tectonics of education means for school leadership at the district level.*

## Thomas Rogers

Much of the work of the recent reform movements seems less a process of wholesale transformation and more the optimization of a 19th-century education system originally intended to deliver a fundamental education to a largely homogeneous student population. However, our definition of the skills needed to succeed in work and life are changing profoundly, just as the student body is changing demographically. The new definition emphasizes not just college-level preparation but critical-thinking and problem-solving skills for all.

These dramatically raised expectations take place against three environmental backdrops, any of which would be challenging alone: new, centralized policy initiatives accompanied by prolonged scarcity of new resources; increasing diversity and poverty in the student body; and the maturation of new educational technologies. Superintendents face a new age and a radically different world.

A lot of the education policy energy in the last decade has been dedicated to fleshing out the standards movement, most notably with the adoption of NCLB and the state analogs that were necessary to come into compliance. In New York and elsewhere, these efforts took the form of a series of decisions that transferred the locus of control from the local school board and superintendent to the state.

With the loss of autonomy came a change in the role of educational leaders. Wholesale restructuring of state assessments, graduation requirements, and corresponding curricula usurped school boards' roles in setting outcomes, while extensive regulation around teacher certification, resource allocation, assessment activities, planning requirements, and state reporting narrowed for superintendents the means to achieve them. The two primary strategies—using student achievement data to target underperforming subgroups and implementing labor-intensive remediation approaches—were focused on the most challenged school districts.

### The Accountability Movement

Hess and Meeks found both school boards and superintendents agreeing that raising student learning across the board (76.5 percent), closing achievement gaps among subgroups (69 percent), and improving teaching (67.5 percent) were either very urgent or extremely urgent priorities. Very few people argue with these goals. (Who would be in favor of lowering achievement, enlarging the learning gap, or undermining teaching?) Yet, these respondents also identified NCLB-era strategies (average yearly progress and state accountability systems) as barriers to accomplishing those priorities (73.3 percent). Similarly, they cited state and federal laws constraining teacher removal (60.8 percent) and principal removal (30.8 percent) as impediments to school improvement. Much of the current reform literature (and management literature generally) illuminates these responses. If high-performing workplaces are characterized by employee ownership of corporate culture and high-performing schools are characterized by deep levels of shared trust among principals and teachers, firing principals and showing teachers the door seem at best counterproductive strategies.

> Hess and Meeks's examination of governance can be found in Hess, R., & Meeks, O. (2010). *Governance in the accountability era: School boards circa 2010*. Washington, DC: National School Boards Association, Thomas B. Fordham Foundation, Iowa School Boards Association.

The notoriety of celebrity superintendents like Michelle Rhee in Washington, DC, and Joel Klein in New York City along with dramatic investments from education philanthropists Eli and Edith Broad and Bill and Melinda Gates leveraged this policy zeitgeist to shape a new reform narrative: Exhaustive reporting of shortcomings and success were meaningless unless they were translated into some kind of consequential performance management system. "If we could replace the bottom 5 to 8 percent of our teachers with average teachers," claimed prominent education researcher Erik Hanushek, "we could move our students' achievement up to that of Canada."

> "I'm a fan of progress; it's change I object to."
>
> —Mark Twain

Tenure battles are hardly new, but with a new Obama administration in 2009, self-styled education reformers found a Nixon goes to China moment—a Democrat who was willing to challenge the teachers unions' influence on education policy.

Meanwhile, the 2008 recession became the first where public-sector employment and education employment dropped. Given the magnitude of the contraction in government revenues, an urgency developed around the need to reduce the workforce through a productivity measure other than seniority, lest talented new teachers be lost while more expensive, but less effective and more senior, teachers were retained.

This urgency, and its implications for the traditional education labor model, has overshadowed the broader and less-controversial aspects of the accountability movement: Common Core State Standards, national assessment consortia, and robust student data systems. Now teaching to new standards, measured with as yet undeveloped assessments and fed into an unproven performance management system, will result in decisions about who will survive the education labor contraction. Understandably this had led to growing anxiety and great apprehension on the part of educators, including teachers and their representatives.

For the states that early on accepted RTTT funds from the Obama administration, the pressure to implement such systems is unrelenting.

*Race to the Top: The Accountability Movement's Triumph*

The RTTT program, legislated within weeks of President Obama taking his seat in the Oval Office, represented a policy watershed. To improve their applications for a significant share of federal funds, states adopted sweeping policy changes. The potential for funding drove more state legislation than the block grants and matching incentive schemes commonly employed as leverage for policy adoption. Moreover, nearly every state adopted policy changes even though fewer than half won RTTT grants. State policy makers took note of this high-leverage, low-cost strategy for policy change. For example, New York mounted similar competitive grant programs, although they have been whittled down by the state legislature and diluted by a clouded policy vision.

> For an account of how the new reform movement grew and developed, see Brill, Steven. (2011). *Class warfare: Inside the fight to fix America's schools.* New York: Simon and Schuster.

Achieving a vision of meritocracy through performance management and teacher evaluation systems, however, requires adding several new ingredients to the education stew. Teachers and principals are understandably leery of subjective evaluations of their work, particularly if compensation changes or termination might result. Yet, objective evaluation data based on student achievement has yet to inspire broad confidence in its accuracy or fairness. To overcome these obstacles, RTTT winners are expected to create new student achievement assessment systems, employ the resulting data in sophisticated, "value-added" measures of educator performance, couple these objective data with subjective evaluations by superiors, and attach high-stakes consequences for underperforming educators (termination) and schools (closure).

**Infastructure.** The infrastructure needed to implement such a system is staggering—a new national curriculum (the Common Core); new assessments of the mastery of that curriculum; state-level data systems to collect and warehouse data; unique identifiers for individual students, teachers, and courses; elaborate statistical systems for making meaning from the data; rules for how to assign statistical significance to the data; rubric systems to force standardization of classroom observations; and proxies for student achievement data for grades and subjects for which there are no suitable assessments. The complexity of the system leaves it ripe for criticism, and adjustments meant to address imperfections have added to the complexity.

**NCLB Waivers.** Roughly half the states that received RTTT funding in the initial rounds were subject to the stinging penalties NCLB imposed for failure to achieve AYP requirements. Just as RTTT drove policy reforms more broadly than grant funds, so too has the carrot of NCLB waivers driven that reform further with a policy of providing amnesty from NCLB provisions in exchange for structural change within states and districts. To the extent that the waiver approach parallels the RTTT theory of action, the two together essentially align all states to the administration's vision of a system organized around college- and career-ready standards and assessments, tougher annual achievement targets for schools, and teacher and principal evaluations based on student test score growth.

### Larger Environmental Changes

The fact that the dominant reform narrative is about accountability and not poverty does not change the fact that large and inexorable environmental forces are at play, principally increasing diversity and poverty, accompanied by constrained financial resources.

1. The glory of American schools lies in their diversity. But this national asset is accompanied by growing poverty. U.S. student poverty has been increasing and now stands at second highest among economically advanced nations, according to the United Nations International Children's Emergency Fund (UNICEF). Simultaneously, the U.S. Census Bureau reports that, for the first time, minority (defined as nonwhite, non-Hispanic) births exceed majority births. The combination of these factors implies that our student body will become ever more ethnically diverse and ever more impoverished.

2. At the same time, addressing the challenges associated with poverty is complicated by diminishing resources. No major political party suggests a new golden age of education funding. Instead, we find a lot of emphasis on recommendations for redeployment of existing resources.

The "bigger, bolder agenda" calls for paying attention to out-of-school factors related to learning. See http://tinyurl.com/q6z8ee. A similar set of proposals encompassing a "whole child" agenda has been defined by the Association for Supervision and Curriculum Development (ASCD) at http://tinyurl.com/5htqlq.

As poverty creates an ever-increasing drag on educational outcomes, it seems likely that the policy views advanced by coalitions such as Broader Bolder Approach to Education will begin to gain traction, while dwindling resources may well make technology an appealing avenue to pursue efficiencies and productivity gains in the public sector, just as it has done in the private arena.

### Leading in the Accountability Age

This is the context in which superintendents must now lead: While a national curriculum seemed unthinkable just a few years ago, 45 states have now ceded control to the national Common Core to be measured by one of the two national assessment consortia. The education labor movement is on the defensive, fighting a multifront war against funding restrictions, pension erosion, seniority setbacks, eroding collective bargaining protections, and economic and political headwinds.

Ultimately, much of the work that consumed superintendents over the past two decades amounted to attempts to wring incremental improvements from an education paradigm rapidly approaching obsolescence. Meanwhile the student body has become increasingly needy due to poverty, greater prevalence of learning disabilities, and a growing number of students for whom English is a second language. Yet, the sum of this work is disappointing, best described as perfecting the 19th-century education system, with longer school days, desks more perfectly aligned, longer and more elaborate multiple-choice tests, one-size-fits-all policies for schools, and the demonization of teachers, unions, and administrators.

The postmodern superintendent could be forgiven for becoming a cynic. But don't succumb to the temptation. Public education stands on the precipice of exciting and dramatic change whose success or failure will be largely determined by your leadership.

Funding, of course, is always a challenge, but superintendents need to make the most of the tools available to them to maximize learning no matter the obstacles. One of those tools is technology.

### The Challenge of Technology

Your emerging leadership challenge is to maximize learning for all, no matter the obstacles. You must make the most of the tools you have available. One of them is technology.

Clayton Christensen's book *Disrupting Class* advances the proposition that disruptive innovation will displace the incumbent education model and will eventually do so at breakneck speed. After assuming charter schools would be a promising disruptive innovation, Christensen abandoned his belief in them and turned to technology. By 2019, he predicts that half of K–12 classes will be taught online. He views this transition as inevitable.

> The argument for disruptive innovations is well laid out in Christensen, Clayton, Horn, Michael B., & Johnson, Curtis W. (2011). *Disrupting class: How disruptive innovation will change the way the world learns.* New York: McGraw-Hill.

Borrowing from the idiom of software versions, educational technology's first two distinct generations experienced modest market penetration consistent with their meager value proposition. We are now entering a third, fundamentally different generation that will profoundly influence the classroom of the future.

**Technology 1.0.** The initial foray into technology consisted of digital versions of an analog equivalent that offered no additional cognitive benefits and cost a lot more. Here, we find distance learning functioning as a giant lecture hall, electronic workbooks that were little more than an expensive way to raise the cost of drill-and-practice worksheets, and low-level, online, multiple-choice assessments. As some experts asked, are flashcards that cost $600.99 (including the price of a laptop) any more effective than those that cost $0.99?

**Technology 2.0.** The next level involved digital versions of an analog modality that drew on unique capabilities of technology but failed to exploit a fundamentally altered cognitive relationship to the material. This involved a trove of teaching materials available in media libraries, students' passive consumption of video (mirroring old-time consumption of the classroom films and filmstrips), and smart boards and online search capabilities. These are undoubtedly helpful, but essentially they are 21st-century versions of blackboards and library card catalogs.

> "The mind is not a vessel to be filled but a fire to be lit."
>
> —Attributed to both Plutarch and W. B. Yeats

**Technology 3.0.** Here, we find the possibility of digital education tools that unlock new cognitive operations for which no predigital analog exists. It sounds like a pipe dream. But, if you find it far-fetched, recall that just scant decades ago, speaking wirelessly to people you could not see was a *Star Wars* fantasy. The idea of looking at distant friends and family while telephoning them was something out of science fiction. The concept of communicating with sister schools abroad in real time was an illusion. And putting the computing power of the Pentagon during the Vietnam War into a student's hands was an implausible notion. Yet, in a few short years, Skype, the Internet, smartphones, laptops, and tablets have breathed life into each of these fantasies.

> The power of emerging technologies can potentially turn schooling on its head as Salman Khan demonstrates with his Khan Academy, which has provided millions of students (young and old) around the world with access to high-quality, online, illustrated lectures on mathematics, statistics, and science. The Khan Academy online lectures are available at http://tinyurl.com/5wdd76w. Khan can be seen explaining his theory of action here: http://www.ted.com/talks/salman_khan_let_s_use_video_to_reinvent_education.html.

Among the trends emerging now, we can anticipate that hardware and infrastructure improvements will improve bandwidth connections and make most smartphone processors extremely powerful. At the same time, the Common Core harnessed to new open- and crowd-sourced courseware offers the possibility of developing new, discrete learning modules and full-blown learning management systems (e.g., the Khan Academy).

We are at a new inflection point in the use of education technology, one that leverages unique technological capabilities to alter, rather than duplicate, the typical classroom experience. Managing this transition, from classroom configuration, to professional development, to actual investments in hardware and software, will require superintendents to develop a new skill set to employ in parallel with the skills already essential to leadership success.

These changes in the structure of accountability, the larger environment, and new developments in technology define the environment in which you as a superintendent must lead. Your job will require you to stay abreast of all of these trends, interpreting them in the local context of your schools and districts, guiding communities and your staff through the conversations that these changes require. The conversations are but a means to an end: Despite the challenges you face, you must remain ever focused on the goal of raising student achievement.

> The National Superintendents Roundtable devoted a major portion of its Fall 2009 and Fall 2012 meetings to technology in education, with presentations from school leaders and senior officials from Microsoft and Apple Corporations. According to Microsoft Global Education Vice President Anthony Salcito, schools of the future are not about technology but about "people, processes, and the environment." Apple Education's Senior Manager for IT and Learning Technologies Stephanie Hamilton agreed, insisting that technology is about changing school culture, not equipment. Business models in schools are not helpful, she noted. In schools, what is required is technology that is learning driven, focused on classrooms, and user centric. Detailed highlights from these meetings are available at the Roundtable's website: www.superintendentsforum.org.

## C. THE "COMMONPLACES" OF SCHOOL LEADERSHIP

*It's very easy for educators to get bogged down in complex theory. They can quickly lose sight of the practical issues involved in educating large numbers of students.*

Robert H. Koff

Nelda Cambron-McCabe

Luvern L. Cunningham

James Harvey

In the 1960s and 1970s, the University of Chicago's Joseph J. Schwab warned teachers and administrators in uncompromising terms of the dangers of overreliance on theory. By its very nature, he wrote, theory "does not and cannot take account of all the matters which are crucial to questions of what, who, and how to teach. . . . [T]heories cannot be applied . . . to the solution of problems concerning . . . real individuals, small groups, or real institutions."

See Schwab, Joseph J. (1978). *Science, curriculum and liberal education: Selected essays.* Jan Westbury, ed. Chicago: University of Chicago Press.

An unknown wag has put Schwab's conclusion a different way: "In theory, there is no difference between theory and practice, but in practice there is."

In place of arcane and complex theory, Schwab argued that an adequate theory of instruction could rest on four relatively straightforward "commonplaces": curriculum, teaching, learning, and community. These were Schwab's stakes in the ground. With them, educators could understand what they were doing. Without them, theory had little meaning.

If those are the "commonplaces" of instruction, what are the stakes in the ground for leadership today? What skills do you have to command as a school leader to do what you were hired to do? What are the "commonplaces" of school leadership today?

We believe there are seven, as shown in Figure 1.1. Although we call them the *commonplaces of leadership,* there is nothing obvious or simple about them. They are, however, stakes in the ground. You cannot be fully effective as a superintendent unless you master them. To develop them completely will require a very deep, clinical exposure to these ideas. It will take a lot of work. In fact, you might just need to unlearn a lot of what you've learned at great cost in time and money. What we describe here will sometimes contradict what you were taught about school leadership.

These concepts have grown out of a major, 20-year investment in a broad, conceptual sweep of the state of education and public affairs in the United States. In that time, with some 300 superintendents who worked with us as colleagues in the National Superintendents Roundtable and the Danforth Forum for the American School Superintendent, we worked with nationally and internationally known experts to apply different dimensions of leadership and organizational development theory to the challenges of school leadership. So, we asked internationally renowned experts on public opinion (such as pollster Daniel Yankelovich; Will Friedman, president of the Public Agenda Foundation; and Kathleen Hall Jamieson of the Annenberg School for Communication at the University of Pennsylvania) to share with us their insights into how the public comes to judgment. We sought the advice of Harvard University's Ronald Heifetz, Martin Linsky, and Marc Roberts about the nature of leadership amid economic, demographic, social, and political change.

We studied schools as learning organizations with Lauren Resnick of the Learning Research and Development Center at the University of Pittsburgh and with the University of Kansas's Jim Knight and Richard Elmore from the Harvard Graduate School of Education. We spent time with Peter Senge examining systems thinking and the five disciplines that

**Figure 1.1**   The "Commonplaces" of School Leadership

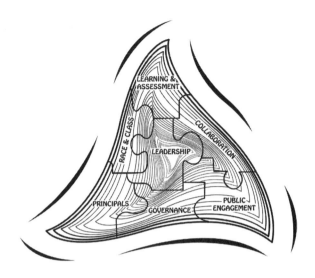

support modern, high-performing organizations. We explored work of the future at Boeing and Microsoft and examined Philadelphia's high school of the future close at hand. Then, we asked Amishi Jha (University of Miami) and Dan Siegel, MD (University of California, Los Angeles, School of Medicine) to help us understand the educational implications of new developments in neuroscience. And we explored how cutting-edge districts are working with emerging technologies with executives from Microsoft and Apple.

We talked firsthand with members of Congress and former members of Congress and made five separate 10-day trips to China, financed by the Chinese government through the College Board, to examine education in the world's greatest developing nation. We then spent nearly two weeks in Europe on a study mission to explore the Program in International Student Assessment (PISA) and schools and education policy in Finland, France, and England.

All of this was illuminated and fleshed out with the personal experiences of the 300 superintendents with whom we worked. This was, in short, an effort to make sure that theory conformed not just with practice but with reality as seen through practitioners' eyes.

> Highlights of all of these meetings, along with photographs and videos, are to be found on the Roundtable's website: www .superintendentsforum.org.

From this activity, we learned that seven issues have become the "commonplaces" of the world of today's school superintendent:

1. **You must *lead*.** You will be expected to lead your school system, not simply manage its operations. The existing governance system—not to mention the demands of NCLB and RTTT—may orient you around making sure the buses run on time, but you have to find a way to reshape governance and union–management relations so that the entire district focuses on learning while creating a compelling vision of the future. This volume will highlight the difference between adaptive and technical leadership, explore systems thinking, organizational development, and leadership theory, and provide you with some advice on how to manage different issues as they ripen.

2. **You must lead within a *governance* structure that is hardly ideal.** In some ways, you have an impossible job. You are simultaneously an educator, manager, budget maker, public servant, politician, community leader, and local preacher. In each of these roles, you are subject to second-guessing by everyone around you, including the board to which you report and the teachers (and their union) you nominally supervise. You must find a way to work with your board and your teachers.

3. **You must understand *learning and assessment*.** You need to understand learning theory and the implications of developing neuroscience for classroom practice. You may have to become a data-driven field scientist to boost student achievement. You will need an expert grasp of what is required of you from federal and state officials in terms of standards—and how those standards are gauged by emerging assessments. These new developments carry with them powerful implications for your community, requiring you to demonstrate a confident grasp of data and analysis that has never before been expected of any public official. This book will provide you with practical advice on how and where to begin—whether you are the only professional in the central office or you oversee an office with hundreds of professionals.

4. **You must worry about *race and class* in your district and set out to close the achievement gap.** Of all the imperatives, this one may be the most challenging, opening up all of the sores and wounds of the nation's racial past while requiring of you a level of patience and dedication that will try most people's souls. In this volume, you will find advice from others who have gone before you and tools for holding difficult conversations.

5. **It goes without saying that you must develop your schools' *principals*.** You will succeed or fail as a leader based on the quality of the leaders you put in place in schools. It's simple. Good schools require good principals. The role of today's principal may have changed even more than

yours. Today's principal must be a hands-on leader of learning. This book provides lessons from the field.

6. **You will have to learn how to** *collaborate.* It is no longer sufficient to oversee a school system that worries about children from kindergarten through grade 12 and from 8:00 a.m. until 3:00 p.m., 180 days a year. You have to worry about your students when they're not in school, persuading the community it needs to invest in them while fending off those who think you should stick to your knitting. The *Fieldbook* has some suggestions to offer and some compelling stories to tell.

7. **You must** *engage your community.* The days of superintendents arriving with a mandate and imposing it on the community are over. You will have to work with your community to create a shared sense of what the community wants to accomplish through its schools. This *Fieldbook* can show you how.

These seven "commonplaces," then, frame the rest of this *Fieldbook.* Our position is straightforward. These issues are the stakes in the ground framing leadership for 21st-century schools. They are the heart of the matter. You must also, obviously, be doing a lot of other things; if you are not intimately engaged in these seven, however, it is hard to know how you can succeed.

Think about that. What is more important to you as a superintendent (or potential superintendent) than leading your district, making governance work, understanding learning and how it is assessed, worrying about race and class, developing school principals, collaborating with other community agencies, and engaging your community?

Simply to ask that question is to answer it. If your priorities are elsewhere, there is a very good chance you are wasting your time.

## D. TOOLS

1. Why not devote one or more sessions with your cabinet to the questions that follow? Find out how assistant superintendents or directors of human resources, elementary and secondary education, finance, and facilities respond. You might be surprised with some of the answers.

2. If you are using this book in a graduate course developing administrators, the reflective questions that follow can be explored by your students at the outset of a term to help them gain a better understanding of the superintendency. At the end of the term, they can be used again to help students reflect on what they have learned and expand their understanding of the superintendent's role in leading a school system that learns.

## E. REFLECTIVE PRACTICE

Before you explore the "commonplaces" in the book, ponder how you currently perceive the role of superintendent.

1. When we say, "You must lead," what aspects of the superintendency come to mind? How do you define leading?

2. How has the new emphasis on standards, accountability, assessment, and choice influenced your understanding of your role as a superintendent? Have these developments changed your relationship with your board? The public? Your principals? Your teachers? If so, how?

3. As you think about your school system, how would you describe the governance structure? Who belongs to the governance structure? What does this mean for the superintendent?

4. What are the superintendent's responsibilities related to student learning, standards, and assessments? How comfortable are you that you have the technical know-how to deal with these issues? If you don't have it, are you comfortable that you have access to the expertise you need within your district?

5. What is the impact of race and class in your school system? What does it mean for student achievement? For equity concerns? For engaging the parents and community?

6. Where do principals fit in your thinking about school reform? What do you expect principals to know when you hire them? How will you prepare them for their role related to the seven "commonplaces"?

7. When you initiate collaborative efforts with others, whom will you invite to the table? Look around. Who is missing? What does that mean for the work that must be done?

8. What does public engagement look like? How will you lead such an effort?

9. Are you optimistic about the future of public education in the United States? If so, how will you manifest that in your leadership moving forward? If not, what are you concerned about? What do you propose to do about your concerns?

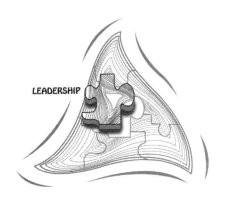

LEADERSHIP

# PART II

# *Leading Your Schools*

*Superintendent Wanted: "A miracle worker who can do more with less, pacify rival groups, endure chronic second-guessing, tolerate low levels of support, process large volumes of paper and work double shifts (75 nights a year out). He or she will have carte blanche to innovate but cannot spend much money, replace any personnel, or upset any constituency."*

What will it take to lead your schools? Can you be the miracle worker sought in the tongue-in-cheek advertisement above who can transform the educational landscape without changing anything? How can you transform education and school structures in your district while facing the daunting obstacles that make the superintendency what has been called an impossible job? This part launches you on a learning journey in which you encounter the first of our seven "commonplaces"— leadership itself.

> The tongue-in-cheek want ad that begins this part of the *Fieldbook* came from Evans, R. (1995, April 12). Getting real about leadership. *Education Week, 14*(29), p. 36.

## A. LEADERSHIP THEORY FOR THE THEORETICALLY CHALLENGED

In imitation of innumerable how-to books for dummies, we were tempted to call this chapter *Leadership Theory for Dummies*. But that threatens to be offensive in a way that *DOS for Dummies* never was. The previous section reminded you of the macro-challenges facing educators everywhere today. This section explores what these developments mean for you as a leader.

For the theoretically challenged, therefore, we want to give you enough information to understand that, as German psychologist Kurt Lewin put it, there's "nothing as practical as a good theory."

Robert Starratt (2003) gives you insight into cultivating meaning and community in *Centering educational administration*. Mahwah, NJ: Lawrence Erlbaum.

The first thing we want to do is review some of the leadership literature. You've heard of a lot of it—from John Gardner in *On Leadership* and Ron Heifetz in *Leadership Without Easy Answers* to Jim Collins in *From Good to Great*. We're just going to touch on this lightly and not go into it in depth, but you might want to check out the resources in the margins of this section as you develop your learning agenda.

Then, we want to put a big theory before you: the notion that your image of the organization you are leading profoundly influences how you understand your role. (In turn, how others imagine your organization powerfully influences how they understand what they expect from you.) You're going to hear a lot about images of organization.

Next, leaning heavily on the work of Ron Heifetz of Harvard University, we introduce you to the distinction between adaptive and technical challenges. You know how to develop a bus schedule or budget. That's technical work. But, how do you help your community understand the role of its schools in economic development or why changing demographics in the district are important? That's adaptive work.

One way to think about how to advance these important issues is by turning your district into a learning organization, one that assesses its own progress. Here, we rely on Peter Senge's fifth discipline work as applied to schools by several of his coauthors and colleagues. This work gives you some sense of what's involved in transforming your district so that everyone—from you and your senior staff to your transportation and maintenance people—is focused on learning.

Finally, we conclude this section with some practical examples from superintendents in the field about how to get started in this work. Theory is fine, but at some point, it has to be put into practice.

We conclude with questions to encourage you to reflect on your own practice. Most people aren't asking these questions. You can't afford to ignore them.

## 1. The Leadership Literature Landscape

*So, you want to be a leader? You'd be surprised how many lessons are out there for you.*

James Harvey

Take, for example, the surprising world of caterpillars as described by Margaret Parkin. As the story has it, two caterpillars were hanging out on a leaf one day when they looked up to see a beautiful butterfly overhead. One of the caterpillars looked at the other and said, shaking his head doubtfully, "You'd never get me up there in one of those things!" The moral of the story: If you want to become a butterfly, at some point, you have to stop being a caterpillar.

Then there are the processionary caterpillars. Each has an instinct, demonstrated by the French naturalist Jean-Henri Fabre, to blindly follow the caterpillar in front of it. As Fabre demonstrated, they are quite capable of following each other around in a circle, ignoring food located nearby, until they die of starvation or exhaustion. The moral of the story is this: Don't mistake hard work, good intentions, and tenacity for accomplishment.

> Want a fun little book that will provide you with great leadership metaphors? Check out Parkin, M. (2010). *Tales for coaching: Using stories and metaphors with individuals & small groups.* London: Kogan Page Limited.

The lesson from the caterpillars is that leadership involves taking risks, sometimes very public risks. Throwing off old assumptions and adopting new ones is how you become a butterfly. And it requires goals, focus, and intentionality. Going around in circles gets you and your district nowhere.

So, what is leadership? Is it charisma? Certain traits? Skills? Power? Leadership behaviors, especially in crisis? As the literature going back to Machiavelli makes clear, it can be all these things and more.

In many ways, as Johnson and Johnson point out, decision making is at the heart of leadership. Leaders have to decide. They find themselves challenged by difficult choices almost on a daily basis. Making decisions, often on the basis of limited data, marks the true test of leaders, frequently involving them in controversy.

> The Johnson brothers provide all the detail you'll ever need on the challenges of working with groups. Johnson, David, & Johnson, Frank. (2012). *Joining together: Group theory and group skills* (11th ed.). Boston: Allyn and Bacon.

Two huge lessons stand out in the literature on leadership and organizational change: Leading effective change demands that leaders (1) get their own emotions under control while (2) developing focused plans on how to move forward.

Whether it is Runde and Flanagan advising leaders to cool down, Patterson and colleagues admonishing leaders to "master their stories," or Johnson and Johnson advocating "smoothing" as a way to manage emotional stress, the suggestions add up to a common piece of advice: Do not let your emotions get in the way of the management and leadership decisions you have to make.

In similar fashion, when Runde and Flanagan advocate the four Rs—recognize, respond, resolve, reflect—or Kegan and Lahey call for a language of commitment expressing what the team stands for, they are talking about agreeing on a plan to get the work done. As school leadership coach and

> Conflict is inevitable in leading change. Here are some useful tools: Runde, C. E., & Flanagan, T. A. (2010). *Developing your conflict competence: A hands-on guide for leaders, managers, facilitators, and teams.* San Francisco: Jossey-Bass; and Patterson, K., Grenny, J., McMillian, R., & Switzler, A. (2002). *Crucial conversations: Tools for talking when stakes are high.* New York: McGraw-Hill.

former superintendent Gene Medina notes in Section G. Don't just talk about organizational change. Get to work doing it. Leading change is not the work of processionary caterpillars.

### A Multipart Intervention

So, you've arrived with a reasonable sense of the challenges before you. The literature suggests you (1) start with the heart; (2) address system dysfunctions; (3) plan in advance on how to deal with conflict; and (4) build a team.

**Start With the Heart.** This advice from Patterson and colleagues parallels an observation from Heifetz: All change involves loss of something precious. Your leadership task is to figure out how to parcel out the change incrementally so that your workforce and your community can deal with it. It is important that staff, teachers, and citizens (who will be expected to collaborate in defining the change and making it a success) have time to describe their feelings about it.

**District Dysfunction.** Patrick Lencioni's compelling fable about corporate leadership—*The Five Dysfunctions of a Team*—provides a lively and useful summary about how the best intentions of team leaders can be led astray by dysfunctions within the leadership team. He describes them as a layer, forming a pyramid, all resting on the most fundamental dysfunction of them all—absence of trust within the team.

What's intriguing about Lencioni's model is that the avoidance behavior evident in many public and private organizations—ignoring results, avoiding accountability, fear of commitment, and avoiding conflict—develops out of the root challenge facing the organization, absence of trust.

> District dysfunction getting you down? Check out Lencioni, Patrick. (2002). *The five dysfunctions of a team: A leadership fable.* San Francisco: Jossey-Bass.

The heroine of Lencioni's fable, Kathryn, continuously reminds her team that they have everything they need to succeed, that the conversation needs to be held around performance issues, not personalities, and then lets each member of the team come to the conclusion that it is their collective dysfunctions that undermine performance.

**Manage Conflict.** There is going to be conflict. There is no way around that. Can you anticipate in advance where it will come from so that most of the negative consequences can be sidestepped? The best way to deal with conflict, if at all possible, is to make plans so as to avoid or minimize it. You can do so by having your team work out agreements in advance about how you will manage conflict. You will also need to develop a consensus on how the group will reach agreement (and define what constitutes consensus). Kegan and Lahey's *seven languages for transformation* might be helpful here. They speak of moving away from language emphasizing complaint, blame, rules, policies, and the like (sound familiar?) toward language that emphasizes commitment, personal responsibility, and public agreement. Potentially, these are very powerful tools to move your group toward dealing with the tasks at hand.

> Sometimes, the way we talk to each other betrays us. Here are some ideas to help make negative conversation positive: Kegan, Robert, & Lahey, Lisa. (2002). *How the way we talk can change the way we work: Seven languages for transformation.* San Francisco: Jossey-Bass.

**Build a Team.** At some point, you have to move beyond acknowledging that change is difficult and conflict must be handled to actually getting on with the task at hand. Here, you want to reach out to the entire workforce and community to invent options for moving forward and reaching agreement on what needs to be done. This isn't simple or straightforward work. As Jack Jennings noted in Part I, educational challenges need to be respected and dealt with in their full complexity.

In this situation, you face one significant disadvantage and two significant assets. First is the disadvantage: The nature of three decades of rhetoric from the national and state levels does not encourage mutual respect, team building, or even capacity building through professional development. It is urgent that team concepts be built into efforts such as Race to the Top (RTTT); otherwise, as the competitive nature of the program implies, RTTT can easily become a zero-sum game encouraging competitive forces that directly undermine the sort of collaborative exploration that effective team and trust building demands.

> Michael Fullan (2001) has done a lot of the work required to apply the latest leadership and organizational development theory to school transformation in *Leading in a Culture of Change*. San Francisco: Jossey-Bass.

But you are not without advantages. Newer staff and teachers will probably be motivated by the latest thinking and new technologies with which they are familiar. Meanwhile, more experienced employees have watched the educational policy train leave the station without so much as a by your leave, much less consultation with local school leaders. There is every reason to believe that, competently led by you, staff and teachers can grasp the stakes involved. It may be too much to expect them to respond enthusiastically, but they have every reason to respond positively given the challenging and perilous environment in which they find themselves.

# B. THINKING ABOUT YOUR ORGANIZATION

Heifetz, Ronald A. (1994). *Leadership without easy answers*. Cambridge, MA: Belknap Press of Harvard University Press offers powerful insights into the difference between adaptive and technical leadership and what is involved in each.

*Forget most of what you think you know about organizational behavior. Put it out of your mind. Much of it bears little relationship to reality. In this section, you will learn about different metaphors and how they shape your understanding of your role and your conception of responsibility. We will also introduce you to the first tool you can apply in leading your district.*

## 1. Images of Organization

### Nelda Cambron-McCabe

### James Harvey

Professor Gareth Morgan of York University in Toronto, Canada, has written compellingly about the images most of us carry in our heads about the nature of organizations and institutions. His work is as applicable to schools, churches, and the nonprofit world as it is to corporations and government agencies.

All organizational (and management) theory, Morgan writes, is derived from images or metaphors that help us understand organizational situations in powerful, yet incomplete, ways. These metaphors are compelling. They extend our insight, help us manage complexity, and assist us in visualizing the similarities between the reality we face and an ideal of some kind in our mind's eye. Paradoxically, of course, these images also distort our perceptions by encouraging us to ignore differences between the reality we face and the ideal we cling to. As Morgan puts it, "ways of seeing become ways of not seeing" as well.

See Morgan, Gareth. (2006). *Images of organization*. San Francisco: Berrett-Koehler for a compelling description of mental images at work in organizational development.

See Figure 2.3, the Ladder of Inference, as a way of working with images within an organization.

Images and metaphors also permit different observers to view the same situation through different lenses. If central office personnel see the district as a structure, they will find plenty of structural elements to worry about. If they think of it as a living, breathing organism, the task of finding ways to nourish the organism takes on new urgency. In a sense, images become self-fulfilling prophecies. That can be dangerous, but there's nothing wrong with this tendency as long as we recognize it.

Morgan describes several metaphors that guide how most of us u.
stand the organizations with which we are involved. These include
following:

- The organization as machine—a mechanistic metaphor of the organization as something made up of interlocking parts that must be
  made to mesh and work together smoothly.
- The organization as organism—a metaphor in which the needs of
  the organization and its environment are emphasized, along with
  consideration of how organizations grow, develop, adapt, and
  decline.
- The organization as a brain—a metaphor emphasizing information
  processing, intelligence, learning, and the possibility of developing
  intelligent learning organizations.
- Organizations as cultures—a metaphor emphasizing values, beliefs,
  norms, rituals, and patterns of shared meaning.
- Organizations as political entities or systems of government—a
  metaphor in which politics, power relationships, and conflict tell the
  major story.
- The organization as a psychic prison—a metaphor where people
  become trapped in their own beliefs about the nature and shape of
  the organization.
- The organization as a site of flux and transformation—this metaphor involves several models, one of which, drawing on theories of
  chaos and complexity, insists that order can emerge from disorder in
  complex, even chaotic, systems.
- Organizations as instruments of domination—this final metaphor
  emphasizes the exploitative aspects in some elements of organizational life.

These metaphors resonate powerfully with much of the dialogue about
organizational life and school administration. For every practical educator
and business leader who wishes that
somehow schools' diverse interests
could be made to work together more
harmoniously (the organization as
machine), there can be found another
assuring the world that order emerges
from chaos (the organization as flux).
For every idealist who is intent on
advancing the concept of schools as living organisms, you will find a self-
styled realist insisting that they are
political entities in which power and
district politics are the predominant

> "Nothing really prepares you for this job. I
> was 22 years in one system, coming up
> through the ranks to become an associate
> superintendent. I thought I was ready.
> . . . The difference to being second in
> command and the superintendent is so vast
> and so unexplainable because of the political
> context of the job."
>
> —Linda Murray, former superintendent,
> San Jose Unified School District, California

forms of engagement. And visionaries intent on creating schools as learning organizations are more than matched by cynics emphasizing that they are power-driven entities, political institutions capable of exploitation.

Here's the beauty of these metaphors. These images give you a chance to understand how you view your organization as well as an insight into how others view it. Imagine that you're trying to shake up the existing order of things while leading a central office wedded to the concept of the district as a machine. You probably won't make much progress unless you help central office employees reframe their thinking. One place to start is with the image of the organization your people hold in their heads (see Table 2.1).

Although Morgan did not characterize his metaphors in this way, you may find it helpful to visualize models of inherited structures of school administration and models of emerging practice. Under inherited images, we find the district described as a machine, a political system, a psychic prison, or even, unlikely as it seems, an instrument of domination. Each of these can be thought of as distinct and different. Table 2.2 shows what these metaphors would look like in your school district. In combination, if these images came to dominate school administration, most educators, we can predict, would not like what they would see. These images imply a return to the schools of the 1950s.

The emerging images, perhaps because they are complex and still developing, are more difficult to describe completely. The image of the organization as a culture is a familiar one. Morgan's work pushes our understanding of learning organizations further. Now we are asked to visualize schools as organisms (emphasizing mutual interdependence among systems), as brains (in which intelligence and control are distributed across the system), and as sites of flux and transformation (emphasizing self-renewal).

Senge, Peter M. (2006). *The fifth discipline: The art and practice of the learning organization.* New York: Doubleday.

Senge, Peter, Cambron-McCabe, Nelda, Lucas, Timothy, Smith, Bryan, Dutton, Janis, & Kleiner, Art. (2012). *Schools that learn: A fifth discipline fieldbook for educators, parents, and everyone who cares about education.* New York: Doubleday. Retrieved from www.schoolsthatlearn.com.

The reality is that, as you shape your view of your district based on the metaphors you bring to it, you also shape and form what you think your job as superintendent actually is (see Table 2.2). You may like what you see (if the district is an organism, your role is that of a gardener or scientist). Or you may not (if the district is viewed as a machine, you're a high-level mechanic).

Take some time to think about the images you hold and the metaphors you like to use. As a school leader, what's the image of your district that comes to mind? The answer to that question shapes how you see your role.

**Table 2.1**  Imagining Your School District

| Image | Nature | Strengths/Weaknesses |
|---|---|---|
| *Inherited Images* | | |
| Machine | Goals and objectives predominate; rational structure; organizational charts; people interchangeable within the system. | Works well where machines work well/Creates a sort of mindless bureaucracy. |
| Political System | Management as political process; identify different styles of government; view politicization as near inevitable and accept conflict as normal; study power and learn how to use to best advantage. | Puts power and conflict center stage while emphasizing the interest-based nature of organization/Breeds more politics and can understate gross inequalities in power and influence. |
| Psychic Prison | Psychic forces encourage or block innovation; frozen mind-sets and unconscious forces make people resist change; irrational things take on power and significance; people imprisoned by their own way of thinking. | Challenges basic assumptions, puts the "irrational" in new perspective, and encourages the management of tension/Focus on unconscious may deflect attention from other forces of control. |
| Instrument of Domination | Power dominates organizational activity; workaholism, occupational accidents, and social and mental stress common; exploitation of employees and customers taken for granted. | Indicates that rationality can be mode of domination and brings ethical concerns to forefront/Metaphor is so extreme it can polarize discussion. |
| *Emerging Images* | | |
| Culture | Organization as unique mini-society; organization reflects people; accept idea that some cultures are uniform, others fragmented. | Emphasizes symbolic significance and interdependence of management and labor in everything/Can manipulate and ignore some dimensions of culture. |
| Organism | Focus on open systems; organizational health, life cycles, and development considered important; adapting to environment encouraged; relationships of species to ecology explored. | Contributes to organizational development/Easily becomes ideology and overstates cohesion in most organizations. |
| Brain | Examine organizational intelligence; interest in learning organizations; use technology to decentralize and distribute intelligence. | Recognizes importance of paradox and provides clear guidelines for learning organizations/May be native if conflicts arise over learning and realities of power. |
| Flux and Transformation | Try to understand fundamental nature of change; look "around the corner"; analyze systemic forces encouraging change; try to encourage organization to shift from one pattern of operation to another. | Leaders get powerful new perspective on role in encouraging change/May imply that leaders and managers just have to "go along for the ride" and are powerless to do much about change. |

SOURCE: Adapted from Morgan, Gareth. (1998). *Images of Organization: The Executive Edition*. San Francisco, CA: Berrett-Koehler Publishers.

**Table 2.2  Acting Out Your Metaphor**

| Image | Nature | Your Role as Superintendent |
|---|---|---|
| *Inherited Images* | | |
| Machine | Detailed rules and regulations govern school operation and curriculum; hierarchical reporting structures; emphasis on control, accountability, and uniform outcomes; separation of planning and design of teaching from classroom delivery. | You are either a mechanic or an organization man or woman. You supervise, monitor, oversee, and enforce rules; you see individuals as replaceable; you subordinate individual interests to organizational goals; you focus on uniform "products." |
| Political System | Competing interests in school and community dominate decision making; interests, conflicts, and power continuously assessed; power relationships always under consideration. | You are a politician. You build coalitions among stakeholders to support schools; you use formal power of position to structure agenda; you think that knowledge is power and use information as a political tool. |
| Psychic Prison | District is trapped in old ways of thinking; blind spots obscure new ideas and pedagogies; district unable to think past current school structures. | You bully people. You use rules to reinforce the status quo; to you, boundaries are a big deal. You encourage "groupthink" so that the district fails to see other options. |
| Instrument of Domination | Inequality in educational opportunities and resources among schools and students is taken for granted. School sites are "battlegrounds" rather than teams or collaboratives. Labor-management strife is rampant, and educators' work is "deskilled" or made teacherproof. | You dominate people. You believe in managerially rational decisions without concern for unintended consequences; you reproduce privilege and advantage of certain groups; and you emphasize organizational efficiency and effectiveness at expense of individual needs of students and teachers. |
| *Emerging Images* | | |
| Culture | Schools may be defined by social processes, images, symbols, and rituals. Or evidence of the competitive spirit of American society may be reflected in schools, which are encouraged to be different or to compete with each other for resources. | You are the superintendent as bard. You lead by developing shared meaning. You shape stories, legends, and myths to create culture. You encourage organizational change through cultural change, and you tend to worry about the symbolic significance of every aspect of schools. |
| Organism | Schools and their environment are viewed as mutually dependent and interactive. The district seeks alignment of interrelated subsystems and collaboration with other community interests. | You are a gardener. You scan the environment for changing conditions. You structure leadership for continuous adaptation and worry about the "fit" between the schools you lead and your community. |
| Brain | Intelligence and control are distributed throughout the system. Flexible, resilient, and inventive systems valued. An integrated information web exists across schools so that leadership can be diffused; schools are guided by core values that shape behavior. | You are a teacher, learner, and problem solver. Through inquiry, you encourage a "learning to learn" orientation in schools. You engage in "double-loop" learning—questioning assumptions and appropriateness of existing norms. You imagine and anticipate new futures, and you uncover forces/structures beneath recurring problems. |
| Flux and Transformation | Educational chaos theory is at work. Schools self-create and self-renew from chaos. Small changes can lead to massive system change (the famous image of a butterfly flapping its wings in Tokyo and precipitating a downpour in New York); meaning and purpose serve as primary points of reference; the key role of relationships and participation in creating the reality of schools is emphasized. | You organize anarchy. You shape and create new contexts to encourage self-organization. You use minimum specifications to create contexts. You nurture emerging context for change rather than controlling change, and you direct attention to "attractors" that pull systems into new forms rather than directing attention to how to resist change. You highlight the tensions between reality and aspirations. |

# C. ENCOURAGING ADAPTIVE LEADERSHIP

*Ronald A. Heifetz helped revolutionize thinking about leadership when he published* Leadership Without Easy Answers *in 1994. He and his team from Harvard University's John F. Kennedy School of Government are greatly in demand all over the world as they help governments, corporations, and nonprofit entities explore their leadership challenges. Heifetz spent quite a bit of time with us over several years talking about the implications of his work for school leaders.*

## 1. Principles of Adaptive Leadership

### James Harvey

### Nelda Cambron-McCabe

"Why are leaders attacked?" is a question very much on Ron Heifetz's mind. "Why are reputations destroyed? Why is it that sometimes national leaders are, literally, assassinated?"

"The complicated academic answer," he suggests, "is that the link between authority and leadership is broken and that some members of the 'tribe' expect complex problems to be solved with technical fixes. The simple answer is that leaders are attacked because what they are asking of us represents a loss—a loss of respect, an important value, a competence, or a privilege. The leader may understand that a gain lies over the hill, but the people being asked to follow can't see over the hill."

And, Heifetz cautions, "Leadership in this context involves the hard work of holding people together and resisting the demands for quick answers." In this situation, the best that you as a school superintendent can do is to ask the right questions, provide information, and frame the issues. "Giving the work back to the people" is what Heifetz calls it. It can be a difficult thing to do, particularly in times of distress or great pressure from federal and state authorities or the local community, because the greater the crisis, the more desperately we look to authority figures for the "right" answer.

Ronald A. Heifetz's *Leadership Without Easy Answers* provides the theoretical framework for taking up adaptive work in your school district. Heifetz, Ronald A., & Linsky, Marty. (2002). *Leadership on the line: Staying alive through the dangers of leading*. Boston: Harvard Business School Press leads you through the practical aspects of doing this difficult but meaningful work. Along with a third co-author, Alexander Grashow, Heifetz and Linsky (2009) have also produced a useful guide to assist you in this work: *The practice of adaptive leadership: Tools and tactics for changing your organization and the world*. Boston: Harvard Business School Press.

### Adaptive and Technical Leadership

"When you think about leadership issues," advises Heifetz, "be aware of key distinctions between technical and adaptive problems." The classic error in both human and animal societies is to treat adaptive problems as if they were merely technical.

The biggest leadership challenges revolve around adaptive problems—new threats, different forces, changes in the environment, shifts in the earth's axis. A leadership challenge is that most people are reluctant to change and want every problem treated as a technical issue that can be solved quickly by those in authority. As one wag has put it: "Everyone is in favor of change as long as someone else changes." Your leadership challenge as superintendent, according to Heifetz, "is to confront the 'tribe' with the gap between its aspirations and current reality." For example, we talk about all children achieving at high levels in our school districts. Disaggregated data, however, paint a very different picture of achievement. Progress on a problem such as this requires both the school and community to learn. It also often demands changes in people's attitudes, values, and behavior.

> Heifetz warns us, "If you have an adaptive problem that you treat as a technical issue, it will take longer to solve than if you confronted it as an adaptive problem from the start."
>
> Many of the statements attributed to Heifetz in this *Fieldbook* were made by him during multiday seminars organized for superintendents by the authors.

Leaders are expected to provide five things for their followers, according to Heifetz. Like mature silverbacks in gorilla colonies, leaders are expected to provide direction so that the group knows where it is headed, protection so that the group can protect itself from attacks, orientation because people do not like to be confused about what their roles are, conflict resolution so that equilibrium can be maintained, and norms because people have to understand what is involved with being a member of a particular community.

All of these things can be provided in both adaptive and technical modes, but they are much more difficult in an adaptive environment. Why is that? Because in adaptive situations, the leader cannot do the community's work. The community has to do it. As leader, you must give the work back to the community. In effect, you have to say, "I cannot solve these problems for you. You have to be involved in developing the solutions."

### *Demonstrate Competence Dramatically on Technical Issues*

If you are telling your board or your community that you can no longer protect them from tough realities, you need some kind of permission to do that, warns Heifetz. But you can't earn that permission if the board or community lacks trust in you.

Heifetz suggests that you gain permission through your technical work. "To obtain the permission you need on the adaptive side, you have to be successful with the technical work first." Nobody will trust you if you blow a hole in the budget or land the board in a disastrous public relations mess.

"But being competent on the basics permits you to challenge people, because you already have built some trust. And, you can always say: 'Look, I passed the bond issue. I renovated the high school under budget. You can trust me on this, too.'"

"Try to sequence the issues," is Heifetz's advice. "First, provide some dramatic demonstration of competence in a technical area. Then try to sequence the adaptive issues so that those that are ripe for resolution come to the fore first. That can be hard, but your key problem is how to be strategic in challenging your own supporters so that you can give them the work at a rate they can stand."

### Get on the Balcony

Think of the dances you once had time to attend. Sometimes, Heifetz notes, you were on the dance floor in the thick of the action; occasionally you took a break, perhaps on a balcony. The metaphorical balcony is often a good place for public officials to find themselves. On the dance floor, you are so preoccupied with keeping time to the music and avoiding other dancers that you never see the whole picture. Heifetz advises the following: Leave the floor, and go up to the balcony periodically. Observe the patterns on the floor. Watch who dances with whom, what kind of music brings out which dancers, and how different people keep time. Do the partners change as the steps become more complicated? The point is to leave the immediate environment occasionally in order to gain a better sense of the overall scene (see Section C.2: Questions for Getting on the Balcony).

### Heroic Suicide or Staying Alive?

How do you develop some strategies for staying alive? "Heroic suicide is not the answer," says Heifetz. Telling everyone else they are wrong, even if they are, is not effective leadership. "Trying to do it alone will not work. How do you survive?" Heifetz lays out a menu of strategies:

• **Don't exercise leadership alone.** Leaders cannot get from the balcony to the dance floor and back again quickly enough. They need partners of two kinds. First, they need allies among the different factions to kindle constructive conflict in each faction. Then, they need confidantes who can serve as reality checks.

• **Externalize the conflict.** Don't make yourself the issue. If people get the impression that the conflict is between you and everyone else, you are dead. Identify the conflict, and give it back to its owners.

• **Listen.** Listen to outsiders. Listen to insiders. Listen to yourself. You conduct electricity from many sources and are a barometer of distress in the system. Your confidantes can help you with this.

• **Distinguish between your role and yourself.** Remember, said Heifetz, "It's not personal." Your emotional health depends on understanding that the attacks on you are rarely personal. People become upset at what you ask them to do, but that is rarely directed at you as an individual, no matter how much it feels that way.

• **Distinguish between a purpose and a sense of purpose.** People die spiritually because they spend a lot of time on one purpose, which they either achieve or fail to reach. Regenerate a sense of purpose in life outside of professional obligations.

• **Find a sanctuary.** Leaders must find a daily or weekly time to think and regroup, and they must be disciplined about finding that time. Just as leaders have to plan on being swept up in the music, so too do they have to plan to get away from it—whether in social activities, spirituality, exercise, or dinner with friends.

• **Give the work back.** Find ways to keep reminding people that you cannot do the work for them. In this task, you'll find yourself continually dealing with work avoidance—staff and others who insist it's too hard, it's not necessary, you're not to be trusted, and you should be ignored. Deal with the avoidance, don't become caught up in it yourself, and insist that the work move forward.

Will these strategies guarantee success? Perhaps not, but without them, it may be difficult to take up the formidable challenges of leading schools without getting badly wounded or pushed aside.

## 2. Questions for Getting on the Balcony

*Identifying the Adaptive Challenge*

- What's causing the distress?
- What internal contradictions does the distress represent?
- What are the histories of these contradictions?
- What perspectives and interests have I and others come to represent to various segments of the community that are now in conflict?
- In what ways are we in the organization or working group mirroring the problem dynamics in the community?

*Regulating Distress*

- What are the characteristic responses of the community to disequilibrium—to confusion about future direction, to the presence of an external threat, or to disorientation in regard to role relationships, internal conflict, or the breaking up of norms?
- When in the past has the distress appeared to reach a breaking point—where the social system began to engage in self-destructive behavior, like civil war or political assassination?

- What actions by senior authorities traditionally have restored equilibrium? What mechanisms to regulate distress are currently within my control, given my authority?

*Directing Disciplined Attention to the Issues*

- What are the work and work avoidance patterns particular to this community?
- What does the current pattern of work avoidance indicate about the nature and difficulty of the present adaptive challenge and the various work issues that it comprises?
- What clues do the authority figures provide?
- Which of these issues are ripe? What are the options for tackling the ripe issues or for ripening an issue that has not fastened in people's minds?

*Giving the Work Back to People*

- What changes in whose values, beliefs, or behaviors would allow progress on these issues?
- What are the losses involved?
- Given my role, how am I likely to be drawn into work avoidance?

---

Adapted from Heifetz, Ronald A. (1994). *Leadership without easy answers.* Cambridge, MA: Belknap Press of Harvard University Press, 254–263.

# D. FROM LONE RANGER TO LEAD LEARNER: ONE SUPERINTENDENT'S JOURNEY

*Former Springfield, Massachusetts, superintendent Peter Negroni was committed to the idea that all children could learn. He came into Springfield with a mandate to make a difference. But things weren't so simple. He had to learn to develop not just relationships and humility but also a learning orientation that was more personal and respectful.*

Peter Negroni

Most superintendents come to their positions after moving up steadily through the teaching and administrative ranks. They are unprepared for the leadership role that faces them. Their careers in the classroom are usually distant memories; their leadership training usually occurred on the fly. An effective superintendent has to relearn what it means to be an educator.

I know this from my own experience. When I became superintendent in Springfield, the system was desperately in need of educational leadership. The staff was insular. There was no overall curriculum. Schools were set up with haphazard grade levels; some elementary schools were K–4, while others were K–6. Some youngsters had to go to as many as four different schools before starting high school.

Adapted from Negroni's experience as described in Senge, Cambron-McCabe, Lucas, Smith, Dutton, & Kleiner, *Schools that learn* (2012), pp. 428–433.

Most critically, Springfield had very rapidly changed from a basically white and black community to an increasingly Hispanic city. Many civic leaders, including school leaders, had not acknowledged that change. Our high school drop-out rate was 51 percent and showed no signs of improving. I came to the district with an overriding personal goal of changing this static, inbred system.

As I look back, I realize that I had embarked on a journey that sometimes quite literally kills people. If one takes on this position as I did—with conventional ideas about the kind of leadership required—he or she might be lucky to last three years. I was fortunate. As I tried to make change happen, I was confronted by the community in a way that forced me to make some painful but essential discoveries. If my experience is typical, successful superintendents go through a four-part journey. They go from being Lone Rangers to being Lead Learners.

### Part One: The Lone Ranger

Convinced that I knew what was wrong with the system, I also assumed I knew how to fix it. Instead of trying to build relationships with the union or the board, I worked around them. Most of the time, I felt that I was way ahead of them. I could change things on my own. And I could change them to suit my preferences.

Take my word for it: You can enjoy some exciting successes as a Lone Ranger. But first, I had three brutal years. I found myself confronting people on an ongoing basis. At public meetings, I would dress down school committee members who didn't agree with me. I would yell, "Well, if you don't see it my way, I can go somewhere else." I knew I might be riding for a fall, but I didn't know how to slow down.

"Convinced that I knew what was wrong with the system, I also assumed I knew how to fix it."

—Peter Negroni

A Lone Ranger cannot implement the necessary changes. Implementation requires something else—a deeper, stronger web of relationships on which the superintendent and everyone else can rely.

### Part Two: Reexamining Relationships

In my fourth year, I started to realize that I would never be able to accomplish lasting change by being a loner. Yet, I still saw myself as the central character in Springfield's story. Everyone else had a minor role.

I recognized that I couldn't go it alone after two crises hit at virtually the same time. The first had to do with teachers' contract negotiations. I still didn't understand that the critical issue wasn't getting the union members to recognize me. I had to learn to recognize them. Second, a candidate for the school committee ran on a platform based on throwing me out of office—and won. Some people in the school system regarded me as a symbol not of the solutions that would save the system but of the problems that had to be eradicated.

Soon after, I talked with Harvard's Ron Heifetz about these stresses in Springfield. He asked what the people who supported the candidate had to lose. He pointed out that the candidate who had triumphed had received 18,000 votes. "Who does she represent?" he asked. "Once you find out what she stands for, you may find out that you represent the same principles." As I began to listen more closely, I realized that Heifetz had offered me a genuine insight. My opponent wasn't anti-school. She didn't oppose high achievement. On the contrary, she cared deeply about the students. She wasn't an opponent at all; she represented a point of view that could be incorporated into the drive for excellence.

> "The critical issue wasn't getting the union members to recognize me. I had to learn to recognize them."
>
> —Peter Negroni

I began to change. I made new attempts to get parents genuinely involved. I made dramatic adjustments in the way I negotiated with the union. My approach to the school committee shifted. I began to solicit the members' opinions about the best way to proceed.

### Part Three: Coaching Instruction

My role began to evolve quite naturally from that of boss to that of coach. I began to create opportunities for others to reflect and act together. This meant allowing others to try things on their own and accepting the occasional failure. Rather than micromanaging, I helped principals, staff, and teachers find their own way.

A good coach raises awareness by asking questions. The best place to start that questioning and creating of opportunities is the classroom. And the best topics revolve around core matters of teaching and learning. My visits, and the nature of the visits, sent a powerful message to the entire system. This is what matters, my visits said. My job is to coach improvement. So, I started to visit classrooms and never stopped. By this phase, I was making 150 classroom visits a year.

I encouraged principals to do the same with teachers at their schools. To support and model this, at the beginning of the year, three or four central office administrators and I conducted 46 school visits in 46 days, with the principal of each school alongside us. Then, the administrators and all 46 principals met to summarize what we had seen.

At one point, I made a presentation about these developments to superintendents in Texas. They were fascinated to discover that a superintendent of a 28,000-student district with 46 campuses could spend almost every day in schools. I know they had trouble believing me. They asked

> "Texas superintendents were fascinated to discover that a superintendent of a 28,000-student district with 46 campuses could spend almost every day in schools. I know they had trouble believing me."
>
> —Peter Negroni

how I did it. I told them I delegated everything else. It was more important for me to be in the schools. The staff would tell callers, "He's visiting schools. That's what he's supposed to be doing." At last, I had stopped managing the machinery and was focused on our core enterprise.

*Part Four: Coaching Community*

We all know that what we do in schools is only part of what educates children in our communities. Then a new Commission on Children at Risk confirmed what I knew in my gut. For students to be successful in schools, they need to be supported by what this commission called an *authoritative community*—one that respects the students and that the students can respect.

A genuine personal transformation takes place for many superintendents as they go through this final phase. They move from being advocates—experts with answers—to conveners of dialogue, in which the right answer might emerge from anyone in the room. In this phase, the superintendent stops managing the machinery altogether and takes the lead in establishing opportunities for people to experiment, innovate, and stretch themselves and the school system.

## E. CREATING YOUR LEARNING ORGANIZATION

Adaptive work as described by Ron Heifetz is difficult and demanding. One useful way to proceed is by applying to schools the principles of the five disciplines developed by organizational development guru Peter Senge and his colleagues. Senge's seminal work, *The Fifth Discipline,* can help you do adaptive work by creating a learning organization. This is where you are going to start seeing the connections between the leadership challenges of adaptive work and many of the major elements of the emerging images described by Gareth Morgan—the organization as a culture, a brain, an organism, and something subject to flux and transformation.

> "As leaders, we play a crucial role in selecting the melody, setting the tempo, establishing the key, and inviting the players. But that is all we can do. The music comes from something we cannot direct, from a unified whole created among the players—a relational holism that transcends separateness."
>
> —Wheatley, Margaret J. (2006). *Leadership and the new science* (3rd ed.). San Francisco: Berrett-Koehler.

Our guide for this journey is Senge's colleague Charlotte Roberts. She introduces us to a new language involving five disciplines, diamonds, ladders of inference, and what lies submerged beneath the iceberg's surface. The rules here aren't as hard and fast as they are in Management 101, but they'll help you a lot more.

## 1. The Five Disciplines

*What does it mean to help people do their jobs better? Or, in terms of reconceptualizing leadership, what is a learning community? Why do schools, of all places, not appear to be effective learning organizations?*

James Harvey

Nelda Cambron-McCabe

These are some of the questions Charlotte Roberts, coauthor of *The Fifth Discipline Fieldbook* (1994), likes to explore. In doing so, she applies the lessons of organizational leadership writ large to the challenges of leadership for learning. Roberts believes that the ability to be a self-learning, self-regulating organization will be what will characterize successful organizations of all kinds in the future—public and private, profit and nonprofit.

"Learning is really about developing the capacity for thinking and interacting with others," she says. A learning organization is an institution that worries about developing its collective intelligence so that it can create its own future. It does so by concentrating on perceived reality, both the reality you perceive and the reality others see.

> Senge, Peter, Kleiner, Art, Roberts, Charlotte, Ross, Richard, & Smith, Bryan. (1994). *The fifth discipline fieldbook.* New York: Doubleday.

"In terms of perceiving reality, think of a diamond," says Roberts. "It has many facets. But most of us see only one facet—the one reflecting our view of the world. As leaders, you need to understand how others view the world. Can you imagine the deeper perspective you would gain if you could see all facets of the diamond? Do you know how others perceive reality? Adults without children? People upset about property taxes? Students who have dropped out of school?"

Illustration by Greg LaFever.

### *The Five Disciplines*

Five cross-cutting, personal, and interpersonal disciplines lie at the heart of creating a learning organization. These ideas promise great potential for improving learning in schools:

**Personal Mastery.** The focus of this work is on clarifying personal vision and aspirations within the context of current reality. Individual learning, says Roberts, is the foundation for organizational learning. Individuals must have a clear view of current reality and an explicit sense of what is important to them. Continually contrasting the vision against current reality can produce positive creative tension to help achieve what's important. Personal mastery that makes a meaningful difference arises from ongoing individual reflection that is supported, nurtured, and modeled by organizational leaders.

**Shared Vision.** We know. You already have one. It's in a folder. But shared vision here is not a document—it's a continuing conversation. The central aspect is common agreement about values, an agreement that forms a collective sense of identity and purpose. With sustained attention and dialogue, the vision grows deeper, ever more complex and more useful.

Roberts warns that leadership is not about "getting your hands on a formula and applying it." Leadership is about creating a vision with others, designing an organization to achieve that vision, and then thinking and interacting with others to make it happen. The old vision in the folder is an internal one. It emphasizes the traditional elements of the school community—the superintendent, principals, teachers, students, parents, and school board. The new vision is much more likely to be all-encompassing, viewing schools and their needs in the context of other local problems including health, housing, employment, economic development, and environmental concerns.

**Mental Models.** Like Morgan, Roberts finds it useful to talk about mental images of how things work. "Think of mental models as a giant jukebox" containing compact discs, Roberts urges. "Most of us have a model of what a good parent is. To recall that model, we select the right CD. Models apply across the board. Who's a good teacher? We pick a CD. What's a good school? We pick a CD. Really, all of these models are a set of abstractions based on experience. We have to understand that if I think one thing and you think another, it does not mean one of us is right and the other is wrong. It simply means we have different mental models."

> Effective tools for surfacing assumptions behind mental models include the ladder of inference and balancing inquiry and advocacy (see Section H: Tools).

An important part of creating learning communities is coming to terms with these different mental models. We must inquire into the invisible assumptions that shape our thinking. What do you mean when you say that "all children will learn at high levels"? Do you mean all, or do you mean most? Or do you mean some, most of the time? How high is high? You may be operating with one set of definitions, while your board and different parent groups are operating with others. Failure to surface these different mental models can lead to all kinds of frustration and confusion as people talk past each other.

**Team Learning.** Team learning is the course work that nobody offers. It's the ability to think and learn together. Most leaders in business and elsewhere probably have an average IQ of 130, says Roberts, but "put them together on a team, and the group IQ drops to 68."

Team learning is a tricky concept. "For team learning to occur," says Roberts, "individuals must suspend their assumptions. It doesn't happen without practice." Unfortunately, many people believe they already use this discipline because they work within numerous groups. Team learning, however, requires deeper conversations and more complex strategies. In the effort to develop team learning, you as an educator have an advantage. Your normal work environment provides a great practice space for applying the skills of dialogue, surfacing mental models, and using inquiry.

> See Section H: Tools for using dialogue and surfacing mental models.

**Systems Thinking.** "This is the ability to see the whole and its parts, and how the parts interact to create what is in front of us right now," according to Roberts.

## 2. Archetypes of Systems Thinking

Embedded in systems thinking is a way of considering organizational behavior as described by nearly a dozen archetypes. Here, we consider briefly just five of the archetypes outlined by Senge. They have clear and unmistakable implications for schools and for school policy.

**Limits to Growth.** This archetype holds that growth cannot continue unabated in an unrestricted, reinforcing dynamic. Something always gets in the way—human capacity, system instability, laws, or regulations. Limits will always be reached. Think of a rapidly growing suburban school system with a reputation for high achievement. To keep up with demand, it must open one or more elementary schools several years in a row and then build middle and high schools. After a few years, the community becomes upset about stagnant or even declining achievement scores because the burgeoning student population has required a dramatic expansion of new teachers, many of them young, inexperienced, and struggling to meet student needs.

**Shifting the Burden.** We will pay more attention to this archetype below in Part IX: So, What Does All This Mean? It holds that it is a mistake to focus on symptoms, while leaving fundamental problems unaddressed. The fundamental problem is what produces the symptom, and until it is taken up, the symptomatic solutions that promise to fix problems quickly will fail. Presented with the opportunity by Peter Senge to apply the shifting the burden archetype to schools, Roundtable members quickly focused on the results of high-stakes assessments as symptoms (low achievement), which might drive discouraged students out of school while leaving student poverty unaddressed.

**Success to the Successful.** When good performance is rewarded with greater resources (on the theory that this will motivate everyone to do better) we are watching the success to the successful archetype at work. One potential drawback is that poor performance (on the part of other organizational units) may be more due to initial conditions than to lack of skill or knowledge on the part of the people in these units. There is nothing wrong with identifying the gap between the highest-performing and lowest-performing units, but its value lies in identifying the gap so that it can be examined, not in reinforcing it with additional resources. Much of the current school "reform" movement (performance-based pay and RTTT, for example) runs the risk of running afoul of the success to the successful archetype.

> To develop your capacity to use archetypes, see Kim, Daniel, & Anderson, Virginia. (1998). *Systems archetype basics: From story to structure.* Waltham, MA: Pegasus Communications.

**Tragedy of the Commons.** This archetype goes back to agricultural practices in Europe that set aside a commons for shared grazing for local residents. With no one responsible for monitoring how much each individual took from the commons, overgrazing was common. As demands on the commons increased (because individuals increased their draw and disregarded others' needs) the commons' ability to perform diminished. These factors can be seen at play in today's public schools. Vouchers and charters draw money and frequently students with the highest motivation out of traditional public schools, leaving them with fewer resources to respond to students with greater learning needs. Conversely, the expansion of special needs programs, even in relatively wealthy districts, constrains budget resources for other programs. Challenges such as these threaten public schools' capacity to serve the common good.

**Fixes That Fail.** Fixes that fail can be thought of as a special version of shifting the burden. When subsystem symptoms are addressed in isolation of the larger system, the fix can be predicted to fail and in fact make the situation worse (unlike shifting the burden, where the response may result in modest improvement even while the fundamental issue is ignored). Mao Zedong's great sparrows campaign was designed to increase agricultural production by preventing birds from eating stored grain. Millions of birds were killed as part of the effort, but unchecked insect populations then destroyed grain on the stalk, leading to a massive famine that killed millions.

Peter Senge talks about systems thinking as a "shift of mind." Instead of looking at events for cause and effect, we seek out the interrelationships and the deeper patterns behind the events. The iceberg metaphor (see Figure 2.1) illustrates this shift of mind; we look for patterns, the forces at play, and ultimately, the mental models that limit our thinking.

Figure 2.1   The Iceberg

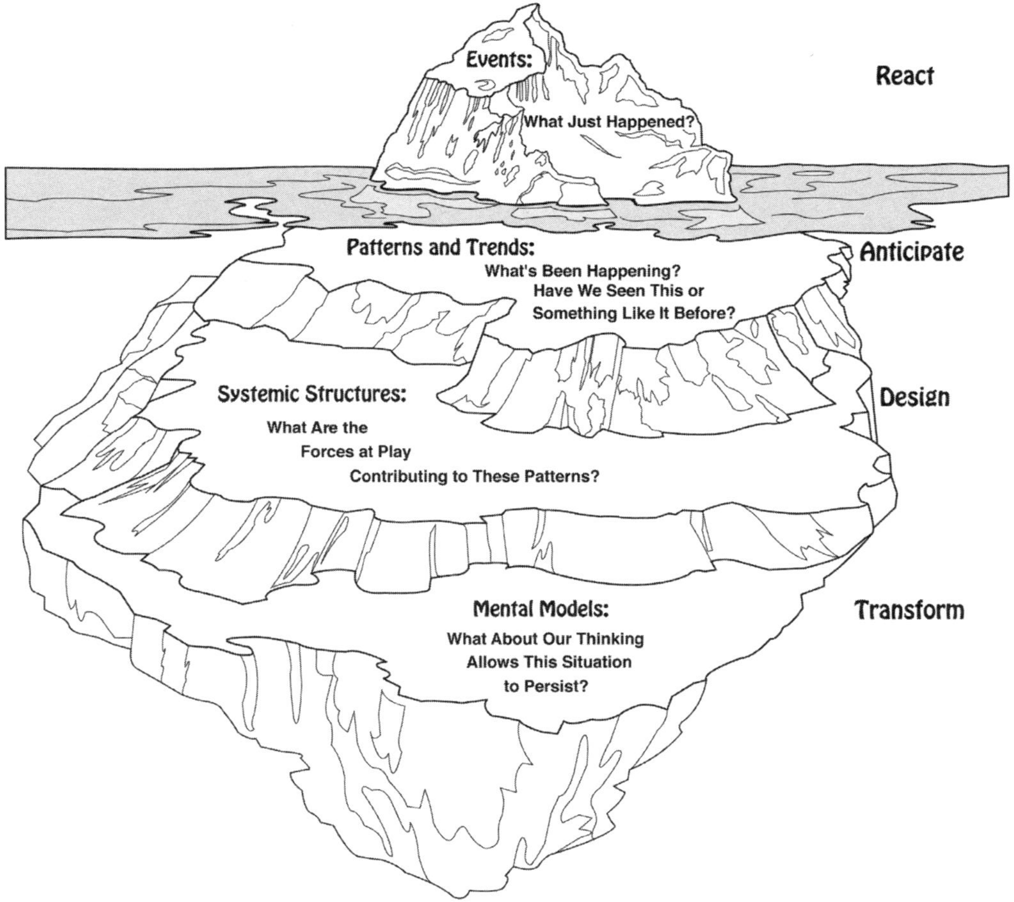

React

Events:
What Just Happened?

Anticipate

Patterns and Trends:
What's Been Happening?
Have We Seen This or
Something Like It Before?

Design

Systemic Structures:
What Are the
Forces at Play
Contributing to These Patterns?

Transform

Mental Models:
What About Our Thinking
Allows This Situation
to Persist?

Illustration by Greg LaFever.

47

## 3. The Iceberg

*The purpose of this exercise is to identify and reflect on a district problem using four levels of questions that create the foundation for a systems thinking process. In this exercise, you are challenged to worry about events, patterns, systemic structures, and mental models.*

### Gary Wegenke

*Step 1: Events*

*Identify a problem in your school district, school, or classroom that has been going on for weeks, months, or possibly years.*

*Reflect on the events (and their details) that have caused the problem to persist. How have you and others responded to these events? What have you done or what have others done collectively to manage the events in an effort to resolve the problem? Are you reacting to the event in an effort to seek causes and determine effects?*

From a systems perspective, schools are complex organizations intertwined with multiple constituencies. Seldom do events represent an isolated issue. Yet, often events are treated as separate problems leading to searches for quick fixes. Typically, this means looking for some action that has been used to manage this event, or something like it, in the past. You need to ask: Who is responsible? Were procedures followed? How do we prevent this from happening again?

Take the problem of the achievement gap. As an example, the Heartland School District superintendent realized that state data revealed significant achievement differences by race, ethnicity, and income. What should the district's leadership do in the face of this information? One approach would be to convene some kind of ongoing, districtwide consideration of what the data mean and how to respond. Such a discussion might reveal that board cutbacks in teacher aides and professional development had severely affected schools in the poorest part of town. But the Heartland school board went for the quick fix of spinning the release of the state data. When the superintendent tried to discuss systemic causes for the achievement gap, the school board president quickly squashed the discussion, noting the board's plans to consider a resolution expanding the number of days devoted to test preparation.

> For educators new to systems thinking, check out Meadows, Donella. (2008). *Thinking in systems: A primer.* White River Junction, VT: Chelsea Green.

### Step 2: Patterns and Trends

*Explore the event or problem you identified in Step 1 at a deeper level. What's been happening? Have you been here or somewhere similar before? Chart the data and events over recent years. Do patterns or trends emerge?*

Heartland, predictably, was hammered in the local newspapers. It took a step back and regrouped. School leaders knew that budget reductions and cuts in programs and services were not new. They graphed the patterns and trends over the prior 10 years and discovered a budget that had been driven by increases or decreases in state and local revenue rather than a set of clear priorities. Reductions in revenue had narrowed educational options just as the student population grew and schools became more crowded and diverse. Heartland officials had been in a reactive mode, responding quickly to budget developments by attempting to maintain current initiatives or minimizing the impact of financial cuts. School leaders and concerned community members could now understand this cycle and try to break it.

### Step 3: Systemic Structures

*As you consider the patterns and trends you identified in Step 2, what forces, internal and external to the school district, are contributing to these patterns and trends? What permits them to continue? What structures must be changed in the school district to shift these patterns?*

As the Heartland school board and superintendent explored the issues before them, they recognized the influence of multiple interest groups in the budgeting process. The squeaky wheel got the grease. Parents of upper-income children argued for gifted and talented programs. The Heartland Volunteers testified in favor of athletic programs. And the teachers' union lobbied for seniority as the sole criterion for making staff reductions. The board began asking itself, "Who's supposed to do the right thing for all students?"

### Step 4: Mental Models

*Examine the structures you identified in Step 3. What is it about your thinking and others' thinking that allows these structures to persist? What shifts in attitudes, beliefs, and behaviors must occur to change these forces and structures?*

The mental models we hold of our organizations influence structures and interactions within the system. Too often, these images remain hidden and obscure. To transform a system, they must be brought to the surface and examined. Skills of reflection and inquiry are central to unearthing mental models.

Like the Heartland school board and superintendent, you can use the iceberg model to begin engaging in systems thinking. With experience, you will find that the process is nonlinear as you move back and forth among the various steps, and you will discover that your iceberg is only one in a sea of icebergs.

## F. BUILDING A CORE LEARNING GROUP

*Few school leaders are as experienced as Dr. Les Omotani in using the five disciplines in schools. He employed these principles in both West Des Moines, Iowa, and Hewlett–Woodmere Public Schools in New York prior to his retirement. This section provides a glimpse of how Dr. Omotani and his administrative team changed the way they worked together.*

### Les Omotani

I've frequently been asked why I (or anyone) would want to be a school superintendent. As my career matured, I became clearer and clearer about why I was there. It was about building a community of learners who could create an organizational structure and culture to maximize the opportunities for students. As such, the most important thing that you can do as superintendent is to place a high priority on setting aside time on the job for learning together. It's definitely the key; there's no way people can learn new ways of thinking, new ways of doing things, or new habits if they're just trying to fit a discussion in on top of everything else they've got to do.

Adapted from "Creating a Core Learning Group," published in Senge, Cambron-McCabe, Lucas, Smith, Dutton, & Keiner. (2012). *Schools that learn*. Reprinted with permission.

The move to valuing collective learning represented a fundamental change for me. In the first half of my administrative career, those around me expected me to know what was going on, to have answers, and to make decisions. I was comfortable with those expectations, thinking that was what I was supposed to do. Quite frankly, I gained a lot of recognition and reward for doing that well. But that leadership role was more about winning compliance than commitment. Many people did things because they were told to do them by me or other administrators in our district. It wasn't that we were telling them to do bad stuff; the stuff made sense, but it wasn't their own. That was the way things worked in traditional organizations.

I moved to seeing leading as learning with others, serving and caring for people, and ensuring the best possible learning environment for both students and adults. It is a more powerful way of leading, resulting in more impressive outcomes. The school system is everyone's work, their learning, their creation; and you can't predict where it's going. Wherever it goes, it'll go there because you've struggled as a group with it and believe it's the right direction. We relied on the strengths and the experiences of one another; we made better decisions by pulling in multiple perspectives on the system.

> "In schools we're living in new times. If we don't have practices like systems thinking in place, then the political structure will take over because of uncertainty and scarcity. We've seen that the old frameworks don't work. With systems in place, you react and think more collaboratively and critically."
>
> —Joyce Bisso, superintendent of Hewlett–Woodmere School District

As I moved into the superintendency in the Hewlett–Woodmere Public Schools, I felt that developing a community of learners with a group of administrators had to be my top priority. As a core learning group, we could not only make better decisions but also create the conditions for everyone else in the school community to learn. Our learning would ripple through the system, opening up opportunities for faculty and students. We would trust, as Meg Wheatley puts it, that meaningful conversations could change our world.

A community of learners, however, doesn't just form on its own. It requires deliberate work to create the right conditions; its members must acquire new skills. In my experience, people think that they know how to talk with each other, but they do not. Traditional ways of interacting in meetings do not lead to thoughtful, productive dialogue. If we want to build collective intelligence and action, we must learn new rules for engagement.

*Convening the Core Learning Group*

A district leadership team (DLT) already existed at Hewlett–Woodmere when I got there. Principals and selected central office administrators regularly met. But over the years, according to several members, the DLT had become a dreaded two-hour meeting with talking heads giving out information. Agendas could consist of 15 or more items with minimal time for speakers to get their points across or time for discussion. If you were at the bottom of the agenda, forget it; maybe next time. Few, if any, opportunities existed for individuals to learn from each other.

So, we expanded the DLT to include 28 central office administrators, principals, and assistant principals. We invested significant resources in preparing them with sophisticated skills to lead organizational learning. Many of the members said that for the first time they felt they'd been given permission to bring their whole selves into our interactions. Through the processes used, even short warm-up activities like check-ins, we unlocked a yearning to know one another better, to build stronger relationships, to be able to trust more, and to depend on each other. As a group, we found our interactions rewarding, energizing, and reinforcing.

"Trust that meaningful conversations can change your world."

—Wheatley, Margaret. (2002). *Turning to one another: Simple conversations to restore hope to the future.* San Francisco: Berrett-Koehler, p. 145.

When we first started down this path, the administrators couldn't envision a two-hour meeting, let alone a full day on the learning disciplines and dialogue. That was too much time away from their offices or buildings. But they soon reached a point where they wanted more time to interact with each other. This is typical in systems where leaders come together in this way: Even if they've been traditionally focused on their units, schools, or departments, they begin to see the interrelationships and bring their own energy to the process.

### The System Holds the Plan

In our first conversations, we decided that the core group would be ongoing and embedded in our practice. We set aside one day a month during the school year to learn together; individually, we would practice our learning every day. Conducting this development and learning right here in the district, as opposed to in an external setting, would turn out to be critical to our success. Sending a few people away to specialized training or bringing someone in for a day or two has never worked in my experience.

Typical staff development programs have specified content and a fixed timeline with progression planned in advance. We simply said, "Let's learn and practice together." We moved along an evolutionary path, where the learning in each session set up the next. The initiative to move our learning along came directly from the core group.

Though I had led numerous sessions about the fifth discipline concepts elsewhere, I felt that I could not be both the teacher and the learner in this core group. That was a pivotal decision. I convinced Nelda Cambron-McCabe, an author of this book, to be our facilitator and guide. Being present as a learner gave me a feel for how the other individuals in the group experienced the learning; I don't think you can understand that unless you are in the sessions as a participant. It requires deliberate patience and restraint from you as superintendent, so that you don't dominate or others don't get in the habit of looking to you for guidance. I took it as an opportunity to practice listening and reflection. I truly believe that the core group saw this as our work, not mine.

Rather than follow a linear path of spending one day on each discipline, Nelda proposed that we integrate them. We began with an all-day session examining the five learning disciplines together. We decided then to spend our second session on what it meant to learn together, focusing heavily on team learning and mental models. In that session, we learned about and practiced many of the tools in *Schools That Learn,* including the ladder of inference, inquiry and advocacy, and double-loop learning (see Section H: Tools). We were introduced to concepts; equally important, we engaged in practice exercises that forced us to use each idea or skill. We made them our own by applying them in our day-to-day work in the schools.

> The ladder of inference became a prominent visual in every core group learning session.

In the third session, at the core learning group members' request, Nelda introduced systems thinking. We created examples from within the school district to illustrate the archetypes. The group found the concept of the iceberg to be so powerful that they decided that the next session would be devoted to it. For that session, small groups of administrators prepared by developing real case problems in their specific areas of responsibility. We then analyzed these using the iceberg. Each group presented its case and analysis as everyone else listened and engaged in conversation about the issues. This activity promoted team learning in multiple ways. Individuals gained better appreciation for dilemmas facing other administrators, everyone received valuable feedback about their issues, and people had an opportunity to practice their listening and inquiry skills.

This evolutionary approach became the model for our planning. Shortly after each session, we scheduled a conference call with Nelda and several core group members. We talked about the last session, what team members were experiencing in their work, and where they needed further assistance. From that conversation, the group agreed on the focus for the next session. The power of this format is its evolving nature. No one saw this as in-service or professional development; rather, it was the way we came together to do our work.

### What We Learned

Did it make any difference? Yes, it did. The dreaded DLT meeting became a substantive learning space. We moved from a dozen agenda items per session, with three or four people reporting and everybody else listening, to sessions where the group controlled the direction. This was such a profound change that people commented about it frequently. DLT members didn't want to miss the meetings. We no longer needed to use meeting time to read information; we put information on our web page. Our meetings were for interaction.

In addition, our interactions changed substantially. Individuals listened closely to each other, raising questions for clarification and wanting to understand. In the meetings, almost everyone talked. Our extensive work on holding meaningful conversation gave us a language to support each other. Someone would say, "We need to hear from everybody because we can't read minds." Saying simple things such as, "There's a reason why everybody's around the table," makes a difference.

To embed this work organizationally, we worked on a lot of fronts at once. Each member of the team was comfortable with different approaches—some modeling the thinking and ideas, and others modeling the application of the tools and strategies. In general, team members listened more in the schools. They asked more questions. The impact was noticeable; staff in the schools would ask, "What's going on with the DLT?"

For me personally, the greatest lesson was the importance of letting go of the need to offer rapid solutions. I learned to say to people, "Confusion is OK; it's normal; it's to be expected. Just trust the process because we're going to be fine." I watched people who were frustrated with this process hang in there awhile; then, all of a sudden, they got it. It's hard to describe the energy that this generated within the group. At first, because of members' concerns about the time taken, we agreed to limit most sessions to four hours. But, by the second session, the core group members said, "That's simply not enough time; we need full days."

Maybe the most important lesson I learned is that it's not about creating a learning organization; it's about supporting the learning of individuals as they figure out how to collaborate.

> "A safe, trusting relationship does not mean that we must agree on everything. It does mean, however, a safe place to express our differences and to engage those differences to make better decisions for our schools. That requires trust."
>
> —Les Omotani

For school leaders who want to follow this path, you must always keep the focus on trust. It required an ongoing effort on my part, and you will need to constantly look for opportunities to build on that trust. Stay mindful that trust is fragile, and be aware that, if you're not living out these principles, then you risk the trust of those around you. If you fail to listen and hear all team members, you will lose trust. As a leader, I learned that I could not expect others to engage in inquiry unless I modeled it in my interactions.

## WHAT'S NEEDED TO DO THIS WORK?

Allow the learning journey to evolve; traditional professional development doesn't work.

Develop trust within the team, and continuously build on it.

Conduct development and learning within the district with the entire team; sending a few people away for training does not help the team.

Learn and practice together the skills to hold meaningful conversations.

Use school system issues as a practice field.

Establish a culture that says it's OK for school administrators to take time away from their buildings for their own learning and development.

Bring the school board along on the journey through sharing the team's learning and new language (i.e., mental models, ladder of inference, etc.).

# G. FROM THEORY TO PRACTICE

*While it's easy to talk about learning organizations and systems thinking, putting all of this into practice is difficult. Here, we get some advice from experienced educators about the day-to-day realities. An experienced headhunter talks about how to apply successfully for a superintendency, and experienced superintendents discuss how to lead and thrive in this challenging leadership position.*

Lee Pasquarella

## 1. Getting the Job

Landing the perfect job is tough, says Lee Pasquarella of Cascade Consulting, a boutique educational talent search firm that likes to look at unconventional candidates for the superintendency. "I'm not impressed with experience," says Pasquarella in his direct fashion. "I'm much more interested in accomplishments. I'm also more comfortable with people who don't have all the answers but are happy to live with the questions."

"The search process is no mystery," he emphasizes. "You need to understand it to succeed. Hard work and attention to detail pay off."

Among the tips Pasquarella offers are the following:

- Know who you'll be interviewing and their interests and biases.
- Don't be surprised by the questions. Develop a list of what you expect to be asked, and then practice the answers.
- Think in terms of accomplishments, not functions.
- People size you up in the first five minutes. Dress conservatively; make eye contact; smile; be pleasant but not chummy.
- Letters and résumés are important—not in guaranteeing an offer but in getting you as far as the interview.
- Make the letter short, sweet, and effective. An introduction should say why you're interested in this particular job; the body should explain why you're the right person; and the conclusion should restate your personal philosophy and why it fits with what the district seeks.
- Pay attention to the normal courtesies and expectations around writing. Don't write to Mr. Smith and address him as Ms. Smith. Proof your materials carefully to weed out grammatical howlers, and double-check your facts and statistics.
- Maintain the three C's during an interview: cool, calm, and competent. You know you can do the job; make sure the interviewer does too.

## 2. Implementing Systems Thinking in a District

*Gene Medina served as a superintendent for 15 years, including 9 years in the North Kitsap District in the state of Washington. Here, he reflects on the importance of organizational development, systems thinking, and mental models in developing an effective and successful superintendency (a collaborative, interdependent team of district leaders).*

## Gene Medina

North Kitsap is a district enrolling about 7,000 students on 12 campuses. From the beginning, I was committed to using systems thinking to design and implement plans to build a learning organization focused on improved student and adult learning. If a district is to evolve as a learning organization, leadership must focus on clear communication, clear goals and action plans, collaborative working relationships, capacity building, and interdependence among its learning communities. So, it was important that I focused on developing a dynamic, focused, and interdependent leadership team that connected with members' personal passions.

If I learned anything through these experiences, it was the importance of taking action, doing the work, and learning together by doing the work rather than getting caught in the trap of analysis paralysis. If we simply begin doing the work by applying our knowledge and skills and being open to learning together, we can learn and do wondrous and incredible things to improve learning. Fullan said it quite simply, "Ready, fire, aim." Do the work because the aiming comes later.

So, what's involved? It begins with you. You must know what you value and believe. It is vital for others to know and hear what is important. What is our work, and why are we doing it? What is nonnegotiable?

Where to begin? You need to know how things are done around here. Obviously, a lot goes into that (see Figure 2.2 for a map of some of the major elements of organizational culture). I recommend school district leaders review and assess the district and school culture, particularly the learning culture. How do we learn about how things get done around here? What are the core beliefs and values of the organization? How are things communicated? What are the district and school goals? Are they aligned? How do individuals deal with conflict? Are differences valued? What are the district norms? What is OK behavior? And what is not OK? What do members of the district believe about children, learning, and their responsibilities as professionals? Understanding these elements can create a foundation for your leadership and planning work.

Where does systems thinking fit into this? Peter Senge identified systems thinking as the *fifth discipline,* or systems thinking in the context of four other disciplines: personal mastery, mental models, shared vision, and team learning. Over time, I have come to understand that systems thinking is a way of seeing or perceiving a system as a whole. To understand a system and think systemically, you need to see the connections among events, patterns, structures, mental models, and vision. (See Gary Wegenke's iceberg metaphor in Figure 2.1.)

Let me illustrate. If we are curious about why children are not improving in their reading and math performance year after year, then look to

**Figure 2.2**   Elements of Organizational Culture

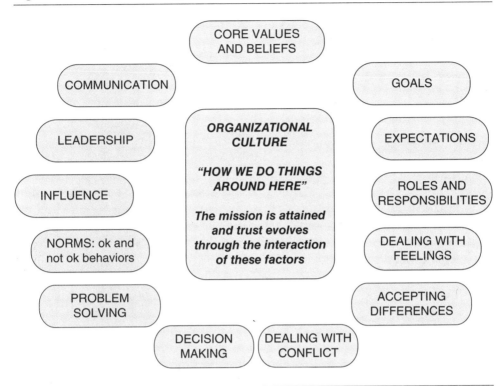

SOURCE: Gene Medina. Used with permission.

events (what is done in classrooms, what is the focus of teachers' and administrators' training activities), review the use of instructional time and teacher and administrator training time (what patterns exist), and identify what structures exist (how instruction is organized and implemented and how teacher and administrator training is organized).

This can lead us to uncover the mental models that drive instructional practices and professional development and, in turn, the real vision for doing the work. Several questions may help: What do the events, patterns, and structures tell us about what staff members believe about success for all children? Do they have doubts about students succeeding? Do some demonstrate by their actions that certain children are worth more effort than others?

Understanding the flow from events to mental models and vision is powerful and can provide valuable insight into the system. While we can focus on aligning the instructional program (goals, core standards, assessment and instructional resources), we also must assess the alignment between what people say they want (words) and what they actually do (actions). Understanding the events, patterns, and structures enables us to discover the real beliefs and underlying drivers in the system.

> "I began my work at North Kitsap by writing and sharing a one-page piece titled 'Superintendent's Core Beliefs and Values.' Additionally, I drafted my expectations for others and myself and shared these with the administrative team, asking them to do the same."
>
> —Gene Medina

I began my work at North Kitsap by writing and sharing a one-page piece titled "Superintendent's Core Beliefs and Values." Additionally, I drafted my expectations for others and myself and shared these with the administrative team, asking them to do the same.

After interviewing all administrators and many of the district classified staff, I found no clarity of purpose and little communication among the district support staff who did not meet together. So, I reviewed roles and responsibilities, interviewed staff, conducted an organizational systems review, and reorganized based on our core focus: improving learning. We created an executive team, which I referred to as the *superintendency*—and we moved right into team building with the administrative teams (district-level leaders and school administrators) and district office support team. I thought it was important that we design a leadership framework that illustrated our core focus and work—improved learning for all—while enabling members to practice and exhibit behaviors consistent with new ways of doing things. I found that old practices linger, and it is helpful if there are many opportunities to practice new behaviors and norms.

For example, as part of this effort, the district executive team expected all members of the district-level support team (directors, secretaries, clerical staff, etc.) to spend at least an hour a week in a school. This created unexpected anxiety. We found that about one-third of our district office staff was uncomfortable going into schools. They were so focused on their own little corners of the world—instructional program management, student records, payroll, human resources—that they hadn't been in a school for years and had no understanding of what happened in them. As we explored this concern, we found that it wasn't really resistance but anxiety. Through their feedback and collaborative conversations, we came upon the ideas of partnering (visiting schools in pairs or trios) and providing training similar to training we provided school volunteers.

Then, something truly exciting evolved. Several secretaries, administrative assistants, and district office clerical staff began developing their own training. It evolved into district office staff viewing themselves as ambassadors to our communities. We were developing organizational capacity and commitment to our new work. We were building a new system with new cultural norms. (Compare Les Omotani's experience in Hewlett–Woodmere, where the dreaded DLT was transformed from a boring bureaucratic function into an exciting learning community, as described in Section F: Building a Core Learning Group.)

You cannot create a learning organization working solely with your administrative staff and teachers. You also must bring the board along.

Growing the board, helping it develop, is one of the great challenges of district leadership. It's also one of the most rewarding aspects—for district staff and students. It is essential that board members with their enormous responsibilities become learners along with all constituencies in the system. Building a learning organization takes time. It is a challenge to listen to different perspectives and try to understand them. But the investment is time well spent. Through discussion and dialogue, you learn, you grow together, and you create common ground. You will find it pays big dividends tomorrow in the form of new energy in your community and powerful learning in your schools.

## 3. How to Thrive as a Superintendent

*Frank Hackett, superintendent of schools in Pembroke, Massachusetts, completed a study in 2011 on the characteristics of superintendents in Massachusetts who thrive in their positions, defined broadly as being satisfied that their jobs are aligned with their values in promoting success for all children. Here, he shares insights with us that echo elements of Heifetz and Senge.*

### Frank Hackett

To understand what makes superintendents effective, I recently held in-depth conversations with five Massachusetts superintendents generally thought to be thriving in their jobs. Among their peers, they had reputations of being able to confront difficult challenges, navigate their way through problems, and even improve their own levels of functioning in the process. They were performing at high levels despite the increasing complexity, ambiguity, and demands of the job, a combination of elements creating high levels of stress and forcing many experienced leaders to consider retirement or other employment.

What makes them different? Well, experience helps. Managing the technical elements of the job is important. The longer superintendents have been around, the greater the likelihood that they stay on top of, for example, the fiscal elements of district administration. But tenure isn't why superintendents maintain passion for their work.

Three factors are associated with superintendents who are seen to be (and who see themselves to be) thriving. They are attuned to their own values. They have a strong sense of moral purpose (and of their own role as a teacher). And they actively enhance their own well-being by continuing their learning and expanding their self-awareness.

### *Attuned to Embedded Values*

Thriving superintendents are attuned to their own values, and they are keenly aware of when the situations they face present conflicts with those values. This feature of successful superintendents provides them with an ability to view the many adversities they confront as opportunities to make positive change. As a result, they approach these issues with both a strong sense of purpose and the expectation that they will succeed. Because thriving superintendents understand the underlying value conflicts, they can help their school communities focus on the values involved, not the conflict. And because these superintendents are aware of their own values, they can appreciate the values of others and have some insight into how those values might be influencing behaviors, up to and including personal insults. In the effort to reach common ground, these superintendents enable a more respectful and open dialogue about values. Because they use values as a touchstone, these superintendents tend to encourage long-term, transformational change.

### Strong Sense of Moral Purpose and Role as Teacher

The moral purpose of these superintendents is found in the work. They express this as a sense of obligation, a duty to make conditions better for those with whom they work and, more specifically, for the children they serve. Superintendents who thrive transcend their own self-interests and the historical practices and culture of their school communities (and, at times, their own political well-being) to move their systems toward a higher sense of purpose in serving the common good.

> Several years ago during a Philadelphia Kiva (see Part V for a description of a Kiva) devoted to the ethical dimensions of education, a superintendent from the West Coast, who at the time was waging a fight against a virulent cancer, was asked if she considered education to have a moral purpose. "Oh," she responded immediately, "of course. Every night, I pray for all the students and families in my district."

In my discussions with these leaders, they were likely to view themselves as essential contributors to the local common good. They tended to ground their sense of themselves as leaders in a deep commitment and care for others, particularly for children. As a result, they respond to dilemmas in ways that show their dedication to their people, to the system they serve, and to deep change in their school communities. Superintendents who thrive exhibit an obligation to expand the awareness of the school community through teaching and guiding others. Essentially, they embrace the role of teacher.

### Enhanced Well-Being Through Self-Awareness and Learning

Thriving superintendents protect and enhance their own well-being through self-awareness and learning. They think deeply about their own values and beliefs in the face of the conflicts they confront. They also understand changes in their practice as a result of being open to other viewpoints. Thriving superintendents have a high tolerance for the ambiguity and messiness of the issues they face. Because they are self-aware, they are able to protect themselves emotionally, often exhibiting an ability to put themselves in others' shoes, while understanding the sometimes unacceptable behavior of people around them.

I concluded that the main difference between superintendents who thrive in the face of adversity and those who wilt seems to involve a self-reinforcing mixture of confidence and mastery. Having mastered one difficult situation, these superintendents are confident they can handle future challenges. Here, all three elements—values, moral purpose, and enhanced well-being—come together. Thriving superintendents paint on a larger canvas, a canvas devoted to bringing social change to their school communities. They view the dilemmas they face not as problems to be solved but as opportunities to make a difference on a large scale. This commitment renews their enthusiasm and helps these superintendents bring everyone around them to higher levels of performance.

# H. TOOLS

## 1. The Ladder of Inference

*Charlotte Roberts gave this Michigan superintendent the ladder of inference and other tools to help her district understand what was happening around it. Mary Leiker, former superintendent in Kentwood, Michigan, describes what she learned.*

### Mary Leiker

The ladder of inference (see Figure 2.3), together with several related tools, helped me improve the interaction in our administrative team and with and among school board members. I see the ladder as a way of breaking apart and slowing down my thinking and opinion formation as well as the thinking of others. Typically, we reach hundreds of conclusions each day and act on those without thinking about how we reached those conclusions.

**Figure 2.3    The Ladder of Inference**

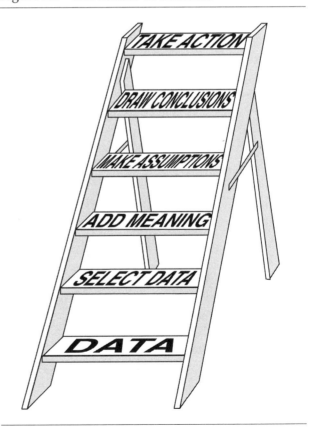

Illustration by Greg LaFever.

The ladder of inference can force us to make our thinking visible to ourselves and to others. An action that seems to occur instantaneously actually begins with the data we observe. From that data pool, we select certain information, add our own personal meanings, make assumptions based on those meanings, draw conclusions, and take action. Because of our own unique experiences and our beliefs about the world, you and I can see the same event and describe the outcome quite differently.

When we reach an impasse, backing down the ladder provides a mechanism for us to learn together. Because we've run up the ladder so often with our built-in assumptions, individually, we reach similar conclusions each time. We fall into a mental habit, which can easily become a prejudice. Working with the ladder (on our own or with others) helps us take off the blinders. Making our thinking visible enables us to bring our best ideas to every issue.

> A detailed description of the ladder of inference can be found in Senge, Cambron-McCabe, Lucas, Smith, Dutton, & Kleiner. (2012). *Schools that learn*.

## 2. The Transition Conversation

### Nelda Cambron-McCabe

### Luvern L. Cunningham

The Transition Conversation process detailed here is one example of support for individuals taking on new leadership positions. This tool provides a powerful process for incoming superintendents to gain an in-depth, systemic perspective on the challenges, opportunities, and barriers they face.

### *What Is It?*

The Transition Conversation consists of a small group of 10 to 15 people convened by the superintendent for an intensive, two-day session prior to the superintendent's entry into a school district. The session focuses on an assessment of the community and its environment and an exploration of leadership strategies that will promote the educational well-being of children.

> Peter Senge's colleague Art Kleiner argues that, in every organization, there is a group of key people "who really matter." To lead, you must understand who that core group is. See Kleiner, Art. (2003). *Who really matters: The core group theory of power, privilege, and success.* New York: Doubleday.

### *Topics and Participants*

Prior to the selection of specific participants, it is helpful for you (as the new superintendent) to think about questions that require the greatest deliberation. Next, identify potential school leaders who can inform your thinking around these issues. These may be individuals who are in similar leadership positions or superintendents who have confronted particular issues and possess certain expertise.

Depending on your context, several insiders may be invited into one or more sessions, but keep in mind that you want an independent assessment, not a restatement of local conventional wisdom. This is a conversation, not a strategic-planning process where you should reach out to all segments of the school community.

### Structuring the Conversation

You should think carefully about how to get the most out of the Transition Conversation. You can take it a step at a time.

### Setting the Stage

Begin your deliberations with a perspectives session. Typically, this will require a full morning to explore the historic context of the school district and community; the current state of the school system and its programs, staff, and students; and the community's expectations of the new superintendent. Individuals who are knowledgeable about the school system and community should be invited to speak about this context.

What you want here are brief, concise presentations, not extended speeches and posturing with numerous charts and graphs. Focus most of the time on asking questions and engaging in interaction with your transition advisers.

### Engaging the Issues

Set aside the afternoon for considering the issues raised in the morning. Ask two or three of the superintendents in the group to facilitate this conversation by beginning with what they heard, what they did not hear, how it fits in the larger local context, and what it means for your leadership. A number of questions can be explored during this period. Here, you want to know what critical issues are facing the district and the community, what needs attention immediately, and which issues are technical as opposed to adaptive.

This conversation can open your thinking to a wide range of perspectives

> Rosa Smith convened a transition conversation when she became superintendent in Columbus, Ohio. "I'm amazed I didn't make more mistakes during my earlier superintendency," she said. "The transition conversation helped me 'think out loud' and shaped my entry into Columbus in very positive ways. Would I do it again? I did! When I left Columbus to assume the role of president of the Schott Foundation, I insisted that my contract include the opportunity for a transition conversation with a President's Advisory Council."
>
> Used with permission from Rosa Smith, former superintendent, Columbus Schools, Ohio.

and important arenas for inquiry. You will see the system through new eyes and different experiences.

### Reflecting on Leadership Strategies

Focus the second day on how to accomplish the work that you must do as the new district leader. This is where you bring the collective learning of the group to bear on your work. What lessons did they learn from their transitions? What would they do differently next time? What do they think you are likely to miss in the beginning months? What parallels do they see between your school district and theirs?

### Follow Up

Don't drop the ball after you take on your new role. Try to reconvene your group at least once during the following year. If it's not convenient for you to get together with them at professional meetings, go to the trouble and expense of scheduling a special meeting. This debriefing can be invaluable as you plan for subsequent years.

## 3. Dialogue: Suspending the Elephant Over the Table

*Sharon Smith from Heartland High excitedly laid out her ideas about how the school might become more student centered by embracing the diverse learning styles of students. It all seemed so logical to her. It would enable alignment of the school's vision (a place where all students achieve at high standards) with what actually takes place in the classroom. Her enthusiastic description of classrooms where students would understand a world of interdependencies rather than memorizing facts and looking for the right answers met a brick wall. Her teammates' response boiled down to, "We could never do that. It would never work here." With that, the conversation was quickly diverted to something that would work.*

> Linda Lambert, in her work with constructivist leadership, notes that a leader's primary role is leading conversations. A leader "opens, rather than occupies, space." See Lambert, Linda, et al. (2002). *The constructivist leader* (2nd ed.). New York: Teachers College Press, p. 64.

> You will find great conversation-starter ideas in Wheatley, Margaret. (2002). *Turning to one another: Simple conversations to restore hope to the future.* San Francisco: Berrett-Koehler.

### Barbara Omotani

Sharon was frustrated. No one even tried to understand this teacher's contribution, leaving her feeling her ideas were not worthy of consideration. She sat silently as the meeting continued.

### Dialogue: Creating a Common Understanding

Surely, you remember the old story about the six blind men and the elephant? Each identified the animal as something different, depending on where he touched—a wall (touching the side); a rope (grabbing the tail), or a tree (feeling a leg). Dialogue is a way to suspend the elephant over the table so that everyone can get a good look at it and describe what they see to everyone else.

It is critical to understand that dialogue is a conversation with the center, not the sides. Rather than participants taking sides, it encourages thoughtful consideration of all diverse perspectives and views. These perspectives go to the center of the table for deliberation and understanding. With dialogue, individuals release the need to defend or justify their mental models. The purpose is learning. (See sidebar: Necessary Conditions for Dialogue.)

> A concise description of dialogue and ways to make conversations more effective can be found in Senge, Cambron-McCabe, Lucas, Smith, Dutton, & Kleiner. (2012). *Schools that learn.*
>
> A *talking stone* can be used as a technique to encourage listening. The individual holding the stone talks; everyone else listens and cannot add ideas until receiving the stone.

## NECESSARY CONDITIONS FOR DIALOGUE

As you begin your work in dialogue, pay attention to the conditions identified here. Each condition requires new skills that all of us have to acquire and practice if we are to engage productively in learning conversations.

**Suspend Judgment.** It's easy to judge someone else's ideas as being good or bad, right or wrong. In dialogue, however, judgments must be set aside. This critical ability to silence the critic in your attic is especially important when the other person's thinking differs from yours.

**Listen.** When most of us say we're listening, we're really just waiting to talk. Listening in a dialogue session is truly hearing and seeing the larger picture of what everyone is saying. It is listening with the intent of discovering others' mental models.

**Reflect.** Reflection is thinking in silence before judging or making a decision. It is pausing between thoughts and actions, consciously slowing down conversations to avoid jumping to premature conclusions. A place to start your reflection is to ask questions: How are the ideas connected? What does this mean for our work?

**Surface Assumptions.** Mental models arise from the assumptions we carry around in our heads. Making progress toward a common vision depends on surfacing and examining underlying assumptions that get in the way of realizing the vision. Often, we don't want to explore assumptions because it is uncomfortable to expose and confront differences within a group. Dialogue provides a safe space to share assumptions and understand their impact on the organization.

**Inquire.** Inquiry involves two dimensions. First, we invite others to critique our thinking: "I've laid out my reasoning here. What do you think?" Second, we seek to understand others' thinking: "Can you tell me more?" Inquiry requires an open mind. You need to be curious about all possible sides of the elephant suspended over the table.

## I. REFLECTIVE PRACTICE

Obviously, we've given you a lot to bite off on leadership. Here, we give you an opportunity to chew on some of these issues. We ask you to think about what you've read so far and apply it to the school situation in which you find yourself.

The exercise that follows can help you reflect on the concepts in this section. It should help you personalize the material and tailor it to your own use while deepening understanding of your leadership challenges. Working with partners from your administrative team provides an opportunity to practice the skills of dialogue.

Here are some key questions for reflection and for consideration.

*What are the values* that guide your district? As a leader, what do you think is important in the district, and how do you try to symbolize and give voice to those values?

*If you had to create an image of your district right now,* what would it be? How about the board, staff, principals, and teachers? Are they similar images and metaphors or different ones?

*What do I need to survive?* Do individuals in my district understand the distinction between technical and adaptive challenges? If not, how do I create a common understanding of this framework?

*What is needed to ensure that all children can succeed?* What are the structural impediments to progress here? What mental models do educators and community members hold regarding children's chances for success? What is it about my thinking and behavior that gets in the way of children learning?

*Can I map the iceberg?* How about systemic structures impeding learning? Have we talked about the mental models that drive the systemic structures?

*Where am I, and where is my staff,* on the ladder of inference around specific issues? Do we engage in dialogue to surface these understandings? If you "suspended the elephant" over your staff table, how would different people describe the issues?

*Where is your balcony?* How often do you get to it? Who are your confidantes and your critical friends? (Here's a hint: If there's no balcony, or you can't reach it, or if you can't identify your confidantes and critical friends, you are in a lot of trouble.)

*Where do you stand* on the spectrum from Lone Ranger to Lead Learner? Can you figure out how to move yourself along the spectrum?

*Map in your own mind the similarities and contrasts* among Morgan's organizational images, Heifetz's adaptive challenges, and Senge's mental models. Do they track? Do they differ? If so, how, and what does that imply for your district?

*Ask your board and your leadership team* to go through the same organizational images exercise. How do their perceptions match yours? Are they comfortable with exercises such as this? If not, what does that imply for your relationship with them?

# PART III

GOVERNANCE

# Coping With Governance Challenges

Clearly, we want you to adopt a new take on leadership, but as Part I emphasized, you are being asked to do so in the midst of a transformed governance framework. Until the last two decades, schools were popularly thought to be a local obligation, a state responsibility, and a federal interest. Faith in the local control of schools could always be taken as a given in any discussion of school administration. All of that has changed since No Child Left Behind (NCLB) was enacted by the federal government in 2001. NCLB demanded that schools in virtually every district in the United States meet annual performance standards, insisted on qualified teachers in every classroom, and encouraged the growth of charter schools and for-profit entities providing supplemental services for students. This general approach accelerated with Race to the Top (RTTT), part of the Obama administration's stimulus package. RTTT put billions of dollars behind transformation models for schools performing in the bottom 5 percent, efforts requiring local boards and superintendents to fire principals and replace up to 50 percent of the teaching staff.

Meanwhile, as funds for schools shrank in 2012, states accelerated their efforts to create charter schools and vouchers, while concerted pushes in states such as Indiana, Michigan, New Jersey, and Wisconsin set out to reshape collective bargaining laws.

In the face of all this, we shouldn't pretend that the traditional meat and potatoes of organizational management don't make a difference. They do. Power struggles with school boards remain a challenge. When you cross local union leaders, you'll make local headlines. And no one will tolerate your failure to balance the budget. You have to lead. But you have to manage, too.

This part of the *Fieldbook* guides you through the minefield of new thinking about governance, the growing privatization of public education, and superintendent-board-union relations.

# A. PRIVATIZATION

## 1. The Growth of Charters and Vouchers

*It's possible of course that the whole thing was sheer coincidence. If so, governors and state legislatures accomplished something truly remarkable in 2011. Faced with the greatest state budget shortfalls in history, they arranged for the greatest transfer of public assets to private schools ever contemplated. It may be serendipitous, but only in the sense that novelist Emma Bull defined a coincidence as "the word we use when we can't see the levers and pulleys."*

James Harvey

The sheer scale of the 2011 effort to privatize public education through vouchers and charters is staggering. "School may be out for the summer," noted a July editorial from the *Wall Street Journal*, "but school choice is in. . . . This year is shaping up as the best for reformers in a very long time." No fewer than 13 states enacted or expanded charter or voucher legislation in 2011, while 28 states had legislation pending.

An earlier version of this article appeared in the Association for Supervision and Curriculum Development's (ASCD's) *Educational Leadership (69)*, December 20, 2011. Reprinted with permission. Learn more about ASCD at www.ascd.org.

Meanwhile, states were grappling with the largest state budget shortfalls on record, according to the Center on Budget and Policy Priorities. Massive budget holes—totaling $110 billion in 2009, $191 billion in 2010, and $130 billion in 2011—had to be filled, patched, and spackled. The combination of the end of the federal stimulus in 2011 and shrinking state and local revenues in the face of high unemployment and the collapse of the housing market meant that perhaps 84 percent of all public school districts expected to be cutting essential services in 2011–2012— paring back classes, eliminating language offerings, laying off teachers, and slashing summer school and extended day programs—according to a June 2011 report from the Center on Education Policy (CEP).

### The State of Play

Did governors and state legislators respond to the crisis CEP described by rushing to shore up public schools? Many did not. Tax credits, vouchers, and charters were all the rage in many states. Louisiana strengthened the state income tax break it provides for private school tuition. North Carolina permitted parents of students with disabilities to claim tax credits for expenses related to private school tuition. There was talk in the

Tar Heel State of a system of public schools designed around vouchers. Governor Scott Walker of Wisconsin, who engaged in a bitter dispute with public employee unions over collective bargaining, lifted the cap on the number of students in Milwaukee's Parental Choice Program, the nation's original voucher effort.

Even national figures got in on the act. While voting to cut $11 billion out of federal education funding for fiscal 2011 (including cuts in Title I, Striving Readers, literacy, teacher quality, math and science, education technology, and special and vocational and adult education), the U.S. House of Representatives found the money to maintain charter and choice funding. At about the same time, the U.S. Supreme Court turned its back on long-standing Court precedents with a 5–4 vote that ruled in favor of an Arizona school voucher program that critics argued improperly directed taxpayer funds to religious schools. Nine years earlier, on another 5–4 vote, the Supreme Court in *Zelman v. Simmons-Harris* also ruled that Cleveland's state-enacted school voucher program did not violate the U.S. Constitution.

### *The Levers and Pulleys Behind the Coincidence*

When advocates of charters and vouchers take credit for their commitment to choice and the needs of low-income children, do not be beguiled. The altars before which many of them genuflect are those of the business world—deregulation, markets, and contempt for public service. Those altars are the levers and pulleys behind the year's events.

The 2011 developments were the culmination of a 30-year assault on public services in general and public education in particular. Grounded in arguments in favor of free markets and letting citizens decide how to spend their own money, this rhetoric has demonized the poor, catered to the financial power of Wall Street, and disregarded public oversight and regulation, even in basic areas such as food safety.

The truth is this hostility to government has produced an orgy of tax cuts over three decades, leading to unsustainable deficit financing at the federal level. It has also hamstrung governments in states such as California, where citizens' initiatives have required two-thirds of voters to raise taxes but only one-third of them to veto tax increases. Government financing in too many places today suffers not from de Tocqueville's tyranny of the majority but from a tyranny of the minority.

> "Research on the effectiveness of vouchers and charters as educational strategies is disappointing, ambiguous, and unpersuasive at best."
>
> —James Harvey

This particular tyranny has taken public funds intended for the common good and redirected them toward the benefit of the middle class and the wealthy. And it has done so at the precise moment states were staring into the abyss of bankruptcy, forced to gut programs providing nutrition and medical care for low-income children.

*Flying in the Face of Evidence*

Political leaders might find some justification for their actions if they could point to compelling evidence that vouchers or charters provide superior results. With more than 4,600 charter schools enrolling more than 1.4 million students in the United States, charters have become a significant force in education reform. They are a darling of the left, the right, and major education foundations.

On the merits, it is hard to understand the attraction. Research on the effectiveness of vouchers and charters as educational strategies is disappointing, ambiguous, and unpersuasive at best. The impetus behind privatization is based on ideology, not evidence.

In 2009, a pro-charter institute, the Center for Research on Education Outcomes (CREDO), at Stanford University, which had earlier reported encouraging findings on student achievement in charter schools, completed a meta-analysis that integrated longitudinal databases on student achievement in 15 states and the District of Columbia. The jurisdictions involved in the CREDO study educate more than half of all students in the United States and contain more than 70 percent of the nation's charter school students.

The results were sobering: On the basis of student achievement, it was hard to distinguish nearly half of charter schools from traditional public schools. Only 17 percent of charters produced gains that were significantly better than traditional public schools, while 37 percent "had results that were significantly negative." That is to say, in comparison with traditional public schools, charters failed twice as often as they succeeded.

The CREDO researchers handily dismissed criticisms of their methodology. The results stand as the benchmark national study on charter school outcomes.

For the CREDO study see Center for Research on Education Outcomes. (2009). *Multiple choice: Charter school performance in 16 states.* Palo Alto, California: Author. In addition see the summary by Brent Johnson of his study of urban charter schools in Ohio.

Students with vouchers surely do better in their new placements than students in traditional public schools? Certainly that would be true in inner cities? If so, the evidence has yet to appear. Here again, we find dueling studies from advocates on both sides. But reams of credible evidence undermine the case for vouchers.

Through 2009, U.S. Department of Education evaluations of the Washington, DC, voucher program demonstrated no improvements in academic achievement for targeted students. A 2011 account indicated Cleveland public school students often outperformed voucher students on state proficiency tests. In 2011, students in Milwaukee's long-standing school choice program performed worse than, or about the same as, students in Milwaukee Public Schools on the latest statewide tests in math and reading.

"Voucher schools are no silver bullet," concluded Diane Ravitch, author of "The Death and Life of the Great American School System" in *Education Week* in April 2011. "They [voucher schools] should not be embarrassed. But our policymakers in Washington and in the statehouses should be."

A number of studies and analyses have called into question the effectiveness of voucher programs. See, for example, National Coalition for Public Education. (2009, April). Summary of all Department of Education DC voucher evaluations (http://tinyurl.com/9wztedk). Ott, T. (2011, February 22). Cleveland students hold their own with voucher students on state tests, *Cleveland Plain Dealer*, and Richards, E., & Hetzner, A. (2011, March 29). Choice schools not outperforming MPS, *Milwaukee Journal Sentinel*.

### A Bigger and Bolder Approach to Meet the Needs of the Whole Child

Peter Senge argues that leaders need to move away from quick fixes, easy solutions, and silver bullets. Leaders need to understand interrelationships, deeper patterns, and the systems behind the events. They need, in short, to become systems thinkers. In education, this means that quick fixes like charters and silver bullets such as vouchers are no substitute for sustained attention to the needs of the whole child.

One of the perverse outcomes of the current education debate is the exclusion of educators from the school reform discussion at the policy level. Educators have become strangers in their own land, marginalized and silenced through a process of blame, belittlement, derogation, and the assumption of superior insights by people who have rarely spent an adult day in a classroom. Many seem to believe that learning can be reduced to a specific set of skills that can be codified into guides for teaching. The result is the adoption of technical solutions to what are, at heart, complex human challenges calling for difficult, adaptive work involving all stakeholders.

In the face of these assaults on the competence of educators, some analysts and educational leaders have pushed back. A coalition of analysts and advocates put together a plan known as the broader, bolder approach. In a statement released in 2009 that quickly drew several thousand signatures, the broader, bolder coalition insisted that half a century of research had confirmed the impact of social and economic disadvantage on schools and students. In light of that reality, the coalition insisted on the need for evidence-based reform that would supplement school improvement efforts with developmentally appropriate and high-quality early care and education, increase investment in health care services for children and families in poverty, and deal with out-of-school challenges to learning with efforts to provide disadvantaged students with the cultural, organizational, athletic, and academic enrichment programs that middle-class parents take for granted for their children.

Meanwhile, ASCD, an international coalition of educators, has advanced a similar agenda known as the *whole child approach*. A whole child approach to learning, teaching, and community involvement would set out to ensure that every child, in every school, in every community is healthy, safe, engaged, supported, and challenged, according to ASCD. In Part I, Jack Jennings proposed enshrining the right to such an education as a civil right.

Now is the time for policy makers and educators to unite around a bigger and bolder agenda that respects the civic role of the school, recognizes the effects of poverty on achievement, and encourages the development of comprehensive and coordinated services for children, integrated around the school.

Interested in the broader, bolder agenda or the whole child approach? See http://tinyurl.com/9wztedk.

## 2. OHIO STUDY: ACHIEVEMENT IN CHARTER SCHOOLS NO BETTER THAN IN TRADITIONAL PUBLIC SCHOOLS

*Brent Johnson*

In 2011, I completed a study of student achievement comparing traditional public and charter schools in Ohio's Big 8 urban districts: Akron, Canton, Cincinnati, Columbus, Cleveland, Dayton, Toledo, and Youngstown. These districts educate more than 70 percent of African-American students in the state. This was a rigorously designed study. It focused exclusively on student achievement, comparing math and reading achievement in elementary charter and traditional public schools over a three-year period. Using data from the Ohio Department of Education, each of the 94 charter schools in these urban districts was carefully matched with comparable traditional public schools in the same area. The matches were based on average daily enrollment, percentage of Black (non-Hispanic) students, percentage of White (non-Hispanic) students, percentage of economically disadvantaged students, percentage of students with disabilities, percentage of properly certified teachers, and teacher experience.

The results? There were no achievement differences between charter and traditional public schools in Ohio's eight largest urban districts. In the few instances where differences did occur, traditional public schools outperformed their charter school counterparts. Ohio approved charter school legislation in 1997 with the idea that publicly funded charters, permitted to circumvent state and local rules and regulations, could raise student achievement. Ohio has been actively involved in this experiment for 14 years. At best, however, charter schools are doing no better than traditional schools. The results of this study raise a fundamental question: Is it worth $2.8 billion to continue funding charter schools that do not raise the quality of education for urban students and their communities?

# B. THE CHALLENGES OF PUBLIC ADMINISTRATION

James Harvey

Richard C. Wallace, Jr.

When it comes to difficult challenges in public administration, the task of overseeing a school system, particularly in urban communities, ranks right up there with the positions held down by police chiefs, city managers, and public transit directors. Some school superintendents are responsible for systems that enroll more students than a state university, while being the largest providers of food, transportation, and routine health screening in their communities. Many districts—urban, rural, and suburban—are the largest employers in the area.

The very complexity of these organizations explains why toil, turmoil, and turnover are the lot in life of the superintendent, especially in big cities. The conventional wisdom that the position of superintendent changes every two years probably overstates the case, but newspapers around the country continually report on unpleasant terminations of superintendents' employment. Sometimes, it's a budget crisis that precipitates the rupture. Often, it's a disagreement with the union that undoes the incumbent. Too frequently, it's a clash with a board member or a faction of the board over micromanagement of the district. In 2001, the Public Broadcasting Service (PBS) broadcast a two-hour special describing life in the fast lane for an urban superintendent and concluded it was the "Toughest Job in America."

School superintendents have long complained about the governance challenges of their work. Board members are supposed to provide democratic oversight of public schools. Yet, too frequently, members are named in off-year elections with low voter turnout.

> The American public was introduced to the complexities of the superintendent's assignment in 2001, when PBS broadcast "The Toughest Job in America," produced by the Merrow Report. Narrator John Merrow is the regular education reporter on PBS's *News Hour*. A discussion about the program can be found at http://tinyurl.com/ametsdj.

Indeed, turnout can be so low that as few as 5 percent of local citizens can elect board members, a situation rife for manipulation by special interest groups, whether the issue is restoring creationism to the curriculum or boosting teachers' salaries.

Although many boards are able to avoid these problems, the possibility of mischief around board elections is always present. So, too, is the human tendency of individuals on the board to mistake their oversight role for the opportunity to straighten out management. Board meddling and micro-management is a near-universal complaint of school system leaders.

Another near-universal challenge is how to work with teachers' unions. Although adequacy of teachers' salaries and the perquisites of seniority receive a lot of attention in public discussions, most members of the public are just now beginning to realize how central these issues are in school union–management relations.

The fact is that teachers' incomes don't stack up well with the salaries paid to other professionals with college degrees. Their bargaining units never let management lose sight of that reality. While management may feel that computers, new textbooks, or revisions to the curriculum are the most important educational priority of the coming year, many union officials are inclined to look at every dollar spent elsewhere as money unavailable for salaries. And, while reformers demand that the best teachers be put in the most challenging schools, unions insist that seniority (and the prerogative of choosing where to work that accompanies seniority) is a sacred cow.

Teachers' unions, of course, are simply one of the bargaining units that many superintendents work with. In large districts, it is not unheard of to have another half dozen or more unions representing different groups such as bus drivers, carpenters, electricians, maintenance personnel, and cafeteria employees. If you wind up in one of these districts, you'll find yourself bargaining with all of them.

In Homer's epic, Odysseus was required to pilot his boat through a narrow and treacherous strait. His vessel was threatened on one side by the flesh-eating Scylla and, on the other, by the whirlpool Charybdis. You're not likely to be devoured by the board or drowned by the union. But you're going to have to pilot your district through the very stormy waters raging between these two sides. This part of the *Fieldbook* provides you with some useful charts and navigation aids. And it suggests ways of working with your board and your unions.


## C. CHANGES IN STATE AGENCIES

*Michael Gorman, an educator and coach for 37 years, has served as superintendent of schools in two New Jersey districts. Since 2006, he has been superintendent of the state's Pemberton Township schools, enrolling more than 5,000 students.*

Michael Gorman

While policies at the national level have developed and evolved, profoundly affecting expectations of superintendents (see Part I), state education agencies, once regulation-encrusted barnacles on state government, have also taken on new life. A top-flight education agency head who returned to his former shop after a decade away immediately noticed the difference.

David Hespe, chief of staff to the New Jersey Commissioner of Education in 2012, served as commissioner of education in the Garden State under former Governor Christine Todd Whitman. "In philosophy, vision, and structure," Hespe told the National Superintendents Roundtable in June 2012, "there is no comparison between the Department of Education I entered in 1997 and the one that exists today. They are very different places."

He goes on to describe a department that is more focused on school performance and outcomes, as distinct from the entity he led, which was part of a hierarchy in education that "focused on making sure that everyone did what they were supposed to do." He considers this change in New Jersey to be typical of the changes experienced by state education agencies around the country.

"In 1997 we thought our job was compliance," notes Hespe. "When it came to school improvement, we told people what to do. But, if you made a list of low-performing schools in 1997 and compared it to the same list today, there'd be very little change. So, you'd have to say that in terms of our efforts in the state since 1997, the compliance approach has not been very successful."

A good symbol of the changes afoot can be found in New Jersey's request for a waiver under NCLB. Today, observes Hespe, the state, like states everywhere, is focusing on schools, not on districts. It is now moving away from telling districts what to do to an emphasis on doing more alongside the most troubled schools. "We want to bring in expertise in data, leadership, organizational development, curriculum and evaluation. We want to be partners. There are 2,500 schools in New Jersey and, instead of worrying about them all, we're focused on the 200 schools that need the most help."

Hespe describes a new state education agency worrying about four key initiatives: an NCLB waiver from the U.S. Department of Education; educator effectiveness; college and career readiness; and educational transformation. In this effort, he insists, his agency is trying hard to listen to what local officials have to say.

Hespe acknowledges that the New Jersey Department of Education is experiencing difficulty finding the right people to put on its own bus, to use an image from Jim Collins's *Good to Great*. State department employees face a salary cap of $141,000, and it's hard to find outstanding people willing to go to work for the state at that level of salary, he concedes. Challenged as to whether Governor Christie's decision to cap salaries for local Garden State superintendents has not been a boon for surrounding states (who are hiring experienced superintendents from New Jersey), Hespe insists that the situation presents the state with a great opportunity: Districts are hiring ambitious, young administrators from elsewhere. Is the rancor between educators and the governor that seems so divisive to people outside the state interfering with good government in New Jersey?

Hespe thinks not, dismissing the issue as a clash between the personal styles of the governor and the head of the state teachers' association.

Apart from the politics of the change, the larger lesson from Hespe is that state education agencies are moving away from worrying about process and regulatory equity for all schools to performance and equitable outcomes in the most challenged.

# D. WORKING WITH IMAGES OF ORGANIZATION

## Luvern L. Cunningham

Remember what we had to say earlier about images of organization? Try to apply some of those images to the problems you're encountering with board members and union leaders (see Tables 3.1 and 3.2). You may think you're leading a district that, like a finely tuned learning organization, assesses its own performance and works to improve it. But your board members may have a much different metaphor floating around in their minds. They may think of the district as a finely tuned machine, disciplined in its pursuit of standards, with a curriculum and administration aligned around achievement of those standards. To them, you're not a leader but a mechanic. At their most unpleasant, they may see you as little more than a board flunkey because the image that they could never describe in public (or perhaps even admit to themselves) is of a system based on politics and power.

Meanwhile, your union may be working in concert with an entirely different image. You say you want to create a learning organization, a district that functions like a brain. So does the union. But it puts a political twist on the metaphor, insisting that the components of the organization (specifically the union's members) have to conceptualize how this learning organization will be designed. Far from being a partnership involving all, the union may be intent on minimizing your role in reshaping the organization you're supposed to lead.

Knowing which metaphors drive your board members and unions may not entirely solve the challenges they pose for your working relationships. But they will help you understand why some of the games you see around you are being played, and they may give you some ideas about how to deal with them.

# E. WORKING WITH YOUR BOARD

*Nothing can make life better for a harried school superintendent than a board united behind her. And nothing can make her life more miserable than a badly divided board that routinely votes 5–4 or 4–3 on every significant issue before it.*

**Table 3.1** Inherited Images of Organization: How the Board and Union Behave

| Inherited Images | The Board | The Union |
|---|---|---|
| Machine | No-nonsense bottom line; runs a tight ship<br>Chair runs the show; short meetings; low-profile superintendent<br>Limited citizen participation<br>CEO/board of directors philosophy<br>Oriented around results<br>Rigid reporting lines<br>Power sought and respected<br>Diversity not a priority | Well prepared for struggle of negotiations<br>Attracts support from other labor unions<br>Influences other bargaining units<br>Listens to national leadership about strategy<br>Skilled in building and maintaining membership<br>Salaries and benefits outweigh learners' interests<br>Top labor lawyers handle negotiations<br>Top leaders do not always reflect the rank and file |
| Political System | School board is first step on political ladder<br>Many candidates for board vacancies, often soliciting war chests<br>Board meetings broadcast on radio or TV<br>Polling often used; citizen participation championed<br>Students are a means, not an end<br>Members seek personal media coverage<br>Committees and task forces are popular<br>Will sacrifice superintendent for political advantage | Leaders well known inside and outside jurisdiction<br>Skilled and muscular lobbying is a strong suit<br>Always has best institutional memory around<br>Secures favorable settlements, even in hard times<br>Plays on constituencies' heartstrings<br>Monitors and nurtures special interests<br>Understands neighborhood and community media<br>Active in all elections, including those for school board |
| Psychic Prison | Salutes tradition<br>Supports back-to-basics curriculum<br>Educating kids for the 1950s<br>Opposes innovation, outsiders, technology, and sex education<br>Board meetings are formal and by the book; turnover low<br>Seeks and supports conservative administrators<br>Little participation in state associations<br>Fiscal conservatism is demanded and rewarded by reelection | Contract provisions followed to the letter<br>Focused on salaries and benefits<br>Hidebound on educational issues<br>Building representatives are enforcers<br>Building representatives often play hardball<br>Expects loyalty from the rank and file<br>Leaders usually tougher than board or superintendent<br>Lukewarm on standards and assessment |
| Instrument of Domination | Relishes local control and fights to protect it<br>Take-no-prisoner approach with management and union<br>Oriented around fiscal conservatism and accountability<br>Prefers weak superintendents and administrators<br>Promotes loyalty through nepotism and sole-source contracts<br>Punishes those who challenge its power<br>Disinterested in achievement gap or issues of race and class<br>Boards usually appointed and new members resemble old | Prepared to strike; hangs tough in negotiations<br>Leadership dominated by former middle and high school teachers<br>Uses rumor mill to inform membership<br>Threatens school officials from time to time<br>Disinterested in achievement gap or issues of race and class<br>Teachers' working conditions oppressive<br>Devoted to "I teach . . . you learn" pedagogy<br>Little sympathy for organizational development |

**Table 3.2** Emerging Images of Organization: How the Board and Union Behave

| Emerging Images | The Board | The Union |
|---|---|---|
| Culture | Improving academic achievement for all children is basic<br>Diversity reflected in board membership<br>Equity is a prominent and consistent value<br>All sectors invited to speak to the board<br>Policies in place to honor multiple views<br>Members participate in state associations<br>Members represent a broad range of constituencies<br>Members adamant about advocating for financial resources | Consistently supports school improvement<br>Respects diversity and supports closing the achievement gap<br>Committed to closing the achievement gap<br>Local traditions are important<br>Endorses minority recruitment and professional development<br>Sensitive to community cultural change<br>Supports policies for family leave and health benefits<br>Acts on assumption that school cultures reflect community |
| Organism | Leading members understand systems thinking<br>Joins professionals in support of academics<br>Organizes celebrations to reward good work<br>Builds and sustains collaborations to meet needs<br>Selects a superintendent with community-building skills<br>Uses committees to do its work and worry about board growth<br>Engages media in educating the public<br>Exploits technology for organizational growth | Joins in system's efforts at school improvement<br>Comfortable working with the superintendent<br>Supports reform and accountability<br>Participates in local, state, and national educational movements<br>Incorporates learning needs into contract<br>Leaders are also learners<br>Unusually strong capacity for fiscal analysis<br>Invests in union development |
| Brain | Focused on schools' educational mission<br>Supports a community-of-learners philosophy<br>Supports site-based management<br>Champions excellence in student performance<br>Works collaboratively with colleges and universities<br>Creates partnerships with private research centers<br>Sees unions as allies in development<br>Adopts high personnel standards | Leadership embraces organizational development<br>Joins the board and administration in search for new strategies<br>Strong commitment to standards and reform<br>Considers itself to be a learning community<br>Bargained contracts reflect its commitments<br>Engages in research<br>Committed to technology and its application to learning<br>Invests union resources in the learning community concept |
| Flux and Transformation | Restless and impatient with the status quo<br>Prizes innovation and change<br>Challenges tradition<br>Endorses alternative routes to licensure<br>Frequent challenges to board leadership positions<br>New-age administrative leadership sought and applauded<br>Supports the concept of multiple ways of learning<br>Willing to take fiscal risks in pursuit of goals | Members aware of changing environment and possibly anxious<br>Prospect of membership growth exists if change is threatening<br>Possibility of backlash from anxious members must be considered<br>National and local leaders struggle to understand change<br>Opportunities exist for new rank-and-file leaders to emerge<br>Partnerships with superintendent and board look attractive<br>Focus on children and their achievement is a winning political strategy<br>Fusion of technology in curriculum embraced |

*Working with a representative board, whether elected or appointed, is like performing in front of a panel of Olympic judges every day. Few members of this panel hand out 10s. In this section, we help you through the board thicket by describing typical challenges of board work and summarizing decades of experience from successful superintendents.*

## 1. Getting It Right With the Board

### Luvern L. Cunningham

Most people wind up reporting to an individual, a single superior. On occasion, a professional may have to make a report of some kind to a committee, but that's fairly infrequent, not a daily occurrence. The "line" relationship is really with an individual.

As a school superintendent, you are placed in a unique employment system. It is hard to think of any other in the world that is similar. You will be hired by a collective known as a school board or a school committee; you will be expected to report to this group; and your work will be approved or challenged by it, sometimes on a daily basis.

Your tenure in office demands that you satisfy the expectations of this group. If it's a nine-member board, you must carry with you on every significant issue at least five votes. But that's a very uncomfortable working margin, because the board's makeup can change on short notice. Ideally, you should have the support of all nine board members. You should be so lucky to live in that administrative paradise. Many superintendents are happy with a working margin that provides them with six out of nine votes of support and consider themselves in Eden if they can count on seven votes consistently. Smaller seven- or five-member boards, of course, make your margin for mistakes with the board even narrower.

Now, here's the rub. Satisfying the expectations of the board (which is required if you are to survive in office) may or may not coincide with what is required if you are to succeed educationally in the district. To prosper in that sense, you have to raise standards, close the achievement gap, develop your principals, and work with issues of race and class. Sometimes, this work can put you at cross-purposes with the board. There's a tricky balance here. You can be successful by one measure—surviving on the job. But can you survive and succeed educationally?

Getting it "right" with the board will be a key issue in your long-term success. Here are some ideas that promise to help.

### Get Off to a Good Start

You should make sure that student learning is a central element in how the board will judge your success. The time to have this conversation is not after the board has decided it's unhappy with you because you've started moving principals around (in order to get the most effective administrators where they're most needed). The conversation has to begin during the recruitment phase (see Part II, Section H: Tools: Transition Conversation). As one superintendent said, "We thought the board hired us to make change. It turns out it hired us to make the crisis go away. So here we are making change and it's not exactly what they wanted."

### Use Your Honeymoon Productively

No matter how troubled your school system is, you will enjoy a honeymoon in your new community. This is the period when the board members talk about what a great person they selected. The union leader insists that, unless you succeed, the schools cannot succeed—and unless the schools succeed, teachers can't succeed. You'll get good copy and positive coverage in the local newspapers. You can do no wrong. You may even walk on water. It may last FDR's proverbial 100 days. It may last a year or longer. However long it lasts, several things are apparent. First, life is wonderful. Next, the honeymoon will come to an end. And finally, you will want to use every opportunity during the honeymoon to strengthen the hand you've been dealt. Don't waste this time. Use it productively:

- Reestablish the understandings reached during the selection process about district goals and objectives, particularly those related to learning. You don't want board members to forget why they hired you.
- Make and cement relationships with internal and external constituencies. You must pay attention to both your internal and external audiences during this honeymoon period.
- Insist on a candid, independent, external review of the district and its potential problems. Surface major issues early in your tenure so that most reasonable people in the community will not lay the blame at your feet.
- Give the district the bad news about the problems you've diagnosed and the medicine that has to be prescribed. You may have to clean up some problems you've inherited, but you shouldn't put yourself in a position of taking the blame for them.
- Analyze community opinion and resources. You need a very good sense of the community and its needs.
- Cement your relationship with the board while putting your administrative team in place. There's a concept of relational distance about the appropriate role of the board with respect to central office staff; you need to defend your staff from board intrusion.

There's a lot to be done during the honeymoon period. If you're too busy basking in the warm glow of the first 100 days to do the work required to stabilize your position, you may find yourself in the same position as a lot of newlyweds. When reality sets in, both sides begin exploring phone book entries under *lawyers—divorce.*

> Analyze community opinion and resources. You need a very good sense of the community and its strengths and needs. See Claire Sheff Kohn's ideas in Section H: Tools for how to proceed.

### Work on the Relationship to Sustain It Over Time

Like any relationship, the one between you and your board requires work. It requires a lot of attention over a long period of time. One experienced and highly successful superintendent found that quarterly meetings, which provided him with formative evaluations, worked wonders for the relationship. Some superintendents have found that many of the learning organization tools related to inquiry and advocacy, mental models, and team learning have had a significant impact on their relationship with board members (see Part II: Leading Your Schools). However you structure this relationship, building it should always start by recommitting to the goals and objectives you've already agreed on.

### Time to Go?

When it's time to go, you want to exit with dignity. Don't worry. In most instances, you'll know when that time has arrived. Board members will forget the agreement to focus on learning and will begin second-guessing you about portable classrooms or reporting relationships in your office. Board turnover may become more frequent, creating instability. What had been a relationship of mutual self-respect begins to deteriorate. Those newspaper stories about your imminent demise? They appear more and more regularly. And the board chair seems less and less interested in knocking them down.

What to do? Sometimes, it depends on where you are in the contract cycle. If the contract is about to expire, it will either be renewed, or it will not. But if you have questions about the shape of the new contract and whether it is fair to you or not, it's probably time to think about updating your résumé.

The reality is that, unless the relationship has become irretrievably broken, most boards will want to treat you with respect. And you should treat your board with respect. The best solution here is often simply facing up to the obvious: Get together with the board chair to obtain agreement that your lawyer and the board's will work to plan a smooth exit that is fair to both parties. That's how you leave with your dignity—and that of the board and the community—intact.

## 2. TIPS ON WORKING WITH THE BOARD

*Your relationship with your board will make or break you. Here's what experienced superintendents advise.*

*Richard C. Wallace, Jr.*

Pay attention to this relationship. Don't assume that lack of friction is good news. Problems can sneak up on you out of the blue. Below are some ideas for managing and nurturing a good relationship:

1. Regular workshops to address policy and to provide ongoing evaluation to the superintendent can be career savers.

2. When you are hired, establish in writing, from the word *go*, the ground rules of your relationship with the board. These ground rules should include the formal terms of your evaluation.

3. Ideally, you should get the board to agree on its priorities early in your tenure. Use research, data, needs assessment, and focus groups to help the board agree on priorities. Then, use those priorities as the touchstone against which you assess board requests for staff work.

4. Work with the chair to minimize board micromanagement. When individual board members cross the line, you need to confront them immediately. Also, develop a conflict-of-interest policy to protect the board and your staff from themselves.

5. Insist that all staffing issues, including hiring and firing of principals, are your responsibility. You can't give this fundamental management role away to the board.

6. Empower the board to succeed by helping members make policy, address constituent concerns, and run a perpetual campaign in support of the schools.

SOURCE: Adapted from The urban superintendent: Creating great schools while surviving on the job. *Report of a Colloquium for Former Urban Superintendents, Council of Great City Schools* (September 2003).

### 3. School Finance 101: No Surprises Around Money

Richard C. Wallace, Jr.

As superintendent, you can probably survive quite a bit of bad news. But there is one surprise where you will be held personally accountable. It is the shock of finding that the district has been spending more money than it has. It doesn't matter that there is a chief financial officer (CFO) in charge of the budget. All that will count is that both the board and you failed in your fiduciary responsibility to local taxpayers. Depending on how serious the shortfall is, a financial meltdown in your district is very likely to cost you your job.

Mishandling the budget is one of the surest ways to grease the skids for your exit. Here's how to get a handle on district finances.

1. Regular, annual, external audits are not irritations but potential career savers.

2. In addition to audits, you need a financial analysis that explores how money is used, how much is received by formula and from soft sources, how much is committed (and to what), and how much is discretionary.

3. If you don't understand budgeting, get a tutor or go back to school. You can never be confident that you are on top of issues in your district unless you have a full grasp of the budget. Without it, you are not in command of your district; your budget director is.

4. Worry about building the financial literacy of your board members. For a surprisingly high proportion of board members, the most complicated financial bookkeeping they have ever dealt with is a household checking account.

5. Checks and balances are basic. One person should approve and another should write checks. And it's always a good idea to require two signatures on any check. Even in the nonprofit world, money has a remarkable habit of disappearing unless people keep their eyes on it.

6. The small odds and ends of district finance can create huge headaches. Establish procedures to monitor schools' independent activity funds. And discourage board or staff use of district credit cards.

7. While you need to understand the budget, you should stay out of the details. It's typically hundreds of pages of minutiae. What you need to grasp is broad strategy and a sense of the budget options available to you to influence student achievement.

8. It's a good idea to allocate a minimum of 1 percent of the budget for professional development.

9. The budget needs to reflect district priorities, and it also needs to reflect yours.

10. If you are interested in a particular theme related to student achievement, fund this theme at the outset. It will be hard to finance it after everything else has been funded.

SOURCE: Adapted from The urban superintendent: Creating great schools while surviving on the job. *Report of a Colloquium for Former Urban Superintendents, Council of Great City Schools* (September 2003).

## F. WORKING WITH YOUR UNIONS

*There's no question that union–management relations have become more toxic in the last 10 years. In 2011 and 2012, rancorous disputes between public officials and union leaders were common. In Wisconsin, protests saw 100,000 or more protestors occupying the state capitol in opposition to Governor Walker's plans to take away public unions' right to collectively bargain over health care and pensions, to limit pay increases to the rate of inflation, and to end automatic dues collection by school districts. Similar protests greeted passage of Governor Mitch Daniel's proposals to make Indiana the first Rust-Belt state with a right-to-work law barring union contracts from requiring nonunion members to pay union dues. Governor Chris Christie of New Jersey referred to teachers' unions as "political thugs," while Mayor Rahm Emmanuel found himself dealing with the first Chicago teachers' strike in a generation in part over his plans to close 100 regular schools, open 60 charter schools, and implement a major new teacher evaluation system based, somewhat, on student achievement.*

*The ramifications of these developments will play out for years in courts before superintendents will know where they stand legally. Meanwhile, you have to work with your staff, your teachers, and your unions. This section provides you with some rules for the road.*

James Harvey

Apart from teachers, it's hard to find anyone who has much that is positive to say about teachers' unions. In public discussions of school reform, unions are often demonized as reactionary bulwarks against change, staunch advocates of the status quo. On occasion, teachers join in the criticism, and in recent years, thoughtful union leaders have tried to rethink how organized labor can improve its relationship with district management.

In many ways, union critics have a strong case to make. Union leaders imagining the school system as a political entity can easily convince themselves that they've waited out reform superintendents before and they can again. "Here comes another one!" is the cynical response. When superintendents who are trying to terminate incompetent teachers find themselves tied up in seemingly endless and costly hearings and procedural due-process snarls, they can easily decide that the potential benefits aren't worth the cost.

> "We have to end this process in which outbreaks of war between the union and district interrupt periods of chronic, long-term, festering resentment. In war, anything goes, with lots of casualties."
>
> —Adam Urbanski, President, Rochester Teachers' Association (in a superintendent roundtable meeting)

In some ways, however, the case isn't immediately self-evident. On a state-by-state and community-by-community basis, some of the worst schools in the United States are found in states without unions. If unions are the problems their critics make them out to be, there's little evidence to support that in states with political cultures opposing collective bargaining.

Here's the issue: Outside critics can afford to carp about unions and criticize teachers, but you have to work with the union. Teachers are your workforce. And here's a related reality: If organized labor and unions disappeared off the face of the earth tomorrow, you would still need a labor-relations strategy for dealing with your teachers. What would it be?

### A Legacy of Union–Management Strife

It's hard to recall now, but 50 years ago, the National Education Association (NEA) counted administrators among its members, considered itself to be a professional association, and looked down its nose at the upstart American Federation of Teachers (AFT), which was busy organizing teachers. In those days, teacher salaries and benefits were low, and salaries for elementary and secondary teachers differed substantially. It was a profession dominated by women presumed to be supplementing their husbands' incomes. These women would be in the workforce for a short time, anyway, because they would undoubtedly return to the home as soon as their children arrived. In a world such as that, teachers' strikes were inconceivable.

All of that started changing around the mid-1960s as the AFT succeeded in organizing more militant teachers, and the NEA realized that a new era was at hand.

### Trade Union or Professional Union?

In a sense, what is at issue is whether teachers' unions will be trade unions or professional unions. If you are successful in working with your union to develop a more professional orientation around labor-relations issues, everyone will win. You will have an easier time bargaining with the union. Your community will see that unions are as concerned with learning, accountability, and teaching as a genuine profession as they are with grievance procedures and protecting teachers' rights. Teachers will benefit the most. They will be paid like true professionals and will enjoy the authority and status that teachers elsewhere in the world enjoy.

Want to read the case against teachers' unions? You need *The New York City teachers' union contract: Shackling principals' leadership.* New York: The Manhattan Institute, 1999. It argues that school principals' hands are tied by contracts requiring seniority-based hiring and rigid work schedules that impede the dismissal of poor teachers and keep principals from putting the right teachers in the right jobs.

The case for teachers' unions? A nonideological defense of the value of teachers' unions can be found in the September 2011 issue of *Forbes.* Arguing that, in a democratic society, teachers cannot be bypassed in reform, columnist Erik Kain argues that unions are valuable "not because they are a model of efficiency or because they are always right or because I think there is no need for reform. . . . No, I support teachers unions because they are the best chance this country has to improve and strengthen public education *for the long haul.*" See *http://tinyurl.com/3sf6q7z.*

## 1. A Primer on Labor–Management Relations and Contracts

### Luvern L. Cunningham

Few district employees, and even fewer citizens, know much about the details of local union contracts. Labor negotiations occur mostly behind closed doors, sheltered from public view. Some contracts are very brief and others very lengthy. Here are some key points to keep in mind about bargaining and contracts:

- Collectively bargained agreements brought benefits to many school district employees throughout the 20th century.
- Not all districts or states have unions or collective bargaining. In many states, collective bargaining for public employees is prohibited (as it is for private employees).
- Bargaining processes and outcomes vary from district to district and state to state. There is no single process that fits all. In 2011 and 2012 several states eliminated what are known as *fair share agreements,* which require all teachers to pay union dues in recognition of the benefits they receive from collective bargaining.
- The teacher contract is a "sacred text," exercising great influence over day-to-day school operations and efforts to improve schools and student achievement.
- Memoranda of understanding between the union and the district often constitute what has been called the *contract behind the contract.* Pay attention to such memoranda; they extend and often complicate the contract.
- Contracts with other employee groups have similar influences, often in terms of the length of the school day and the school year, access to school facilities, and standards of maintenance.
- Some longtime union heads are the most influential district leaders, often overshadowing superintendents and board members if considerable turnover exists.
- Despite the lack of detailed information available to the public, salaries and fringe benefits attract the greatest public interest.
- Contract sections governing professional development; selection of materials; and teacher qualifications, assignment, seniority, and evaluation profoundly influence student learning.
- In many districts, schisms between labor and management have existed for years, accompanied by a climate of acrimony that makes negotiations about learning difficult.
- The local balance of power is often disturbed when state and national union leaders offer support to district labor leaders as the negotiating process gets under way.
- Evaluation of district employees, especially teachers and administrators, can be a source of great conflict and hostility, even in the case of professionals deemed incompetent by superintendents.

- An interest in professional unionism is emerging at national and local levels, suggesting that unions play a central role in issues such as teacher accountability, program quality, and implementation of standards-based reform.

## 2. Do's and Don'ts in Contract Negotiations

*David Alfred, executive director of the statewide Employee Relations and Negotiating Network in Washington, is responsible for a collaborative effort between the statewide association of superintendents and the statewide human resources association. He helps district leaders organize themselves for negotiations and creates a statewide community for district leaders to think about employee relations. He also provides bargaining and negotiations training and negotiation and labor relations crisis support.*

James Harvey

"It's important," says Alfred, "to understand the distinction between classified employees and certificated employees in most states." In Washington, for example, classified employees legislation contains a specific prohibition against striking, but the law regarding certificated employees, including teachers, is silent on whether they can strike. Although teachers are not prohibited from striking by law, precedent prohibits them from doing so. Courts in the state of Washington have consistently held that teachers do not have a right to strike. Whenever the possibility of a teachers' strike develops, school boards almost invariably seek court injunctions prohibiting such a strike.

Alfred describes three distinct bargaining styles: traditional adversarial bargaining, collaborative and trusting bargaining, and what he described as interest-based bargaining, in which participants on both sides come to the table as problem solvers. While he's a big believer in the concept of interest-based bargaining, says Alfred (you have interests; we have interests), it requires a lot of training, "takes forever," and has had a hard time taking root.

> A limited right to strike exists under state law for public employees in Alaska, Colorado, Hawaii, Illinois, Minnesota, Montana, Ohio, Oregon, Pennsylvania, and Vermont. Alaska law has been interpreted as prohibiting teachers from striking even though most other public employees are permitted to strike.

Collective bargaining is a tricky area, and it is likely to test board–superintendent relations unless everyone understands their roles, according to Alfred. The board's role in bargaining, he says, is to set policy, be the public's voice, and ratify the agreement. That's it. They are not the bargainers. They should not be at the bargaining table and, ideally, should be united in support of whatever agreement is negotiated, whatever the size of the board. Here are key issues, according to Alfred:

- If a strike is a possibility, unite the board behind your approach. If the board is not unanimously ready to take a strike, it will cave in before it should, or disagreements within the board will become public knowledge, undermining the district's negotiators.

- Agree on the district's philosophy. Don't bargain away management's prerogatives. If you want to settle in the worst way, you probably will.
- Prepare, prepare, prepare. Take only well-considered proposals to the table.
- Never bargain off templates or proposals from the union. Listen to the union; then bargain off your proposals.
- Be ready for employee bargaining units to attack individual members of the management team, including the superintendent, personally, by name, and in public. The employees want to get board members to the bargaining table, and you just have to live through this.
- Communicate regularly with the community and staff about progress in the negotiations—otherwise, the employee bargaining unit gets to drive the public narrative.
- Make sure management communicates with employees in the event the union fails to inform, or misinforms, employees about management's latest offer.
- Understand that unions have extremely well-developed tactics for approaching negotiations (including bringing in national and state-wide reinforcements).
- Unions think very hard about how to slow down management as it deals with financial gaps and the need to implement reductions in force.

It's not unknown for superintendents and boards to agree to contract provisions that will become unworkable in the future, long after superintendents and board members have moved on. Harvard's John F. Kennedy School of Government developed a case study of such a development in Buffalo, New York. There, the three main elements of the governance triangle bought labor peace by relying on unique provisions requiring the state to bail out Buffalo (and other big cities) if it ran out of money. As state finances tightened, of course, this house of cards collapsed. You can find the case study on the website of the National Superintendents Roundtable at http://www.superintendentsforum.org.

- Be patient. Don't be driven by the clock. Take the time to negotiate an agreement you can live with today and the district and the community can live with tomorrow.
- It is especially important to have the district's lawyers take the time to draft language carefully after a tentative agreement has been reached. Shoddy legal draftsmanship can easily give away key provisions you thought you won at the bargaining table.
- In negotiations with unions, says Alfred, remember that there is conflict frequently between the interests of younger teachers and those who are more senior. A savvy district negotiator can often work that tension to the district's advantage.

## 3. Bargain Like a Pro

Richard C. Wallace, Jr.

How do you bargain without giving away the store? Here are the fruits of experience from decades on the front lines involving a dozen big-city superintendents. Follow it to bargain like a pro:

1. Get legal advice in negotiating and administering contracts. The superintendent of a major urban district never sits at the negotiating table. That is a task for staff and attorneys.

2. Try to obtain a uniform negotiating calendar unless you're prepared to have the district endlessly tied up in negotiations, union by union.

3. Encourage collaboration around the main thing—student achievement. Ideally, the contract becomes a living document that adjusts and changes continually as understanding of student achievement evolves.

4. Make the contract the instrument for advancing student learning. If it isn't in the contract, it's not really the main thing.

5. Think of negotiating as a problem-solving mechanism, not a source of conflict. Ideally, it should be a perpetual tool for problem solving.

6. Keep language about the calendar out of the contract. It's likely to be too restrictive. Also, make sure that you don't agree to noneconomic provisions with financial implications.

7. Find ways around problems. No union representative can abandon the union's position on seniority. Insist that the superintendent has the right to assign personnel for the good of the district. Handle assignments on an exception basis if need be. Unions also want good schools.

8. Leaders and members are different constituencies. Often, the leader is far ahead of members on key educational issues. In the same vein, you should inform all teachers of changes in the contract. That way, you define the change, not a bargaining or building representative.

9. Work with the board chair to have one spokesperson for the board's position during negotiations. You can't negotiate if the board is a Tower of Babel.

10. Don't agree to grievance procedures that create more trouble than they're worth. The grievance procedures should not become a source of grieving.

11. Keep up to speed on what's happening with union reform. Some of the most progressive ideas about how to advance learning are coming from union leaders themselves.

12. Watch out for union–board relationships. It's not a good sign if the union knows of the board's position before you do.

13. Remember that the contract is the union's "sacred text." If it isn't in the contract, it's not important.

SOURCE: Adapted from The urban superintendent: Creating great schools while surviving on the job. *Report of a Colloquium for Former Urban Superintendents, Council of Great City Schools* (September 2003).

# G. THE SMALL-DISTRICT SUPERINTENDENT

*Urban education receives a lot of attention in the United States; urban systems often enroll 100,000 or more students. Most people are surprised to learn that more than 50 percent of the school systems in this country enroll 1,000 or fewer students. What's life like in a small-district environment?*

Janie Edmonds

When I signed on as superintendent of a district with fewer than 1,000 students, I had no idea how many ways the role of the superintendent would differ from the same role in the 6,300-student district that I left. In my eighth year in the same small district, my perspective is much better informed. The best and the worst of this wonderful district is its size.

The primary and most obvious difference between the two superintendencies is that one is a job of delegation coupled with all of the associated mentoring and monitoring roles that effective delegation demands. The job in a small district, lacking a staff of specialists to whom you can delegate, means that you, the superintendent, necessarily are truly a hands-on leader, a mentor and doer rather than a mentor and monitor.

Here are some of the features of a small district, as I have come to understand them, organized around administration, student achievement, and parental involvement.

### Administration

• **Nature of the Work.** Nothing says it better than roll up your sleeves. You'll be wearing a business suit, but the variety of tasks that you'll engage in directly is endless. It's never boring. While working in the larger district, I was taken aback when a (very) small district superintendent called me at the last minute to apologize for not arriving to lead a cochaired county-wide meeting. He had to stay behind to cover a class because a substitute teacher wasn't working out. This example highlights the hands-on leadership you need to be willing to provide.

• **Hats.** "Hats?" you ask. This is about how many you will wear. You will wear as many as can be stacked without them all tumbling down. You will achieve a deep understanding of every role in school leadership. That's invaluable for your career and leadership. As a small-district superintendent, you are human resources. You are the budget specialist. You are the mentor to all other administrators and to some teachers, particularly those who teach a discipline that you taught and know well. Some superintendents serve as business administrators as well. Others assume leadership of special education. Some serve as principal of a school, too. The possibilities are unlimited.

• **Personal Privacy.** What's that? All public leaders give up much of their personal privacy. In a small community, where everyone knows nearly everyone else and where word travels as fast as an electron between energy levels, people know you well. People will wave at you in your car, and students will grin and wave wherever they see you, bringing the pleasure that being pleasantly recognized usually does. All of the cheery and intrusive aspects of social media will find you in person if you hold a highly visible position in a small community.

• **Bureaucracy.** Bureaucratic layering is minimal in a small district, so people are more likely to find their way to you with their problems and with their appreciation. Though problems that work their way up the organizational chart are not smaller, you will find more flexibility in decision making because fewer people were involved in the decision before you. Systems analysis is more readily accomplished as well.

• **Cost of Administration.** Per-pupil costs for individual administrators will be necessarily larger. This may raise eyebrows around budget time. Lower the eyebrows by reminding people of how precariously high your hats are stacked. There is no way around this truth. Per-person administrative costs are higher in smaller districts.

• **Budget Challenges.** Even temporary declines in student population create discomfort and diminished morale among the faculty. Teachers' jobs are at stake, and anxiety is high. Budget cuts can be devastating in small districts, threatening the arts, guidance, media centers, extracurricular activities, and athletic teams. I found shaving but not eliminating programs to be effective. Reducing positions to four-fifths or even 50 percent is painful, but the likelihood that you can restore programs is much better if the program remains in place.

• **Manageability.** Few individual situations are too hard to manage. You are, after all, an experienced administrator. There can be far too many issues on your desk far too often. That said, with fewer buildings to visit, fewer people to know, fewer records to sift through when deciphering situations, and quick access to any teacher or student, obstacles of scale are minimized. You will quickly identify your allies and readily build a network of critical friends in the community.

*Student Achievement*

• **Instruction.** Student interests are more easily kept at the center of all that you do in smaller places because you know people so much better. Smaller districts have a bonus when it comes to achievement too. When you and every one of your administrators can know every teacher well enough to understand each teacher's strengths and needs, programs and professional development can be better targeted to improve instruction. Remember the excellent 6,300-student district I mentioned earlier? I was asked there if I observed every teacher's work every year. The answer was in the numbers: There were 510 teachers and 180 school days per year. To visit every teacher's classroom would take 170 days, assuming I could schedule three teachers a day. Observing was a delegated, shared task, and there were teachers I didn't know. Exceptional academic supervisors did visit every teacher's class there every year, but most of my insights were necessarily secondhand.

• **Discipline.** A teacher's ability to give more attention to each student is supported by smaller numbers. Fewer disciplinary issues accompany more individual attention and districtwide consistency. That leaves more time for learning. It's a great scenario, and it's a great support for teacher and community morale. You will surely find that it creates an environment where issues such as harassment, intimidation, and bullying are seldom brought to your door, which means, of course, that everyone feels safer and can focus better on learning.

• **Relationships.** At the heart of the advantages of smaller places are the relationships that a small scale supports. Relationships foster dedication and familiarity, and they encourage personal interaction and a resulting sense of personal safety. Students know each other, all of the teachers, and their administrators, including you. They can take learning risks with less apprehension. Achievement is enabled.

• **Sense of Identification and Belonging.** These characteristics make it matter more for you to try to do well. You matter, as a person and as a student. You matter as a superintendent who is a person too. Others are rooting for you and counting on you because they know you. They care if you do well. That doesn't eradicate every problem, but it does soften the impact.

• **Curricular and Other Opportunities for Students.** Because the number of opportunities will be smaller, you will want to ensure that they are chosen and monitored with great attention. Partnerships are key here. Online learning can augment curricular programs, and learning effectively online is an increasingly important skill. While there may be fewer offerings, the likelihood that a student will be able to participate in an Advanced Placement class, on an athletic team, or in an extracurricular organization is enhanced. The percentage of students who can have active leadership roles in student government or extracurricular activities is increased.

- **Retention of Students.** An enhanced sense of identification and belonging helps reduce drop-out rates. Smaller class sizes make your small public school district competitive with private and public charter schools, which are valued for their smaller class sizes and ability to give more attention to each student.

### Parent and Community Involvement

- **Attention to Individuals.** Parents in a small community recognize you, the superintendent, and expect one-on-one time with you whenever they feel they need it. That's usually a good thing, though it lengthens your day. If your children's parents recognize that their children are doing well and that you care a great deal for that to be true, they value you a great deal. Time spent with parents is time judiciously spent.

- **Knowing Names and Families.** It's entirely possible for you to learn many names, especially those of parents who are highly visible or have large families. My pharmacist and a salesperson at a local department store have known my name since the first time I shopped in their stores. The sense of personal interest that it seems to represent keeps me going back time after time, though neither is the best deal in town. We love to be known. In schools, it can earn you casks of human capital.

### A Major Challenge

One of the most significant issues a small district faces is the challenge of remaining innovative in the face of pressures to be insular. It's a particular issue for teachers. If, for example, you have only four teachers at a particular grade level, and the district provides them with regular, recurring blocks of time to work together, ideas quickly get a little stale. After a while, the four teachers have shared all of their best ideas—and a lot of their good but not best ideas too! Somehow, you have to give teachers (and administrators) opportunities to learn in partnership with people from other districts who have had different sets of experiences.

This is just a small slice of how very different the experience of a small-district superintendent is from those of colleagues in larger places. What matters most is that you match your style and preferences to the nature of the district you serve. The days are long, and the responsibilities are heavy, but in a place that fits you, the rewards are frequent and make your days much more satisfying.

## H. TOOLS

### 1. Build an Entry Plan

*Despite our emphasis on the importance of including everyone in district planning, it's probably not wise to show up on the first day of work without some idea of what to do on Monday. Claire Sheff Kohn, who served as a superintendent in four districts in two states (New Jersey and Massachusetts), outlines how you can prepare an entry plan into a new district.*

## Claire Sheff Kohn

I wanted to learn as much as I could about the system and community and believed that spending time and effort up front would reap long-term benefits. I knew the demands of the job would hijack my schedule soon enough, so I wanted to protect against that by drafting a comprehensive entry plan clearly laying out what information I would gather and how, from whom, and according to what timeline. I expected to put out some fires, but I wanted to keep the focus on students and instruction, using the entry process as the first step in building the foundation for the future work of the district.

So, how to begin? Here's one way:

> Here are two useful references to help superintendents promote powerful learning: City, Elizabeth A., Elmore, Richard F., Fiarman, Sarah E., & Teitel, Lee. (2009). *Instructional rounds in education: A network approach to improving teaching and learning.* Cambridge, MA: Harvard Education; Curtis, Rachel E., & City, Elizabeth A. (2009). *Strategy in action: How school systems can support powerful learning and teaching.* Cambridge, MA: Harvard Education.

*Write a preliminary outline of your entry plan, which can be finalized after soliciting input from a coach or mentor and a handful of other trusted colleagues.*

In the preliminary outline, you include the purpose of this process, the initial list of stakeholders to be interviewed, a few open-ended questions to be asked of each group, the mechanisms for gathering data, the timeline to be followed, a statement that the findings will not be presupposed, a note that areas for further study will be identified, and an explanation about how and when the findings of the study will be reported publicly.

### *Determine Who You Need to Talk To*

You can anticipate who should be on a preliminary list of stakeholders—school committee or board members, administrators, employee bargaining units, town officials, local media, parent and student groups, and more. But you'll need help identifying groups unique to your new district as well as the names of key individuals and their contact information. Start by asking board members, central office staff, and building-level administrators to review your preliminary list and add to it. Then, you can get out letters or e-mails of invitation with the entry plan enclosed, and start scheduling group and individual meetings.

*Undertake a comprehensive document review, and figure out how to vet this (and other data) with the leadership team.*

As part of the interview process and during review of budgets and websites, you learned a lot about enrollment and demographics, student achievement, staffing levels, and the financial status of the district. Googling the district and scanning the local papers for issues and news also helped. Now that you have the job, an important part of the entry process is to get up to speed as quickly as possible on the many details involved in any school district. You'll need to explore student achievement data, school improvement plans, district goals, strategic plans and policies, employee contracts, school committee minutes, written evaluations of faculty and staff, and organizational charts and staffing plans. That's just for starters. You'll also need to get on top of recent state department reports, student discipline data, the technology plan, special education, reports on the program of instruction, school accreditation, annual town reports, and legal matters such as grievances and arbitration.

After reviewing this array of documents, touch base with people you trust, including your leadership team, to test your initial thoughts. You want to promote a highly functioning leadership team through shared purpose and clarity about the work of the district. This is the foundation on which you and your team's success in the work of the district will be constructed.

*Begin to visit schools and classrooms with your principals (and later with a coach or mentor).*

The only way to get a true grasp on the quality of instruction in the district is to get into schools and classrooms. You will need to schedule specific times to be out in the schools observing classrooms with your principals. Think of yourself as a coach to your principals, one who keeps them focused on the instructional core, instructional practice, and the improvement of student achievement. If the district has a classroom-observation method in place, use it. If not, work with your principals to create it.

*Develop a method for organizing the data collected with an eye toward making the writing of the entry report relatively easy and painless.*

Your entry plan process will take months to complete and involve enormous amounts of data. You need to figure out how to organize all of the information into a coherent whole so as to make the writing of the entry report relatively easy. As you collect information, work with your administrative assistant to keep track of the data and organize it. I use an online application for tracking projects. I like to put together a binder of entry plan artifacts—such as letters, notices, and surveys. I also keep a journal in which I record important issues, facts, and other notable items as I go through the process. Tap a coach, a mentor, and other trusted colleagues for other ideas. One of the things you'll need to sort out is what you want to include in the report and what to keep for your own personal understanding.

School systems are complex organizations. Entering a new system is daunting, but I believe developing an entry plan will put you in a better position to lead. The point is to listen and learn in the hope of making the complex into something more manageable. The goal? That's simple: to work in partnership with others to make this district as good as it can be so that your students can be as successful as they can be.

## 2. How Well Is Your Board Functioning?

### Luvern L. Cunningham

Board effectiveness will determine your effectiveness. The checklist in Table 3.3 will help you to get started. It can be used for either discussion or assessment.

## 3. Leading While Surviving Professionally and Emotionally

*Richard Wallace, Jr., served as superintendent for many years in Massachusetts and Pittsburgh, Pennsylvania. Here are some ideas he developed with other large-city superintendents to help school leaders survive.*

### Richard C. Wallace, Jr.

Recall from earlier that Ron Heifetz said that leaders can quite literally be killed. He was talking about national leaders and the risk of assassination many of them run. You may be threatened physically. Some school leaders are public figures, and while it is rare, it is not unknown for some superintendents to require 24-hour-a-day security in the face of threats they have received. Gunfire broke out at a Panama City, Florida, school board meeting in 2010, as an aggrieved citizen turned his anger on the board and the superintendent.

Still, the bigger risk you run is of character assassination. That's never fun, and it can be painful. Don't think for a minute that your spouse will enjoy reading the caustic comments of parents or teachers in the local newspaper. You may have to worry about insults your children will hear at the local school. In the face of this kind of unpleasantness, how do you maintain your sanity and sense of self? You need to worry about protecting your inner self and your family.

You have a district to lead. Your district is full of families relying on you to educate their children. The board may be worried about proper deference at meetings. The union may be complaining about unreimbursed time from teachers. To the families in your community, however, these are sideshows. They want their children educated. How do you do that while surviving professionally and emotionally?

Experienced and successful superintendents offer two key pieces of advice. The first protects you professionally: Make sure you have seven elements—elements that are necessary to lead any organization—in place.

**Table 3.3    How Well Is Your Board Functioning?**

Circle the appropriate number below:

(1 = Very Poor; 2 = Below Average; 3 = Good; 4 = Excellent)

*The School Board . . .*

| | | | | |
|---|:-:|:-:|:-:|:-:|
| . . . spends most of its time and energy on education and student achievement. | 1 | 2 | 3 | 4 |
| . . . believes that advocacy for the educational interests of children is its primary responsibility. | 1 | 2 | 3 | 4 |
| . . . concentrates on goals and uses strategic planning to accomplish its purposes. | 1 | 2 | 3 | 4 |
| . . . works to ensure an adequate flow of resources and equity in their distribution. | 1 | 2 | 3 | 4 |
| . . . harnesses the strengths of diversity and integrates special needs and interests into the goals of the system. | 1 | 2 | 3 | 4 |
| . . . deals with controversy in an open and straightforward way. | 1 | 2 | 3 | 4 |
| . . . leads the community in matters of public education, seeking and using many forms of public participation. | 1 | 2 | 3 | 4 |
| . . . exercises continuing oversight of education programs and their management, draws information for this purpose from many sources, and knows enough to ask the right questions. | 1 | 2 | 3 | 4 |
| . . . works out, in consultation with the superintendent, separate areas of administrative and policy responsibilities and how these separations will be maintained. | 1 | 2 | 3 | 4 |
| . . . determines the mission and agenda of each committee, ensuring coherence and coordination of policy and oversight. | 1 | 2 | 3 | 4 |
| . . . establishes a policy to govern its own policy making and policy oversight, including explicit budget lines to support those activities. | 1 | 2 | 3 | 4 |
| . . . invests in its own development, using diverse approaches that address the needs of individual board members and the board as a whole. | 1 | 2 | 3 | 4 |
| . . . uses policies and procedures for selecting and evaluating the superintendent. | 1 | 2 | 3 | 4 |
| . . . uses policies and procedures for evaluating itself. | 1 | 2 | 3 | 4 |
| . . . collaborates with other boards through statewide associations to influence state policy and how state leadership meets the needs of local schools. | 1 | 2 | 3 | 4 |
| . . . understands the role of the media and its influence on public perceptions and avoids manipulating the media for individual political gain. | 1 | 2 | 3 | 4 |
| . . . supports local control and is vigilant in safeguarding the rights of communities to determine what constitutes the educational well-being of children and their families. | 1 | 2 | 3 | 4 |
| . . . provides, in cooperation with the superintendent, for the orientation and preparation of new board members. | 1 | 2 | 3 | 4 |

This section is adapted from The urban superintendent: Creating great schools while surviving on the job. *Report of a Colloquium for Former Urban Superintendents, Council of Great City Schools* (September 2003).

The next nurtures you personally: Build shelters and create structures in which to protect yourself emotionally.

*Organizational Leadership*

As a school leader, you should be worrying about these seven organizational elements as well:

- You must have the right people. You can't do it all yourself, so you need good people in key leadership roles at the district and school levels.
- You must have access to data about your system's performance. Otherwise, you are probably operating in the dark. You can't really understand your organization's strengths and weaknesses.
- You need an effective delivery system. Having the right people or right ideas doesn't do you much good if you can't deliver what you set out to provide.
- Logistical systems are essential. Getting the bits and pieces of the organization moved around and where they need to be when they're required is often the difference between success and failure—in schools and corporations as well as in military campaigns.
- You need a communications system. You need to be able to communicate effectively both within the organization and beyond it. Without such a system, you are unable to affect what goes on in your organization or communicate its needs and accomplishments outside the system.
- You absolutely have to have a methodology for evaluating the first five elements. This may well be the area of greatest organizational weakness both in and out of schools. Everyone understands the importance of people and communications systems; fewer realize how important it is to evaluate every aspect of organizational operations.
- Finally, you need to understand that leadership success is a process, not a destination. You must endlessly recycle your understandings developed during the evaluation throughout the first five elements, engaging in what organizational theorists have lately come to call continuous improvement across every facet of organizational life.

This list might lack the complexity and detail of many educational theories, but it possesses the elegance and virtue of simplicity. You don't have to be charismatic to lead your district. If you are going to lead it effectively, however, you should be worrying relentlessly about this short list.

*Emotional Survival*

One of the things you will have to adjust to as superintendent is the realization that criticism comes with the territory. You'll need to develop a tough skin. Being on the receiving end of personal attacks, delivered either face to face or anonymously, is not easy on you or your family. Given the demands of this job, and the very high level of stress it imposes, superintendents have to be strong individuals. You will have to be, too. This is not a position for the faint of heart. It will not sit well with people still struggling to sort out their values. The first essential is that you know something about yourself.

Knowing yourself and your strengths and weaknesses is critical. Nobody is perfect. No superintendent is ideal. But, at some gut level, superintendents must understand what they stand for and how they are likely to respond to stress. They should also understand their own personal biases. A superintendent inclined to blame students for failure is unlikely to be an ideal leader in a district with a lot of vulnerable children. A leader who likes to scapegoat teachers may find it hard to inspire their trust. Ideally, you will welcome challenge and respond well to it. But, if you're inclined to head for the hills when unexpected surprises develop, you need to find people who can shore you up in that area. Make no mistake about it—stress, unexpected surprises, and downright unpleasantries are part of the job.

There are some tried-and-true methods of minimizing personal stress. Get used to the idea that, whatever you decide, you're wrong! "Should we close school this morning because it's beginning to snow and the forecast indicates a possibility it will get worse?" The answer is, "Yes," according to many parents worried about their children's safety. "Who are you kidding?" say others, already en route to work without child-care arrangements in place. "Should we offer extended-day services at cost to help parents in the workforce?" "Of course you should," say parents desperate for affordable and safe day care. "Over my dead body!" may be the response of local taxpayers.

> See Wallace, Richard. (1995). *From vision to practice: The art of educational leadership.* Thousand Oaks, CA: Corwin.

In a district enrolling several thousand students, whatever you decide will offend someone. Don't let the criticism slow you down. Do what you think is the right thing and move on. Otherwise, you will be immobilized.

Next, it may take the patience of Job, but while critics are busy personalizing their attacks on you, you must take care to focus on issues, not people. No matter how ugly things get, your responsibility is to stick to substance. The public needs to understand that your priorities are high-quality education, children's safety, and responsible administration of the public's business. The naysayers will say what they have to, regardless of what you do. Don't get down in the mud with them. Former Omaha, Nebraska, superintendent Norbert Schuerman used to like to quote an old farmer's saying: "When you wrestle with a pig, the pig has fun, and you get dirty!" Get used to the idea that conflict is the price you pay for leadership.

> Remember a smart farmer's warning: "When you wrestle with a pig, the pig has fun, and you get dirty!"

Finally, put yourself first. It's not selfish to say that. Unless you can preserve your sense of self, you cannot do what you went into education to do—help all children learn at high levels. To put your district's children at the top of policy priorities, you have to put yourself first. Otherwise, you are no good to them. So, worry about maintaining your sense of self. Understand your strengths and weaknesses. Think about your values. Don't take any of it personally. And get up on the balcony every once in a while with people you trust to get your bearings and renew your commitment.

You'll find all of these efforts time well spent.

### 4. Ten Ground Rules for Survival

Richard C. Wallace, Jr.

How do you survive in the hothouse of the superintendent's office? Here are 10 rules of the road from successful former superintendents.

*Ten Rules of the Road for Survival*

1. The main thing is to maintain student achievement as the primary objective; that is, never take your eyes off learning.

2. The most important element of the main thing is belief in students.

3. If what you are doing does not improve what happens in classrooms between teachers and students, it is probably not worth doing.

4. Accountability means making a year's worth of difference in the life of every student, every year.

5. It doesn't matter what you decide, you're wrong! Conflict is the price you pay for leadership.

6. Don't take it personally. Remember, if you wrestle with pigs, you get dirty, and the pig has fun.

7. Listen to the people around you. They can keep you from falling flat on your face.

8. Leaders make their own good days. When leaders create real value for citizens, the public will respond enthusiastically.

9. Making permanent change means changing the things that are permanent.

10. All leaders are in transition whether they succeed or fail.

SOURCE: Adapted from The urban superintendent: Creating great schools while surviving on the job. *Report of a Colloquium for Former Urban Superintendents, Council of Great City Schools* (September 2003).

# I. REFLECTIVE PRACTICE

The always formidable difficulties of school governance have become even more challenging in an era of high standards, greater accountability, and questions about the efficiency and effectiveness of government generally. The stakes have never been higher for you or for the students and families in your community.

This section provides an opportunity for you to reflect on how you can respond to these challenges. Here are some key questions you should be considering.

*What's your experience with internal conflict in the district?* Do you find yourself whipsawed by competing demands from boards, unions, and the central office? Or do these different power centers work reasonably well together?

*Are you troubled by micromanagement by your board?* Or is that not a significant issue in your experience?

*Does the board (or do individual board members) say one thing and do another?* How do you account for shifting opinions about what to do on the board and among its members? Is there anything you can do to help stabilize the board around a central mission?

*Where do social media fit into the governance equation?* Have you and the board established guidelines to define who speaks for the board, especially in an age of instantaneous communication via social media?

*What about the union?* Is your union more influential in the district than either you or the board? Or are you fairly comfortable with the role of the union and how it wields its influence in district affairs?

*Are you able to put teachers where you most need them?* Or do you find that seniority or other provisions in the agreement dictate teacher assignments?

*Are there significant differences between your images and story lines and those of your board and union?* If so, what are the implications for district governance? Could these differences explain some of the disputes and tension in your district?

*Are you confident that district finances are in good shape?* What have you done to guarantee that the day never arrives when your CFO calls you to announce a major budget shortfall?

*What have you done to encourage more openness about change in the union?* Has it helped? Was it a waste of your time?

*What have you done to preserve your sense of self?* Where's your balcony? Who's your critical friend? What do you do to preserve a sense of your own value?

# PART IV

# *Learning and Assessment*

T he new discussion in education focuses, as it should, on learning and high achievement for all students. The goal of high achievement for all is to be attained through standards and assessment. The consequence is that educators and policy makers are bombarded on a daily basis with national and international assessment data that purport to assess the state of American learning. But very rarely do these assessments define what learning is.

On occasion, they try to draw lessons for best practice or improved policy, but it is not always clear what lies behind these judgments or how reliable and useful they are. For example, a lengthy report on lessons for school reform based on the Program for International Student Assessment (PISA) administered by the Organization for Economic Cooperation and Development (OECD) casually offers up Hong Kong and Shanghai as examples of how education in China is changing. But the fact is that Hong Kong and Shanghai bear almost no resemblance to the rest of that great nation. Perhaps most remarkably, this lengthy report mentions the Communist Party of China (CPC) only once and comments benignly on the five-year plans for educational policy developed by the CPC's Politburo. Indeed, what the National Superintendents Roundtable heard from Finnish officials during a visit to Europe in 2012 is as applicable to China as it is to Finland and the United States: "It's not possible to move the education system of one country into the culture of another."

This part of the *Fieldbook* reviews briefly the shape of the new policy discussion in the United States. It then examines emerging principles of learning organized around what cognitive psychologists sometimes refer to as the *malleability of intelligence.* Essentially, this is a concept that hard work at learning can make one smarter. Here, we draw on research from cognitive psychologists and neuroscientists such as Lauren Resnick at the Learning Research and Development Center (LRDC), University of Pittsburgh; Amishi Jha, leader of the Jha Laboratory at the University of Miami; and Dan Siegel, MD, of the University of California, Los Angeles (UCLA), School of Medicine. Their work suggests that ability is not fixed but malleable, that student effort can create ability, that student focus and concentration can be improved, and that emerging insights from neurobiology carry clear educational implications. This leads, in turn, to a discussion of the Common Core State Standards, on which so much of the hopes of the educational policy community rest, before taking up the achievement gap and value-added assessments of teachers.

## A. THE SHAPE OF THE NEW DISCUSSION

James Harvey

You may not remember what launched the standards-based reform movement, but most old-timers would date it to April 26, 1983. That's the day the National Commission on Excellence in Education arrived at the White House with an alarming report for President Reagan asserting that the nation was literally at risk due to the poor quality of education in the United States. One of the remarkable things about the reform movement spawned by that report is that the energy behind it continues to this day.

First out of the box with reform suggestions were governors, eager to promise greater flexibility and independence at the local level in return for better results. Next, President George H. W. Bush partnered with Bill Clinton, then governor of Arkansas, to create six ambitious National Education Goals, beginning with the idea that all children should start school ready to learn; that is, that they would have access to world-class preschool programs. The United States would also be first in the world in math and science achievement by the year 2000. Building on that theme, the first President Bush had his secretary of education (Lamar Alexander, later a U.S. senator from Tennessee) develop America 2000. This was a program to encourage choice in schools, create model schools in every congressional district, develop new school designs through the New American Schools Development Corporation, and involve the communities in worrying about the *other 93 percent* (the portion of time students spend out of school between conception and age 18).

President Bush's political opponents were not attracted to America 2000, and most elements of the president's proposal (with the exception of New American Schools) disappeared when Governor Clinton defeated President Bush in the 1992 presidential campaign. Clinton's Department of Education developed a standards-based reform agenda based on a concept of alignment. The idea of alignment was to improve system performance by conforming educational standards with assessments, classroom practice, and teacher education. Anxious about charges of federal interference in local education and disrupted by his political opponents, President Clinton's Goals 2000 program made this a voluntary activity on the part of states.

As Jack Jennings and Tom Rogers wrote in Part I, standards-based reform morphed fairly quickly into test-based accountability, a development that only accelerated when the new Obama administration took office and launched the Race to the Top program (RTTT). Since then, change in the standards and assessment movement has moved at warp speed.

### Race to the Top

Within weeks of taking office, the Obama administration had secured congressional passage of the American Recovery and Reinvestment Act (ARRA), a fund of some $767 billion widely known as the stimulus package, designed to help deal with the 2008 near-collapse of the American (and global) banking and economic systems. Included in ARRA, without public scrutiny or attention, was $4.35 billion for a new program known as RTTT, intended to spur innovation and reforms in American education. This is a huge pot of money in any era. In fiscal 2009, the federal government was spending approximately $14.5 billion on Title I of the Elementary and Secondary Education Act (ESEA, essentially No Child Left Behind [NCLB]), the largest program of federal aid to elementary and secondary education. It provides funds for students in districts with high numbers or concentrations of children in poverty. In one fell swoop, RTTT increased funding for the same population by 30 percent. These new funds were doubly appealing to states and districts facing their own economic problems as the Great Recession decimated the sales and property tax revenues funding local schools.

A significant feature of RTTT was that, for the first time, funding for special programs for low-income students depended not on their status as low-income students but on their residence in a state willing to agree to the federal requirements for receipt of these funds.

The original RTTT contemplated a competition among states. Two other features of RTTT should be mentioned: By 2012, the U.S. Department of Education proposed to spend $400 million on a separate competition involving school districts. Second, in 2010, as part of RTTT, the department awarded grants to two state consortia intent on developing assessments tied to the Common Core initiative. That initiative was established by a collaborative effort involving the National Governors Association (NGA) and the Council of Chief State School Officers (CCSSO). The Common Core standards have been endorsed, as this book goes to press, by 45 states and the District of Columbia.

In sum, within eight short years, the educational landscape has been transformed. Education, once thought to be a local responsibility, is now driven increasingly by national and state imperatives. Top-down, technocratic solutions (many drawn from the business world and relying on complex data systems) have been imposed on schools, regardless of the complexity of local challenges. Competition for federal funds among states and among districts has been established as one way of doing business. And teachers now face the prospect of competing with each other for performance-based salaries. It is a very brave new world out there.

# B. PRINCIPLES OF LEARNING

Traditionalists have thought of intelligence as a fixed asset with which people were born. You might fall short of taking advantage of your full intelligence, but you only had so much to work with. (And, in consequence, there were implications for schools: There were limits to what individual students could be expected to learn.) New developments in neuroscience challenge these dated ideas. We can now think of intelligence as something to be developed. It is the ability, among other characteristics, to think and reason, to plan out work and tasks, to solve problems, and to think in complex and abstract ways. Biologically, the basis of intelligence revolves around connections between and among neurons in the brain, a developmental task that is especially important in early childhood but continues into adult life. As intelligence is something to be developed, it follows that we need to rethink outdated notions about limits on what individual students can learn. Lauren Resnick has spent a career at LRDC thinking about these issues, and she shares her insights into the educational implications of these developments with Richard Wallace, former Pittsburgh school superintendent.

## 1. Effort-Based Education

*Superintendents find Lauren Resnick's model—with its challenge to the traditional thinking that inherited ability determines what a student can learn—extremely persuasive. Resnick notes that schools are built on the assumption that aptitude governs achievement. She counters with the argument that a student's effort creates ability. That is, students can "become smart by working at the right kinds of learning tasks." This section introduces you to how the Principles of Learning can be used to shift the day-to-day work of educators toward an effort-based focus.*

Richard C. Wallace, Jr.

Does aptitude primarily determine what students learn in school? Lauren Resnick denounces this deeply rooted conception of learning in numerous settings with superintendents and principals. Her decades of research on how students learn have led to the development of nine Principles of Learning grounded in the belief that educators can harness student effort to create ability (see Table 4.1).

For extensive background on the work of the Learning Research and Development Center (LRDC) at the University of Pittsburgh, see http://www.lrdc.pitt.edu/.

Table 4.1    Principles of Learning

1. **Organize for Effort.** Replace the assumption that aptitude determines how much students can learn with the belief that sustained, directed effort yields high achievement. Support means setting high minimum standards, matching the curriculum to the standards, providing expert instruction, and giving students extra time if needed.

2. **Establish Clear Expectations.** Define explicitly what we expect students to learn so that school professionals, parents, community members, and students can understand it. When expectations are clear, students can take responsibility for their own learning. All children are given a chance to work toward demanding expectations.

3. **Insist on Fair and Credible Evaluations.** Assessment processes must be aligned with the standards and curriculum. Students and parents must find assessments fair, and community members and employers must see them as credible.

4. **Recognize Accomplishments.** Everyone likes recognition. If we expect hard work from students, we should celebrate their authentic accomplishments.

5. **Create Academic Rigor in a Thinking Curriculum.** Thinking and problem solving are the new basics of the 21st century. Thinking requires a solid foundation of knowledge. Curriculum must include commitment to a knowledge core, high thinking demand, and active use of knowledge.

6. **Accountable Talk.** Teachers should encourage *accountable talk* in their classrooms—talk that is accurate, uses appropriate knowledge, encourages rigorous thinking, and responds to and develops what others in the classroom have said.

7. **Socialize Intelligence.** By calling on students to use the skills of intelligent thinking—and by holding them responsible for doing so—educators can teach intelligence. Interactions with others are critical in constructing understanding and meaning.

8. **Encourage the Self-Management of Learning.** If students are to develop as learners, they must be encouraged to develop and use an array of self-monitoring and self-management strategies.

9. **Understand Learning as Apprenticeship.** The historic value of apprenticeship to learning can be brought into schools by encouraging learning environments in which complex thinking is modeled and analyzed and by providing mentoring and coaching as students undertake extended projects.

SOURCE: Adapted from materials provided by the LRDC, University of Pittsburgh.

> "The view emerging today is that effort creates ability. That is to say, smart isn't something you are, it's something you become."
>
> —Lauren Resnick

Resnick has adopted an *incremental view of intelligence*. That is, intelligence is something that expands and grows. "It's not true," says Resnick, "that the brain is fixed at the end of the first year; the brain's capacity to learn and adapt continues throughout life." She argues, "People can get smart." If students believe this, they invest more energy when confronted with something new. However, it's not simply brute effort that leads to greater mastery. Resnick clarifies: "Incremental thinkers are particularly likely to apply self-regulatory, meta-cognitive skills when they encounter task difficulties, to focus on analyzing the task and generating alternative strategies. Most important, they seek out opportunities to hone their skills and knowledge, treating task difficulty (and thus occasional setbacks) as part of the learning challenge rather than as evidence that they lack intelligence. They get on an upward spiral in which their intelligence is actually increasing. Meanwhile, their peers who think of intelligence as fixed try to avoid difficult tasks for fear of displaying their lack of intelligence. They enter a downward spiral by avoiding the very occasions in which they could learn smarter ways of behaving."

Resnick argues that targeted effort is what you and your administrative and teaching peers should be pursuing. It's counterintuitive, given the conceptions we've inherited, Resnick acknowledges, "but the view emerging today is that effort creates ability. In other words, smart isn't something you are, it's something you become."

Schools can consciously set out to "socialize intelligence," believes Resnick. That is, they can routinely challenge students to engage in strategic problem solving and self-monitoring of what they know. These two attributes—strategic problem solving and self-monitoring—are really what metacognition is all about, she says.

"We can't teach intelligence but we can socialize it," argues Resnick. "Kids will get smarter. In fact, that's what we do with gifted and talented programs and it's time we took those techniques to all children." It's also what first-rate private and parochial schools do, too.

Schools that set out to socialize intelligence will challenge students, expect them to act smart, provide them time to act smart, and hold them accountable for their work. "Educators have to be very demanding for this to work," Resnick says. But if it does work, it develops students with a set of beliefs, skills, and dispositions that are powerful tools for learning. These students will be convinced that difficult problems can yield to analysis. They will be confident in their own talents and abilities. And they will be able to monitor their own development well enough to know when to ask for help.

She concludes: "What we need to be about is ensuring that children are using their minds all day, every day, and in every subject." We need to set students on the "upward getting-smarter spiral."

Think about that. You have the children in your schools for only per-haps 10 percent of their time. You can't afford to waste it. If you don't use 100 percent of school time for socializing intelligence, we won't make it.

# C. EMERGING ISSUES IN NEUROSCIENCE

In October 2012, the National Superintendents Roundtable convened a fascinating meeting in San Francisco to explore the educational implica-tions of emerging, new knowledge in neuroscience and neurobiology. During this three-day meeting, Amishi Jha, leader of the Jha Laboratory at the University of Miami, addressed issues of student attention, while Dan Siegel, MD, from the UCLA Medical Center, outlined what he termed the *living brain* and thought out loud about the educational implications of emerging, new scientific knowledge. (See also Part VII: Collaborating With Your Allies for additional presentations on neuroscience and the implica-tions for education, especially for preschool education.)

## 1. The Neuroscience of Mindfulness

### James Harvey

Amishi Jha of the University of Miami has worked with a diverse range of leaders over the years, from the Vatican to the U.S. Department of Defense. Her work focuses on the basic neural mechanisms of attention and work-ing memory, each self-evidently important in both classroom management and learning.

Much of the impetus for her work rests on an insight from the philosopher William James: "The faculty of voluntarily bringing back a wandering atten-tion, over and over again, is the very root of judgment, character, and will."

Wandering attention, notes Jha, can be seen in scans of the brain. Today's neuroscientists, in fact, can actually identify regions of the brain in which certain types of cognitive activities develop. Mindfulness she defines as "a mental mode characterized by present-moment experience without conceptual elaboration or emotional reactivity." It is "about hold-ing steady in the present," not worrying about the past or "visualizing catastrophes in your future."

Mind wandering, Jha reports, tends to be about worry. It is, in fact, the default mode of the brain, as attention and working memory are "hijacked by pre-occupation with self." The default network is REST: rapid, ever present, self-related, thinking. It can be tamed via medication, psychotherapy, computer-based training, and also mindfulness-based training. Research indicates it seems to help reduce stress in a variety of situations. In health, it

> "The faculty of voluntarily bringing back a wandering attention, over and over again, is the very root of judgment, character, and will."
>
> – William James

seems to improve the quality of life for people with chronic pain, human immunodeficiency virus (HIV), cancer, and psoriasis. Stress related to depression, anxiety, post-traumatic stress disorder (PTSD), and Attention Deficit Hyperactivity Disorder (ADHD) has been ameliorated with mindfulness training. And it helps improve a number of relationships—in marriages, between parents and children, and in the workplace.

The default mode of mind wandering is not entirely negative, she emphasizes. Experiencing off-task thoughts during an ongoing task has both positive and negative aspects, as can be seen in Table 4.2.

It is possible both to reduce self-related preoccupation through mindfulness training and to increase the capacity of working memory capacity, concludes Jha. Educators should consider more training in contemplation and mindfulness education. And they can start by understanding that "the ability to multi-task is a myth. Switching from one task to another exhausts the human capacity to focus because the brain can only do one thing at a time."

> "The ability to multi-task is a myth."
>
> —Amishi Jha

### 2. The Embodied Brain

#### James Harvey

Dan Siegel aims to provide a scientifically grounded, integrated view of human development to promote the growth of vibrant lives and healthy minds. He focuses on interpersonal neurobiology and an approach known as *mindsight* and describes an "embodied brain" as the foundation of the approach. The embodied brain is made up of what most of us think of as the brain in the skull, plus the spinal cord and a "spider web of interconnected neurons throughout the body."

> An overview of Siegel describing his hand as a model for the brain is available at http://tinyurl.com/y8soyah.

Using his hand as a model for the brain, Siegel led the Roundtable through the different areas of the brain and the functions they govern.

The following hardly does justice to the presentation, but he started with a

Table 4.2   Aspects of Off-Task Thoughts

| Positive | Negative |
| --- | --- |
| Creative problem solving | Difficulty performing task |
| Better planning for future | Rumination and worry—choking under pressure, stereotype threat, performance anxiety |
| Insight | Distractibility |
| Visioning positive outcomes | Visioning catastrophic outcomes |

simple request. He asked the audience to hold up their open hands and think of the wrist as the spinal cord and the heel of the hand as the brain stem. Then, he said, "Bend your thumb across the palm of your hand and fold your four fingers over the thumb." The thumb represents the limbic region of the brain, protected deep within the skull. Within that broad model of the brain, he described the following functions:

- The spinal cord is the neural cord providing head-to-body connections.
- The brain stem governs independent, unconscious bodily functions— whether you are awake, or bleed, or breathe. It also governs fight, flight, and freeze responses to stress.
- The limbic area, on top of the brain stem, governs motivation, emotion, appraisal of meaning and value (is something worth paying attention to?), implicit memory (e.g., fear of dogs), attention and awareness (which are required for deep learning), and attachment (the four Ss: safe, seen, soothed, and secure).
- The cortex, on top of the limbic area, is an incredibly complicated, layered, wrinkled mass of neural tissue. The frontal lobe (the middle knuckles of the fingers) contains the executive function, governing intentionality and decision making (based on the information it obtains from the other lobes). The rear (occipital) lobe at the back of the hand is where we find the visual cortex, and it is responsible for sight. The parietal lobe (on top) manages sensory information and spatial recognition. And the temporal lobe (the fingertips) processes external auditory stimuli and assists people in understanding and forming speech.

Each of these portions of the brain is awash with a network of neurons that help organize the central nervous system, Siegel emphasizes. In the amazing instrument for learning that is the human brain, the cortex and limbic system fire off up to 100 billion neurons, making trillions of synaptic connections instantaneously throughout the body and the embodied brain.

**Implications for Education.** Embedded in each of these stages are many implications for learning. The neural core is mostly unformed at conception, so stress in utero (e.g., drugs or alcohol) can easily be embedded in the limbic or brain stem regions. Substance abuse "plays havoc" with the normal development of neurons, says Siegel, and "there is now some evidence that stress influences brain development." The effects can be transmitted from generation to generation, apparently: Children and grandchildren of slaves or Holocaust and famine survivors demonstrate "epigenetic molecules" that seem to pass traumatic memories on genetically.

> Siegel has published extensively on neurobiology. See, for example, Siegle, Daniel J. (2012). *Pocket guide to interpersonal neurobiology: An integrative handbook of the mind.* New York: W. W. Norton; and also Siegle, Daniel J. (2012). *The developing mind* (2nd ed.). New York: Guilford Press.

The limbic area obviously governs important learning functions involving motivation, emotion, paying attention, and the like. Children and adults can be educated to focus more and to extend the amount of time between emotion and action (e.g., anger and striking out). It is here also that families and schools need to pay attention to the four Ss: safe, seen, soothed, and secure. Patterns of relationships with parents and schools shape how our minds work, reports Siegel. In the limbic area, he says, there is the reactive state of *no*. The reactive state leads to fighting, fleeing, freezing, or collapsing; it also induces shame and fear in young people. But there is also the receptive state of *yes*. In the receptive state, children and adults can be encouraged to learn, grow, and take risks.

> Expectations and emotions also play a part in individual success. According to the work of Martin Seligman, former president of the American Psychological Association, optimistic salespeople sell more, and optimistic students get better grades. See, for example, Seligman, M. (1990). *Learned optimism*. New York: Knopf; and Seligman, M. (1996). *The optimistic child*. New York: Houghton Mifflin.

The prefrontal cortex is key to learning. It's here that intentionality and focus develop. Beyond that, it is the area in which the most important outcomes of education are developed: reflection, relationships, and resilience.

As a medical student, noted Siegel, he had an epiphany. Medical students are not competitive with each other, he says. Their competition is with death, and to defeat it, they collaborate with each other. Students should not be competing with each other either, he says; they should be collaborating to solve the challenges of the world.

## D. COMMON CORE STATE STANDARDS

Within the educational policy community, there is a lot of excitement about the promise of the Common Core standards for improving education across the United States. The section that follows outlines the hopes animating those developing the standards, a cautionary note about the difficulty of implementing standards from a prominent educational think tank, and the anxieties of some local educators about what they will mean in practice.

### 1. The Case for the Common Core

#### James Harvey

As the Brookings Institution noted in 2010, "Unlike most countries, the United States does not have national education standards, no single set of expectations for what all American teachers should teach and all American students should learn. It never has. A question that the rest of the world considers foundational to its national school systems—deciding the content of the curriculum—sits in the hands of local authorities."

Local control has extended far deeper than local school districts. Former U.S. Secretary of Education Rod Paige reported that one reason he insisted on a common curriculum in English and language arts when he was Houston's school superintendent was that he discovered several dozen different reading curricula in place in the district's elementary schools. Students transferring within the district ran the risk of missing critical elements of reading instruction or repeating work they had already covered. In fact, as the 2010 Brookings account concluded: "Even students transferring from one teacher to another within the same school may . . . learn a different curriculum than their former classmates."

Efforts to establish national curriculum guidelines in the administration of President George H. W. Bush met with disastrous political results. Led by Diane Ravitch, Bush's assistant secretary in charge of the Office of Educational Research and Information (now the Institute for Education Sciences), the effort built on an attempt to develop a national curriculum in mathematics championed by the National Council of Teachers of Mathematics. The federal standards initiative funded professional associations and consortia of teachers and scholars to develop national standards in history, English language arts, science, civics, economics, the arts, foreign languages, geography, and physical education. But it collapsed in 1994 when Lynne V. Cheney, chair of the National Endowment for the Humanities, attacked the developing history standards (which had not been released) as models of political correctness because they paid too much attention to the nation's historic failings and not enough to the nation's great men (or great women, either). In the ensuing uproar, radio commentator Rush Limbaugh said the standards should be "flushed down the toilet."

Meanwhile, according to Ravitch, a turnover in administrations (from George H. W. Bush to Bill Clinton) short-circuited any effort to oversee the standards-development exercise. The new Clinton administration, which had had nothing to do with developing the standards, disowned the effort.

So, when the National Governors Association (NGA) and the Council of Chief State School Officers (CCSSO) announced a new effort to develop Common Core standards in mathematics and reading during the second term of the George W. Bush administration, it was something of a historical event. As the Brookings Institution notes, the "Common Core standards project brought together experts in both reading and math to develop a set of standards that would be, in what became a mantra, both 'higher and fewer in number' than existing state standards. The standards are voluntary—states choose whether to participate—but for the first time most American students will study a uniform curriculum through at least the eighth grade." (These are defined as Common Core standards, not federal standards, although they have the effect of being national.

There's something disingenuous about that because federal leaders from both parties have encouraged the effort and the Obama administration put several hundred million dollars behind the development of assessments to validate the standards.)

The Common Core standards were developed very quickly. A draft of the experts' recommendations circulated for a few months, and the standards were announced in 2010. In September of that year, the U.S. Department of Education awarded grants totaling $330 million to two consortia to develop annual assessments aligned with the Common Core standards. As of August 2012, 45 states and the District of Columbia have signed on to the standards. Plans call for the assessments to be administered for the first time in the 2014–2015 school year.

Supporters of the Common Core view them as providing a consistent, clear understanding of what students are expected to learn so that teachers and parents can know what they need to do to help students. The standards are intended to be robust and relevant to the real world, reflecting the knowledge and skills that young people need for success in college and careers. With American students fully prepared for the future, supporters say, communities will be best positioned to compete successfully in the global economy.

The standards are said to have been built on the highest-quality models from states across the country and from countries around the world, according to CCSSO and NGA. They should provide teachers and parents with a common understanding of what students are expected to learn. Consistent standards are intended to provide appropriate benchmarks for all students, regardless of where they live.

The standards, in both mathematics and English and language arts, define the knowledge and skills students should have within their K–12 education careers so that they will graduate from high school able to succeed in entry-level, credit-bearing academic college courses and in workforce training programs. Courses in other subjects may be available in time, but as of early 2013, only two curriculum areas have been targeted. The standards are intended to be

- aligned with college and work expectations;
- clear, understandable, and consistent;
- rigorous and require application of knowledge through higher-order skills;
- built upon strengths and lessons of current state standards;
- informed by other top-performing countries; and
- evidence based.

Implementation is a state function and is likely to roll out through the next several years. Implementation obviously implies development of curriculum (and materials and textbooks) to make the standards real, along with assessments to judge whether the standards make any difference.

## 2. A Think Tank Examines the Common Core

### James Harvey

A major source of information on education policy in the United States is the Brown Center at the Brookings Institution in Washington, DC. As it is not responsible for supporting or creating initiatives such as the federal National Assessment of Educational Progress (NAEP), PISA, the Trends in International Mathematics and Science Study (TIMSS), or the Common Core State Standards Project, the Brown Center feels no need to act as a cheerleader for any of them. On the contrary, it feels free to look at all of these efforts objectively, calling things as it sees them.

Supporters of the Common Core, therefore, need to take into consideration an analysis from the Brown Center at the Brookings Institution. The Center's Tom Loveless concluded that these standards would not make much difference in American classrooms (or on student performance). Loveless examined the major arguments in support of the Common Core and was unimpressed by what he saw:

- Several prominent critics have examined the Common Core standards and, comparing them to state and international standards, concluded that they do not represent much of an improvement. The math standards, in particular, seem to be inferior to existing standards in Massachusetts and California.
- An unusual coalition of educators, conservatives, libertarians, and small-government advocates issued a manifesto denouncing federal support for the assessment effort, worrying that it would lead to "a one-size-fits-all, centrally controlled curriculum for every K–12 subject . . . [that] threatens to close the door on educational innovation, freezing in place an unacceptable status quo and hindering efforts to develop academically rigorous curricula, assessments, and standards that meet the challenges that lie ahead."

There is no evidence to support the claim that high-quality standards promote academic achievement, reports Loveless. Prior research shows little correlation between ratings for the quality of state standards and state NAEP scores. Higher performance standards don't produce higher performance: States with high, more-rigorous cut points for proficiency do not have stronger NAEP scores than states with less-rigorous cut points.

Would common standards reduce variation in attainment? Probably not, concludes Loveless. While it might reduce between-state variation, most

For the Brown Center's analysis of the Common Core, see The Brookings Institution. (2011, February). NAEP and the Common Core State Standards. In *How well are American students learning?* Washington: Author. *The 2010 Brown Center Report on American Education*, *2*(5) (http://tinyurl.com/bga4yo5).

variation exists within states, and if standards alone were up to the task, existing state standards should have eliminated those variations. "It is highly unlikely," he concludes, that Common Core standards introduced in 2014 will reduce variation within California any more effectively than the existing California standards, which have had 50 years to do so, with little effect.

Standards are aspirational, reports Loveless. "[L]ike a strict diet or prudent plan to save money for the future, they represent good intentions that are not often realized." The problem is that curriculum can be understood as *intended, implemented,* and *achieved.* Standards define the intended curriculum. The implemented curriculum, on the other hand, is what teachers actually teach. The achieved curriculum is what students learn. The Common Core standards sit on top of a system teeming with variation in terms of the implemented and achieved curriculum, says Loveless, and "will probably fail to dramatically affect what goes on in the thousands of districts and tens of thousands of schools that they seek to influence."

"Don't let the ferocity of the oncoming debate fool you," he concludes. "The empirical evidence suggests that the Common Core will have little effect on American students' achievement. The nation will have to look elsewhere for ways to improve its schools."

### 3. Local Educators Look at the Common Core

#### Bernard Josefsberg

#### Jonathan Budd

Here's an imaginary conversation about the Common Core standards between two experienced educators—one a district superintendent, the other a high school English teacher. Josefsberg is superintendent in Easton-Redding District 9 in Connecticut; Budd teaches in the district's Joel Barlow High School.

*Bernard Josefsberg, Superintendent*

I have to say that, when you look at public perceptions of education, it's easy to understand the appeal of the Common Core standards. I recently heard a keynote presentation from a distinguished professor repeating the lamentable tale of American results on international tests—"below the international average and well below that of the top achieving countries."

Both the illness and the remedy were familiar and disquieting. Even more disquieting was the professor's fervor for the Common Core (and accompanying Next Generation testing). However much our current educational condition may be incoherent, flaccid, and gauzy, to that degree will the Common Core and accompanying testing reverse it all—or so the distinguished professor led us to believe.

Based on what I know about educational reform, I am more than a little skeptical that the Common Core is anything more than a technical refinement on a well-worn approach.

*Jonathan Budd, English Teacher*

The implication of the Common Core is that (1) standards don't currently exist, (2) standards do exist but are inadequate, or (3) adequate standards exist but are locally contingent. A lot of this is expressed as, "The Algebra you learn in Mississippi shouldn't be different from the Algebra in Connecticut or Oregon."

Regardless of the argument, the Common Core presents an opportunity to refocus our energies, to accept implicit and explicit critique, and to tell our stories of what we do well and why and what we can do better and how.

Commenting in late 2012 on the looming implementation of the Common Core within 18 months, a North Carolina superintendent worried that federal and state officials needed to slow down. He said, "We really don't know what's in these standards. We don't have curriculum for them. We don't know what they'll mean for principals and teachers. We need to train ourselves about the implications of the standards and the assessments. Then we need to train the principals and teachers. And we have to develop new curriculum and texts or online materials. All within 18 months. This is a huge sea change in expectations for local performance. We should take the time to do it right, because if we get it wrong, we won't get the chance again for a generation."

*Bernard Josefsberg*

I'm all for burnishing our public image, but as a matter of educational leadership, I'd rather do so through exceptional educational experiences that lead students to learning rather than by continuing the beatings until morale improves.

At this point, I worry that we no longer have a choice, and that an insistent zeitgeist is setting us up for failure through its primitive view of human motivation and development. We've seen this movie before. But the zeitgeist is powerful. I find myself forced to dance in step with it despite my reservations.

This work is very difficult. It can't be achieved through policy fiat. I worry that, in the frenzy to respond, we will cut adrift many of our most challenged students because shallow thinking that demands more rigor, more competition, and more naming and shaming of teachers will ignore the need for more depth, more deep thinking, and the human capacity to step back from ourselves and laugh at our own foolishness.

*Jonathan Budd*

I think that's right. It's not clear how Common Core will influence student engagement, motivation, and learning. We also have to appreciate the link between student as learner and teacher as learner.

Most people agree that we need students to become independent thinkers, but apparently independence doesn't apply to teachers. We're being told what to do. Let's be honest. Nothing is less appealing, to child or adult, than simply being told what to do.

*Bernard Josefsberg*

I'm worried that we're being set up for a fan dance in which cheap tests hide behind fans labeled Common Core standards. Allan Luke's 2011 American Educational Research Association (AERA) Distinguished Lecture, titled "Generalizing Across Borders: Policy and the Limits of Educational Science," is very informative in this regard.

Luke, from Queensland University in Australia, draws attention to the entanglement of government, foundations, and test-producing conglomerates:

> Check out Allan Luke's 2011 AERA Distinguished Lecture on the limits of educational science at http://eprints.qut .edu.au/41118/1/C41118.pdf.

> We are pushed to take on the new common sense of accountability through narrow metrics and through standards that do not always do justice to what is educationally sound and culturally meaningful. There is a silencing process that goes on. . . . [T]he normative, the ethical, the cultural—matters of value—have quietly slipped from policy discussion . . . overridden by a focus on the measurable, the countable, and what can be said to be cost-efficient and quality assured.

We get a lot of hand waving and assurances about high-quality assessments, but I'm not sure we get the real thing. Setting standards is one thing; testing to those standards is quite another. There is little reason to believe that tests that are only incrementally better than what we've experienced for a decade will warrant the confidence of those of us in the field. Slapping a BMW ornament on a Honda doesn't make it a BMW, any more than slapping a 21st-century-skills label on existing assessment items make them worthy of the name.

I agree with Linda Darling-Hammond and Ray Pecheone that "an assessment system that promotes high-quality learning" should be tightly integrated with standards, curriculum, and teacher development—and it should also be developed in partnership with teachers and use multiple measures to evaluate students. If we could be assured the Common Core assessments met those criteria, I'd join the crowd beating the drum for them.

*Jonathan Budd*

I'm not so sure about that. I push back against the standards inherent in large-scale assessment, even as those standards are articulated by Darling-Hammond and Pecheone.

Several years back, one systems analyst for a district in which I worked concluded that greater copy room efficiency could be gained if teachers were required to present all materials for copying at least 48 hours ahead of when the copies were needed. Wisely, the school principal understood that the goal of a school is not making copying easier for the copying room but making teaching easier for teachers. This half-baked scheme was withdrawn, but its cousins remain still in all sorts of ways, many implicit, in school communities.

> For a scholarly commentary on assessment, see Darling-Hammond, L., & Pecheone, R. (2010). *Developing an internationally comparable balanced assessment system that supports high-quality learning.* Center for K–12 Assessment and Performance Management (http://tinyurl.com/a2t87vg).

As we consider ways to emphasize the importance of assessment to the teaching–learning enterprise, we ought to think as broadly and critically as we possibly can. Yes, we should endorse multiple measures, but multiple measures that arise naturally from strong teaching and strong learning.

*Bernard Josefsberg*

Listen closely to our workplace dialogues, and consider the terms we use, the meanings they convey, and the understandings they produce—or, for that matter, obscure. Educational technospeak dominates our discourse and reveals an impoverished professionalism.

As local educators, we function as the medium through which political authority and monied interests work their will. Were that will undeniably beneficial to our students' life chances and educational needs, then I would be the first to encourage us to do our part, step up, and enact faithfully the Common Core and its assessments. But I'm not sure that will is beneficial. Wordsworth's powerful lament about the materialism of the Industrial Age comes to mind:

> *The world is too much with us; late and soon*
>
> *Getting and spending, we lay waste our powers;*
>
> *Little we see in Nature that is ours;*
>
> *We have given our hearts away, a sordid boon!*

What will it profit us as a nation if we busy ourselves with aligning and assessing, in the process of laying waste our powers as educators, giving away our instructional hearts in a sordid deal that confuses first-rate standards with third-rate assessments?

# E. THE ACHIEVEMENT GAP

James Harvey

Richard C. Wallace, Jr.

As a new superintendent, you have quite a challenge ahead as you grapple with emerging accountability provisions of NCLB and the even newer requirements of RTTT. Although there seems to be broad agreement that the most onerous of NCLB's requirements must be modified, the achievement gap remains a troubling educational reality.

Never before in the history of American education have school leaders been called on to follow student achievement as closely as they are now. Perhaps they should have been, but they were not, and you are unlikely to have been well prepared. Where to start?

You will be expected to speak authoritatively about the differences among performance tests, achievement tests, and aptitude tests. The language of criterion-referenced and norm-referenced test items should be second nature to you. And naturally, you will be familiar with the strengths and weaknesses of machine-scored versus hand-scored test items (and their financial implications). Does that all sound too much? Turn to websites such as those maintained by the Educational Testing Service (www.ets.org) and Achieve (www.achicvc.org) to get a handle on the distinctions.

Next, you'll need to know which tests are most appropriate under which circumstances. (The reality is that your state education agency will define the assessments you use, but you need to know enough about these assessments to understand their effect within your community.) Try to avoid getting trapped in a situation in which a test that might be perfectly appropriate for a specific purpose is asked to do double or triple duty. Tests that are acceptable for program evaluation purposes are likely to be entirely inappropriate for making judgments about individual students. Results from the National Assessment of Educational Progress (NAEP), for example, provide only estimates of the performance of groups of students (not individual students). These estimates are applicable only at the national, regional, and state levels. With the exception of some trial urban districts, NAEP results tell you nothing about performance in your district, much less about performance in specific schools or individual students. International assessments such as the Trends in International Mathematics and Science Study (TIMSS), the Program on International Student Achievement (PISA), and Progress in International Literacy Study (PIRLS) typically provide estimates only at the national level. You might want to turn to groups such as the National Center for Fair & Open Testing (www.fairtest.org) to learn more about these distinctions.

So, the stage has been set by NCLB, RTTT, and the Common Core. You will have to raise student performance. You will have to raise the performance bar. And you will have to close the achievement gap.

Denial, of course, is routine in schools as elsewhere. Too often, "successful" districts rely on average test-score results as evidence that the achievement gap is someone else's problem. Yet, even "successful" districts find themselves surprised when averages are pulled apart by school, income, and ethnicity. Invariably, they find the averages conceal as much as they reveal. The reality is that you do not have many choices in terms of data usage. Ignoring data is not an option anymore. You won't be able to hide behind the false security of districtwide averages. How do you proceed?

After nearly 50 years of federal encouragement, the achievement gap has not been closed. It won't be closed with wishful thinking in the next decade, either. Here's the deal that you should insist on making with the public around the achievement gap.

1. We'll do our part, but the community needs to do its. We can do it, but the resources need to be put in place to get it done.

2. The resources include equalizing funds within districts, developing out-of-school community assets, and improving early education programming.

3. We will insist that the school board provide ample resources to students with the greatest need.

4. We will create a no-excuses mentality by infusing a sense of urgency about this issue within the district. Specifically, we will improve the level of expectations for poor and minority children, and we will use data to drive the discussion about the achievement gap.

5. We will communicate the sense of urgency by insisting that the district no longer ignore race and class, the 800-pound gorilla in our schools, and by putting the best principals and teachers in the schools that need them the most.

6. As part of the effort to close the achievement gap, we will also hold families and the community accountable. The best predictor of a student's performance is not race, income, or even parental education. It is whether the child comes to school. We cannot educate children who are not in class.

7. We will identify outstanding schools, teachers, and principals, and we will celebrate their accomplishments.

SOURCE: Adapted from The urban superintendent: Creating great schools while surviving on the job. *Report of a Colloquium for Former Urban Superintendents, Council of Great City Schools* (September 2003).

### 1. It's Not Good Enough: A Personal Perspective on Urban Student Achievement

*Here are some inspiring comments from school administrator Diana Lam, an immigrant from Peru with a doctorate from Harvard who served as a superintendent in Massachusetts, Idaho, Texas, Rhode Island, and New York. She reminds us not to ignore children's dreams. In the words of the Nobel laureate William Butler Yeats: "In dreams begins responsibility."*

#### Diana Lam

If 50 percent of students in a poor urban high school enroll in college, it's hailed as a success story. But if only 75 percent of students in some suburban high schools go on to college, heads roll.

For too long, many Americans have expected too little of poor and minority children and the schools that teach them. The legacy of low expectations for poor and minority children has infected our schools, poisoning the futures of children who suffer the misfortune of growing up in America's cities. I am not interested in blaming socioeconomic factors or municipal budgets for the failure of children to reach high standards. These are excuses that paper over a harsh reality—every day in America, poor and minority students are deferring their dreams, while we argue about what's going on.

> Some school systems recognize that emotional intelligence plays a significant role in students' success in and out of the classroom. Many turn to Golman, Daniel. (1995). *Emotional intelligence: Why it can matter more than IQ.* New York: Bantam.

For me, the problem of low expectations is neither an abstract issue nor a debate about other children. It's deeply personal. Had I grown up with the yoke of low expectations around my neck, I would be someone else entirely. I grew up in Peru in a family of modest means, the daughter of a Chinese father and a Peruvian mother who had never finished elementary school. While their lack of formal education and their need to work endless hours to support the family limited their ability to help me in school, they instilled in me a respect for education. They also expected great effort from their daughter. My parents' influence was critical, yet exceptional teachers also shaped my life.

As a young girl, I dreamed of one day going to college in the United States. At the age of eight, I stood, my heart in my hand, and shared this dream with my third-grade teacher. How easily she might have squashed my hope and crushed my heart. A different teacher might have thought to help me by scaling back my dream to something more manageable, perhaps to learn a craft or go to secretarial school. But my teacher believed in me, breathing energy into my hope and mapping out the route to attain my ambition.

My third-grade teacher was gifted, for she knew that the power of children's dreams is the greatest inspiration in the world. She understood that the commitments children make in the deep recesses of their hearts explain incredible acts of courage and risk taking, the forces that truly shape societies. Her belief in me paid off. At the age of 16, I won a scholarship and moved to the United States to attend college. I carried with me the immigrant's dream of unbounded opportunity in a country where the air itself was filled with hope. A free and democratic society guarantees many rights to its citizens, but none is more precious than the legacy of hope that things will get better.

> "My third-grade teacher was gifted, for she knew that the power of children's dreams is the greatest inspiration in the world. She understood that the commitments children make in the deep recesses of their hearts explain incredible acts of courage and risk taking, the forces that truly shape societies."
>
> —Diana Lam

As a child in Peru, I was challenged by my teachers. They supported me. The roots of my work as an educational reformer grew there in the safety of a community where I was equipped with the intellectual faculties to pursue my sense of justice in the world. It's time to show the next generation that their dreams, too, have roots in reality and that their teachers, also, will give wings to their dreams.

## 2. Whistling Past the Schoolyard

*Studies in the state of Washington and elsewhere reveal that minority students are found in the bottom deciles of the achievement distribution at rates three to five times those of white students. Despite progress in closing the achievement gap, progress isn't nearly fast enough. States are (sensibly) levering minority students close to the standards bar. What is needed is a slingshot, not a lever.*

James Harvey

Mary Beth Celio

The happy chatter from state leaders and educators about improved student performance on the state assessments is just so much whistling past the schoolyard. The dreams of many minority students and their parents are quietly being buried. The road ahead for minority students is much rockier than most of us want to believe.

### Problem Unfolding Out of Sight

Everyone is entitled to celebrate progress, but out of sight, an educational catastrophe is looming. Because reports based on averages and incremental improvement conceal almost as much as they reveal (even when reported by race, gender, and ethnicity), the scale of the problem is easy to overlook. The racial achievement gap in most communities and states is more severe than most officials appear to understand or acknowledge.

In many communities and states, African-American, Native-American, and Latino students stand about half the chance of meeting standards in reading and mathematics as students who are white or Asian American. Closer analysis reveals a harsher reality: It's not just that fewer of the minority students in trouble meet the standards; it's that they are not even close. Their performance abysmally misses the mark. As Part V of this *Fieldbook* discusses, achievement challenges for minority males are particularly difficult, much more imposing than those facing minority females.

There is no way to sugarcoat the facts: Across states, in cities and on farms and reservations, minority students in trouble are found at the bottom of the educational barrel at rates three to five times higher than they should be. At current rates of improvement, even after 10 years, roughly half the gap will persist. We need to stop kidding ourselves about what it will take to fix this problem.

> When analysts consider college graduation rates at age 24 by income level, very troubling disparities emerge, reports Kati Haycock of the Education Trust. By age 24, fully 48 percent of young men and women from high-income families have graduated from college; among low-income young adults, the rate is only 7 percent. Haycock concludes, "This suggests that, unless you believe the children of the rich are seven times smarter than the children of the poor, there is something terribly wrong."

### What to Do?

Familiar nostrums aren't going to change things. There needs to be direct, focused attention on the kids at the bottom of the pile using every weapon in the state's arsenal.

**Focus.** In the most troubled schools, focused effort to improve instruction should be the primary order of business. Financial incentives to get the best teachers and principals into these schools are essential. And school leaders should be freed up to reconfigure staffs, add to and alter how time is used, and try out new technologies and teaching methods. If it takes more money, it takes more money. Business as usual in these schools is unconscionable.

**Revitalize Communities.** We also need to step up to the plate on out-of-school influences on learning. Minority students are concentrated in schools with a lot of poverty. Over the years, one constant in educational research is the powerful relationship between income and achievement. As poverty goes up, test scores go down.

> The American Institutes for Research (AIR, 2010) has developed a range of resources related to student achievement. See, for example, *Student learning expectations gap can be twice the size of national black–white achievement.* Washington, DC: Author. See also the AIR's website for additional information at www.air.org.

Poverty and its accomplices—unstable neighborhoods, single-parent homes, violence, and high rates of unemployment and substance abuse—explain as much as 60 to 70 percent of achievement differences in many studies.

In a technical sense, statisticians speak of poverty as "predicting" low achievement. As a practical matter, this doesn't mean poor kids can't learn, but it does mean the odds are stacked against them. Poverty doesn't explain everything, but it explains a lot.

For schools serving the most troubled neighborhoods, public officials need to think about complementing school-based efforts with community-revitalization strategies. Neighborhood investment programs to stabilize housing, build home ownership, generate economic development, and create jobs are all needed. And policy should encourage the efforts of faith- and community-based organizations to repair the shattered fabric of neighborhoods and families.

None of this will be easy, but as Albert Einstein is said to have suggested, it's a form of insanity to repeat the same approaches over and over in hopes of getting a different result. And, for decades, we've been pretending that schools alone can fix the achievement problem. Families and communities have a responsibility, too.

Regardless of changes in assessments or the new Common Core standards, we need to understand that, although schools need to do better, they also need help. If we don't act soon on that knowledge, we may as well continue whistling past the schoolyard. Because behind school walls, the dreams of too many minority students are being deferred, drying up, in the memorable phrase of poet Langston Hughes, like raisins in the sun.

This is not a problem in your district or state, you say? Don't kid yourself. Wherever you are, this is precisely the problem you face.

# F. VALUE-ADDED ASSESSMENT OF TEACHERS

## James Harvey

In recent years, there has been an explosion of interest in the relationship between teacher quality and student outcomes. Everyone understands the importance of good teaching in school improvement and student learning. There's very little argument about this. Teachers are, by most any standard, inequitably distributed among students. Poor students are far more likely than their wealthier counterparts to be matched with teachers who have little experience, are graduates from less-selective colleges, and possess fewer credentials.

However, the political will to address teacher inequities has so far failed to match the strength of the rhetoric decrying the problem. But new federal and state policy initiatives suggest that political will and rhetoric are beginning to develop. There's also a lot of misinformation, combined with some misunderstanding, of what the research would mean in practice. In some ways, educators, policy makers, and editorial boards have jumped to conclusions that aren't fully justified in the data or research.

One of the most exciting findings of educational research in recent years comes from the work of two economists, one in Tennessee named

William Sanders and another at the Hoover Institution at Stanford, Eric Hanushek. Their analyses indicate that, if you could provide the best teachers to low-achieving students for between three and five years in a row, you could close the achievement gap (compared with low-achieving students being assigned to the "worst" teachers). This is a very promising argument, as it affirms the importance of teachers and teaching, if anyone needed that affirmation. It also points to some possibilities for policy that, although potentially uncomfortable for adults in the field, would undoubtedly benefit low-achieving and especially low-income and minority children.

That's the research at the basis of a lot of the assertions we hear today. For example, it's said that teaching is the most important determinant of student learning. It is argued that the quality of teaching overwhelms everything else as a predictor of achievement outcomes. We see this in policy pronouncements, advocacy pieces, and editorials and opinion pieces every week. It's also the basis for a lot of policy directions in the RTTT, the broader educational stimulus package, and what seem to be the emerging policy directions for Title I, as laid out in the Obama administration's Blueprint, issued in March of 2010.

But the research behind this is suggestive, not definitive. The work of Sanders and Hanushek is based on statistical modeling, not empirical research. The models took large state bases and looked at student outcomes after the fact; they then distributed high- and low-achieving students among their teachers. In fact, nobody followed students for three or five years and confirmed that students with the best teachers for several years in a row produced achievement results that were 50 percent higher than students assigned to the worst teachers. The hopeful outcome is based on an ideal: an imputed result that extended one year's analysis and added up the gains (for high-achieving students) and the losses (for low-achieving students) that might be obtained if students had the best teachers (defined as those in the top 15 percent in terms of student results) for five years running.

But it turns out, according to a sober analysis from the National Council on Teacher Quality (*If Wishes Were Horses*), that the chances of any student getting the best teachers for five years in a row are about 1 in 17,000. Those odds are far better than the chances of winning a state lottery, but they are still not great odds. And the chances are undoubtedly lower for disadvantaged students because they tend to be concentrated in schools with a lot of challenges that are staffed by the most junior teachers.

So, trying to make sure that the top one-seventh of all teachers are assigned to the students who need them the most is a challenging assignment. As a practical matter, as any superintendent can understand, it promises to turn school systems inside out and upside down. Perhaps that sort of shaking of the system is required. Perhaps that's what has to be done. But no one should pretend that it's easy or can be done overnight. It's going to be very hard and will take a lot of time. And it's not clear right now that we have the tools to do it well.

As this discussion has developed, an important wrinkle has been added. Many argue that it would be unfair to compare student outcomes for teachers assigned to classrooms in which students start out far below the bar with outcomes for teachers in classrooms with students at or above the bar. The proposed solution is to look at the *value added* by teachers, that is to say, achievement growth of the students in the classroom, no matter where they began. There's a certain logic and sense of fairness to this approach. How well is it likely to work?

> **Rankings Tanking in Corporations.** The forced ranking of employees pioneered by GE about 30 years ago is often used to justify teacher evaluation and rankings. But, just as the practice gains a head of steam in education, it is falling out of favor in the corporate world, according to recent accounts. The proportion of high-performing companies using employee rankings fell from 49 to 14 percent in the last two years. Why? The practice undermines the teamwork that is essential to business success, according to corporate leaders. See the *Los Angeles Times* (August 13, 2012) at http://articles.latimes.com/2012/aug/13/business/la-fi-employee-evals-20120808.

## 1. The Case for Value-Added Assessment

*For several years now, Dan Goldhaber has been directing a project on Teacher Quality and Human Capital, a joint effort of the University of Washington and the Urban Institute. Among other issues, the project has looked at state licensure testing, labor markets, the measurement of teacher performance, returns to skill and wage premiums, and the politics of reforming teacher pay. One of the issues Goldhaber discussed with the Roundtable in 2010 was the potential of value-added estimates of teacher job performance in making tenure decisions.*

### James Harvey

Dan Goldhaber supports the idea of using value-added methods as part of teacher evaluation, but he makes it clear that putting into practice what seems so simple in theory will be hard. One of the hopes of proponents of value-added assessments is that administrators and policy makers will be able to identify which teachers add the greatest value to student outcomes, potentially offering a mechanism to weed out ineffective teachers, reward the most competent, and assign the best to students and schools facing the greatest challenges.

Traditional metrics for assessing teachers leave a lot to be desired, Goldhaber notes. Most standard evaluation devices—possession of a teaching credential, years of experience, holding tenure, in-service assessments, and financial rewards for continuing education—fall far short of the mark. Few tenured teachers are dismissed, he argues. Although one survey of eight districts revealed that administrators believed between 2 and 7 percent of tenured teachers should be out of teaching, typically less than 0.5 percent are dismissed each year.

Still, despite the surface appeal of the value-added concept, a lot stands between the ideal and the reality. Goldhaber's research suggests the following:

- While it is true that "teacher quality is the most important schooling factor influencing student achievement," schooling itself (that is, all school effects, not just teachers) accounts for about 20 percent of achievement variation.
- Out-of-school factors far outweigh school variables in explaining achievement outcomes. Teacher quality itself accounts for about 8 percent of student achievement variation, according to a study Goldhaber completed in 2002 for the Hoover Institution.
- A single year's data on teacher effectiveness is likely to include a lot of noise; a more accurate picture of individual teacher effectiveness requires multiple years of assessment data—at least three and perhaps as many as five years.

Other potential troublesome issues include ignoring untested areas (history, the arts, and the civic purposes of education); narrowing of instruction to tested areas; corruption of the assessment system by cheating and hiding low-growth students; the imprecision of cut-point scores; what to do about teachers who are competent in one teaching area but not another; apportioning credit among multiple teachers; the reality that a teacher can be effective in one school situation and not in another; and the real possibility of discouraging teacher collaboration.

> For an accessible review of the relationship of student performance to school and teacher quality, see Goldhaber, D. (2002). The mystery of good teaching. *Education Next*, Spring 2002.

The case for value-added assessment is hardly overwhelming and depends, even a supporter like Goldhaber acknowledges, on multiple years of data. One of the significant potential shortcomings is the potential discouragement of teacher collaboration. It's hard to see how schools can create professional learning communities (PLCs) that encourage teachers to learn among themselves while simultaneously pitting teachers against each other with value-added measures designed to inform decisions about teacher compensation and employment.

## 2. The Case Against Value-Added Assessment

*Henry Braun of Boston College is one of the distinguished mathematical statisticians in the United States, indeed in the world. Before joining the Boston*

*College faculty, he spent years working on large-scale assessments for the Educational Testing Service. In 2010, he shared with the Roundtable his work chairing a committee of the National Research Council (NRC) looking into value-added assessment. He also went on to describe what he was at pains to insist were his personal conclusions about high-stakes assessment, not those of his NRC committee.*

## James Harvey

Braun takes as his text the question, "Value-added: Is it the silver bullet, or is it just a bullet?" Random assignment of subjects in an experiment is the gold standard of research, notes Braun. But students are not assigned to classrooms randomly. Still, "the public buys into the construct that if good teachers are critical to student learning, why can't evidence of student achievement be used as an indicator of school and teacher quality?"

The research literature on this is very complex, he notes, so the NRC appointed a committee to look into the question. The committee pulled together several commissioned papers and held a two-day conference on the subject in 2007 before issuing a report in 2010. The report pointed to several measurement and analytic challenges, including these:

- the need for very high standards for assessments used to make high-stakes decisions;
- the possibility of changing educators' behavior with unintended consequences;
- the difficulty of attributing student growth to specific teachers in team-teaching situations;
- the reality that test scores reflect a narrower set of educational goals than most parents and educators hold for students;
- the fact that all test scores are susceptible to measurement error;
- the need for equal-interval scales that permit consistent ranking of schools, teachers, and value added (so that a 10-point jump from 30 to 40 equals a 10-point jump from 60 to 70), a requirement most tests do not meet;
- the difficulty of vertically linking tests from grade to grade to compare growth;
- bias introduced by nonrandom assignment of students to teachers and teachers to schools;
- challenges to precision and stability in the face of small class sample sizes, leading to year-to-year fluctuations in estimates of teacher effects; and
- challenges to data quality, including missing or faulty data.

These are hardly trivial issues. Turning to his personal views on the matter, Braun notes, "Given what I know and my knowledge that a lot of what is being said is inaccurate, it is wrong for me not to speak."

On pay for performance, Braun points out that evaluations of the concept produce contradictory results. The latest study from Vanderbilt indicates that even bonuses as high as $15,000 are ineffective. What value added is really measuring, he said, is not the effectiveness of teachers but the effect of being in a particular classroom. "Suddenly this becomes just a teacher issue as though nothing else in the class mattered."

If, he cautioned, policy makers continue to insist on value-added measurement, they should be aware of Campbell's law: "The more any quantitative social indicator is used for social decision-making, the more subject it will be to corruption pressures and the more apt it will be to distort and corrupt the social processes it is intended to monitor."

## 3. A New Model for Teacher Evaluation and Compensation

*Teacher evaluation, especially value-added evaluation, has become a third rail of school reform proposals in recent years. Here, Steve Price, former superintendent of Hazelwood schools in Missouri, and Circe Stumbo, president of West Wind Education Policy, Inc., Iowa City, describe a thoughtful approach to implementing such evaluation approaches. The article is a product of both authors, but it is written in Price's voice.*

Steve Price

Circe Stumbo

Personnel evaluation is one of the most important sets of policies and practices that superintendents can use to drive change. Between 2010 and 2011, evaluation skyrocketed in prominence as a strategy for instructional improvement and achieving improved student results. Several forces contributed to this explosion of interest:

- technical advances in the use of student achievement data to make determinations about educator effectiveness;
- rhetorical opportunities to use the results of current evaluation systems to discredit teachers unions; and
- the federal government's interest in evaluation reform combined with an unprecedented opportunity to fund very large competitive grants for state education agencies (the $4 billion of RTTT, the $3 billion School Improvement Grants program, and the $54 billion state stabilization program, all part of the Obama administration's stimulus package).

The convergence of these interests creates both pressures and opportunities for reform. In the wake of major changes in federal and state policy, some school leaders will think of the evaluation system redesign task as an exercise in compliance. Others will see this as an opportunity to bring personnel systems into alignment with a vision for improving teaching and learning and use it as a lever for change.

*Taking Charge of the Agenda*

Unfortunately, the tone of the politics surrounding state and federal initiatives has been highly adversarial. Teachers have been portrayed as largely ineffective, lazy, and overpaid—and teachers' unions are viewed by some as protecting incompetence. Many argue the process of revamping evaluation is tantamount to getting rid of bad teachers.

For others, however, the drive for more useful evaluation systems is grounded in a commitment to supporting improvements in professional practice. For decades, education reformers have been striving to determine how well teachers and leaders are performing and, based on that information, how to help them improve.

As the dust settles on the federal pressures to revamp evaluations, districts are going to be provided with the chance to press for evaluation reform. I believe this is a golden opportunity that superintendents should seize. Providing high-quality feedback to teachers and principals on areas for improvement can serve to build a district's capacity for change. I approach evaluation as an opportunity for constructive change. Whether you are going to be forced to change your evaluation system or you see changes to your evaluation system as a lever for improvement, diving into systems reform is both necessary and perilous. No matter what, you can—indeed must—take charge of the agenda and use it to your advantage.

*Driving Toward Effective Practice and Improvement*

An evaluation system must embody your district's vision for learning, teaching, and leading. This, as it turns out, is no small task. In one district in which I launched a redesigned teacher evaluation process, it was developed in an environment in which several important strategic goals were already in place. These goals included advancing four critical strands of our reform work: professional learning communities (PLCs), systems thinking, race and equity, and assessment literacy.

These strands were grounded in a few basic principles:

- The focus of the strands would not change. These learning targets would remain stable and predictable over time.
- The strands would be integrated like a tightly woven fabric and not treated as four separate initiatives.
- Adequate resources and time would be provided to support the necessary professional development and organizational structures needed to assure success.
- Strand learning would be job-embedded in a safe environment that encouraged risk—without punishment for failure.
- The strands would be aligned with an evaluation system that supported professional growth first and foremost.
- The organization would be flattened out to support a culture of shared leadership and learning across job classifications.

As the district moved into the work of redesigning their evaluation system, we crafted a theory of change that demonstrated the relationships between the strategic strands and evaluation (see Figure 4.1).

PLCs provide the locus for the work of assessment literacy, race and equity, and systems thinking. All of this is underpinned with an educator evaluation and professional growth system that informs and supports the vision. This foundation supports the old adage, What gets measured gets done.

This is great in theory. However, the predominant work around educator evaluation has been born out of a different theory of professional practice and change. And states also have their own standards and ideas about what should go into teacher evaluation systems. How do you take charge of the agenda and at the same time navigate between the many federal, state, and local ideas about what an evaluation system ought to be? Table 4.3 on the following page outlines the steps that need to be taken, but it all rests on trust.

### Build a Culture of Trust

First, you develop a culture of trust between teachers and administrators. It was noted in Part II of this volume that trust is the essential underpinning of every successful organization. As Anton Chekhov put it, "You must trust and believe in people or life becomes impossible." It's also impossible to implement a reform agenda supported by an effective educator evaluation and professional growth system without trust.

Unfortunately, a union-versus-management mentality has crept into too many districts. The 2012 Chicago teachers' strike, the first in that city in about 25 years, is a clear sign of the climate surrounding the task of evaluation system redesign. As you move into evaluation redesign, you'll

**Figure 4.1**    Teacher Evaluation as the Foundation of Professional Development

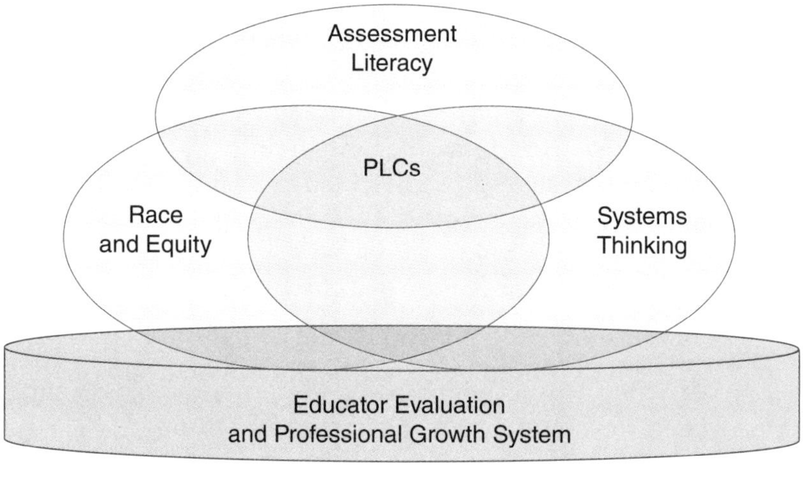

Illustration by Circe Stumbo.

hear a lot of emotional stories about the history of union–management relationships in your district. Lines will be drawn. You'll be asked to take sides, and you'll have to in some way. After all, you're management.

You will have to address this situation when you come across it. It is one of the endless conflicts within a district. In my last district, I promised the staff and union that I would work hard to improve the administration's relationship with the union, but I knew increasing levels of trust would only come through demonstrated actions over time. I spent a significant amount of time in the schools and the community. I initiated the teacher evaluation redesign concurrently with the administrator evaluation redesign. We set up a communications subcommittee to help all staff understand and buy into the collaborative process the committee was using. We established a dedicated site on the district web page outlining the research supporting the evaluation redesign process. We included a list of frequently asked questions and updated the list frequently. A communication subcommittee crafted a variety of techniques and tools to involve and inform the broader staff. And we developed a community-friendly presentation about the evaluation redesign and reform initiatives. All of these things began to have a cumulative effect on understanding the need for change and acceptance of what was involved, but I can't pretend the work was fully successful or complete when I left the district.

### Conclusion

As a school leader with many years of experience as a superintendent, I can assure you that your system of educator evaluation (for both teachers and principals) can be a strong lever for change in your district. Whether you are required or constrained by state and federal mandate or you

---

Table 4.3   Redesigning Evaluation Systems

Starting with a vision and building a culture of trust are just the first steps in a complex process of redesigning evaluation systems.

1. Start with a vision of equity, systems change, and educator effectiveness.

2. Create an inclusive, trusting environment for the design, implementation, and review of the evaluation system.

3. Define the purposes and uses of the evaluation system—and how it supports the vision.

4. Select criteria aligned with the vision for teacher and principal effectiveness.

5. Craft your system of evaluation and support.

---

embark unencumbered on your system (re)design, start your journey not with discussions about the technical issues of measurement but rather with a clear statement of the vision, goals, and relationships you want your evaluation system to support. With that grounding, you can ensure not just a comprehensive approach but a coherent one as well.

## 4. Another Model

*Here is quite a different conception of how to improve both teaching and learning. It describes the work of the National Commission on Teaching and America's Future (NCTAF). Tom Carroll, NCTAF president, told the Roundtable in 2010 that the isolated, stand-alone practice of teaching must yield in the 21st century to team-based approaches to improving student learning.*

### James Harvey

Tom Carroll's outlook on the teaching challenges facing American schools could hardly be more different from that of advocates of performance-based compensation. He directly takes up the issue of the importance of teacher collaboration. Carroll is president of the NCTAF, which has issued several landmark reports on teaching in recent decades.

"Once in a generation we have the opportunity to redefine public education," declares Carroll. "We are at such a point now. The problem is we are busy trying to fix a 19th- or 20th-century notion of teaching, when what we should be doing is creating a new vision of learning for the 21st century."

The challenge, he says, is moving from an emphasis on teaching and leadership to an emphasis on learning for everyone within the school—administrators, teachers, and students. "Today, teachers are on their own. Each individual teacher is busy developing his or her abilities. There is no effort to build common resources for the entire teaching community within the school."

Carroll argues that a teaching organization (what we have now) uses batch processing in the search for efficient transmission of knowledge. What we need, he suggested, are "learning organizations that facilitate co-created learning environments and make use of ubiquitous learning resources that can be customized to meet individual needs." In such an environment, everyone wins because every learner can thrive.

For decades, he points out, it has been known that 50 percent of new teachers leave the profession in the first five years. They leave because they are poorly prepared, have little support, and cannot find a rewarding career path.

### Fixing Old Notions of Teaching and Learning

Educators and their organizations have a responsibility to reshape old notions about teaching and learning into a paradigm that fits the 21st century, according to Carroll. They have a "professional responsibility to create 21st century learning organizations, learning spaces, and learning places." Just as law and medicine moved from the individual practice of Perry Mason and Dr. Kildare in the 1950s to legal and medical teams in the 21st century, so too education must make the transition to teams if it is to meet its responsibilities to parents, students, and taxpayers. So far, we have succeeded only in moving from the stand-alone teacher of the 20th century to the stand-alone teacher of the 21st, says Carroll wryly.

> Law and medicine moved from the individual practice of Perry Mason and Dr. Kildare in the 1950s to legal and medical teams in the 21st century. Education must make the same transition in teaching, says Tom Carroll.

### A New Model

Carroll calls for replacing the current emphasis on teaching and teacher evaluation with a learning ecology for schools. We are all familiar with two different kinds of teams, he says. There are *independent teams*—for example, Olympic track or skiing teams—within which members work together but perform independently and even compete against each other. Then, there are *interdependent teams,* that is, teams made up of individuals dependent on each other for the team's success (hockey or basketball teams). These are the teams in which, in an old coach's saw, "there is no *I* in the word *team.*"

There's no *I* in the word *teacher,* either, is Carroll's message. Schools need interdependent teams of teachers, not independent teachers or independent teams. When reform or demands for teacher quality or performance-based compensation become all about individual teachers, learning suffers. "Teachers have a collective responsibility for student learning," notes Carroll, who says that a 21st-century view of learning should consider teachers as an "interdependent learning community" focused on four "learning age competencies":

- **Core Competencies** in language arts, reasoning, information literacy, mathematics, sciences, and social sciences necessary for adult success;
- **Creative Competencies** including creative expression in the arts, critical thinking, innovation, collaborative problem solving, and resourcefulness;
- **Communication Competencies** in languages, digital media, social networking, and content creation technologies; and
- **Cultural Competencies** including cultural understanding, personal and communal responsibility, adaptability and resilience, an ability to engage in productive teamwork, and active citizen participation.

Educators across the country are actively working to develop these new learning cultures in their schools. NCTAF's publications cite Richard Murphy School in Boston as an exemplar. At Murphy, teaching has become an open transparent process, in which teachers regularly observe and work with each other to improve their teaching practice. The teachers at this K–8 public school have redefined their roles, as they have become members of a professional community composed of accomplished teachers, novice and student teachers, and teacher coaches. School-wide teams of teachers meet on a weekly basis to develop and refine a collectively built body of teaching knowledge and skills that can be customized to meet each student's learning needs. The members of these school-wide teams talk about "our students and our school" instead of "my students" or "my class." The students are majority minority, with over 75 percent being school lunch eligible. In 1999, over 50 percent of the 4th grade students were in the failing category on state tests. Today, the majority of the students are performing in the advanced and proficient levels.

Interested in the approach advocated by the NCTAF? See Wehling, Bob. (Ed.). (2007). *Building a 21st century U.S. education system.* Washington: National Commission on Teaching and America's Future. Retrieved from http://nctaf.org/wp-content/uploads/2012/01/Bldg21stCenturyUSEducationSystem_final.pdf

Murphy, reports Carroll, emphasizes individual learning plans for all students, a distributed leadership model in which teachers govern and manage the school, and an environment that encourages teachers to take risks. Teachers see themselves as learners within the school.

The Murphy School is not the only site pioneering professional learning communities for teachers. Three thousand miles away in Sherwood, Oregon, Sherwood schools are part of a statewide effort to reshape teaching and learning through the Creative Leadership Achieves Student Success (CLASS) initiative. This experiment aims to expand career paths, improve performance evaluation, provide outstanding professional development, and explore new teacher compensation models. Leaders of the effort describe trust as the essential glue holding it together. Leadership is defined as a culture that begins in the classroom, encouraging strong bonds and relationships between and among teachers and emphasizing active research to guide practice and collaborative teams.

In the face of these on-the-ground experiments, value-added approaches come across as yesterday's solution applied to the problems of today and tomorrow. "What does the Murphy example say about value-added assessment?" asks Carroll. "It's not encouraging. Value is added through team learning, not through individual accomplishment or competition between teachers."

# 5. Central Office Best Practice Around Learning and Assessment

*Pam Ansingh served as a coach with the Washington State Leadership Academy and continues to work with district leaders to improve teaching and learning. As part of her doctoral work at Seattle University, she surveyed central office administrators to determine best practices in the state of Washington in 2011–2012. Here is a summary of what she learned.*

## Pamela J. Ansingh

State and national standards have drastically changed what students learn and how teachers teach and leaders lead. In K–12 education, it is no longer enough that students put in the required seat time, while teachers present lessons. What matters now is the answer to these questions: Are students learning the content as put forth in the standards, and how well are students learning the intended curriculum?

How prepared are central office administrators to lead school districts in the face of these new demands and changing student populations? This study involved a survey and interviews with central office staff in Washington State districts performing in the top 5 percent of all state districts as measured by state assessment results in reading, writing, and mathematics. Sixteen of the 296 districts in the state took part. I wanted to know the following:

> An outstanding national overview of central office changes can be found in a Wallace Foundation–funded study: Honig, M., et al. (2010). *Central office transformation for district-wide teaching and learning improvement.* Seattle: University of Washington, Center for the Study of Teaching and Policy (http://tinyurl.com/by62wqp).

- Are there common leadership attitudes and actions practiced by central office administrators in support of teaching and learning in these top districts?
- If so, what are they?

> Another highly useful analysis of effective district practices in the state of Washington is the following: Abbott, M. L., Baker, D. B., & Stroh, H. R. (2004). *From compliance to commitment: A report on effective school districts in Washington State.* Seattle: Washington State Research Center, Pacific University (http://tinyurl.com/co9j4ap).

What I found confirmed much of the literature on the importance of instructional leadership; the need for ongoing, contextual professional development; the importance of coherent systems thinking; and the need for trust and transparency of action. These were the findings:

*Top districts build capacity through instructional leadership that emphasizes data, involves instructional staff, and encourages instructional leadership on the part of central office staff.*

Administrators in top districts tend to believe the following:

- Instructional leadership requires the knowledge and use of data and is demonstrated by central office administrators' participation in data review opportunities one to four or more times per month.
- Building the capacity of the instructional staff is an important factor in student achievement and is demonstrated as central office administrators involve principals, teachers, and others in instructional decisions two to four or more times per month.
- Student achievement is positively impacted by the effectiveness of district instructional leadership and requires attention from central office administrators the majority or all of the time.

*Ongoing, contextual professional development is encouraged via learning walks or walkthroughs and frequent central office collaboration with principals around work practices.*

Administrators in these districts believe the following:

- Conducting classroom learning walks or walkthroughs is an effective means to guide professional dialogue on improving instructional practices, and the best district administators conduct them with building principals one to four or more times per month.
- Effective professional development relates to actual work practices so that central office administrators collaborate with principals on work that is focused on the improvement of teaching and learning one to four or more times per month.

> For more on walkthroughs, learning walks, and coaching, see Part VI: Developing Your Principals.

*Administrators in top-performing districts are committed to building coherence through systemic change that encourages the use of common assessments, curricular materials aligned to state objectives, and districtwide instructional frameworks and common standards.*

They believe the following:

- Student achievement is increased by the use of common assessments to measure student progress.
- Achievement is increased by the use of common curricula aligned to state standards.
- It is important to use a districtwide instructional framework that provides commonly agreed-upon effective instructional practices.

- Student achievement is increased by the use of common, agreed-upon practices for effective instruction.
- The development of state standards is a positive step, although some frustration exists with frequent changes in the standards.

*Administrators in top-performing districts support transparency of interactions and a district culture of trust.*

They reported this:

Creating a culture of interpersonal trust between the superintendent and other instructional leaders in the district contributes to effective collaboration that positively impacts student achievement.

Many district leaders spoke of the transparency in their districts, not only in terms of data but also in terms of relationships and interactions that they believe have contributed to the high levels of trust as well as improved student achievement. Others shared that they use collaborative goal setting and that the practice of transparency supports progress toward the goals. As one district administrator put it: "The term transparency of results means for me anyway, that we aren't afraid of what our results are and we put those results in front of people."

In reference to their collaborative culture, one central office administrator explained, "What separates (districts) is they take great ownership for how their kids are performing. They take great ownership of how their teachers are performing, their principals, all the way through. They are constantly looking for ways to help people improve."

> For the complete study, see Ansingh, P. J. (2012). *An exploratory study of central office best practices in Washington's top 5% performing school districts.* Seattle, WA: Seattle University.

### Concluding Thoughts

Roles and expectations have indeed changed for district leaders. Administrators heavily trained in site-based thinking and management skills no longer fit the educational leadership bill whether at the school, district, or university level. District-level leaders must adapt to their new roles as instructional leaders and contributing members of a larger system that is integrated and interested in the advancement of student achievement for all.

The advent of the K–12 Common Core standards will only hasten the need for quality leadership at the central office level. No longer able to survive as collections of parts, effective district leadership must weave a more highly aligned system connected by the goal of improving student achievement. In this new era, central office administrators must intentionally shape and guide the work needing to be done in terms of improving achievement for all students.

## G. TOOLS

### 1. Effective State Accountability Systems

#### Luvern L. Cunningham

Researchers at the University of Washington developed the following description of an effective state accountability system. How does your state stack up?

An accountability system should have the following:

- Fair, reliable, relevant, and understandable indicators of school performance
- Predictable and consistent incentives for performance
- Opportunities for schools to build their capacity, ensuring tools and resources for schools
- Flexibility for schools to adapt to help their students learn and meet state standards of performance
- A safety net, providing functional learning opportunities for students when school improvement is not possible
- A comprehensive public information campaign that helps schools and the public understand the process
- An independent body guiding the system and providing a check and balance on the political oversight of the system

> The American Evaluation Association issued a position statement on high-stakes testing in Pre-K–12 education. It went on record to oppose the use of tests as the sole or primary criterion for making decisions, arguing that such use creates serious negative consequences for students, educators, and schools. You can find this statement at http://www.eval.org/EPTF.asp.

### 2. Assessing Your State's Accountability System

#### Luvern L. Cunningham

Accountability is a high-stakes part of life in the school trenches. Table 4.4 is a checklist to help you review your state's assessments.

**Table 4.4**  Accountability Checklist

| Our State Accountability System: | Yes | No | Not Sure |
|---|---|---|---|
| 1. Uses multiple measures of student performance to arrive at judgments of the success or failure of the state's educational system. | | | |
| 2. Meets all the requirements of the No Child Left Behind legislation at the state and local levels. | | | |
| 3. Ensures that the accountability system does not underserve (or do a disservice to) segments of the student population. | | | |
| 4. Aligns state academic standards, curriculum, and assessments. | | | |
| 5. Provides comprehensive information so that teachers, principals, central office administrators, parents, and community leaders can understand the accountability process. | | | |
| 6. Provides regular, understandable reports to the public on the performance of the state's educational system, including plans for improving its performance. | | | |
| 7. Reports annually and comprehensively on costs. | | | |
| 8. Assures practitioners that standards guide test development and other instruments of measurement that are a part of the accountability system. | | | |
| 9. Spells out clearly the placement of management and oversight responsibilities within the accountability system, including segments that may be delivered through outside contracts. | | | |
| 10. Places school accountability in the context of public and community accountability for the well-being of children and youth outside schools, including mental health, substance abuse, juvenile justice, and correctional programs. | | | |

NOTE: Yes = +1; No = −1; Not Sure = 0. Add your responses together to determine your score: 7–10 points—Congratulations; 4–6 points—Needs work; 1–3 points—You're not failing anyone on these results, are you? 0 or below—Legislature flunks.

143

## H. REFLECTIVE PRACTICE

Here are some key ideas you should be considering.

*Are you sure* that the educators in your district understand the pressures on schools today? Do you understand these pressures? Do your teachers and principals?

*What about the details of NCLB* and its adequate yearly progress requirements? Are you confident that everyone understands what this entails?

*When issues of race and class and the achievement gap* come up in your district, do people fall silent? Or are they able to discuss these challenges openly? Is there a different answer to these questions in your community and in your school buildings?

*Have you created, or are you creating,* the infrastructure that will permit you to track progress in closing the achievement gap? Do your principals and teachers comprehend that this is your first priority?

*Have you become a connoisseur of data?* If not, where do you find the skills and confidence to understand what is happening in terms of closing the achievement gap?

*Are you confident in discussing* the economic and demographic facts of life with the business leaders in your community? With teachers and administrators? With community groups? Are you the only one talking about these things, or have you managed to transform this into a community conversation?

*Compared with the national demographic picture, what is the picture in your district?* What about individual schools? What do your principals and teachers make of these data? Do your principals and teachers understand where your students go (and what they do) after graduation?

*Do you track critical data monthly (i.e., attendance, suspensions, etc.)?* Is this publicly posted for teachers in each building to follow district and school progress? Is it accessible to parents and other interested groups in the community?

*Has your community agreed on standards for student performance?* What level is expected? Has this information been broadly disseminated?

*Have you closely examined students' assignments* and the work they produce? Does this review reveal that all students are expected to achieve at high levels? Or do your schools expect less from certain groups of students?

*Are students with the greatest needs receiving more resources* (i.e., best teachers, enrichment opportunities, etc.)? Who speaks for these students?

*Is your district speaking with one voice?* Or are different parts of your district telling different people different things?

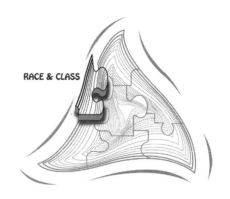

RACE & CLASS

# PART V

# *Addressing Race and Class*

I t is as true today as it was two generations ago. Race remains what Swedish sociologist Gunnar Myrdal once described as the great "American dilemma." The legacy of centuries of oppression and prejudice remain with us, now made even more complex by burgeoning income inequality, clear class differences between and within groups, and growing diversity in the American population. How do you close the achievement gap? How can schools live out their historic promise of providing a second chance to all Americans in a society where inequality seems not to shrink but to grow? Discussions about race and class are among the most explosive and difficult you will ever hold as a superintendent. In this part of the *Fieldbook,* you will learn some of the things to do and to avoid when trying to hold these difficult conversations. You'll also learn about what's going on inside schools—and what's going on outside them that might help you in your work. Finally, we look at some sobering data about the crisis facing young men of color in the United States.

## A. WHY RACE AND CLASS?

*Until No Child Left Behind (NCLB) came along, most of the discussion of school reform paid little attention to an unpleasant secret. Schools of all kinds, urban and rural, generally don't do a good job serving children of color and poverty. Race and class shape student achievement in ways both subtle and obvious.*

Howard Fuller

James Harvey

The short answer to the question of why worry about race and class is that you probably cannot succeed as a school superintendent unless you worry about it. Nationally, 44 percent of all public school enrollment is made up of minority students—African-American, Hispanic, Asian or Pacific Islander, or Native American. About 20 percent of all children aged 5 to 17 live in poverty, with the proportion of poor minority children exceeding 40 percent and the number of African-American children living in severe poverty doubling in recent years. While it is true that there are more white children who are poor than minority children, the proportion of minority children who are poor is much higher.

And these children are nearly as segregated today as they were in the days of legal Jim Crow. About one-half of white students attend public schools that enroll 10 percent or fewer minority students. About 2 percent of white students attend schools with enrollments of 75 percent or more minority students. Data for minority students are, of course, reversed: About 4 percent attend public schools with less than 10 percent minority enrollment. Nearly 50 percent of minority students attend public schools with enrollments that are 75 percent or more minority.

When these students arrive in your classrooms, what will their teachers look like? By that, we mean, will the teaching force bear any resemblance to the students they are teaching? The answer, unfortunately, is no. While the students are members of minority groups, young, and about evenly divided between boys and girls, the teaching force is primarily white, aging, and overwhelmingly female. More than four out of five teachers in the United States are white (about 86 percent); two-thirds of them are 40 years of age or older; and nearly three-quarters are women.

The dynamics of race and class are becoming ever more complex. In 2003, for example, the United States Bureau of the Census announced that, for the first time, Hispanic Americans were the nation's largest minority group. In the lifetime of superintendents launching their careers today, white Americans will become a statistical minority of the population.

Here, we begin to address these issues. Conversations about race and class are difficult to have. We explore that at the outset. Then, we look at the basics, what's happening both inside and outside schools. We explore the

Want a stunning insight into how class plays out in modern life? A picture is worth a thousand words. You'll probably have to find it on the Internet, but get your hands on a copy of *28-Up*, a documentary by filmmaker Michael Apted, who also directed *Coal Miner's Daughter* and *Gorillas in the Mist*. Starting in England in 1964, he filmed 14 young people from different economic backgrounds at seven-year intervals beginning at age seven. The aspirations of wealthy young people were shaped by their parents, and most aspired to attend Oxford or Cambridge University. Generally, that's where they wound up. Children from low-income families were left to work out their own educational destinies, and most opted for less-demanding curricula and immediate work. That couldn't happen in the United States, you say? What about all those legacy admissions to Ivy League institutions?

challenge of closing the achievement gap. Next, we examine the assets students depend on in the effort to succeed in life before we turn to some questions and issues for reflection. Finally, we suggest some tools you can use to begin the conversation.

> "When a community of people discovers that they share a concern, change begins. There is no power greater than a community discovering what it cares about."
>
> —Wheatley, Margaret. (2002). *Turning to one another: Simple conversations to restore hope to the future.* San Francisco: Berrett-Koehler.

Why should you worry about race and class in the long run? Because our society cannot long function while it tolerates the class, income, and racial differences that are evident to anyone who takes the time to look. If it was true, as President Lincoln said nearly 150 years ago, that this nation cannot "endure half slave and half free," it is equally true that the nation cannot endure half wealthy and half poor, with the differences defined more by race, privilege, and class than by ability, merit, or effort. To say the same thing another way, unequal outcomes in a democracy might be defended on the grounds that everyone had an equal chance at the start. But if it turns out that significant numbers of students were not treated fairly at the outset, there can be no defense for unequal results.

## 1. Holding Difficult Conversations

*In the United States, conversations about race and class are nearly inevitably stilted, stylized, and difficult. Neither majority nor minority participants seem able to express honestly and openly what's on their minds, at least in formal, public settings. Many people prefer to avoid the discussion, considering it to be the thinnest of ice on which to set foot. But it is a discussion that has to take place, a conversation that has to be held. Here are some examples of how to proceed and tools you might use as you begin this dialogue in your district. We don't pretend it will be easy, and you may make mistakes. With the help of the tools here, however, you can begin the engagement and experience some success.*

### Howard Fuller

The great silent dialogue in American education is about race and class. It's silent because so little is ever said publicly about the topic. The reality is that Roundtable and Forum superintendents didn't find this discussion any easier than you will. We found it difficult. You will too. But you're going to have to engage it.

Careful planning, honesty, determination, and sometimes just plain luck can help you broach these topics. Several factors appeared to be particularly valuable in framing the discussion:

- structuring meetings around powerful individual stories;
- improving comfort levels by breaking large groups into smaller and smaller units; and
- using skilled facilitators to help draw out the discussion.

By the same token, several situations need to be avoided, lest they sabotage the conversation. These range from lack of adequate preparation to trying to deal with difficult issues in large groups. The tools provided later in this part give some suggestions on how to work around these land mines.

*Stories*

Forget about the experts at first. Try to find some people who are willing to share their lives with you. Find some very successful people, from very diverse backgrounds, all of whom started out life with huge obstacles in their paths. If you can find people like that, just listen to what they have to say.

> "How do we frame a conversation about this so that our country's story has a happy ending? Because if it doesn't work for some of us, it can't work for any of us."
>
> —Peter Negroni, former superintendent, Springfield, Massachusetts

What you will hear is powerful. And it's often painful. Imagine sitting in a meeting in which four complete strangers share the following with you: being forced to listen to racist jokes in the classroom as a child . . . living a childhood of Appalachian poverty so severe that privies were unavailable . . . understanding, even as a child, that the deck was loaded against people who looked like you . . . trying to console your children scarred by racial slurs . . . waging a 70-year fight to obtain the honorable discharge and medals a father had earned but never received . . . confronting the prejudice and biases that divide even minority groups . . . examining the many ways in which class and caste blight dreams, divide society, and stunt American growth.

This is raw and tough stuff. But if you can set up the dynamics in which speakers can share material such as this—and you, your staff, your teachers, and your community can hear it—you will have made a tremendous start with the discussion. This conversation will leave you with new understandings of the dynamics of race and class in our life and schools. And it might leave you shaken.

> "How you talk about this is critical. I remember saying to some of my African-American colleagues, 'If you keep venting like that, nobody will say anything because you're blowing our white friends out of the room.'"
>
> —Lynn Beckwith, Jr., former superintendent, University City, Missouri

Among the storytellers we listened to in one experiment with this approach were the following: Beatriz, a national education leader who is Latina; Jacqueline, an African-American woman who deferred her college plans to work as a parent activist; William, a professor emeritus at a Big 10 campus, who grew up poor and white in Appalachia; and Bernard, also an African American, now president of a foundation, who grew up in the North, during World War II, struggling with racism. Listen to their tales.

**Beatriz.** "I married an African-American man," she began her story. "Now head of his own manufacturing firm, he was blacklisted by the chair of his Ph.D. program for objecting to the chair's racist speeches. I have had to console my children after they heard racial slurs. And I've also had to encourage them when they were challenged for not being black enough."

She concluded her story by noting that the responsibility for addressing this state of affairs "rests with both blacks and whites. Both have prejudices to overcome; and both must recognize that unity is the only solution."

**Jacqueline.** Born in Chicago, Jacqueline moved to Milwaukee as a child. She recalls that, at one point, flyers were distributed in her neighborhood announcing a Ku Klux Klan rally near her house.

At Roosevelt Middle School in Milwaukee, she found herself attending what was thought to be "one of the worst schools in the city. Predominantly African-American and Hispanic in enrollment, a majority of its teachers were from minority groups." At the end of eighth grade, said Jacqueline, she was transferred to another school with a majority enrollment of white students. "The idea was that we'd get a better education with white kids."

Unable to get health care coverage, child care, or financial aid to go to college in her 20s, Jacqueline put off her college dreams in favor of consulting and civic activism. "I still have my own personal goal of going to college to become an engineer. But before I do that, I have to defer it to help eradicate racism, classism, and genderism."

**William.** This presentation was framed by class. He grew up a poor Appalachian white boy in the 1930s, in a part of America little changed from the 19th century. So poor that the children literally evacuated outside the kitchen window (because there was no privy), he grew up in a largely

> For a powerful story to share with others, see Adichie, Chimamanda. *The danger of a single story, TED talks* (http://tinyurl.com/ycq3msk). Adichie, an African novelist, cautions, "The single story creates stereotypes, and the problem with stereotypes is not that they are untrue, but that they are incomplete. They make one story the only story."

> Immigration trends profoundly influence schools and communities across the nation. For an intriguing look at the experience of immigrant children in four schools (Wisconsin, Colorado, Connecticut, and Iowa), see Center in Child Development and Social Policy. (2003). *Portraits of four schools: Meeting the needs of immigrant students and their families*. New Haven, CT: Yale University.

> Raymond Terrell and Randall Lindsey can help you develop your own personal narrative as you journey toward culturally proficient leadership. Their book, *Culturally Proficient Leadership: The Personal Journey Begins Within*, published by Corwin Press in 2009, has received widespread recognition for assisting school leaders as they attempt to communicate and collaborate across cultures.

dysfunctional family in which his alcoholic father ultimately deserted the family and "my mother went crazy trying to deal with that."

William and his brothers and sisters used to run to the road to see a car go by, there were so few. They learned to pole coal off the top of passing freight cars with a stick, so that they'd have something to heat their shack. "A good poler could get a bushel of coal off a train easily. A bad one could easily get the pole driven through his body."

William's view of education's role in this is rich and textured. He noted, "My school could easily have destroyed me. It did not. Instead, it became my second home. It was the source of my sense of self-worth."

**Bernard.** "My generation, those of us over 65 years, was never confused about racism in the United States," said Bernard at the outset of his remarks. "We pursued full citizenship, accompanied by all its rights and responsibilities, as hard as we could. We knew what we had to do, and we had few illusions about how much help we would get. We loved America even when it had trouble loving us back."

The product of a strong family, whose father had a second grade education and whose mother possessed a college degree, Bernard grew up in the steel-company town of Gary, Indiana.

> "We loved America, even when it had trouble loving us back."
>
> —Bernard

One story tells it all: Bernard discovered that, although his father was entitled to several medals for his service in the army during World War I, he had never received them. "Seventy years after the armistice was signed, I finally obtained, from the Pentagon, the decorations and awards my father deserved. My mother and brothers and sisters never knew he'd earned them."

### Small Groups

Large groups of people cannot process powerful information such as this. When the group is large, people may listen to presentations, but they won't talk about them. Increase people's comfort level around this difficult issue for discussion purposes by breaking down large groups into smaller ones. This rarely fails and almost always works. (See the tools for holding the conversation throughout this section.) In almost no small group will you encounter the dynamics that often develop in large groups: One or two individuals start to dominate the discussion so that the conversation turns into pro forma, sometimes angry, speeches and lectures.

### Skilled Facilitators

Skilled and experienced facilitators are another key ingredient. They should include the broadest diversity possible: Latino scholars; African-American activists; community leaders; and parents, teachers, and advocates for the disadvantaged are all good candidates. Working with a structured format helps. It should invite participants to explore their own understandings of issues related to race and class. In well-facilitated, small-group discussions, we learned the following:

- Prejudice is not confined to any ethnic group but cuts across them all. Class is a common issue. Even people of color are divided along class lines.
- Board members and superintendents are frustrated by these issues; they want to change these dynamics; they have less power to do so than they thought.
- People in small groups are often initially uncomfortable, afraid of saying the wrong thing. They get beyond that, but it is difficult.
- You can't get to a comfort level on these issues in one afternoon, and no amount of time is enough unless people are willing to struggle together.
- Adults are the problem, not children.

"The problem is changing," says one former superintendent, a Hispanic who was banned from hotels in the South under Jim Crow. "It used to be a black–white issue. Now we're talking about a more complex problem of diverse groups of white people and people of color competing with each other."

## 2. Sabotaging the Conversation

### Howard Fuller

### James Harvey

Just as skillful preparation can make it possible to hold the conversation, sloppy or careless preparation can sabotage it. We don't always get it right. The reality is that, on occasion, the discussion of race and class is frustrating and incomplete. You can learn from the mistakes we made.

Three things consistently threatened to sabotage the conversation:

1. poor preparation;
2. large groups, particularly those in which participants could not maintain eye contact with everyone; and
3. careless and insensitive language.

*Poor Preparation*

Preparation may be the single most important factor in the success of any meeting about race and class. This cannot be overemphasized when convening a group around volatile matters that customarily are ignored in our society.

> Race and class are areas where you can't succeed by making it up as you go along.

At various points in our planning, we turned to external experts when we felt we had reached roadblocks. In one instance, this was less than satisfactory for the group because of poor planning. The planning group had outlined general expectations for a three-day meeting, but we turned over the detailed planning to someone who had been quite successful with our group previously. Unforeseen events in this individual's schedule resulted in lack of planning for the meeting and, consequently, in a meeting that was awkward and counterproductive. You must ensure that preparation receives your full attention when you embark on discussions of race and class in your district.

### Large Groups

Don't create a situation in which you find large groups assembled for long periods over several days. You're inviting discomfort and conflict, particularly if you're unclear about the agenda. While we're at it, make sure that large-group circles, established so that everyone can see everyone else, are properly shaped. At one of our meetings, despite efforts to form a circle, some participants found themselves looking at the backs of the heads of several of their neighbors.

This experience reinforces an earlier learning experience. Small-group discussions to lay out the dimensions of the effort go well, but it is hard to maintain a sense of unity and purpose in the group as it expands. Some members dominate the discussion, sometimes expressing anger, while others withdraw. The lessons here are straightforward: Understand that the problem will not be solved in one or two meetings. The conversation has to be relaunched every time it is brought up. Large groups should be avoided until the people involved have developed considerable experience holding the conversation in smaller and more-intimate environments.

### Careless and Insensitive Language

Language matters. Use of inappropriate terms can wreck the entire effort. Even people with the best of intentions can stick their feet in their mouths. When that happens, the best way to proceed is bring it up, challenge stereotypes, and move on.

An especially vivid example of this occurred at a meeting at the end of a lengthy day. The day began early and finished late. It ended, disastrously, with dinner and a major presentation followed by three respondents. The final respondent, a Native American woman, reported that, as an educator, she had always sought the "schools nobody else wants," schools in which student problems were the most difficult. "Most of my illegal students," she lamented, "were 'wetbacks' desperate for an education in an American school."

The use of this racially loaded term (not once, but several times) so offended several people that, the following morning, the group agreed to set aside the meeting agenda and discuss the incident. Three views emerged. First was the thought that the term is as offensive to Latinos as the worst racial epithet is to African Americans. Second was the view that, although the term is offensive, the word used to disparage African Americans is immeasurably more corrosive. Third, several people ascribed the incident to a slip of the tongue, brought on by a long day and the lateness of the hour. All agreed that holding this difficult conversation was essential to group learning.

Again, the lessons here were instructive. Don't overtire people when dealing with a difficult topic like this. Don't use language carelessly. When it happens, the group should not tolerate it. After raising the issue, accept an apology and move on.

### 3. Crisis Facing Minority Males

#### James Harvey

Within the next generation, the educational destiny of the United States will be driven by demographics and gender. If equity, social justice, economic competitiveness, and a level educational playing field for males and females continue to be important goals for this society, American leaders must deal with long-standing racial and ethnic inequities in educational outcomes. Nor should they ignore emerging evidence that boys and young men increasingly lag behind girls and young women on important measures of educational experience, achievement, and persistence. Where these trends intersect, the combination of gender, race, and ethnicity produces toxic outcomes for minority men.

> "In this ranking of the worst for males [comparison of bachelor's completion rates for young males] the U.S. was the worst of the worst."
>
> —Mortenson, Thomas G. (2008, October). *Educational attainment and economic welfare, 1940 to 2008* (Number 196). Oskaloosa, Iowa: Postsecondary Education Opportunity.

These findings emerge from the data available on minority achievement in the United States, analyzed by gender. The conclusion is unavoidable: Males in general lag behind females—and young men of color in America are in a crisis.

When demographic and educational change in the United States is examined, there is a mixture of very good and very bad news.

- Within a generation, the United States will be a much more diverse nation. Indeed, by midcentury, no racial or ethnic group in the United States will be a majority. Greater diversity will undoubtedly be a national asset in a more globally connected world.
- Many minority groups, including traditionally disadvantaged groups, are producing record numbers of school and college graduates.

- However, the fastest-growing populations in the United States are those minority groups with the lowest levels of educational attainment.
- If current population trends and educational attainment levels continue, the general educational level of Americans will probably decline by 2020.
- Across the board, young men are not persisting in school or achieving at the same levels as young women.
- The challenge of responding is most acute for the most disadvantaged men of color. At just about every stage of the educational pipeline, they lag behind minority women in terms of achievement, persistence, and school and college completion. Gender enrollment and completion gaps in higher education for the most disadvantaged minority groups are shockingly high.

### A More Diverse Nation

There is little mystery about the immediate future. The U.S. population under the age of 18 already exists; these young people have been born. They will grow up to be the adults of the next generation. The Bureau of the Census projects that minorities will represent more than half of all children in the United States by 2023, and that the entire U.S. population will be 54 percent minority by 2050.

But, as "the other" becomes a majority, diversity becomes a great potential asset in schools, the workforce, and society. Greater diversity, far from being a cause for alarm, is something to be cherished in American life.

### Minority Educational Progress

Faced with growing diversity, the United States can take pride in substantial progress in recent decades in the levels of educational attainment of minority Americans. Many challenges remain, but a history of success exists, a foundation on which to build.

With regard to minority populations, here is what the data reveal for young Americans aged 18 to 24:

- For African Americans, the proportion holding high school credentials was about the same in 2006 as it was in 1986 (about 84 percent).
- Meanwhile, the proportion of Hispanics holding high school credentials increased from 59 to 65 percent.
- School completion rates for Asian Americans and Native Americans in 2006 were 91 and 71 percent respectively; trend line data to 1986 on these populations are not available.
- With regard to college attendance, enrollment rates for young African Americans (18 to 24) increased from 22 to 32 percent, while Hispanic enrollment rates increased from 18 to 25 percent.

- With respect to degree attainment, the number of associate's and bachelor's degrees awarded increased for all racial and ethnic groups, with minorities accounting for almost half the growth in associate's degrees conferred and 35 percent of the growth in bachelor's degrees.

Despite the clear need to accomplish more, there is a promising record of some progress in advancing minority educational attainment, a record on which the nation must build.

### Fastest-Growing Minority Populations

As valuable as that progress is, the increases outlined above represent growth from a low base. Though there has been progress, graduation rates for the most disadvantaged Americans still lag considerably behind those of white Americans (and of Asian Americans, generally, but not of Pacific Islanders). That is to say, the fastest-growing populations in the United States are those minority groups with the lowest levels of educational attainment, while an aging, white workforce increasingly enters retirement or approaches it. Unless current educational imbalances are corrected, American society is likely to see an increase in the proportion of the population with less than a high school diploma while witnessing a decline in the proportion graduating from high school, entering college, or attaining an associate's degree or higher.

### Differences in Educational Outcomes by Gender

There has long been a widespread belief that education in general systematically favors males. While that may have once been true, it is no longer. The data leave no doubt that girls and women today consistently outperform boys and men in terms of achievement and educational attainment. It is essential to acknowledge this new reality even in the face of another reality: The agenda for girls and women is itself incomplete. Boys of color are significantly behind on the achievement and school completion scales; girls and women of color are only comparatively better off, and they also face their own challenges.

The most recent data available on high school completion rates and the proportion of young men and women age 25 to 29 with associate's degrees or higher are crystal clear. Across the board, the results for women are superior to those for men. This

Source: The College Board Advocacy and Policy Center. *The Educational Crisis Facing Young Men of Color.* Copyright 2010. Reproduced with permission.

gender gap extends across all racial and ethnic categories—white, black, Hispanic, AAPI, and Native American and Alaska Native.

With regard to high school completion, women consistently outperform men—by 4 percent for white women, 9 percent for African-American

*The Urgency of Now*, a 2012 50-state report on public education and black males, confirms much of the College Board report. North Carolina (58 percent), Maryland (57 percent), and California (56 percent) have the highest graduation rates for black males. New York (37 percent) and Illinois and Florida (47 percent) have the lowest. Arizona (68 percent), New Jersey (66 percent), and California (64 percent) have the highest graduation rates for Latino males; New York (37 percent), Colorado (46 percent), and Georgia (52 percent) have the lowest. The report urges moving from a standards-driven reform agenda to a support-driven agenda that provides all students with equitable access to the resources required for success. See Schott Foundation for Public Education. (2012). *The urgency of now: The Schott 50 state report on public education and black males*. Cambridge, MA: Author.

and Hispanic women, 2 percent for Asian American women, and 7 percent for Native American women. Meanwhile, boys in general seem to be twice as likely as girls to be labeled learning disabled and seven times more likely to be diagnosed with attention deficit or attention deficit hyperactivity disorder as girls.

### Challenges for Minority Males

It is very hard to avoid the obvious: The educational crisis facing young minority males is formidable. Across the board, males from all racial and ethnic backgrounds are likely to be suspended at about twice the rate of females. While the rate of suspensions for Hispanic and Native American males is considerably higher than that of white males, the rate for black males is almost three times as high. Status drop-out rates for 16- to 24-year-olds tell a similar story: Here, while black males are more likely than whites to be dropouts, the rate for Hispanic males is almost four times that of whites.

### Implications

Two basic data points are critical with regard to projected levels of educational attainment. First, the youth population in the United States is becoming more racially and ethnically diverse. Second, despite some encouraging progress in educational attainment, minority groups with the most disappointing levels of educational attainment are growing the fastest, while an aging, white population approaches or enters retirement.

Important American values of justice and equity are involved here. An America that hopes to provide equal opportunity must begin with equal access to an education of high quality in schools, colleges, and universities.

There also are critical economic issues in play. Individual and national standards of living are likely to be threatened if the United States does not respond to the developments outlined here. What we have in this confluence of educational, demographic, and retirement trends is a situation in which well-educated, older Americans can be expected to retire to be replaced by more poorly educated minority citizens.

## 4. THINKING ABOUT EDUCATING MEN OF COLOR

The challenges facing minority Americans take place in different policy contexts. Some of these contexts are outlined below.

### African Americans

- African Americans disproportionately attend urban schools, many of them large.
- Ninety percent of African Americans are concentrated in California and the belt of states running from New York through the South and Southwest, the Midwest and Texas.
- Fifty-four percent grew up in female-headed families in which young people are more likely to be poor and less likely to have strong male role models.
- One study indicates that African-American girls may challenge bias and discrimination, while boys may not.
- Another study suggests that black males experience depression, anxiety, guilt, and hostility at levels considerably higher than girls.

### Hispanics

- Hispanics and Latinos are found everywhere, in cities, suburbs, and rural areas.
- Ninety percent of the Hispanic population lives in the states of Washington, Illinois, and California and in the Southwest and along the Eastern seaboard states, from New York to Florida.
- Many Hispanic and Latino homes do not use English as the primary language.
- Cultural backgrounds vary widely. The college attendance rate of Cuban Americans is 45 percent; for students whose heritage includes Mexico or Puerto Rico, it is about 30 percent.
- One study indicates that girls in urban barrios see achievement as a way to resist cultural stereotyping; young men, on the other hand, see cutting class as a way to socialize with peers while escaping negative judgments and conflict in school.

### Asian American and Pacific Islanders

- Although the U.S. Census recognizes 48 ethnic categories of Asian American and Pacific Islanders (AAPI), a major challenge in examining the AAPI population is lack of data in general, limited disaggregation of data by ethnicity and culture, and very little data on AAPI males.

*(Continued)*

(Continued)

- While Hawaii and California are the states with the largest proportion of residents who are Asian or Pacific Islander, California had the largest number (4.5 million), followed by New York (1.3 million), Texas (806,000), New Jersey (648,000), Illinois (551,000), and Hawaii (498,000).
- In Washington State, AAPIs speak more than 100 languages; 40 percent of AAPI students speak a language other than English as their primary language; in 16 Washington school districts, these students account for 10 percent or more of enrollment.
- AAPI students experience alienation and marginalization in schools to varying degrees. Filipino and Southeast Asian American students are most at risk of being considered low achievers and gang members by teachers.

## Native Americans

- These students are very likely to attend remote, rural schools.
- The Department of Interior recognizes 562 tribal entities in the United States.
- Native Americans are concentrated in Alaska, the plains and mountain states, and the Southwest. In seven states, 5 percent or more of the population is Native American or Alaska Native: Alaska, New Mexico, South Dakota, Oklahoma, Montana, Arizona, and North Dakota.
- Ambivalence about school is common. Discontinuity between Native American and Western ways of learning often leads to disagreement.
- English may not be the primary home language.
- School social and behavioral norms may contradict tribal cultural norms.
- One-third of Native Americans are born into poverty, often to a mother who is not a high school graduate.

### 5. Taking Risks Around Race

James Harvey

This is a true story about a superintendent whose advocacy around issues of race and class upset powerful leaders in his community. Let's call our superintendent Phil Smith. He's an articulate leader, a tall, good-looking, well-built man in his early 50s. His commitment to children and public education is hard to miss. Yet, after nine apparently successful years as a school superintendent in the Midwest (including seven in his last district), he found himself circulating his résumé nationally, unemployed and looking for work amidst a national recession.

It's not a situation he expected to be in, he says. Indeed, he hoped to end his career in this school district, but after initial success passing bond and building levies, his ambition ran afoul of local irritation at taxes amidst a recession and anger from white, working-class constituents in his community (and his schools) about his commitment to equity. The district enrolls roughly 5,000 students, about 24 percent minority with about three-quarters eligible for free or reduced-price lunches. More than 40 percent of the students are drawn from backgrounds of rural (white) poverty, most attracted to the area because of manufacturing jobs.

It all started well enough, notes Phil. He began his work stressing equity in broad terms—race, class, gender, and income. But a conversation with Glenn Singleton, coauthor of *Courageous Conversations About Race,* turned him in a new direction. Class, income, and these other factors were important but not the essential point, argued Singleton. Race, racism, and the racial achievement gap

> A 2007 estimate from the National Center on Higher Education Management Systems ("Adding It Up," November 2007) held that eliminating the degree gap between underrepresented people of color (including men) and white Americans would produce more than half the degrees needed to meet the goal of providing 55 percent of young Americans with two- or four-year degrees. The 55 percent goal has been endorsed by several other prominent groups, including the Bill and Melinda Gates Foundation, "Postsecondary Education: Focusing on Completion," November 2009; Commission on Access, "Admissions and Success in Higher Education: Coming to Our Senses," December 2008; State Higher Education Executive Officers, "Second to None in Attainment, Discovery, and Innovation," *Change Magazine,* September–October 2008.

have to be addressed in schools "intentionally, explicitly, and comprehensively" if true progress is to be made. Newly convinced, Smith hired Singleton as a consultant to build district- and school-level equity teams trained in the Singleton framework, one that emphasized passion, practice, and persistence around issues of race.

As the effort matured and took shape, resistance to courageous conversations and the equity work developed. Drawing language directly from his reading of Heifetz, Smith describes "assassins" who began to circle around the central office. Led by several dozen "angry people" associated with the power elite in the community, the group was upset that Smith's emphasis

> An important resource as you pursue work related to race: Singleton, Glenn, & Linton, Curtis. (2006). *Courageous conversations about race.* Thousand Oaks, CA: Corwin.

on race in the schools threatened existing relationships. One of the leaders of the effort was secretly distressed, also, that his grandson was being exposed to a set of ideas that the boy's parents accepted but the grandfather found foreign.

Internally, Smith also encountered hostility. Intent on hiring more minority teachers and administrators, he was shocked to be confronted one morning in a school building by a young teacher who had not been selected for an administrative position: "I guess if you're white around

> The superintendent was shocked to be confronted one morning in a school building by a young teacher who had not been selected for an administrative position: "I guess if you're white around here, you can't be an administrator anymore."

here, you can't be an administrator anymore." Smith still fumes about that: "Imagine a teacher with the gall to say that to the superintendent."

The revolution started in a private meeting called to develop a strategy to lower local taxes as the economy tanked in 2008. At the end of the meeting, one of the participants said, "Let's talk about this superintendent." Behind the scenes, a strategy for unseating Smith emerged: The "assassins" encouraged two well-known local conservatives to run for the five-member board and financed their campaigns. Once installed, the new members made up the lion's share of a three-member majority (on a five-member board) demanding Smith's ouster.

Smith is philosophic about what happened. "I did a lot of good," he says. "It's a better school system than when I arrived. We started closing the achievement gap. People have pride in their schools. The new buildings are a source of great community satisfaction."

He's also reflective. "If I made a mistake, it was in not paying attention to what Heifetz advised: Leadership is about giving people discomfort at a rate they can tolerate. I may have been a bit too full of myself, too. I felt that if I had made the transformation, others could also."

A big part of Smith's disappointment with the outcome is that the district made it clear to applicants to replace him that the board had no interest in continuing this work. The district, a leader in a statewide equity group, even abandoned that work.

"Knowing what you know now, would you do anything differently?" he is asked. "If I were doing this again, instead of starting from the top, I think I would not go full scale right away. I'd look around the community to find people who wanted to change, and I'd build from there."

Still, Smith is at peace with himself. Although he says, "I now question how effectively I led the effort," he also says, "I'm comfortable with what I did. I can sleep at night. I believe I did the right thing, and I've left behind people and some institutional capacity to deal with issues of race."

## B. SUPERINTENDENTS CONSIDER RACE AND CLASS

*Want to know what your peers, as superintendents, consider when thinking about race and class? Here are results from one of the few studies that asked the men and women who sit behind the superintendent's desk how they view these challenges. The short answer is that they see the issue as complex and underdeveloped with a lot of work still to be done.*

Linda Powell Pruitt

*Has race, class, and the achievement gap been an issue in your district? Has there been a critical incident in your district related to these issues?*

In answer to this question, almost all respondents started on safe ground. They first described their districts in terms of student demographics, generally including percentages of ethnic groups, issues of language and bilingual instruction, and some sense of the dynamics of recent immigration. Some went beyond that description to talk about teacher, administrator, and board race and class percentages and how those interacted in the climate of the district. Several mentioned race and class dynamics in hiring decisions at the district level and in board composition, elections, and negotiations.

Those who saw the achievement gap as important painted a similar picture. Student population is changing dramatically, teacher and administrator ranks are changing far more slowly, and political processes are not changing at all. This creates a climate where teachers no longer know the students or their communities. Often, politicians understand neither. Structures of power and privilege remain intact and do not look like the students being served. Teacher preparation programs were criticized because they do not provide new teachers the skills necessary to work with young people today.

Respondents characterized and described the issues of race, class, and the achievement gap in a broad range of ways. These descriptions ranged from "not an issue" to "there is nothing in the district that race doesn't influence." This seemed related to a basic underlying factor. If the issue was framed as being narrowly about test scores, then race (and maybe class) were not issues, especially if the district was all white. Many were very poor districts, for which poverty was the major issue. Others saw the achievement gap as a symbol or measure of the district's racial climate. One stated, "What this is really about is not just high test scores, this is about breaking down stereotypes [about low-income students]."

However, there seemed to be an unexamined agreement that it was the presence of students of color in a mostly white system that made race an issue. Adult behaviors or district policies were less often framed as an immediate issue. Three respondents said that it

> This study examines perceptions around race and class from 17 members of the Forum for the American School Superintendent. Each participant responded to a set of open-ended questions around race, class, and the achievement gap. A comparison group of 6 California superintendents (bringing the total respondents to 23) is also included in the analysis because no significant differences were found between this group and the Forum participants. The superintendents responded to questions about critical incidents, problems, resources, and remaining challenges.

> "When you look at the results society achieves for poor and minority children, you begin to suspect at some point that these results are intentional."
>
> —Peter Negroni, former superintendent, Springfield, Massachusetts

was their professional, political, or ethical issue even though their district could "live with" a gap between white, middle-class children and poor children of color. One superintendent stated that, while it was not a particular issue in the district, "nationwide we have a tremendous race and class issue to be worked on." Several mentioned including a commitment to this question in their preliminary contract negotiations with a district.

In districts with multicultural student populations, disaggregated data was universally seen as important in starting a conversation about the gap. Being able to demonstrate and quantify the existence of a gap was important in harnessing community energy as well as in measuring progress toward closing it. However, one respondent pointed out that the related challenge was fighting the causality explanation for achievement scores: that the color or class of these students causes their low scores.

In some communities, closing the gap is associated with lowering standards. Several superintendents noted that it was critical to communicate with the community in a reassuring way. The goal had to be stated as raising achievement for all students while raising achievement for poor children more quickly. Several stated that they routinely faced the following questions: "Why are you spending money on this [efforts to close the gap]?" and "Why are you [just] interested in 'these' kids?"

Critical incidents named included publication of disaggregated data, controversy over programs to support minority hiring and retention, hiring and placement of principals, and an employee's use of a racial epithet. Several superintendents went out of their way to mention the heated nature of debates about bilingual education; it is very hard to build common ground and support while defusing English-only rhetoric.

All in all, a picture emerges of superintendents interested in exploring issues of race and class who are either not quite sure how to proceed or making the effort to swim upstream in their districts.

*What problems or obstacles have you experienced in other conversations about these issues?*

Almost all respondents used this question as an opportunity to talk about varied and specific problems and obstacles in their own districts. One superintendent described a basic tension in how the achievement gap is framed: "I think we still operate from the premise that we have 'broke' kids and it's a matter of fixing the kids rather than it is our responsibility, as professionals, to create the outcomes we want."

Several superintendents reported a general feeling of hopelessness in communities of color; community members are accustomed to doing badly on standardized tests and having overall low-performing schools. One superintendent was concerned that the community had given in to a "dynamic of resignation." Another stated that the public tended to "judge school quality on the basis of their perception of the students who attend."

One superintendent was surprised by the initial response that raising issues of diversity was seen as divisive; one board member held a strong belief that the conversation itself would be damaging.

Another respondent expressed a strong sentiment held by many: "The obstacle is the mind-set of generations of bad habits on race and class issues." Denial by the mainstream community that America is a class-oriented society leads to a blindness to the differing and

> "There seemed to be an unexamined agreement that it was the presence of students of color in a mostly white system that made race an issue."
>
> —Linda Powell Pruitt

powerful constraints on poor, rural children. Several focused this mind-set on teachers. Persuading them to change their attitudes about whether students can and will achieve at higher levels is a huge challenge. One respondent stated flatly that teachers are a problem because they live outside the community and have no connection to the culture of the students. Too many of them are "just there to get a check."

Dwindling resources and union tensions are a major issue. In some districts, resources have been cut every year in recent memory, while needs have continued to grow. Failed bond issues, past deficits, salary freezes, and contentious challenges like school closings demand much of the superintendent's attention. Tensions with the union were mentioned by most superintendents in unionized districts. Conflicts often occur over improving or changing classroom practices for underperforming students. Perceived as anti-teacher, these measures are sometimes resisted by union leadership although welcomed by the rank and file.

*What resources, actions, or attitudes have you found helpful in addressing race and class issues in your district?*

In keeping with their assumption that the children were the primary site of the problem, some superintendents initiated direct programs to improve the academic achievement of students of color. These superintendents were inclined to promote more diversity among extracurricular activities and encourage afterschool tutoring and mentoring programs for minority students.

Others, however, reported working on interventions to improve school culture. They might invite a theater group to work with students using stop-action and discussion techniques. Some encouraged racially mixed groups of older students to work with middle-school groups that are student facilitated. *Changing the testing environment*, defined as communicating clearly the meaning and importance of statewide testing to students and to parents, was also heavily favored by these superintendents.

Some superintendents focused on instruction as the intervention with the greatest and quickest impact. These respondents were attracted to direct instruction at the high school level and to promoting literacy and improvement in all subjects. Generally, providing greater access to better instruction was heavily favored. "Providing the basic kids with some of what we give the gifted kids," was one respondent's comment. Also mentioned were the efforts to eliminate barriers for students underrepresented in advanced courses, to provide open access to all Advanced Placement courses, and to have the district pay for the Preliminary Scholastic Assessment Test (PSAT) for every student.

Others took a larger view that included parents and families. These respondents wanted to encourage greater parental involvement, and some of them were inclined to support full-service schools that would help provide low-income students and children of color with more social services. Favorite solutions also included intensive professional development for teachers, administrators, and board members; diversity training for all employee groups on an ongoing basis; and staff development oriented around communications, curriculum, meeting the needs of all learners, and social cooperation.

One respondent described focusing "very precisely on the skills that students need to do well" on the state achievement tests and requiring "very high quality professionalism as opposed to programs with a lot of catchy names." This means that teachers understand "the variables of motivation, how to approach students who come from non-middle-class backgrounds and have an excellent knowledge of curriculum."

"Just identifying the issue" of the achievement gap was noted as a critical act. Making the leadership acknowledge the gap exists and that it is unacceptable has been important. The superintendent must be proactive, positive, and persistent—one superintendent described "maintaining a relentless focus on the issue" as his most difficult assignment.

*What do you think remains unaddressed about these issues in your district?*

Superintendents were clear that the agenda is both difficult and underdeveloped; it is far from settled, and much remains to be done. Their comments were as varied as their districts:

- There is a real challenge to creating the belief that all children can learn and that most parents support the success of their children. One respondent noted that the community as a whole hasn't grasped the difficulty of dealing with race and class.
- One superintendent asked if districts are "afraid to be successful," and several others raised variations on this theme. This fear leads to a sense of resignation on the parts of school staff and communities. "While education used to be seen as the way out of poverty, now poverty seems to be used as a reason for children not getting an education."

- What are the unexpected outcomes of some of our efforts? In one district, successful African-American students graduate from a racially integrated high school and go to colleges where they become part of black-only groups. Is that a success? Another noted that their success-oriented philosophy had inadvertently hurt the community by promoting the idea that, once you go to college, you "don't come back here."
- The recruitment of teachers—especially teachers of color—who have the knowledge, skills, and attitudes to be successful with all students is a perennial problem.
- The role of the media in communicating and interpreting issues of race and class was mentioned as a problem by many. One superintendent noted that, during his tenure, the media had moved from being positive and supportive of initiatives to covering events in a manner "designed to create an adversarial environment" in the district.

*Key Themes*

Several themes emerged from these conversations, issues cutting across individual views and district realities.

1. **Each superintendent's situation was highly idiosyncratic.** Each told a detailed and specific story that included the history of his or her district, the economic climate, the roles and fates of previous superintendents, and the like. One suburban superintendent said candidly, "I have it much easier than some of my colleagues."

2. **The respondent's race and class identity was also a key factor.** A complex form of achievement gap exists among school leaders. Superintendents demonstrated dramatically differing levels of proficiency in their ability to talk about race and class as personal, professional, and political issues in education. Superintendents of color all indicated that they brought different perspectives to these issues than their white colleagues. Superintendents of color were also more likely to report personal attacks as relatively routine (although painful) parts of their job than were white superintendents.

3. **The issue of authority or who is in charge was woven throughout many of the stories.** Some superintendents described particular difficulties in change initiatives in their districts. Resistance seemed most likely to any intervention that focused attention on systemic rather than student issues and that threatened a shift in adult power. One respondent noted that, for some superintendents, encouraging shared ownership for outcomes implied they might be "losing some of their authority."

4. **There was wide variation in complexity of professional understanding of the role of superintendent.** Many images emerged from these

interviews, including manager, moral leader, orchestra conductor, and politician. The complexity in these differing images seemed directly related to a sense of what one respondent labeled as *efficacy*, or the belief that leadership actions could help close the achievement gap.

5. **Superintendents often understand the dynamics of race and class along the lines of Heifetz's continuum of adaptive–technical change** (see Part II: Leading Your Schools). Most see issues of race and class as classical adaptive work for leaders. Others gravitate toward the issue as a technical problem. These respondents are more inclined to focus on answers instead of raising questions and to encourage the dissemination of information and workable solutions. Both groups are interested in what they can do themselves, and with their communities, to make progress.

6. **Examining race and class is a continuing struggle.** Several respondents expressed the sentiment that "these issues had been circled" for a long time and now might be the time to "meet them head-on." Participants acknowledged concern about the willingness and capacity to engage in a deep conversation about these issues. One noted, "There are significant issues that we have to get out [on the table]. This whole issue of race and class weaves its magic by the fact that it's usually avoided rather than confronted."

It's undoubtedly true that these issues continue to challenge educators. Why wouldn't they? They continue to challenge the nation.

## C. CAN WE CLOSE THE GAP?

*When superintendents talk about student learning, they often refer to an achievement gap between middle-class children and those from a lower socioeconomic status (who often are members of minority groups as well). For urban superintendents, one of the most important tasks in assisting student learning is to concentrate on those who are most at risk educationally to try to close this gap. A 2003 study for the Wallace Foundation surveyed superintendents in the 100 largest districts in the United States and followed up with telephone interviews. This is what they had to report.*

Howard Fuller

James Harvey

During the interviews conducted as part of this Wallace Foundation–funded study, all superintendents—majority and minority, men and women—universally agreed on the nature and severity of the challenge. Nobody said, in effect, this is not a problem or the problem is overstated. Here are typical comments:

"No question about it. There are huge problems in terms of minority drop-out rates and the achievement gap."

"The achievement gap is a very big problem. In my former district, Hispanics and African Americans range from the bottom quartile to the lower end of the third quartile, low-income Caucasians range from the middle of the second quartile to the middle of third, and middle-class whites range from the middle of the top quartile to the 90th percentile."

The survey results, as well, show that most superintendents are deeply troubled by the achievement gap. Nearly nine out of ten (89 percent) agree or strongly agree with this statement: "The racial achievement gap between students is a critical and chronic challenge." Across the board, therefore, widespread agreement exists that the achievement gap is perhaps the most compelling educational issue of our time.

With regard to whether current efforts to eliminate the gap are adequate, the study received different answers from survey respondents who were asked to put their answers on paper and from interviewees who were interviewed personally and in depth.

> For a thorough and scholarly examination of the achievement gap in the United States, see Jencks, Christopher, & Phillips, Meredith. (Eds.). (1998). *The black-white test score gap.* Washington, DC: Brookings Institution.

Of the superintendents surveyed who see the achievement gap as a critical and chronic challenge, a majority (67 percent) believe that the programs the district has in place are capable of closing the gap within five years. In contrast, interviewed superintendents felt that what they were currently able to do was not enough.

## 1. Race and District Complexity as Factors in Superintendents' Responses

Both the race of the superintendent and the complexity of the district affect the response to the survey question about the possibility of closing the gap. Figure 5.1 demonstrates these contrasts between superintendents from highly complex districts (defined as districts in bigger cities with larger enrollments, more schools, and both more minority students and more students living in poverty). In more complex districts, minority superintendents are less likely to dismiss the achievement gap and are more optimistic about closing it in five years.

Some survey superintendents, both majority and minority, deny the existence of an achievement gap. Nearly 1 in 8 white superintendents (13 percent) reported that the gap is not a problem. Only 1 in 16 minority superintendents (6 percent) shared that view.

Figure 5.1   More Complex Districts

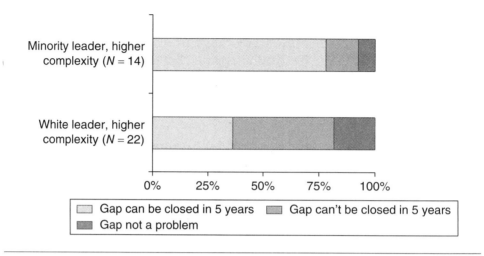

Interestingly, for both white and minority superintendents, those in highly complex districts are more likely to report that the gap is not a problem than are those in less-complex districts. Nearly twice as many white superintendents in highly complex districts agreed the gap is not a problem, compared with those in less-complex districts: 18 percent compared with 10 percent. Although 7 percent of minority leaders of highly complex districts reported the gap is not a problem, no minority superintendent in a less-complex district did so.

It is difficult to interpret these results. Some superintendents may have felt uncomfortable making racial achievement comparisons. Others may have believed that an achievement gap is not a problem "in my district." It is also conceivable that racial minorities are so highly concentrated in some highly complex districts that the achievement gap as traditionally understood is meaningless because few white students are enrolled.

> The complete report from which this research is abstracted is titled *An Impossible Job? The View From the Urban Superintendent's Chair*. It's a report to the Wallace Foundation from the Center on Reinventing Public Education at the University of Washington and can be found at http://tinyurl.com/axa4m4l.

Beyond that, we find a paradox. Although, in general, minority superintendents are much less likely than white superintendents to dismiss the existence of an achievement gap, they are also much more likely to believe the gap can be closed in the next five years.

Once again, it is difficult to interpret these findings. Perceptions, attitudes, and value systems may lie at the root of these differences. It is possible that minority superintendents view the achievement gap as their primary personal and professional challenge and believe they have the will and the tools to meet it. Meanwhile, white superintendents in the most highly complex districts may view financial issues or pressures of state accountability systems as the major issues while finding little reason to be optimistic that the gap can be closed in five years.

Despite the misgivings of a fairly sizable group of surveyed superintendents, the reality is that most superintendents, whether minority or white, agree that they will have the problem of the achievement gap under control in half a decade.

The confidence of most superintendents in the survey stands in stark contrast to the opinions of interviewed superintendents. The superintendents who were interviewed reported that they were unable to do the minimal things necessary to make a start in closing the gap. They were up front about the frustration they experience due to their inability to put the best teachers where they are most needed. They have trouble focusing resources on schools, classrooms, and children needing the most help. Even these elementary, small, first efforts—so clearly essential to any effort to close the gap—are beyond their authority.

The following are typical of the comments received during the interviews:

> "To close the achievement gap, you need to be able to change how every dollar is spent. This means reallocating funds away from existing programs and maybe even schools in middle-class neighborhoods."

> "Middle-class parents are often the biggest challenge. They want their children's schools unchanged. It matters a lot to them that their schools have lots of languages and lots of science options; they also know that major investments in schools serving the disadvantaged would threaten what they now enjoy."

The upshot, according to the interviews, is that superintendents find themselves talking a good game of reform, but many believe that what they are doing will not be enough.

An excellent book recommended for discussions of race and class is Tatum, Beverly Daniel. (1999). *Why are all the black kids sitting together in the cafeteria?* New York: Basic Books.

## 2. Schools Can't Do It Alone

*A generation or two ago, it wasn't unusual for policy makers and the public to believe that school achievement problems in low-income neighborhoods needed to be approached in a pincerlike campaign. One pincer would operate inside the schools, which were thought to be pretty good and simply needed to be improved and beefed up. The other would operate outside the schools and would work to eliminate the disadvantages in health care, housing, jobs, and community infrastructure in many neighborhoods. Reforms of recent years have swept both pincers away and replaced them with an accountability-based demand that schools improve student performance and close the achievement gap. This section attempts to restore some of the balance of that earlier conversation.*

## James Harvey

In the 1980s, researcher Joan Bergstrom at Wheelock College in Boston reported a finding that people had trouble accepting. From birth through age 18, Bergstrom said, nearly 80 percent of a student's waking time is spent outside school. Schools were never intended to do it all, and they can't do it all by themselves, she concluded. By 1991, Secretary of Education Lamar Alexander pointed to the fact that a child spends 93 percent of his or her time from birth through age 18 outside of school, and argued that this time is an important asset in the school-reform agenda. He and former President George H. W. Bush advocated a community-reinforcement element to school reform as part of their America 2000 strategy. Like the national goal of school readiness, the community element of America 2000 disappeared from the public radar screen. You cannot afford to let it disappear from yours.

In a sense, what will be required here is a commitment to building a bridge between the curriculum of the school and the curriculum of the home and neighborhood. Finding ways to help school personnel access the richness of students' experiences outside school; providing incentives to encourage staff to live in the community; empowering parents to become more knowledgeable about the system; and developing reciprocal relationships so that community centers, voluntary organizations, libraries, and churches become part of the community's educational fabric—all of these activities are important. They can help make sure no child is left behind outside of school. The goal is no small order. It should be to weave together the neighborhood's fabric so that good schools are able to work with caring families in strong and healthy communities.

## 3. An Asset-Based Approach

## James Harvey

Here's an exercise for you. At your next staff meeting, ask your teachers and administrators to think through, in private, what and who accounted for their success. After they've had a few minutes to think about that, ask for a show of hands. How many people thought of a parent? How many thought of another adult who acted as a mentor and sounding board? How many thought of a teacher? How many thought of a particular school? You will almost certainly capture everyone in the room with those four categories, but just to be sure, ask if anyone came up with other possibilities.

Most public discussions about young people focus on what's wrong with them. The subtext of much of what we hear about race and class is that things would be better if only these young people were white and middle class. Yet, according to research developed by the Search Institute in Minnesota, a much more productive approach would be to concentrate on the assets of young people, not their deficits.

This research defines as important some 40 family and community assets related to the development of children, teenagers, and young adults. Some constellation of these assets, not all of them, is important. Most young people can draw on about 20 of them as they grow up, which turns out to be a kind of critical mass for adult success. Kids with fewer than 10 of these assets in their lives are likely to wind up in trouble; those with 30 or more normally hit the ground running when they reach adulthood.

There's something terribly wrong with the way we talk about young people in our society, argues Clay Roberts from the Search Institute. On one level, we devote pages of newsprint and hours of media time to negative portrayals of teenagers. But this emphasis ignores the fact that 95 percent or more of youth do wonderful things with their time.

On another level, according to Roberts, professionals talk about young people in ways that have nothing to do with the reality of teenage lives. "As a junior high school history teacher, I used to listen to the kids outside the school on Friday as they waited for a ride home," he says. "The conversation was always the same: What are you doing this weekend? Any good parties? Who got drunk last weekend? Who might get wasted tonight? Who's getting some? And who isn't?"

> Delpit, Lisa. (1995). *Other people's children: Cultural conflict in the classroom.* New York: The New Press is a treasure trove for teachers, especially those teaching in culturally diverse classrooms; it is equally important for superintendents and other school administrators. It is a marvelous book filled with the wisdom of practice.

These are the things typical teenagers think about, argues Roberts. Yet, we behave as though kids need programs. "They don't need programs, what they need are people." Roberts calls for a new emphasis on asset building.

These 40 assets are based on research involving almost 100,000 6th through 12th graders in 213 towns and cities across the United States. (See Sections C4 and C5 in this chapter for details.) Externally, the assets involve the following:

- Support from family and neighborhood
- A sense of empowerment
- Clear boundaries and expectations
- Constructive use of free time

The internal assets involve these:

- Commitment to learning
- Positive values
- Social competencies
- Positive sense of self

Schools are important in young people's development, but they are not the only thing, according to Roberts. A lot of the assets come from the home and the community, not the school. "The best predictor of a child's success is whether that child came from a healthy, strong, supportive family," asserts Roberts. "The second best predictor is bonding with school." However, it is clear that combinations of assets are much more important than any single asset. The more assets young people have, the better their chances of avoiding destructive behaviors later, says Roberts (see Table 5.1).

**Table 5.1**   Power of Assets

| Negative Behaviors | Youth With 0–10 Assets | Youth With 11–20 Assets | Youth With 21–30 Assets | Youth With 31–40 Assets |
|---|---|---|---|---|
| Problem Alcohol Use | 53% | 30% | 11% | 3% |
| Illicit Drug Use | 42% | 19% | 6% | 1% |
| Sexual Activity | 33% | 21% | 10% | 3% |
| Violence | 61% | 35% | 16% | 6% |
| *Positive Behaviors* | | | | |
| Succeed in School | 7% | 19% | 35% | 53% |
| Value Diversity | 34% | 53% | 69% | 87% |
| Maintain Good Health | 25% | 46% | 69% | 88% |
| Delay Sexual Gratification | 27% | 42% | 56% | 72% |

The data on 100,000 middle and high school students indicate that youth with the most assets are far less likely to engage in high-risk behavior involving alcohol, drugs, violence, and sexual activity than those with fewer assets. Fully 53 percent of students with 10 or fewer assets experience problems with alcohol abuse, for example. By contrast, only 3 percent of those with 31 or more assets to draw on encounter the same problem. The patterns involving illicit drug usage, sexual activity, and violence are very similar.

Conversely, the more assets young people can draw on, the more positive their attitudes and behaviors. More than 50 percent of young people with 31 or more assets succeed in school, compared with just 7 percent of those with 10 or fewer. Similar positive patterns prevail on such attitudes and behaviors as valuing diversity, maintaining good health, and delaying gratification.

Roberts offers a self-evident truth when he says, "Those of us who came from difficult circumstances know that some of the most important people in our young lives had a vision for us that we didn't have for ourselves. They believed in us when we couldn't believe in our own future."

One of the challenges you will face in dealing with race and class is how to create situations in which more and more assets can be provided to young people who need them.

## 4. Twenty External Developmental Assets

*Support*

- Family Support. Family life provides high levels of love and support.
- Positive Family Communication. Young person and parent(s) communicate.
- Other Adult Relationships. Young person receives support from three or more nonparent adults.
- Caring Neighborhood. Young person experiences caring neighbors.
- Caring School Climate. School provides a caring, encouraging environment.
- Parent Involvement in Schooling. Parent(s) are actively involved in helping the young person succeed.

*Empowerment*

- Community Values Youth. Young people perceive that adults value youth.
- Youth as Resources. Young people are given useful roles in the community.
- Service to Others. Young people serve in the community one hour or more a week.
- Safety. Young person feels safe at home, at school, and in the neighborhood.

*Boundaries and Expectations*

- Family Boundaries. Family has clear rules and consequences and monitors young person's whereabouts.
- School Boundaries. School provides clear rules and consequences.
- Neighborhood Boundaries. Neighbors take responsibility for monitoring young people's behavior.
- Adult Role Models. Parent(s) and other adults model positive, responsible behavior.
- Positive Peer Influence. Young person's best friends model responsible behavior.
- High Expectations. Both parent(s) and teachers encourage the young person to do well.

*Constructive Use of Time*

- Creative Activities. Young person spends three or more hours per week in lessons or practice in music, theater, or other arts.
- Youth Programs. Young person spends three or more hours per week in sports, clubs, or organizations at school or in the community.

- Religious Community. Young person spends one or more hours per week in activities in a religious institution.
- Time at Home. Young person is out with friends with nothing special to do two or fewer nights per week.

## 5. Twenty Internal Developmental Assets

*Commitment to Learning*

- Achievement Motivation. Young person is motivated to do well in school.
- School Engagement. Young person is actively engaged in learning.
- Homework. Young person reports doing at least one hour of homework every school day.
- Bonding to School. Young person cares about his or her school.
- Reading for Pleasure. Young person reads for pleasure three or more hours per week.

*Positive Values*

- Caring. Young person places high value on helping other people.
- Equality and Social Justice. Young person places high value on promoting equality and reducing hunger and poverty.
- Integrity. Young person acts on convictions and stands up for her or his beliefs.
- Honesty. Young person tells the truth even when it is not easy.
- Responsibility. Young person accepts and takes personal responsibility.
- Restraint. Young person believes it is important not to be sexually active or to use alcohol or other drugs.

*Social Competencies*

- Planning and Decision Making. Young person knows how to plan ahead and make choices.
- Interpersonal Competence. Young person has empathy, sensitivity, and friendship skills.
- Cultural Competence. Young person has knowledge of and comfort with people of different cultural, racial, and ethnic backgrounds.
- Resistance Skills. Young person can resist negative peer pressure and dangerous situations.
- Peaceful Conflict Resolution. Young person seeks to resolve conflict nonviolently.

*Positive Identity*

- Person Power. Young person feels he or she has control over "things that happen to me."
- Self-Esteem. Young person reports having high self-esteem.
- Sense of Purpose. Young person reports that "my life has a purpose."
- Positive View of Personal Future. Young person is optimistic about her or his personal future.

## 6. Deficits or Assets in Over-the-Rhine?

*Tom Dutton, professor of architecture at Miami University, Ohio, has been working in the Over-the-Rhine neighborhood of Cincinnati since 1981. He and Peter Block, author of* Community: The Structure of Belonging, *spent a weekend with the Roundtable in Dutton's Over-the-Rhine Center for Community Engagement. Here is what we learned from them.*

### James Harvey

For two decades Tom Dutton has been bringing architecture students from Miami University in Ohio into the Over-the-Rhine community to design new housing and service possibilities for small businesses. His Center for Community Engagement, established in 2000, is located in the community and has provided a base for a semester-long urban residency program for his students for the last four years.

Over-the-Rhine (so named because it was originally a German community on the other side of a major canal that came to be called "the Rhine") is typical of many urban minority communities, reports Dutton. In 1950, it had a population of about 30,000, 95 percent or more of them white; in 2000, population had plummeted to 7,500 and was 80 percent African-American. It is a maze of contradictions. Median income in the community is $10,000, but it boasts the city's symphony hall—home to music, ballet, and opera—while also housing the second-largest homeless center in the state. Business interests in the city want to revitalize and gentrify it because it is right beside downtown convention hotels, but local residents wonder what will happen to them in a new, hip, upscale Over-the-Rhine.

A confluence of factors has reshaped urban America, says Dutton. Interstate highways bypassed and often split cities. Urban manufacturing facilities have been abandoned in favor of high-rise offices housing services and finance. Fully 90 percent of the home loans made by the Federal Housing Administration (FHA) since the 1930s went to suburbia instead of cities. The combination of these factors has wrecked urban minority communities in the United States, he says.

People in Over-the-Rhine want everything most of us want, he said. They want jobs. They want nice places to live. They want drugs off the street. They want less crime. But elite public discourse on the community focuses on what's wrong with it, not its strengths. There is, therefore, a powerful elite consensus in favor of gentrifying the neighborhood, a process that has inevitably led to tossing poor and minority renters out of their communities and replacing them with white owners. Some people refer to it as *econocide*—a way of "arranging for the disappearance of the losers."

### *Rebuilding Community*

Peter Block, author of *The Answer to How Is Yes* and *Community: The Structure of Belonging*, is a big fan of Dutton's work. The "brilliance" of the work, says Block, is that Dutton understands relationships within the community and has involved students so that they see the community's gifts, not its problems. How do we move, asks Block, from conversations that focus on deficits to those that encourage giftedness? And how can educators facilitate these conversations?

In an insight applied to Over-the-Rhine that could just as easily be applied to American education, Block notes that the problem mentality tends to dominate the conversation. It is a mentality that is interested in assigning blame. To the media, says Block, news "is only what's negative. If you see a positive story in a paper, it's called a 'human interest' story, not a news story." All of this "leads me to think we need to create our own agenda—and it needs to be an agenda that is painstakingly built on creating relationships, not something built by a stranger showing up with a plan."

We need a new narrative around the outcomes we want, notes Block, a conversation around the positive, not the negative. It must be a narrative that understands that the community relies on a strong social fabric. It is the fragmented nature of our communities that is pulling the United States apart, he argues.

We must understand, concludes Block, that we need connection before content and that the small group is the unit of transformation—because, in the small group, everyone's voice can be heard. Beware of people offering help, is Block's advice. "Don't offer it yourself. Telling people they need help says that something's wrong with them. Get into the habit of encouraging people's gifts."

Block reports that three questions can get the conversation going at any meeting. Each should be discussed in turn in small, *knees-together groups* (three-member groups, sitting with knees 9 inches from each other) and then discussed with the larger group before the next question is posed:

- What brought you to this meeting? Why was it important for you to come?
- What struck you about the previous conversation?
- At what crossroads do you find yourself at this point in your life?

The answers are less important than the questions and the conversation they generate. A good question, says Block, should be personal and ambiguous and provoke a modest amount of anxiety. We need to think anew, he concludes, about the new narrative that's important to America. "What is that narrative? Parts of it include some straightforward observations: This country is not as white as it thinks it is. Things aren't going as well as you believe they are. We need to consider new possibilities for how to bring the classroom into the community." But the big question each of us needs to ask ourselves is, according to Block, "What am I doing to create the world I want?"

## 7. A Pastor Looks at Assets

*A pastor, who by chance ministered in Cincinnati's Over-the-Rhine community, addressed some 400 community leaders and clergymen and -women at a gathering on community development convened by the Danforth Foundation in 2004. His remarks confirmed every argument advanced by Roberts, Dutton, and Block. Here's what the Rev. Damon Lynch III, senior pastor of New Prospect Missionary Baptist Church in Cincinnati, had to say.*

### James Harvey

In trying to solve social problems, government has focused on a glass that is half empty, according to the Rev. Damon Lynch III. "Government has focused on what's not there and then poured billions of dollars into emptiness. My own community of Over-the-Rhine in Cincinnati has every human social service agency known to human beings. And we have more churches than we need! We have a church between every two social service agencies. Yet Over-the-Rhine is still considered the worst community in the city. How can that be?"

*Unless You're Deficient, You're Not Important to Me*

Communities, said Lynch, are places where people share their gifts. And building communities requires focusing on strengths, assets, gifts, and abilities. At his church, he reported, he once asked all of the people sitting on the left side of the aisle to pretend they had a gift for a person sitting across the aisle. He then invited the people with gifts to give their gift to those across the aisle. The people on the right side of the aisle had the opportunity only to receive a gift; they could not give one.

Afterwards, he asked people how they felt about this. Remember this was all pretense; nothing had changed hands. "The gift givers felt terrific. They felt wonderful. They had offered a gift to someone across the aisle. But the gift receivers felt cheated. They'd been shortchanged. It was an unnatural transaction. They had not been made part of the community because they did not have the opportunity to share their gift."

Government cannot fix communities by focusing on emptiness, is Lynch's message. "I can't help you unless I can label you. I can't make you part of my caseload unless you're somehow deficient. Then you become important to me."

### The Three A's

Social service agencies and churches need to start focusing on the three As, he says. Acknowledge that everyone is gifted. Affirm those gifts. And then, activate them. It's not enough to acknowledge and affirm; the gift must be put to work.

Illustrating how that can operate, Reverend Lynch told a story about alcoholic and homeless Clint in Over-the-Rhine. Pushing a shopping cart full of junk and detritus that was all he possessed, Clint demanded money from Lynch one morning.

"I refused and went 'pastoral' on Clint. 'Come to church,' I said. Clint then went 'deficient' on me. 'I can't help myself. I'm just a poor alcoholic.' I said, 'That's OK, the church is full of them.'"

"But it had no effect, and this went on for weeks. I'd go 'pastoral' and Clint would go 'deficient.'"

"One day I learned that Clint was a skilled artisan. He 'points' the bricks in buildings. That is, he scrapes out old mortar between the aging bricks and replaces it with fresh mortar to maintain structural integrity. I was pleased to learn this. So, the next time I saw Clint, I said to him, 'I understand you're a tuck pointer.'"

"You should have seen the response. He straightened his shoulders. For the first time I can recall, he looked me right in the eye. And he said the most amazing thing: 'I'm the best there is. I'm the brick doctor.' What a change. Now I'm no longer 'pastoral' and he's no longer 'deficient.' I'm the guy with a building that needs attention and he knows that he's the best brickman in Cincinnati."

To make a long story short, against the advice of the elders of the church, Lynch saw to it that Clint got a job pointing the brick walls in one of the church's old buildings. Clint seized the opportunity.

"And then we held a little ceremony with the elders and the community to celebrate the completion of this work and the reopening of the building. Who do you think showed up? Sitting right up front was Clint the tuckpointer. And of course he'd brought old deficient Clint the alcoholic into the church with him."

The problem is that, although the church and the community need Clint the tuckpointer, 15 agencies in Over-the-Rhine need Clint to be an alcoholic; otherwise, he's of no significance to them, concluded Lynch.

"We need to stop looking at young people as 'dropout-this' and 'unwed-that,'" he notes. "We need to identify and cherish people's gifts and strengths."

# D. TOOLS

## 1. Kiva: A Tool for Talking

### Luvern L. Cunningham

Think of the Kiva as a tool for talking, a technique for improving organizational learning and deepening social and political understanding. It has been used successfully for decades in many contexts where difficult issues require intense reflection and analysis.

*Kiva* is a Native-American term from the American Southwest. It defines a sacred meeting, a place for the practice of tribal democracy, where communities reunite for rituals or ceremonies. Its distinctive architectural features (circular, often around a fire pit) facilitate conversation, encourage all to speak, and designate levels of authority among tribal members. It incorporates several levels of seating and participation. The most influential tribal leaders occupy the seats closest to the fire. Leaders with less influence are seated in rows consistent with their power, behind the first row. All are encouraged to speak.

### *How to Make a Kiva Work for You*

Modern American communities aren't tribes. Seating people by influence won't work. But you can define orders of seating based on roles, responsibilities, accountabilities—or anything that bonds people. Because Kivas are designed to clarify issues rather than confront opponents, they can be used to improve community understanding of even very controversial topics. For example, the objective of a Kiva might be to talk about the recent announcement that a local employer is leaving town, implementation of a new math curriculum, or racial tension in a local high school. Kiva participants could include students, parents, teachers, and administrators, all sharing their perspectives. At most normal school meetings, adults would dominate this discussion. Students would feel shut out. Even many parents would defer to teachers and administrators. In a Kiva setting, students and parents can both be explicitly invited into the conversation. In some cases, you might even want to mix and match the different groups; for example, do girls in the school experience racial tension differently from the boys? How do they handle it?

During the discussion, it is important to keep a detailed record of what is said (so that participants see that their points of view are being heard) either through newsprint or electronic feedback mechanisms or both. Then follow-up can be planned.

*It sounds useful. What about the nitty-gritty of organizing one?*

## Purpose

Clarity of purpose is essential. The Kiva concept will be novel to most participants. Particularly with difficult, complex, and emotion-laden problems, the purpose must be clearly stated. When race or class is on the table, a focus on who is at fault will only encourage acrimony. What the community needs to worry about is this: "What's the situation, and how can we improve it?"

## Physical Arrangements

Attention to the arrangements of tables and chairs sounds trivial, but it is not. The basic configuration calls for chairs set in rows in either square or circular arrangements around a central, open square (see Figure 5.2). The number of rows depends on the number of groups taking part. Usually, three or four groups (and hence rows) make up a Kiva. The members of the first group to respond to the facilitator's questions are seated in the front row. Seated directly behind group one are members of the other groups who will come to the front in a predetermined sequence. This is important: Everyone participating in the Kiva has an opportunity to express his or her views. The Kiva is set up so that power based on seniority or authority is not permitted to silence people. When those seated in the front row (e.g., administrators) are finished, they move to the back row, and every other row moves toward the front. Then, different actors (e.g., teachers, parents, taxpayers, and students) enjoy the opportunity, in turn, to offer their unfiltered opinions on the subject at hand (e.g., curriculum or school funding).

> A typical Kiva layout begins with a moderator in the center of a square surrounded by three different circles of participants. Observers can be seated on two opposite corners of the square with notetakers at the two remaining corners.

> Read the description in Section 2, The Kiva in Action, of the Kiva held in a jail. Do you think a similar process might be used in your district? Do you have staff members who could be trained to facilitate? Should nondistrict facilitators be recruited to do this work?

## Group and Kiva Size

If there is an ideal Kiva size, it is between 24 and 48 persons as primary participants. This means that the

**Figure 5.2**  Kiva Layout

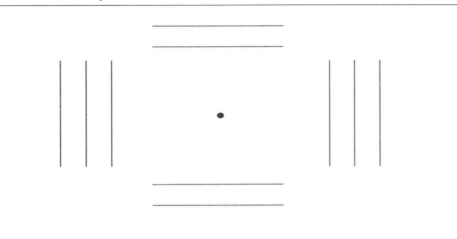

individual ring size around the open square ranges from 8 to 12. Participants are organized in rings from inner to outer. The immediate audience is limited only by the size of the room.

### Facilitation

A Kiva is managed by one or two trained facilitators who lead discussion, elicit observations and ideas, and maintain control of the dynamics while exhibiting flexibility. Facilitation is both an art and a science. Too much control is inhibiting; too little is unproductive. All comments must be honored and treated with respect. A bit of humor helps. Neutrality is essential; don't disparage anyone's contribution. And time limits must be observed.

### Time

Kiva planners have to pay attention to time. The gravity of the problem and the number of participants (and their groupings) help determine time allocations. Fairness in time allocation is critical. If your Kiva about racial tension is divided into groups of Anglo, African-American, and Latino parents and students, you must allocate time equally among the three groups. Facilitators will only create a disaster by providing significantly more time to one group than to the others.

### Questions

Good questions from the facilitators are key. They must be clear and connect to the goals of the Kiva. Long, involved questions are often misleading and hard to follow, frequently introducing unnecessary confusion or discomfort. Some common questions should be asked of each participant group to ensure understandings of perspectives across groups. Questions can come from several sources, including the facilitators.

### Physical Environment

Selecting the right place for the event contributes to effectiveness. Elbow room, good acoustics, comfortable seating and room temperature, microphones if necessary, and water all make a difference. Good lighting and easy access to restrooms help too.

### Audiences

If there is an audience, and most often there is, members are seated behind the participants with care to ensure that audience members are able to see and hear. Should there be radio or television audiences, provision must be made for their technical needs.

### Expert Observers

Two or three known and respected leaders, recognized for their ability to observe and comment, are invited to bear witness. Such commentary adds meaning, content, and value, and it provides a basis to build on for succeeding meetings. Before the event ends, a facilitator invites commentary from the observers and expresses appreciation for their contributions.

The next section, on a Kiva held in a jail, gives you a sense of how the Kiva can be used.

## 2. The Kiva in Action

### Luvern L. Cunningham

The scene is a jail in a major midwestern city, a facility for males aged 12 to 18 serving sentences of two years or more. Most are African-American, and some are guilty of appalling crimes, often drug related—armed robbery, rape, or murder. The jail is very old. Actually, it was once a school. On the former basketball court, people of all ages are seated on worn, squeaky folding chairs. The purpose is to begin to look at possible intergovernmental collaboration to improve the life chances of these young prisoners. An event unique in the jail is about to begin—a Kiva.

This Kiva is arranged to talk about the past, present, and future of 48 incarcerated young men. Three groups are seated in the Kiva's concentric rings, with observers behind them. The first group consists of 12 prisoners, all volunteers at this Kiva. The second is made up of prisoners' families—parents, grandparents, and guardians. The third row holds professionals from the jail, schools, and the city's juvenile justice system. Each ring has about 12 active participants. Each ring (row) comes to the front row in sequence. Security is tight. Observers represent city hall, district school administration, the state juvenile justice office, and some state and local politicians.

Two respected community members serve as facilitators: one a young African-American male probation officer, the other an elderly African-American woman. They enter the circle to begin the Kiva. They are skilled. Although they thought carefully in advance about the questions, their approach is flexible. While their demeanor is relaxed, the questions are penetrating. Some of the questions are addressed to all of the participants; others differ depending on the row.

The room is pin-drop quiet at the start. Answers from the prisoners are short, sometimes hostile. Some heads are down, avoiding the eyes of the facilitators. Those in the second group, the family representatives, are slow to respond, language halting at times, emotions on

> "You will fail and feel uncomfortable many times. When a person begins this process and it fails the first time, you can't just say, 'Well, I tried and it didn't work, so I'm out of here.' If you'll continue trying, you'll see great strides forward. We have to insist that all children have the opportunity for a wonderful life."
>
> —Diana Lam, former superintendent, Providence, Rhode Island

edge. Guilt, sorrow, anguish, and hopelessness are in the air. The participants in the professional row—candid, direct, and insightful—are given to speeches at times, but each member is sympathetic to the needs of the young men. Each group has 30 minutes. Then, the observers comment. The observers are all over the lot. Many are defensive, clearly protecting their parts of the political and administrative infrastructure. Politicians, for the most part, talk in high-minded platitudes.

All the participants and observers talked about why the young men were in jail. They explored what life is like inside. They talked about their hopes for what would happen on release. Would the street take over? Would they go back to gangs? Would they be incarcerated again? Or was there some hope they would return to school or work? The programs of the professionals were described and critiqued, sometimes ridiculed.

From this Kiva, with its direct exposure and interaction among differing groups, new possibilities emerged. The schools, the probation department, and the juvenile justice authorities began exploring how to collaborate. Records began to move more quickly among agencies. Jail personnel began to attend professional development programs at the schools. School administrators and counselors visited the jail, where they saw firsthand what happens to school dropouts and how jail personnel work with angry, aggressive young males. Public officials acquired new insights into gang behavior and insisted that school officials and the mayor's staff meet together with male and female gang leaders.

What did the Kiva contribute? First, it offered an ordered environment for conversation. Second, it provided a neutral process to hear people out. Third, it guaranteed balanced participation from diverse groups in a compressed format. It hardly needs to be said that it encouraged communication among different groups, along with summarization and the opportunity to plan follow-up.

Was it worth it? Perhaps not, if you define success as immediately solving every problem. But certainly so by a more reasonable standard. That miasma of silence and hopelessness that pervaded the old gym at the outset? As the Kiva ended, it had been replaced with chatter and a sense of cautious optimism for the future.

> Lindsey, Randall, Robins, Kikanza, & Terrell, Ray. (2009). *Cultural proficiency: A manual for school leaders.* Thousand Oaks, CA: Corwin provides a wealth of individual and group activities to assist you in this difficult work.

## 3. Microlab, Peeling the Onion, and Active Listening

### James Harvey

You will find yourself struggling with how to hold these conversations, sometimes successfully, sometimes less so. Here are some of the tools that worked for us:

*Small-Group Discussions*

The smaller, the better.

*Skilled Facilitators*

Sometimes involving a facilitator with a vested interest in the issue, but with no vested interest in the organization sponsoring the discussion, works well.

*Stand Up and Cross the Line*

Launch meetings by inviting participants who are already seated to stand up and cross whatever line seems to divide the room. (Progress from easy through challenging questions. If you were born in August, cross the line. If you have children, cross the line. If you have ever been robbed, cross the line. If you have had a family member jailed, cross the line.) You'll be amazed at how fast racial and ethnic differences disappear as people start answering these questions.

*The Microlab*

This is a structured, timed conversation (see Tools: Microlab Guidelines and Sample Questions by Emily White later in this section). It involves only four people who are not observed. Divide all participants randomly into groups of four who are required to sit closely together, facing each other. Friends and relatives should not be together. Using lots of I words, individuals are encouraged to take a minute each on each of the following questions (which are presented one at a time as each question is answered):

- How would you describe your background?
- What are your strengths and weaknesses?
- What is something you never want said again about the particular group you identify with?
- As a leader, what's your strength in dealing with diversity?

*Peeling the Onion*

This is a protocol involving 4 to 12 people to develop an in-depth understanding of an issue, situation, or opportunity. It uses active listening to honor complexity and to avoid premature advice and solution finding (see Tool: Peeling the Onion Protocol by Emily White later in this section).

You need to remember that, sometimes, these efforts will fail. But failure presents an opportunity to try again. Sometimes, disappointment may develop because expectations about what is possible in the short run are poorly stated. As the Stages of Collaboration outlined in Table 5.2 emphasize, different goals require different strategies and diverse leadership approaches. It is likely that a purpose such as encouraging more congenial relationships may be easier to attain than equally worthwhile, but more challenging, goals such as working jointly together. At all stages, active listening from everyone is encouraged.

> "I have not failed. I've just found 10,000 ways that won't work."
> —Thomas A. Edison

*Tool: Microlab Guidelines and Sample Questions*

This was an exercise led by Emily White at a meeting for superintendents. It was designed to be taken back to superintendents' districts.

*Microlab* is a term for a small-group exercise that addresses a specific sequence of questions and promotes active listening. It uses a timed process. The microlab is useful for team building, democratizing participation, and strengthening diversity work because it is about equalizing communication and withholding judgment. It affirms people's ideas and helps build community.

*Aim:* The purpose is to help participants learn more about themselves and others and to deepen the quality of collegial sharing.

*Size:* It works best with same-size groups of three to four people.

*Time:* Microlab takes 15 to 45 minutes with less time for groups of three addressing two to three questions and more time for groups of four addressing three to four questions. Allow time for the whole group to debrief at the end.

Collaboration

| her/Meetings | Leadership Looks Like . . . |
|---|---|
| ...ty | - Anecdotes shared<br>• Coaching/mentoring focus on helpful suggestions<br>• Working to lessen competition and isolation<br>• Appreciation and gratitude often expressed | • Meetings informative, free flowing<br>• Learning many things/not necessarily connected<br>• Analytical/reactive<br>• Centralized<br>• Maintains tradition |
| Helping and Assisting | • Coaching and mentoring are top-down; follow-through is inconsistent<br>• Feedback becomes more descriptive, less judgmental<br>• Focus is less on complaints, more on conviction | • Problem-specific help given when requested<br>• Encourages ongoing goodwill and regard<br>• Focus is on meeting needs of individuals<br>• Beginning to look at needs of community as a whole |
| Sharing: Validating and Valuing Existing Practice | • Existing ideas are pooled<br>• Mutual reinforcement of habits that are not always questioned deeply<br>• Cooperation is stressed<br>• Productive use of conflict begins | • Agendas are structured to allow time for sharing of practice, not just manage business<br>• Language and habits of discourse are shaped<br>• Critical thinking and appreciative listening are taught |
| Working Jointly: Building a Community of Leaders and Learners | • Critiquing of work, giving and getting feedback<br>• Sharing of responsibility<br>• Peer coaching/openness to critique become norms<br>• Time together enhances understanding and imagination<br>• Go from individual to collective practice<br>• Problems seen as symptoms for community concern, not just individual intervention<br>• Both veteran and new voices welcome | • Meetings transformative<br>• Use of structures and protocols is a norm<br>• Problem prevention, being proactive are norms<br>• Openness and trust developed within and among groups<br>• Norms are set with group<br>• Teachers learn reflection<br>• Encouraging team to view school as community<br>• Assumptions are always questioned |

SOURCE: Adapted from Michael Fullan and Andy Hargreaves, *What's Worth Fighting for in Your School?* (New York: Teachers College Press, 1996).

The time limit in this exercise provides safety. Crisp time boundaries help people take calculated risks and highlight aspects of listening. Sample questions might be "Describe your childhood." "Can you remember something that hurt you emotionally as a child?" or "What names have you been called that you never want to be called again?"

### Directions From the Leader

"I'll be directing what we're going to be sharing. It's not an open discussion. It's about listening and sharing nonjudgmentally. I will pose one question at a time. Each person gets approximately one minute to answer it in turn. The challenge is that no one is to talk or ask questions when it's someone else's turn [active listening practice]. I will time the activity and tell the groups when they should be halfway around their circle and, when time is up, to go on to the next question. So, this is an opportunity for some openness and honesty, respecting confidentiality. When someone says something in your group, it is not to be repeated by anybody else. Can we all agree on that?"

### Guideline for Participants

- Speak from your own experience. Say *I* when speaking about yourself.
- Speak from your own comfort level: not too risky, not too blah.
- Respect shared confidences.
- Silence is OK. The person whose turn it is may need to think before starting.
- There is always the right to pass and go later.
- If someone doesn't get a full turn in one round, he or she should be the one to start in the next.

#### Tool: Peeling the Onion Protocol

This tool and the one that follows (Listening Techniques, Table 5.4) were developed by Emily White for superintendents. You will find them helpful when probing sensitive issues.

Goal:  To develop an in-depth understanding of an issue, situation, or opportunity (see Table 5.3). The exercise uses active listening (see Table 5.4) to honor complexity and to avoid premature advice and solution finding.

Time:  25 to 40 minutes per group, set in advance.

Size:  Groups of 4 to 12 people, with a facilitator.

**Table 5.3**    Steps for Peeling the Onion

| | |
|---|---|
| 1. Presenter describes an issue, opportunity, or incident | 3–4 minutes |
| 2. Clarifying questions from group (brief answers if beneficial) | 3–4 minutes |
| 3. Go round 1. Presenter is silent, taking notes. Group members say: "A question or implication this raises for me is . . ." OR "A deeper issue I'd want to know more about is . . ." | 7 minutes |
| 4. Check in (cross talk)—optional | 2 minutes |
| 5. Go round 2. Presenter is silent. Group members ask: "What if . . . ?" | 7 minutes |
| 6. Open conversation (identify issues that have not been raised or probe a particular point that surfaced) | 5 minutes |
| 7. Debrief process | 5 minutes |

**Table 5.4**    Tool: Active Listening Techniques (Statements That Help the Other Person Talk)

| Statement | Purpose | To Do This | Examples |
|---|---|---|---|
| Encouraging | 1. Convey interest | . . . don't agree or disagree | 1. "Can you tell me . . . ?" |
| | 2. Encourage other person | use neutral words use varying voice intonations | 2. "What happened?" |
| Clarifying | 1. To help you clarify what is said | . . . ask questions | 1. "When did this happen?" |
| | 2. To get more information | . . . restate wrong interpretation to force speaker to explain further | 2. "You stated . . ." |
| Restating | 1. To show you are listening and understanding what is being said | . . . restate basic ideas and facts | 1. "So, you would like your parents to trust you more. Is that right?" |
| | 2. To check your meaning and interpretation | | |
| Reflecting | 1. To show that you understand how the person feels | . . . reflect the speaker's basic feelings | 1. "You seem very upset." |
| | 2. To help the person evaluate his or her own feelings after hearing them expressed by someone else | . . . restate wrong interpretation to force speaker to explain further | 2. "What does this mean to you?" |

| Statement | Purpose | To Do This | Examples |
|---|---|---|---|
| Summarizing | 1. Review progress | . . . restate major ideas expressed | 1. "These seem to be the key ideas you've expressed." |
| | 2. Pull together important ideas and facts | . . . including feelings | |
| | 3. Establish a basis for further discussion | | |
| Validating | 1. To acknowledge the worthiness of other people | . . . acknowledge the value of their issues and feelings | 1. "I appreciate your willingness to resolve this matter." |
| | | . . . show appreciation for their efforts and actions | |

SOURCE: Adapted from *Active Listening Techniques* (San Francisco: The Community Board Program, 1987).

# E. REFLECTIVE PRACTICE

At least twice before, American society has tried to resolve the ambiguities of its racial and economic past through the schools. The first was shortly after the Civil War ended, when segregated schools were established to reinforce the indignities of Jim Crow. That worked in a society in which power and control were powerful images of organization and schools were used as instruments of domination. But the effects on American life were profound, long lasting, and pernicious. The second attempt, in the 1950s, was a nobler effort. It was the hope of building an integrated America by desegregating schools (while largely ignoring segregation in housing, employment, and access to economic opportunity). As noted at the outset of this section, the second attempt ended with about half of minority students in schools that are 75 percent or more minority.

Will the effort to close the achievement gap be any more successful than these two prior efforts? That remains to be seen.

## 1. Thinking About Learners at the Fringes

### Luvern L. Cunningham

The accountability movement marching through American schools is designed to salvage forgotten children and youth. But it might leave some strewn by the wayside. It's not clear that policy makers have thought through carefully what accountability really means for students in foster care; youth in jail; or children who are homeless, are recent immigrants, or do not speak English. Millions of children with special needs run the risk of being overlooked in a general effort to improve achievement. For example, recent research documents that students who move twice in an academic year have far lower grades and perform much more poorly on standardized tests. Data disaggregation, useful as it is, may not go far enough to sort out all these populations and their experiences as learners.

> To see how one community studied mobility, look at Community Research Partners. (2003). *Columbus public schools student mobility research project report.* Columbus, OH: John Glenn Institute, Ohio State University.

As superintendent, you have to be the voice for these learners at the margins. Use the following list of questions to get the discussion started in your community:

- What do you know about kids in your district who are immigrants, homeless, under foster care, under the jurisdiction of other authorities, and are moving between schools in your system?
- How many of each of them are there?
- Have you visited students, for example, in jail? What about those under the jurisdiction of other community authorities?
- What provisions are there for prompt transfer of student records, and other information, to other schools, school districts, or jurisdictions?
- Do you have functioning partnerships with the police, courts, the juvenile justice system, children's services, hospitals and clinics, and other jurisdictions serving your students?
- Would the category of African-American boys be recognized in your district as meriting special attention?
- Are exchanges of professional development programs taking place between and among your schools and the other community institutions serving learners at the margins?
- Are there up-to-date policies and practices within your district, and among other jurisdictions, covering privacy and confidentiality?
- Does the performance of learners in these categories appear in the district's accountability system?
- Are special efforts in place to communicate with parents of immigrant children, foster parents, and parents of those under incarceration or under other jurisdictions?

## 2. Questions for Reflective Practice

Here are some key questions you should be considering. Encourage your staff to think about them, too.

*What's the breakdown* by race and class in your community? How many gated communities? How many trailer parks, units of subsidized housing, and homeless shelters? Line up your teaching staff against these categories. How many of your teachers live in your district?

*If you asked your teachers and staff* about an achievement gap in the district, what would they say? How about parents? Community leaders?

*Is closing the achievement gap a personal and professional priority for you?* How about your administrative staff and teachers?

*Can you be sure that financial resources allocated to individual schools don't contribute to the gap?* Are some facilities newer or better equipped and maintained? Do the most senior and highest-paid teachers cluster in some schools and avoid others?

*Are you able to break down the data in your district by race and clas*s? If so, what does it tell you? If not, why not?

*In an effort to close the gap, what has been tried so far?* Have you tried to reassign teachers? Beef up remediation? Increase enrollment of some groups of students in Advanced Placement and honors courses? What has succeeded? What has failed?

*Have you tried to hold a conversation* about race and class in your district? If so, what happened, and how did you build on it? If not, why not?

*Do your teachers find all the African-American kids sitting together in the cafeteria?* Undoubtedly, they do. Has any thought been given to what that means? Is it a good thing or not?

*What about your board?* Where are board members on issues of race and class? Do they bring up these challenges, or do they wish you'd stop talking about them?

*Have you tried to listen to the voices of students on this issue?* If so, what have you learned?

*What's the status of your relationship with preschool programs?* Do you wonder who these preschool providers are and wish they'd go away? Or have you entered active partnerships with them?

*How about your relationship with community-based programs and churches?* Are they arrows in your quiver as you seek to close the achievement gap or simply other groups out there with which you have little contact?

*Have you explored an assets-based approach to help challenged young people?* How effective was it?

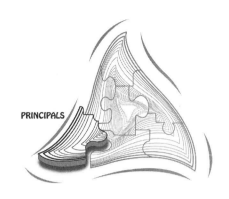

PRINCIPALS

# PART VI

# *Developing Your Principals*

**B**y far, your most significant, substantive challenge as superintendent will be how to focus the intellectual resources of the school district on better teaching and learning. Developing your principals, our next "commonplace," provides your single greatest leverage point. Research and common sense support the importance of strong building-level leadership for improving student learning. In this part, we share a framework that superintendents can use to develop principals as leaders of learning.

A number of teaching and learning models exist to guide educators as they take up these challenges. The Wallace Foundation's leadership work in the course of the past decade has shed significant light on principals and different models of effective school leadership. Here, we include a summary of the Foundation's work, including its relationship to the Interstate School Leaders Licensure Consortium (ISLLC) Standards, along with a specific Wallace product developed by Brad Portin at the University of Washington.

With the help of Ed Fuller (Pennsylvania State University), Richard Elmore (Harvard Graduate School of Education), James Knight (University of Kansas), and Gene Hall (University of Nevada, Las Vegas), we look into the implications of the ISLLC standards for school leaders' development, instructional rounds and walkthroughs, coaching as an effective leadership development strategy, and how to avoid the trap of trying to implement school change while ignoring the anxieties and worries that will inevitably afflict your teachers and staff. The chapter closes with several tools from Otto Graff (University of Pittsburgh) outlining how to mount effective school walkthroughs.

## A. LEADING STUDENT LEARNING

*Few people describe schools as learning communities or learning organizations. As elaborated in Gareth Morgan's metaphors, schools take on mechanical characteristics focused on efficiency, alignment of tasks, and adherence to rules and regulations to ensure uniform outcomes. Superintendents face tremendous challenges in attempting to move schools from this traditional, entrenched stance to one that nurtures collaborative working relationships and learning among teachers, students, and principals. Our work with school districts, however, shows clearly that this is a necessary step for transforming existing schools and must begin with the development of principals.*

### 1. What Does It Take to Lead a School?

Brad Portin

"In the great scheme of things, schools may be relatively small organizations, but their leadership challenges are far from small or simple." That's a central conclusion of a two-year study of the school principalship that I completed with my colleagues at the University of Washington.

As we went about our work, we realized that a lot of the current attention to school leadership looks at all the things principals might do and treats them as if they are the things all principals should do—and that principals should do them all.

> This section is drawn from a useful paper on school leadership developed with Wallace Foundation funding at the University of Washington: Portin, Brad, et al. (2003, September). *Making sense of leading schools: A study of the school principalship.* You can view it at http://tinyurl.com/b9kt97z.

Based on in-depth interviews with educators (principals, vice principals, and teachers) in 21 schools, public and private, in four different cities, we drew five major conclusions about the nature of the principal's work:

1. The core of the principal's job is diagnosing his or her particular school's needs and, given the resources and talents available, deciding how to meet them.

2. Regardless of school type—elementary or secondary, public or private—schools need leadership in seven critical areas: instructional, cultural, managerial, human resources, strategic, external development, and micropolitical.

3. Principals are responsible for ensuring that leadership happens in all seven critical areas, but they don't have to provide it. Principals can be one-man bands, leaders of jazz combos, or orchestra conductors (see Figure 6.1).

4. Governance matters, and a school's governance structure affects the way key leadership functions are performed.

5. Principals learn by doing. However trained, most principals think they learned the skills they need on the job.

From an extensive list of tasks, functions, roles, and duties, the team identified seven common functions of leadership evident in all types of schools and performed by someone in each of them. Table 6.1 lists these seven areas and describes generic actions associated with each.

**Table 6.1**  School Critical Functions and Associated Actions

| Critical Function | Actions |
| --- | --- |
| 1. Instructional Leadership | Assuring quality of instruction, modeling teaching practice, supervising curriculum, and assuring quality of teaching resources. |
| 2. Cultural Leadership | Tending to the symbolic resources of the school (e.g., its traditions, climate, and history). |
| 3. Managerial Leadership | Overseeing the operations of the school (e.g., its budget, schedule, facilities, safety and security, and transportation). |
| 4. Human Resource Leadership | Recruiting, hiring, firing, inducting, and mentoring teachers and administrators; developing leadership capacity and professional development opportunities. |
| 5. Strategic Leadership | Promoting vision, mission, and goals—and developing a means to reach them. |
| 6. External Development Leadership | Representing the school in the community, developing capital, tending to public relations, recruiting students, buffering and mediating external interests, and advocating for the school's interests. |
| 7. Micropolitical Leadership | Buffering and mediating internal interests, while maximizing resources (financial and human). |

These functions were performed in various ways in different schools, as Figure 6.1 illustrates.

In some schools, the seven critical leadership areas (represented by the seven circles) are tightly coupled around the principal. The principal remains centrally involved, if not entirely responsible, for each of the core functions. The top diagram displays what is almost a formula for a beleaguered principal—a one-man band responsible for just about everything in the school, from the lyrics and melody to the bass line and harmonics.

The middle diagram displays a more distributed leadership model. This principal encourages leadership throughout the organization, very much the way the leader of a jazz combo expects her or his musicians to solo. Here, the principal lays down the basic melody line and encourages individual band members to improvise around the theme. This is more of a shared leadership model, sometimes contingent on available talent, sometimes on the disposition of the principal.

**Figure 6.1** Leaders, Responsibilities, and the Seven Core Functions

*Consolidating seven functions within the principal: The Principal as One-Man Band*

The Principal

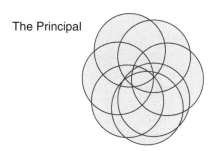

*Shared leadership between principal and other designated leaders in the school: The Principal as Jazz Band Leader*

The Principal

Assistant Principal

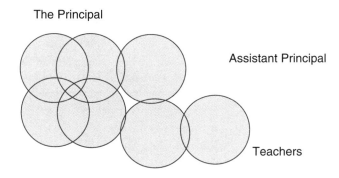

Teachers

*Distinct leadership roles between independent school principals and level heads: The Principal as Orchestra Conductor*

Headmaster

Heads of Upper and Lower
Schools & Other Teacher
Leaders

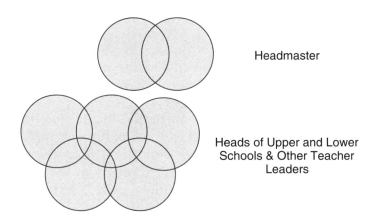

The bottom diagram illustrates how, in other schools, the seven critical leadership areas are even more broadly distributed among various people. Here, the principal is more akin to an orchestra conductor—playing nothing her- or himself, but making sure the many individual parts are expertly performed and harmonize and work together smoothly. In a fascinating video as part of the TED series, conductor Benjamin Zander offered an intriguing insight into the leader as conductor. As a conductor, says Zander, you don't make a sound. "Your power as a conductor depends on making other people powerful. . . . My job is to awaken possibilities in other people." That's true of you as a superintendent, too. Your leadership ability depends on your ability to make others powerful. This particular model accurately describes what is apparent in many private schools. In these schools, the school leader is seen as the headmaster, not the principal.

> You can find Zander's inspiring TED video on the "Transformative Power of Classical Music" at http://tinyurl.com/bsb5rf4.
>
> Zander notes, "It's one of the characteristics of a leader that he not doubt for one moment the capacity of the people he's leading to realize whatever he's dreaming."

Given today's emphasis on instructional accountability, these distinctions are important. In no case was a principal walled off from the instructional work of the school. But neither did all principals present themselves as the instructional exemplar of the school—capable of teaching any class at any time. Yet, even these principals could identify good instruction when they saw it and would incorporate visits to the classroom into their regular practice. But their comments suggest that identifying good teaching is not the same thing as helping others teach well. Clearly, instructional leadership merits the attention it receives in the press and research.

## 2. The School Principal as Leader

*For more than a decade, the Wallace Foundation has supported a variety of research and demonstration efforts to improve leadership at the school level. Through grants, education researchers, and school districts, Wallace has explored the nature of the school principal's role, what makes for an effective principal, and how to tie principal effectiveness to improved student achievement.*

### James Harvey

Although much is still to be learned, it seems clear that the best principals create energy in their schools by attending to five big issues. They encourage a shared vision emphasizing high standards and success for all students; they create a climate hospitable to education; they insist that all adults in the school are responsible for student success; they focus relentlessly on learning by involving themselves in the technical core of schooling; and they organize themselves and the school itself to focus on student learning.

### Organizing Schools to Raise Student Achievement

The successful school principal of the 20th century often embodied the virtues and shortcomings of middle management described in William H. Whyte's 1950s classic, *The Organization Man*. But as the 21st century moves fully into its second decade, principals are more likely to take as their text Jim Collins's bestseller *From Good to Great*. Whyte's complex sociological insights viewed corporate middle managers as risk-averse bureaucrats, beholden to organizational life and unlikely to face significant career consequences as long as they avoided serious blunders. Collins, drawing on lessons from corporate life in the 21st century, argues that effective leadership is about focus, discipline, and constant choice. In short, the modern principal is moving away from the sterility and reliance on the process of organizational life that Whyte found so troublesome toward something that Collins describes as a search for clarity and simplicity: clear objectives, diligence in working toward them, and focus on what is vital—in the principal's case, success for all children. When all is said and done, that is the bottom line pointed toward by a decade of Wallace Foundation support for research on educational leadership.

Effectiveness in today's principal is defined by the ability to create a shared vision throughout the school, to build leadership throughout the ranks, and to sustain a sense of urgency throughout the school's work.

The matter of school leadership was hardly a hot issue 10 years ago. Indeed it was noticeably absent from most major school reform efforts. Even those who recognized leadership as important expressed uncertainties about how to proceed. Today, improving school leadership is high on the list of priorities for school reform. Federal efforts such as Race to the Top (RTTT) call for replacing principals in persistently failing schools. States, through the ISLLC Standards, have defined key parameters to guide principal preparation programs and principal evaluations. And research increasingly points to the critical role school principals play in improving student achievement and closing the achievement gap.

Paying attention to the principal's role is all the more essential as the U.S. Department of Education and state education agencies focus on turning around 5,000 troubled schools, frequently confronting the need for new and more effective building leadership. Indeed, a comprehensive 2010 survey of key education stakeholders—school administrators, state superintendents of public instruction, governors, mayors, state legislators, staff development professionals, and advocates—revealed that these constituencies saw principal leadership as one of the most pressing priorities in school reform. Teacher quality stands head and shoulders above everything else as the top issue, but principal leadership outstrips other compelling issues such as dropout rates; improving science, technology, engineering, and math (STEM) preparation; student assessment; and preparation for college and careers. Policy makers understand that, without effective leadership in each of the nation's 106,000 schools, progress in school improvement is unlikely to be sustained.

> Imagine this: Teachers sharing insights and challenges. Principals leading with trust. A central office that supports principals. All adding up to a synergistic learning system to help all students succeed. That's the vision animating Roundtable superintendent Paul Ash (Lexington, Massachusetts) and his colleague John D'Auria in *School systems that learn: Improving Professional Practice, Overcoming Limitations, and Diffusing Innovation.* Thousand Oaks, California: Corwin Press, 2013.

Thanks in part to the research and innovative projects in states and districts supported by the Wallace Foundation, we now understand the complexities of school leadership in new and more meaningful ways. The field now enjoys powerful evidence on how to proceed and what needs to be done. The simple truth is that, without effective leadership at the building level, school improvement efforts are destined to fail. Significant gains in student achievement are all the more difficult to attain in the face of ineffective principals.

Here is the irreducible minimum of the results of 10 years of Wallace exploration and research:

- There are no documented instances of failing schools turning around without great principals and powerful building leadership.
- The quality of school principals is second only to the quality of teaching in school-related factors contributing to student learning.
- Without first-rate principals, we won't get first-rate teaching (the most significant school-related determinant of student achievement).

The most recent research also demonstrates a dramatic new finding: An empirical link exists between school leadership and improved student achievement. Drawing on both detailed case studies and large-scale quantitative studies, Wallace-funded research indicates that most school variables, considered separately, have only small effects on learning. Individual variables, considered in isolation, do not ramp up learning appreciably. The real payoff comes when individual variables are combined to produce the educational equivalent of a chemical reaction capable of rearranging school molecules and atoms.

Creating the conditions under which that reaction can occur is the job of the new principal. In one school, a principal can put the best hiring practices into effect. In another, first-class professional development can be found. The principal who is able to shore up hiring practices with the best professional development, along with cutting-edge teacher assignment and budget practices, can create a whole that is greater than the sum of its parts. Conversely, failure in any of these areas can weaken the entire effort.

### School Principal as Leader

In a rapidly changing era of standards-based reform and accountability, a different conception of school leadership has emerged. The traditional role of the principal as *The Organization Man*'s middle manager—overseeing budgets, buses, and buildings—has shifted toward the role described in *From Good to Great*, focusing with great clarity on what is essential, what needs to be done, and how to get it done.

This shift brings with it dramatic changes in the expectations of principals. They can no longer be organization men, functioning simply as building managers, tasked with implementing district rules, overseeing regulations, and avoiding mistakes. They have to be (or become) leaders of learning who can develop a building team delivering instruction of the highest order. Ten years of research on principals validates earlier research on essential organizational leadership skills in government, corporations, and the nonprofit world. Effective leaders in schools, like effective leaders everywhere, worry about vision, transformation, values, and organization. If principals are to usher in the achievement gains required today, especially in schools facing the greatest challenges, they need to address five big issues:

1. *Develop and carry out a shared vision* celebrating high academic standards and success for all students.

2. *Create a climate hospitable to education.*

3. *Insist that all adults in the school are responsible for student success* by creating teams and cultivating leadership in others.

4. *Transform the school culture* by focusing relentlessly on learning as the core of schooling.

5. *Organize schools for improvement* by concentrating on data, making maximum use of the principal's time for instruction, and aligning evaluation systems with the school's vision and goals.

Of necessity, each of the five issues outlined above interacts with the other four. It is hard to implement a shared vision around standards and student success in the absence of teams or a focus on learning. And the principal intent on organizing her school for improvement is unlikely to get very far in the face of a toxic school culture characterized by teacher defeatism and student defiance. Even the most heartfelt vision statement simply points toward a goal, one that will never be realized unless the school is organized to move toward it.

> This section summarizes a 2012 paper from the Wallace Foundation (updated in 2013) examining 10 years of research on school leadership (http://tinyurl.com/azcy2ww).

## 3. Help Wanted: Implications for District Leadership

### James Harvey

Imagine you want to place the advertisement below for a principal in the American Association of School Administrators' (AASA's) *School Administrator,* the Association for Supervision and Curriculum Development's (ASCD's) *Educational Leadership, Phi Delta Kappan,* and *Education Week.* You're determined to get the best talent out there. To support such a paragon of excellence, what are you prepared to do?

---

### PRINCIPAL SOUGHT

Come help us build the future! Ideal School District, located in the town of Ideal in the Ideal state, seeks a visionary with strong administrative skills to lead Ideal Elementary, a school with an enrollment of 550 from K–5. The candidate we seek will demonstrate the following:

1. The capacity to serve as an instructional leader

2. A determination to focus on learning, not just teaching

3. A commitment to building Ideal Elementary as a learning community

4. Experience or demonstrated commitment to building a culture of learning based on nested communities

5. A willingness to encourage instructional improvement and enhanced learning by regular and frequent school walkthroughs that provide in-depth knowledge with which to support each teacher's strengths and shore up his or her shortcomings

6. The willingness to create a school culture that respects deep knowledge of instruction and learning—this suggests that the successful candidate will be comfortable working with teachers to improve instruction, offering

*(Continued)*

(Continued)

suggestions to improve curriculum and instruction and recruiting and helping develop teachers loyal to the task of student learning

7. A commitment to professional development as the glue that holds school and instructional improvement together

8. An administrative license in the Ideal state is taken for granted—in addition, the successful candidate will demonstrate several key capacities:

   - Skill in managing a relatively independent school that controls most of its resources, including teacher selection and professional development
   - Commitment to meeting district and school needs around instruction, administration, categorical programs, and parental and community demands

9. Potential for leadership growth

Ideal School District supports principals as leaders of learning. For additional information on the district's vision and expectations for this position, including requirements regarding education, experience, and salary, see www.ideal.k-12 .ideal.us.

*Implications for District Organization and Leadership*

Encouraging the sort of school leadership outlined in the position description will undoubtedly require the best of you and the colleagues on your leadership team. What sorts of changes would be in order? The truth is that only a few districts currently have the capacity to support a leader of learning as described here. In place of drive-by professional development for principals and teachers, a new commitment to building communities of practice is required. Central offices genuinely interested in supporting this kind of school leadership would need to develop the following or have them in place:

• **A Shared Vision of Effective School Leadership.** Monthly principals' conferences to develop a shared set of commitments, principles, and practices should be instituted. Here, principals can explore new instructional practices in a nonthreatening environment and explore school-by-school assessment results. Ideally, the hosting of such conferences would alternate between the central office and individual schools.

• **Specialized Support and Study Groups.** Vision is essential, but vision only gets you so far. Principals also need an array of tools and leadership strategies to implement the vision. Here, the district leadership needs to pay attention to the special needs of specific kinds of principals: new principals, leaders of particularly challenged schools, and principals attempting to meet the needs of specific subpopulations. These study groups should encourage problem sharing, problem solving, and self-reflection.

• **Peer Learning.** Beyond specialized support, you need to encourage communities of practice. Intervisitation among school leaders should be common. Informal buddying among principals should be encouraged by your office. The point is that the task of building a learning organization requires everyone in the school, from students and teachers to principals, to see themselves as learners.

• **Individual Coaching.** As Shakespeare noted, some are born great, some become great, and some have greatness thrust upon them. You can't trust on greatness being thrust upon your new principal; you'll need to help this person develop. The leadership and pedagogical challenges inherent in creating leaders of learning should not be underestimated. Developing a core of principals who are skilled instructional leaders will require individual coaching from the superintendent and leadership team. A focal point of this coaching should be the supervisory walkthrough, in which the superintendent reviews the school's goals and assessment data and then walks through each classroom with the principal to examine students' work, explore how well the students understand their work, and observe teacher performance before making an overall assessment of the school and reviewing areas that need strengthening.

• **Mentoring.** Beyond coaching, the district should set out to provide all principals with mentors, more senior administrators, or principals who can lend their experience and wisdom to junior partners. Mentoring is all the more important for your principals who are struggling. Careful matching of principals to experienced mentors, particularly mentors skilled in leading learning, can help junior school leaders address many issues. Mentors should be expected to visit their protégés' schools regularly, offering guidance on goals, objectives, and budgeting, and developing plans to work with particular teachers.

Beyond the specifics outlined above, the essential point is this: The days of placing principals in schools and leaving them to sink or swim on their own are over. As an instructional leader, you as the superintendent have an obligation to create the conditions in which your principals can become instructional leaders in their own right.

## 4. The Challenge of Principal Turnover

*Ed Fuller is associate professor in the Education Leadership Department at Penn State University. He is also the director of the Center for Evaluation and*

*Education Policy Analysis and associate director for policy at the University Council for Educational Administration. This column first appeared in the Albert Shanker Institute's blog and was then reprinted in Valerie Strauss's blog,* The Answer Sheet *in the* Washington Post, *August 21, 2012. The issue highlighted by Dr. Fuller concerns the remarkably high rate of principal turnover in the United States, at all levels of schooling, and raises questions about the efficacy of replacing principals as a strategy for turning around schools.*

### Ed Fuller

"No one knows who I am," exclaimed a senior in a high-poverty, predominantly minority and low-performing high school in the Austin area. She explained, "I have been at this school four years and had four principals and six Algebra I teachers."

Elsewhere in Texas, the first school to be closed by the state for low performance was Johnston High School, which was led by 13 principals in the 11 years preceding closure. The school also had a teacher turnover rate greater than 25 percent for almost all of the years and greater than 30 percent for 7 of the years.

While the above examples are extreme, they underscore two interconnected issues—teacher and principal turnover—that often plague low-performing schools and, in the case of principal turnover, afflict a wide range of schools regardless of performance or school demographics.

In recent years, those seeking to improve schooling through efforts to increase teacher effectiveness and build teacher capacity have quickly realized that such efforts rely heavily on principal capacity and stability.

Indeed, a number of recent research efforts have found that principal turnover is important for three primary reasons.

First, research has shown that high principal turnover often leads to greater teacher turnover, which in turn can have a negative impact on student achievement and other schooling outcomes, as well as increased fiscal costs.

Second, emerging research and theory has found that principal turnover has direct negative effects on student- and school-level achievement and that the strongest impact appears immediately after turnover occurs.

Finally, research suggests that regular principal turnover can lead to teachers not investing in any change efforts and learning to simply "wait [principals] out." As a result, it also decreases the probability of school improvement. Thus, research suggests that principals must be in place at least five years for the full implementation of a large-scale change effort, including the recruitment, retention, and capacity building of staff.

What does principal turnover look like? I have worked with several colleagues (Michelle Young, Bruce Baker, and Terry Orr) to examine the extent and characteristics of principal turnover, using data from Texas that spans the years 1989 through 2010. There are three important specific findings that illustrate and expand upon the conclusions from the literature discussed above. First, as shown in Figure 6.2, newly hired principals sim-ply do not stay at the same school for very long periods of time, particu-larly in middle and high schools. Strikingly, only 51 percent of newly hired middle school principals remained at the same school for three years, while only 47 percent remained at the high school level for three years. After five years, just 31 percent of newly hired middle school principals remained, and only 27 percent of high school principals. Overall, the average tenure for a high school principal in Texas is just over three years—the average high school principal will not see her or his first freshman class graduate.

Second, the initial level of achievement at the school in the year before the principal arrives is associated with the first-year principal retention rate. A fairly large difference exists in the one-year retention rates between newly hired principals at the lowest- and high-performing schools (with performance measured vis-à-vis nearby schools). Principals in high-achieving elementary, middle, and high schools have higher retention rates in the first year than those in comparable, lower-achieving schools. These initial differences increase further after three years, so that there is a 20-percentage-point difference in the retention rates for middle and high schools and a 15-percentage-point difference at the elementary school level.

**Figure 6.2**    Principal Retention by Schooling Level and 1-, 3-, and 5-Year Intervals

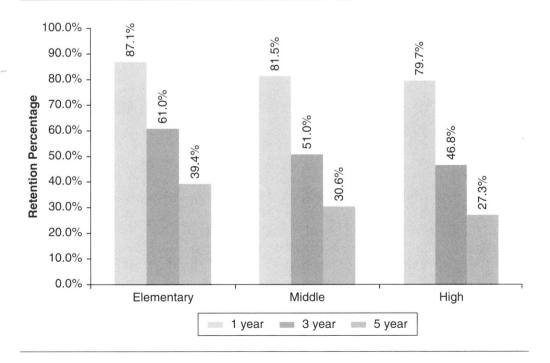

For many years, it has been known that about 50 percent of beginning teachers leave the profession within five years. Recent research from Richard Ingersoll at the University of Pennsylvania reveals that the profession is "greening" as older and more experienced teachers retire to be replaced by younger teachers. Although most teachers are still quite experienced, in 2008, according to Ingersoll, the modal teacher was a first-year beginner (i.e., when asked how many years of experience they had, the most common answer indicated the teacher was in the first year). See http://tinyurl.com/d5eqywc.

In light of these findings, policy makers and analysts might want to reexamine a strategy that relies on replacing 50 percent of teachers in turnaround schools in the expectation that more skilled and experienced teachers will replace them.

Third and finally, the same schools with high levels of principal turnover also have high levels of teacher turnover in the first year. This is especially true at the secondary level. The gaps become larger after three and five years. For urban high schools in Texas with high principal turnover, it is not uncommon to see five-year teacher turnover rates greater than 60 percent.

Despite frequent assertions that one way to improve low-performing schools is to replace the principal and to do so with greater frequency, the evidence suggests serious downsides: Rapid turnover of principals leads to more problems for the school in terms of greater teacher turnover, greater difficulty in recruiting well-qualified or effective teachers, and increased reluctance of staff to invest in reform strategies. All of these issues ultimately have a negative and long-lasting impact on the school's achievement profile.

## B. INSTRUCTIONAL LEADERSHIP

James Harvey

Nelda Cambron-McCabe

When he retired as superintendent of schools in Springfield, Massachusetts, wrote Peter Negroni in the first edition of *The Superintendent's Fieldbook,* a leading national newspaper placed the advertisement for his successor under S for superintendent rather than E for educator. Negroni, now senior vice president at the College Board, reported with some chagrin that applications from building managers and groundskeepers poured in. "Well-meaning applicants paraded their experience overseeing water heaters, cleaning buildings, and collecting rents. It was comical, but not really amusing." (See Negroni's chapter in Part II of this volume.)

But, he said, the blunder reflected an unsettling trend in school administration. For too long "superintendents and principals had become increasingly focused on the machinery and structures of education and on driving up test scores. These issues were more easily comprehended by the public than the messy and often-hidden work of teaching and learning." Superintendents cannot, concluded Negroni, succeed in educating all children to high standards by concentrating on systems at the expense of teaching and learning. "We cannot lead learning if we leave the core of instruction unquestioned, unexamined, and essentially mysterious." Effective superintendents, he declared, need to make the same journey he made at Springfield—going from lone rangers (trying to do it all by themselves) to leaders of learning (working collaboratively on the real business of schools).

Negroni was in the vanguard of a movement in which superintendents and other administrators were asked to abandon their focus on buses, budgets, and books and raise their sights to the challenges involved in becoming leaders of learning, deeply and consciously engaged in improving the instructional core of schooling. They must, in short, become instructional leaders who view time spent in schools and the classroom as the most precious and productive ways to employ their energy.

And it's not easy, he warned. Because their classroom careers are usually long-distant memories, even effective superintendents have "to relearn what it means to be an educator."

### Instructional Leadership

What exactly lies behind the high-blown phrase *instructional leadership*? A Spring 2005 newsletter from the U.S. Department of Education outlined several dimensions of effective instructional leadership for superintendents and principals. Although oriented around early reading instruction, the five hallmarks apply to all levels of K–12 education:

- **Prioritized.** Teaching and learning must be at the top of the priority list on a consistent basis. Leadership is a balance of management and vision. While leaders cannot neglect other duties, teaching and learning require most of the leader's scheduled time.
- **Scientifically based.** Instructional leaders must be well informed about relevant research in order to assist in the selection and implementation of instructional materials and to monitor implementation. Leaders' participation in professional development sessions will help them remain informed and will provide a focus for monitoring.
- **Aligned.** Focus on alignment of curriculum, instruction, assessment, and standards. If student achievement is the goal and that goal is measured by standards-based assessments, the curriculum, instruction, and assessments all must be aligned with the standards.
- **Analytically and Data-Based.** In their focus on improving achievement, effective leaders use multiple sources of information to assess performance. Decisions at all levels must be based on pertinent data. Central office staff can use data to help principals become more effective instructional leaders and to make decisions regarding policy and curriculum.

- **Embedded in a Culture of Continuous Learning for Adults.** Effective instruction is a skill that can never be perfected. All teachers can benefit from additional time and support to improve their practice.

Leaders at all levels of the system have clear and important roles in supporting those improvement efforts.

### Instructional Rounds

"Instructional rounds," report Elizabeth City, Richard Elmore, Sarah Fiarman, and Lee Teitel in *Instructional Rounds in Education,* "sit at the intersection of three current popular approaches to the improvement of teaching and learning—walkthroughs, networks, and district improvement strategies."

**Walkthroughs.** Classroom observation, under different names—walkthroughs, learning walks, classroom visitations, peer observation—is at the heart of instructional improvement, say City and her colleagues. "Unfortunately, the practice of walkthroughs has become corrupted in many ways by confounding it with supervision and evaluation." Descending on classrooms with checklists of things that need to be fixed is "antithetical to the purposes of instructional rounds and profoundly unprofessional."

**Networks.** Establishing networks is also a common strategy in the effort to improve instruction. Professional learning communities (PLCs), critical friends groups, and teacher and principal study groups are all the rage everywhere. Some are well thought out, but many are not. In some cases, "they are simply new labels for meetings that are dysfunctional or disconnected from instructional improvement or both."

**Improvement Strategies.** An improvement strategy "is a precondition for the effective use of instructional rounds," write City and her colleagues. "It is difficult to focus in a productive way on which problem to solve if you don't have a strategy to start with."

Instructional rounds, in brief, are a special kind of walkthrough, a special kind of network, and an improvement strategy that is integrated into practice.

When City's colleague, Richard Elmore, met with the Roundtable in 2011, he announced that his goal "is to build a profession." It takes about 10,000 hours to become competent in complex work, he pointed out. "It's easy to criticize education schools, but the criticism is completely misplaced." The issue is that the only way to learn how to practice in a profession is to learn under real conditions. Think of every teaching hospital in the country on July 1, he challenged. That's the day every intern and resident turns over. But every newcomer who shows up on July 1 has embedded in them a sense of how to proceed. Their challenge is to "build fluency in a core set of practices under close supervision."

Instructional rounds are one way to approach building fluency in core practices, argues Elmore. "We fail to treat induction and early practice as learning," he noted. "We select from the bottom third of college students and then place them in situations guaranteed to produce bad results. Then we wonder why we get these results!" Pointing to Community District #2 in New York City as a model, he noted that the district spent about 10 percent to 15 percent of its budget on professional development, most at the classroom level. "This wasn't the car wash model of spray and pray, but a lot of boots on the ground worried about coaching and paying attention to what students were learning."

Community District #2's efforts involved what Elmore called "brutal conversations about classroom practice. They had none of these conventions about saying nice things first. Then I realized that this is what real professions do."

Working in Connecticut, Massachusetts, Ohio, and Iowa, Elmore has come to the conclusion that advocates such as himself can't just train people and walk away; this is ongoing work. Moreover, he pointed out, even when a school becomes immersed in instructional rounds and says all the right things about the process, improvement might not be stimulated if the school and the staff have not made commitments to each other about what should happen next. We just can't practice instructional rounds to make ourselves feel good, was his message.

Turning to research reported in 2002, Elmore argued that the proportion of variance in student gains in reading and mathematics was dominated by what happened in individual classrooms, compared with differences between schools or between students. We find it hard to acknowledge this reality, said Elmore, although no other nation demonstrates such a large discrepancy between classrooms. He thought that people in the United States did not want to deal with this issue because "a lot of it has to do with things we regard as structurally impossible or politically difficult."

The challenge is how to go from blaming the victim to owning the problem. Canada might point the way ahead, he thought. Canada has jumped from 10th to 4th in the world in mathematics achievement with a common core curriculum and a commitment to high-quality curriculum. "Canadian teachers taken to ordinary, garden-variety classrooms in American schools are horrified at what they see," he reported. One Canadian told Elmore: "I can't report this in the language of rounds, but you people don't have any curriculum, do you?"

"When we explain that the curriculum is the textbook and what teachers do with it, they respond: 'Curriculum is what we teach. Teachers and principals don't make these decisions. They don't want those decisions.' Take that off the table and teachers' energy goes into teaching."

Then, said Elmore, Canadians select for "powerful, driven people who are themselves intellectuals to enter teaching." It's a culture of language, beliefs, efficacy, and legitimacy as educators drive success. Because a cultural transformation is what is required, it has to be *"mano a mano,* one at a time, retail, not wholesale."

A big policy response would be to remake selection procedures, but you can't bank on that in the short run. Another approach is instructional rounds. Done well, "instructional rounds make people extremely uncomfortable," noted Elmore, but it is "at least an opportunity to attack the issue on a retail basis." The issue, he said, is that, in most classrooms, there is no relationship between what the teacher describes as going on in the classroom and what is actually happening.

The instructional core, he emphasized, focuses on three elements: the student, the teacher, and the content. The general rule is that there are only three ways to influence achievement—and if you intervene in one of these elements, you have to intervene in the other two as well. "Individual professional development doesn't address the issue," he said. In fact, it increases the problem Elmore describes because, if instruction across the board is to improve, "all teachers have to benefit." And, "if you change the content without dealing with the teachers, you get low-level teaching of high-level content. You get exactly the same teaching from a different book. We call it 'knocking the edges off the grand piano in order to get it through the door.'" Good teachers with bad material present a different challenge—bored students. "We also have to engage students."

The task, he emphasized, predicts performance. "The work you see students doing predicts their performance on assessments. There's nothing wrong with teacher evaluation, but we're pushing nationally in the wrong direction." Teacher evaluation should be self-evaluation so as to embed the norms of best professional practice within individuals.

Is there a protocol for instructional rounds? Yes, there is. It consists of three simple questions. Its beauty lies in both its simplicity and its complexity. Here are the questions:

1. What is the teacher doing?

2. What is the student doing?

3. What is the task?

### Instructional Coaching

Top athletes, singers, and dancers have coaches. Should you? That was the provocative lead to an article in an October 2011 issue of *The New Yorker* by Atul Gawande, a brilliant writer and physician who described how he came to feel he could benefit from coaching after experiencing what he felt was a plateau in his development as a surgeon. His epiphany involved realizing that he'd just paid a kid out of college to look at his tennis serve, while people like tennis great Rafael Nadal are accompanied by coaches everywhere they go. Gawande checked in with one of his intimidating former surgical professors, now retired, and within weeks was performing in the operating room under the former professor's gaze.

What about other professionals? Gawande cites the work of Jim Knight in improving coaching for teachers. Knight himself had experienced trouble teaching writing in Toronto, "floundering" and "getting nowhere" until "a colleague came into the classroom and coached him through the changes he was trying to make." From that experience grew Knight's interest in a dissertation on coaching at the University of Kansas and obtaining funding to spread the coaching gospel.

Knight told the Roundtable that instructional coaches are on-site professional developers who teach educators how to use proven teaching methods. They employ a variety of procedures to foster widespread, high-quality implementation of interventions, providing on-the-job learning. Instructional coaches adopting the approach developed at the University of Kansas Center for Research on Learning take a partnership approach. They respect teachers' professionalism and focus their efforts on conversations that lead to creative, practical applications of research-based practices. Instructional coaches are thought of as colleagues, friends, and confidants who listen with care and share valuable information with teachers at the time teachers most need it.

**The Meeting of Two Minds.** At its core, instructional coaching involves two people: the classroom teacher and the coach. Coaches work with teachers in their classrooms one-on-one and in small groups. They provide guidance, training, and other resources as needed. Together, the coach and teacher focus on practical strategies for engaging students and improving student learning. Coaches also are often responsible for providing or arranging professional development activities for all teachers in a school or district. At the heart of coaching is the intent to be helpful, not judgmental, Knight told the Roundtable.

Think about what's involved in coaching, urged Knight. "You're asking people to do difficult things that challenge their identity, threaten their sense of themselves, may upset their status, and involve hard intellectual work." Above all, you as principal or superintendent need their commitment—"unless they are committed to the work, they will resist," said Knight, arguing that coaches need powerful emotional intelligence if they are to succeed.

**Significance of Interaction.** Knight told the Roundtable that effective coaching depends on how people interact with each other and is guided by seven principles that ground how coaches work with teachers:

1. Equality (a necessary condition of any partnership)

2. Choice (permitting teachers to be the final decision makers)

3. Voice (encouraging teachers to express their enthusiasms and concerns)

4. Reflection (a reflective, thinking partnership that is a meeting of the minds)

5. Dialogue (the best ideas develop when both partners think their way together through a discussion)

6. Praxis (Aristotle's term for practice as opposed to theory now describes the act of applying new knowledge and skills)

7. Reciprocity (the belief that each learning interaction is an opportunity for everyone to learn)

"Most of the things that work in practice revolve around dialogue, partnerships, and equality," Knight observed. But, he lamented, "most of what is going on to bring school reform to scale points in a different direction, toward school turnaround strategies that rely on mass firings."

**Ten Thousand Hours.** Coaching, he emphasized, is about goal setting, developing explicit skills, precision modeling, and deliberative practice. "You need goals, but you also need a very clear sense of current reality," because you need to be clear about what needs to change.

"It takes 10,000 hours to become expert at anything," Knight observed, echoing Elmore (and Malcolm Gladwell). "Modeling is a big part of what we do, and so is deliberative practice. We need deliberative practice. Talent can only get you so far. In fact, in the end, talent is overrated."

Knight argues for systematic alignment at the school level. School and culture are all part of this, he implies. "You need staff commitment, staff agreement, and staff understanding." He recommended creating a design team to lead the way, led by someone committed to the effort. "You can't choose 'Debbie Downer' to lead something like this!"

# C. FACILITATING CHANGE

*Obvious leadership challenges will confront you as you move forward, mostly the traditional ones of designing, implementing, and assessing programs. But three challenges are not immediately obvious. First is the challenge of understanding the nature of change and what it means in a large institutional setting such as yours. Next is the problem of taking your staff and teachers where you find them and helping them make the leap of faith required to move forward. Finally, you'll find the imperative of bringing the public along and reassuring parents. You won't get far unless you attend to both your internal and your external publics. This section takes up these issues.*

## 1. Nature of the Change Process

Gene E. Hall

Richard C. Wallace, Jr.

We know enough now about the change process from repeated observations that some major themes, indeed principles of change, can be established. We can state with some confidence that these principles will hold true in all cases. You as a superintendent can count on these things. And that's important, because often the only thing that seems to hold true in the midst of change is that all hell is breaking loose. It may be. But these are the principles with which you can ride out the heat. For those of you who like to see these things whole, the 12 principles are laid out succinctly (see box).

---

### PRINCIPLES OF CHANGE

1. Change is a process, not an event.

2. Developing and implementing an innovation are different things.

3. An organization does not change until the individuals within it do.

4. Innovations come in different sizes.

5. Interventions are the actions and events that are key to the success of the change process.

6. Top-down and bottom-up are fine, but horizontal is best.

7. Administrator leadership is essential to long-term and successful change.

8. Mandates can work.

9. The school is the primary unit for change.

10. Facilitating change is a team effort.

11. Appropriate interventions reduce the challenges of change.

12. The context of the school influences the process of change.

SOURCE: Hall, G. E., & Hord, S. M. (2011). *Implementing Change: Patterns, Principles, and Potholes* (3rd ed.). Upper Saddle River, NJ: Pearson, pp. 6–15.

---

We should not need to state the obvious, but here it is anyway. The principles are not mutually exclusive. At first reading, some may seem inconsistent with others. That's because they address selected aspects of the change process—and the principles change as the process develops. And it should be obvious, too, that

It is often noted that the implementation of change itself is the Achilles' heel of educational improvements. A useful book that puts legs under reforms is Hall, Gene E., & Hord, Shirley M. (2001). *Implementing change: Patterns, principles, and potholes.* Boston: Allyn and Bacon.

change is highly complex, multifaceted, and dynamic. If it weren't so complicated, you wouldn't have so much fun with it.

**Change Principle 1.** Change is a process, not an event. This too should be obvious. Change isn't accomplished by having some leader make an announcement or the district requiring some drive-by professional development. Change isn't even the implementation of a new curriculum. Instead, change is a process through which people and organizations move as they gradually come to understand, and become skilled and competent, in the use of new ways. If change is seen as an event, implementation is tactical in nature. That explains why you may hear your assistant complain at a meeting: "What do you mean, they need more training? We bought them the books. Can't they read?"

You need to think about change over the long haul as a process, not as an event.

**Change Principle 2.** Developing and implementing an innovation are different things. Think about it, and this should be obvious too. But it's amazing how many people don't get it. Development and implementation are different sides of the same coin. Whereas development involves everything required to create the innovation, implementation involves everything needed to establish the innovation on-site. On the development side, we find this to be a high-profile activity, are generous with the time allotted to it, and take a large and visionary perspective because, as developers, we are alert and savvy, and we possess the political skills required to understand timing and public relations. Implementation is almost the reverse. There's little glory, it takes time, people often lack patience, and it requires a sort of technical and clinical skill allied to patience, humor, and creativity.

> Thanks to the marvel of modern technology, readers can watch Gene Hall talking about many of these issues at https://vimeo.com/13838354.

What does that have to do with you as a superintendent? Here's just one possibility: Understand that the style of the facilitator required on each side of this equation is different. It's unlikely your developer can implement his or her innovation—or is even very much interested in doing so.

**Change Principle 3.** An organization does not change until the individuals within it do. Ah, there's the rub! Successful change begins and ends with human beings. An entire organization does not change until every individual within it changes. Some people will grasp the change immediately (and buy into it). Others will need additional time. And a few will avoid the change for a very long time.

But everyone sooner or later has to get on board. There's a lot of truth to the old adage about one bad apple spoiling the barrel. The cynic in the faculty lounge is terribly important. Any opposition is important. It has to be dealt with and respected, not ignored in the hope it will go away.

Change Principle 4. Innovations come in different sizes. Innovations can be products (tablets, texts, or assessment techniques) or processes (constructivist teaching, principles of self-esteem in the classroom). Depending on their complexity, innovations can require more resources and

> See Section C2, below: The Hall Innovation Category Scale (HiC) for an educational Richter scale to measure your environment from background noise to educational earthquake.

more time. A new edition of a standard curriculum text can be implemented routinely. That's a small-scale innovation. But a new reading curriculum, with entirely new texts, complex variations in how material is introduced and sequenced, and the need for broad teacher training is a large-scale innovation. It's much harder to implement. Now, think about something like implementing the Common Core State Standards—we're talking about megachange here, and you shouldn't underestimate what's required to implement it.

Change Principle 5. Interventions are the actions and events that are key to the success of the change process. Leaders tend to be consumed with the innovation and its use. They often don't think of the interventions, the actions that they and others take to influence the process. Everyone thinks of training as an important intervention. And it is. But equally important are the one-legged interviews you can conduct about the innovation and how it's developing. If you run into a teacher between classes as you leave a school, you can ignore him or her or chat briefly. (Most teachers have more important things to do than waste their time talking with us. So, it's quick. That's why it's one-legged—because most of us can't stand on one leg for long.) In just a brief chat, therefore, you've already intervened in this teacher's life.

Now, let's assume you use that chat to ask how the new reading curriculum is going in the teacher's class. Any problems he has with it? Any things she likes about it? Asked as a way of obtaining information—and with a genuine interest in the response—you have a good chance of cementing that teacher's commitment to the innovation.

Change Principle 6. Top-down and bottom-up are fine, but horizontal is best. Everyone understands the hierarchy of a bureaucracy. In schools, you, as superintendent, are on top, and teachers and custodians are on the bottom. You might not agree with this, but the public would view the state superintendent as an even more superior person, with state legislators and congressional figures on a plane too rarified for most to comprehend. Top-down and bottom-up change can each work, but both are tough. Mandates from on high get horribly mangled by the time they reach the classroom, and most attempts at bottom-up change collapse because the top cannot bear to relinquish control. Think of a horizontal system instead. At the federal, state, district, school, and classroom levels, everyone is on an equal plane. That's the way to encourage change.

Two reports from the Center for the Study of Teaching and Policy, University of Washington, can help principals as they work with teachers: *Leading for Learning Sourcebook: Concepts and Examples* and *Leading for Learning: Reflective Tools for School and District Leaders.* These materials can be obtained at http://tinyurl.com/4fxve7t.

When horizontal change is encouraged, it depends on everyone doing his or her own job, trusting that everyone else will do theirs as well. Trust is the key to this—the commodity in shortest supply in the school reform discussion.

**Change Principle 7.** Administrator leadership is essential to long-term change success. If you as superintendent are like most people in education, you tend to genuflect when someone advocates bottom-up change on the grounds that those nearest the action have the best ideas about how to accomplish change. It might not make sense for you to believe that (given your position); still, as Ralph Waldo Emerson once said, "A foolish consistency is the hobgoblin of little minds." Think big. Both leadership and grassroots support are needed for change. Without long-term support from leaders and authority figures, most innovations wither up and die.

This principle is a corollary of Principle 6. Everyone has to do his or her job, and you as a leader have to do yours. One of your tasks as a leader of innovation is to institutionalize the innovation so that it survives when the developers leave—and when you leave too.

**Change Principle 8.** Mandates can work. No progressive educator wants to believe this for a second. What? Mandates (inevitably mandates from on high) work? Oh, yes. They can and do—not always, but often enough that they cannot be ignored. A mandate is a strategy with a clear priority and the expectation that it will be implemented. Ending Jim Crow schools in the South was a mandate. So too was compensatory education. No one would deny that both were implemented and, although perhaps neither achieved the results they sought, both changed schooling in America more than any innovation developed by the nation's think tanks or academic institutions.

For the most part, mandates get a bad name because they're announced without being backed up with the supports and other innovations needed to make them succeed.

**Change Principle 9.** The school is the primary unit for change. The key organizational unit for making change is the school. The school's staff and its leaders will make you or break you on any change, whether started from within or without. Obviously, the school is not an island. It can do a lot by itself, but it also needs to move in concert with and be supported by the other components of the system.

No single school is likely to have all the expertise it needs to implement the change you request, demand, or implore of it. Once you understand that the school is the primary unit for change, you should also understand why you need to help support it as it goes about making the change.

**Change Principle 10.** Facilitating change is a team effort. In some ways, this is simply an elaboration of Principles 6, 7, 8, and 9. Change takes leadership. It takes facilitators. It takes principals and teachers. It takes a team.

Understand this: Everyone is in this boat together. Whether they pull together, or bail together, or assign some to pull while others bail, getting the boat safely to harbor requires the best efforts of the entire crew.

**Change Principle 11.** Appropriate interventions reduce the challenges of change. We'll get to this later with "leaps of faith," but for now, understand that hardnosed reformers are wrong when they assert (on the basis of opinion and no evidence) that change is painful and the pain must be endured. Maybe a masochist would pursue change under those conditions, but it's hard to think of anyone else attracted to the idea. Pain is not necessarily the lot of you and your colleagues involved in change. Properly facilitated, change can be fun. It should be rewarding and energizing for you, your staff, your teachers, your children, and your parents.

**Change Principle 12.** The context of the school influences the process of change. Obviously, the physical features of the school and the people in it (along with their attitudes, beliefs, and values) can have important influences on your organization's change efforts. Yet interestingly, a consensus is developing among scholars of schools and corporations about organizational culture and how it relates to the successful implementation of change. When the staff (or corporate officials) collectively reflects with students (or employees) on its work, both staff and officials get a better understanding of what they must do to help their students (and employees) become more successful. (See Part II: Leading Your Schools. All the leadership lessons at the district level are equally applicable at the school site.)

In the corporate sector, this requires a shared and supportive leadership. And that's what's required in schools, too.

## 2. The Hall Innovation Category Scale (HiC)

### Gene E. Hall

Do you need help gauging where you are in your change process? The Hall Innovation Category (HiC) Scale, shown in Table 6.2, lets you get a handle on how far along you are and how many people are on board. The scale illustrates a series of reform strategies that move from talking, to tinkering, to transforming.

Examine the HiC Scale. Where is your district on this scale? Are you talking about reform? Tinkering at the margins? Or are you deep into the hard work of redesign and restructuring required for true transformation? Where is the national discussion? It seems to have moved beyond whispering and telling. It now seems to be yelling and shaking. But is it truly a transformational conversation?

**Table 6.2**   The Hall Innovation Category (HiC) Scale

| Level | Name | Example |
|-------|------|---------|
|  |  | *Talking* |
| 0 | Cruise Control | Teacher in same classroom for many years |
| 1 | Whisper | Commission reports |
| 2 | Tell | New rules and more regulation of old practices |
| 3 | Yell | Prescriptive policy mandates |
|  |  | *Tinkering* |
| 4 | Shake | Revise curriculum |
| 5 | Rattle | Change principal |
| 6 | Roll | Change teacher's classroom |
|  |  | *Transforming* |
| 7 | Redesign | Integrated curriculum |
| 8 | Restructure | Differentiated staffing |
| 9 | Mutation | Changing role of school board |
| 10 | Reconstitution | Local constitutional convention |

## 3. The Leap of Faith

### James Harvey

Gene Hall describes the gap separating where we are in education today and the Promised Land as a yawning chasm. Under most policy prescriptions, a leap of faith is required to get from what are described as today's ugly realities to tomorrow's beautiful possibilities (see Figure 6.3). What explains the resistance to most school reforms is the practical reality that most people aren't willing to make that leap of faith. They may like you. They may even think you're a wonderful person. And if you want to leap out over that chasm and crash and burn, you will make the leap with their best wishes. But only a few will be inclined to jump off the cliff with you. The next few sections will help you bridge this chasm.

## 4. Stages of Concern

### Gene E. Hall

### James Harvey

Researchers at the RAND Corporation, a government-sponsored think tank, sometimes talk about the 17 percent solution in education. By that, they mean that, no matter what innovation is proposed, somewhere around 17 percent of all teachers will sign up, practically right away.

That's useful information to you as a superintendent. It almost doesn't matter what you suggest—school-site budgeting, standards and assessment, reading programs, a new approach to math—17 percent of teachers

**Figure 6.3**    Leap of Faith

SOURCE: Hall, G. E., & Hord, S. M. (2011). *Implementing Change: Patterns, Principles, and Potholes* (3rd ed.). Upper Saddle River, NJ: Pearson, p. 11.

will buy in immediately, some because they want to be cooperative and others because they are firmly convinced that the schools in which they teach can be improved. You can count on enthusiastic support right away. Close to one-fifth of your teaching staff will make the leap of faith with you.

Still, don't mistake the approbation from the people who talk to you for general approval of your plans. Even with 17 percent of the teachers on your side, 83 percent are unaccounted for. Some of these people are disinterested. Others haven't thought about it and don't know much. Some are anxious about what the changes will mean for them. Still others aren't convinced that what you are proposing is the best thing for the children who appear in their classrooms every day. And some, of course, reflexively dig in to oppose any change in the existing order of things. Your challenge becomes how to bring the other 83 percent along. How do you get them to join you in the leap of faith?

Actually, you don't. That won't work. It's unlikely that these people will make the leap. What you have to do is span the chasm for them—provide a bridge across the gap so that leaping is unnecessary.

For more information on this study about stages of concern, see Fuller, Frances F. (1970). *Personalized education for teachers: An introduction for teacher educators.* Austin: University of Texas, Research and Development Center for Teacher Education.

First, some information about what motivates people in the face of change and what kinds of resistance you might expect: In 1970, Frances Fuller at the University of Texas at Austin found that 97 out of 100 students in her educational psychology course rated her course as "irrelevant" or a "waste of time." Faced with these findings, most of us would look for a hole in which to hide our mortification. Not Fuller. To her, the interesting question was this: "What turned on those three smart students?" (All, no doubt, superior people of refinement and good judgment.)

This was a breakthrough question. It turned out that each of the three students had prior experience with children—either as parents or teachers of a church class. So, they enjoyed some background and experience with which to understand and appreciate an introductory course on educational psychology. To them, it was neither "irrelevant" nor a "waste of time" but bore directly on their experience and was a useful way to spend time on a subject in which they were already engaged. Establishing the hypothesis that concerns are a function of experience, Fuller conducted an in-depth study of student teachers. She settled on three stages of concern among student teachers:

- *Self-concerns* do not revolve around teaching or learning, but more around personal issues. ("Can I get a ticket to the U2 concert?") Beginning teachers with such self-concerns will worry about where to park their cars.
- *Task concerns* show up after students have entered student teaching. Now, teaching enters the picture. ("I didn't expect to spend all night grading papers.") The issues are still largely teacher oriented, not student centered.
- *Impact concerns* are the ultimate goal. Here, student teachers (and teachers and administrators and even you as superintendent) begin to focus on what is happening with students and how to improve student results. Now, the comments center on these issues: "My kids understand what I'm trying to do." "I'm taking Saturday's workshop on involving the parents of children with special needs because I think that's a win-win situation for everyone."

In her research, Fuller found that more than two-thirds of the concerns of preservice teachers were in the self and task areas, while two-thirds of the concerns of experienced teachers were in the task and impact areas.

Building on this foundation, University of Texas at Austin researchers developed a seven-stage typology of Stages of Concern. From the lowest levels of awareness to the highest levels of concern, these stages are outlined in the following:

*Seven Stages of Concern*

0. Awareness. Little concern about or involvement with the innovation.

*Self-Concerns*

1. Informational. This is a general awareness of the innovation and interest in learning more about it. These people seem unworried about themselves in relation to the innovation. They are interested in substantive aspects of the change, such as general characteristics, effects, and requirements for use.

2. Personal. Individuals are uncertain about the demands of the innovation or feel inadequate to meet those demands. Anxiety exists about roles in the innovation, including relations to the organization's reward structure and decision making. Financial and status implications of the innovation for self and colleagues may be an issue.

*Task Concern*

3. Management. Attention is focused on processes and tasks of using the innovation and the best use of information and resources. Issues related to efficiency, organizing, managing, scheduling, and time demands are at the forefront.

*Impact Concerns*

4. Consequence. Attention is directed at the impact of information on immediate clients or students. An outward-looking concern, the focus is on the relevance of innovation for students before teachers, evaluation of outcome related to performance and student competencies, and changes needed to increase student success.

5. Collaboration. The focus is on coordination and cooperation with others regarding use of the innovation.

6. Refocusing. The focus is on exploring the more universal benefits of the innovation, including the possibility of major changes or replacement with a more powerful alternative. Individuals have definite ideas about the existing form of the innovation and about alternatives that might be proposed.

SOURCE: Hall, G. E., & Hord, S. M. (2011). *Implementing Change: Patterns, Principles, and Potholes* (3rd ed.). Upper Saddle River, NJ: Pearson, p. 73.

Now, here's what you need to understand. Although, as a superintendent, you may expect most of your staff to support you because they are already lined up in Stages 4, 5, and 6, many of them will still be stuck in Stages 0 through 3.

That is, you have a bit of a leadership challenge. You expect your teachers and administrators to make the leap of faith with you because they are already considering consequences for their students and entertaining ideas about modes of collaboration and how to refocus and improve your plans. But many of your people are disinterested or only mildly curious about what you propose, and some of them are quite worried, if not frightened, by it.

To get them to make the leap of faith, you are going to have to meet them on their own ground. In fact, except for the people already part of the 17 percent solution (probably Stages 5 and 6), most of your staff won't make the leap at all. You're going to have to build bridges (see Section 5: Bridging the Leap of Faith) to get them from where they are in today's ugly reality to where you want them to be in tomorrow's beautiful possibility.

## 5. Bridging the Leap of Faith

Gene E. Hall

James Harvey

If you want people to make the leap of faith, you will have to span the chasm for them. The best way to bridge the gap is to start where your people are and lead them from there (see Figure 6.4).

Figure 6.4    Bridging the Gap

## Today's Ugly Reality

## Tomorrow's Beautiful Possibility

6 - Refocuses and explores innovation to make it more powerful. Needs to be cheered.

5 - Collaborative, interested in cooperation.  Needs support and encouragement.

4 - Interested in impact on students.  Needs data on performance and competencies.

3 - Worried about processes/tasks.  Needs information on efficiency, management, time demands.

2 - Concerned, anxious about innovation.  Needs financial and status information.

1 - General awareness of innovation.  Needs substantive information.

0 - Little awareness of innovation.  Needs general information.

## 6. Your Task as a Superintendent

### Nelda Cambron-McCabe

What must a superintendent do to support principals taking up the challenge of leading student learning? We've laid out an ambitious responsibility for principals that fundamentally changes the very nature of their work. From our experiences, we identified some common behaviors across superintendents that made it possible for principals to lead student learning. Roundtable superintendents elaborate on some of these elements here.

*1. Student learning begins at the top, with the superintendent.*

*Superintendents set the tone by what they do, what they say, and what they value. When student learning is constantly part of your rhetoric and actions, you create a space for principals to engage their staffs and communities. The real question from my learning is "How do we help superintendents understand that their role is to create safe practice fields for principals taking up the student learning challenge?"*

—Les Omotani, former superintendent, West Des Moines, Iowa, and Hewlett–Woodmere, New York

*Superintendents have to understand that principals are the key for improving student learning. Since that's the case, they have to adopt a districtwide framework emphasizing the principal's instructional role. Principals should not have any doubt about their main responsibility. And it starts with the superintendent.*

—Gloria Davis, superintendent, Decatur Public Schools, Illinois

*2. Principals need time to reflect and learn.*

*Successful superintendents build leadership capacity in their principals as school-based instructional leaders. Superintendents encourage school leaders to be reflective in their practice, whether in personal introspection or active dialogue with colleagues, instructional technology specialists, and other district staff. And it includes classroom observations and instructional rounds.*

—Gary Plano, superintendent, Mercer Island Schools, Washington

*Principles must be protected from internal and external pressures that divert their time and energy from student learning. It is a constant, uphill battle to help central office staff understand that we exist to support schools. As superintendent, my role is to clear the way for principals to be the best instructional leaders possible.*

—Suzanne Cusick, superintendent, Longview Schools, Washington

*3. Principals need specific skills and knowledge in creating learning communities to engage teachers and others.*

*Learning communities run counter to the individualistic culture that is found in most schools. As such, we found that our monthly administrative meetings needed to be focused on developing skills to shift this culture. We took a deliberate and systematic approach to prepare school principals.*

—Steve Norton, superintendent,
Cache County School District, Utah

*4. Principals must quit doing some things they're doing now.*

*At the building level, principals are like superintendents and under great day-to-day pressure from parents, teachers, students, discipline, and other issues in the building. Trying to find balance and perspective is difficult. To find time for learning, they may have to let some of those things go or find someone else to take them on. We need to support new models of administration so that principals can be instructional leaders.*

—Morton Sherman, superintendent,
Alexandria City Public Schools, Virginia

*5. Principals must be protected from internal and external pressures that divert their time and energy from student learning.*

*A lot of pressure on principals for administrative work comes from the central office—from finance, personnel, facilities, and so on. As superintendents, we have a responsibility to make sure our office sees its role as supporting the principal's instructional agenda as the essential priority.*

—Lane Weiss, superintendent,
Saratoga Public Schools, Saratoga, California

*6. Principals must model leading student learning as a fundamental way to change what happens in schools.*

*We have to model the behaviors we expect from principals and teachers. One of the things that make "Walkthroughs" very powerful is that they model what we expect from the principal. You're not just telling principals to walk through the classrooms, you're doing it with them.*

—Steve Price, former superintendent,
Hazelwood Schools, Missouri

*7. Superintendents and school boards must create new policies, structures, and practices to frame the student learning agenda.*

*To lead successful schools, where each student has the opportunity to succeed, you must reexamine every program you offer, every practice in place, every school/home/community relationship you have developed. Otherwise, you will just keep on doing what has always been done and it no longer works. Business-as-usual will not solve the educational problems we face or prepare our students for the world of tomorrow.*

—Louise Berry, superintendent,
Brooklyn Schools, Connecticut

*8. The new expectations for principals must be clearly understood by all.*

*By affirming instructional leadership through policy, superintendents ensure that this core belief is both actionable and at the center of principals' work. Superintendents need to champion school boards' efforts to adopt policy that acknowledges and codifies instructional leadership as a key role in the academic achievement of all students. This policy must be arrived at through a vetting that honors the real work involved, celebrates gains, and contains professional accountability for all parties.*

—Steven M. Ladd,
superintendent, Elk Grove, California

*9. Superintendents must raise the tough questions.*

*Our goal is to ensure that ALL students achieve at high levels. While the vast majority of Lexington students perform very well on standardized tests, there are groups of students who continue to struggle. If we truly want all students to succeed in our schools, then all principals, teachers, school board members, and residents must rethink what we are doing, even if it makes some people uncomfortable.*

—Paul Ash, superintendent, Lexington Public Schools,
Lexington, Massachusetts

*10. Distribute leadership in your district.*

*Every administrator in our district is an instructional leader. Our administrative team has identified an instructional framework for focusing the entire district on key research-based best practices. Collaboratively, they are developing the*

> Interested in the broad moral purpose of schools? See Fullan, Michael. (2001). *Leading a culture of change.* San Francisco: Jossey-Bass.

*curriculum, articulating expectations and developing a monitoring tool. As a team, they will analyze our implementation data and identify interventions and supports for teachers. This collaborative model provides the foundation for the way teachers will work in professional learning communities to share practice and improve their craft.*

—Yvonne Curtis, superintendent, Forest Grove
School District, Forest Grove, Oregon

## D. TOOLS FOR INSTRUCTIONAL LEADERS

### 1. Nine Tools for the Instructional Leader

*Superintendents found Otto Graf's on-site work with their principals to be invaluable as the principals took up the challenge of instructional leadership. Graf raises provocative questions that force a reconsideration of the business-as-usual stance prevalent in schools and provides tools for principals to shift their orientation to teaching and learning issues.*

Otto Graf

Ask any principal to list the top priorities of his or her job, and most will include instructional leadership. Next, ask the principal to review his or her work calendar to see how the use of time corresponds to this priority. In most cases, the time devoted to the role of instructional leader does not begin to match the priority given that role.

Taking up instructional leadership involves a shift in perspective. This begins by making questions about student learning central to each day's work.

All instructional leaders should be able to put their hands on the following tools easily:

1. **Data.** Collecting and analyzing data about student performance, classroom by classroom and subject by subject, is imperative.

2. **Clinical Supervision.** Principals need to be comfortable assessing and guiding teachers based on actual observation of their classroom performance.

3. **Self-Evaluation.** Encouraging teachers to collect and analyze their own data about what's going on in their classroom is powerful.

4. **Videotaping.** The videotape offers vivid accounts of the lessons and what teachers and students are doing.

5. **The Portfolio.** Ideally, portfolios should capture the work of both students and teachers.

6. **Peer Observation and Collegial Discussions.** Nothing convinces a teacher about the merits of a new approach more than counsel from colleagues and peers.

7. **PLCs.** Encourage every adult in the building to understand that they're all in this together.

8. **The Walkthrough.** This tool provides a fresh ritual for collecting data and sharing perceptions.

9. **The Debriefing.** This essential corollary to the walkthrough permits verbal and written feedback to individual teachers and the whole faculty about learning in the school.

   - How can I have an impact on what happens, in every classroom, for every student?
   - How can I ensure that every child is held to and enabled to meet high standards?
   - How will I talk to teachers and students about what is being learned and how performance is evaluated?

## 2. The Walkthrough

*The walkthrough observation technique creates a fresh ritual for collecting data and, afterward in a debriefing, sharing perceptions and ideas. In a sense, it brings the teacher and the principal into the cultural center of instruction. The walkthrough provides a very real indicator that instruction and learning are the priority in the school. It also signifies that the teacher and principal play major roles in the instruction and learning process. Over a period of time, walkthroughs can forge a relationship between the principal and teacher as colleagues who work closely together in the area of instruction. Principals and teachers begin focusing on those things that make a difference in improving academic achievement. The process of coaching each other becomes a significant factor in shaping what happens in the school.*

Otto Graf

How often did you as principal conduct a walkthrough? To be part of the culture of the school, a walkthrough should be conducted on a regular basis. Most principals set a goal to see every teacher a minimum of two times per month. Over the course of a school year, a principal can take 20 snapshots of a teacher's classroom. Using multiple snapshots, principals can collect important data about the implementation of the curriculum, the differentiation of instruction, the performance of students, and the ability of students to evaluate what constitutes good work. Here's the 14-step process.

1. *Conduct a preliminary walkthrough* to learn important information about the staff, students, curriculum, and school. The goal of this

walkthrough is to see the school in operation and to begin collecting baseline data around a wide spectrum of instructional practices.

2. *Conduct a walkthrough meeting* with the staff. This meeting sets the stage for the walkthrough and helps to establish clear expectations for the staff's participation. Specific school goals, special programs, or areas of focus for the school should also be reviewed at this meeting.

3. *Establish guidelines* for all participants in the walkthrough. Clear expectations need to be established concerning professional behavior for individuals involved in this process. Participants must maintain the highest degree of confidentiality regarding what is observed in the classrooms. While feedback is important, negative or judgmental comments to others regarding teachers or students are not appropriate.

4. *Establish the focus* for subsequent walkthroughs. Principal and teachers work together to identify specific elements of effective instruction that they wish to implement. This step includes the identification of *look-fors*—precise descriptors of teaching strategies that tell the observer what the strategy looks like when applied in the classroom.

5. *Connect the look-fors* to established standards. Look-fors in the classroom should reflect the district's standards for curriculum and instruction. This is an important step in developing a common language and a matching set of indicators for instruction and learning.

6. *Create an agenda for the walkthrough.* The principal should establish an agenda specifying look-fors for the walkthrough and communicate them to everyone involved. The exact number of classroom visits may vary, but a typical walkthrough includes five to ten classrooms.

7. *Identify data* to be collected (e.g., student learning behaviors, student work, teacher behaviors, materials used, physical arrangement of the classroom, and class activities).

8. *Collect data.* The person conducting the walkthrough should collect data. Note specific examples of effective practices and exact details about the implementation or use of look-fors.

9. *Observe student behaviors* that influence learning. The walkthrough should focus primarily on student work. Walkthrough participants may observe students' behaviors, level of engagement, and quality of work. Talking to students about what they are doing and how they evaluate their work presents a wonderful opportunity for assessing teaching and learning.

10. *Validate effective practice.* The walkthrough begins as a process for validating powerful teaching practice, effective use of guiding principles of learning, and effective learning strategies demonstrated by students.

11. *Debrief with teachers.* Debriefing with teachers and, in some instances, with students is a critical step in the walkthrough process. (See Table 6.3 for debriefing options.) Feedback based on observation is a powerful tool.

12. *Debrief staff.* Providing feedback to the staff as a whole is critical. This process begins by validating effective teaching and learning practices and encouraging their continued use. As the process develops, ample opportunities exist to engage teachers in sharing ideas and strategies with each other to create a strong learning community.

13. *Coach each other.* The walkthrough provides an excellent opportunity for participants to talk about instruction and learning and to coach each other. While this process begins with the principal and other administrators walking through classrooms and the school, engaging teachers in the process improves everyone's learning.

14. *Create a new school culture* emphasizing improved teaching and learning. The walkthrough should be seen as part of the culture and not as an event. To make this process a part of the culture, principals must establish a visible and continuing presence in classrooms.

**Table 6.3**    Debriefing Options Following a Walkthrough

*Oral Feedback.* Provide verbal feedback to teachers about something observed during the walkthrough. Be specific and connect the feedback to look-fors or elements of effective instruction.

*Written Feedback.* Write a general narrative about what was observed during the walkthrough and distribute the information to the entire staff. The narrative includes specific examples (without identifying a particular teacher or classroom) and evidence of how look-fors are present in the school. Short e-mail notes to individual teachers can be effective, also.

*Debriefing the Faculty.* Conduct a short meeting to debrief the faculty immediately after completing the walkthrough. The meeting is generally held after school, and attendance is most often voluntary. This meeting begins with a general overview of effective practices observed during the walkthrough and specific evidence of look-fors employed in classrooms. Feedback is focused on what is present in the school and not on individual teachers.

*Group Conference.* Conduct a group conference with teachers to highlight and validate the teachers' use of effective practices and implementation of look-fors. The conference begins with a general overview about what was observed during the walkthrough. This is followed by giving each teacher one or two specific examples of effective teaching strategies or look-fors that he or she demonstrated during the walkthrough.

*(Continued)*

(Continued)

*Growth Conference.* Conduct a group conference focused on improvement. To create a specific growth objective for the conference, use framing questions, identify areas of consideration, encourage teachers to complete self-reflection sheets, examine student work, or share instructional artifacts from students and the classroom.

*Clinical Supervision Conference.* Conduct a one-on-one conference with a teacher to reflect on the teacher's performance or the performance of his or her students.

*Study Groups.* Form small learning communities. Provide the time and resources for teachers to meet and discuss instruction and learning. Study groups can explore new strategies and research, share best practices, and engage in action research projects in classrooms.

*Other Tools.* Videotape lessons, prepare professional portfolios, examine student work, share teaching artifacts, review teachers' lesson plans, and devise projects.

# E. REFLECTIVE PRACTICE

## 1. A Teaching or a Learning System?

*How do you differentiate between a teaching system and a learning system?*

### Nelda Cambron-McCabe

Reflective practice has been an integral part of our work in the Roundtable and the Forum. Often, this was personal reflection, but at other points, it included engaging each other in dialogue around a particular issue or concern. In one session with superintendents and their school board members, we posed the following question: How do you differentiate between a teaching system and a learning system?

These questions can help a group of teachers, administrators, and others reflect on their understandings about teaching and learning and the implications for students' learning.

- How do you differentiate between a teaching system and a learning system?
- What does a teaching system look like in a classroom?
- What does a learning system look like in a classroom?
- Is there a difference in expected outcomes?
- What is the student's role and responsibility in a teaching system? In a learning system?
- How does change occur in a teaching system? In a learning system?
- What constitutes success in a teaching system? In a learning system?

## 2. Questions for Reflective Practice

Here are some key questions for reflection and for consideration as you develop your principals.

*What do you expect* principals to know about the principles of learning? Have you identified the specific responsibilities principals have for student learning? Have your actions established student learning as the main priority of the school district?

*Do you know how much time* principals spend on activities related to student learning? Are principals' performance appraisals related to student learning?

*Where do you stand* on the question of whether intelligence is inherited, developed by hard work, or socialized? What about your teachers and administrators?

*How do you support your principals?* Do you have programs in place to provide coaching or conduct school walkthroughs? What other approaches do you pursue?

*Regardless of the specifics of what you do, how well do you support your principals?* Do you provide regular opportunities throughout the year for principals to engage in conversations about student learning and students' work? Have principals designed their own professional development plans to promote their own growth and learning?

*How well does your administrative team support principals?* Think about your "cabinet" or whatever you call your top administrators. Go through the same assessment with the team. How happy are you with these results?

*Does the change process* described here make sense to you? Or do you think change can be imposed? How do your principals view change? Have you engaged principals in conversations about the change process?

*Let's assume you're ready to make the leap of faith.* How many people will leap with you? Have you sympathetically thought about the concerns they might have so that you can work to address those concerns?

*Are you confident* that you have a good strategy for engaging parents and the public about student learning? Are you able to state succinctly what you hope the students in your district will know and be able to do? Are principals and teachers able to do the same thing? What about parents? Would the answers support each other or conflict?

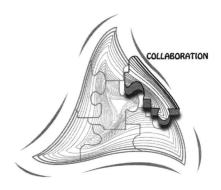

COLLABORATION

# PART VII

# *Collaborating With Your Allies*

Viewers of *CBS Evening News* were undoubtedly startled to turn on their televisions on June 9, 2011, and learn that 84 percent of the students in Whitney Elementary School in East Las Vegas, Nevada, were homeless. That was 518 students out of 610. At the time, government estimates indicated 900,000 American children had no real home. A few weeks later, CBS's *60 Minutes* reported on school bus routes running past "motels for the homeless" in Seminole County, Florida, a report that was followed up in November with the revelation that some families could no longer afford the motels and many children in Seminole County were living on the streets or in cars.

Homelessness, child neglect, juvenile violence, breakdowns in child protective services, inadequate foster care systems, lack of access to preventive health care—all of these things influence your ability to do your job. They are not your responsibility, but increasingly, these challenges spill over onto your campuses.

This part of *The Superintendent's Fieldbook* highlights the need for collaborative structures with other government agencies, describes how to build them, and shares with you the stories of some successful collaborations around early care and education.

The CBS homeless reports on Whitney Elementary and Seminole County cited here can be found at

http://tinyurl.com/ahamp2h

http://tinyurl.com/4k53ggk

http://tinyurl.com/cr6bbnm

Why should you worry about any of this? Because increasing numbers of children from very troubled backgrounds are showing up in your classrooms, and you cannot educate them effectively unless your community addresses their needs.

## A. WHAT IS COLLABORATION?

James Harvey

Why aren't the children in your community learning more? Why are so many young people in trouble in so many different ways—experimenting with drugs and alcohol, dropping out, becoming parents while scarcely more than children themselves, or running afoul of the juvenile justice system?

A big part of the answer to these questions is that many American families are in trouble. They are in trouble everywhere. Accounts of families who were apparently secure in the middle class with stable jobs and equity in their homes but suddenly found themselves out on the street in the Great Recession due to job loss and inability to meet mortgage payments became a staple of press coverage after 2008. In many inner cities, families are in crisis, facing unemployment, homelessness, and ongoing drug-related street violence. Another part of the answer is less obvious but equally significant: The service delivery system itself is shattered. The human service delivery system has become so fragmented and diffuse, cumbersome, inefficient, and underfunded, that it's hard to make it work. It often fails to meet the needs for which it was designed. Much of the good work you struggle with in your schools can be undone in an hour by a careless caseworker reviewing a family file or a parent finding him- or herself suddenly cut off from access to health care and medicine. Inevitably, failures in these other systems wind up creating problems in your schools.

Collaboration is more than cooperation. Cooperation implies agencies sharing information with other units of government. Collaboration implies agencies working together. It is an organized and conscious effort to break down the silo walls separating different agencies serving families. Collaboration is intended to make sure that children don't fall between the cracks and that vulnerable families receive the services they need efficiently and with dignity. Typically, the services involve things such as maternal and child health care, child welfare and protection, parental employment and income support, housing, early care and education, job training and youth employment, and delinquency programs and juvenile justice.

That's an awfully broad area of responsibility. You need some familiarity with it all. Outside the safety of school walls, a lot of young people are in danger of sinking. The difficult and tedious work of collaboration may be the best lifeline you can throw them.

This section of the *Fieldbook* introduces you to the concept of collaboration, explores what is required to make it work, and describes some successful collaborative models.

Just as leading learning demands new images and mental models from you, so too does collaboration require a profound conceptual shift. This section examines that conceptual shift and suggests that thinking of young people's assets instead of their deficits may be a key to improving service delivery to vulnerable families.

## 1. Build Boats, Not Houses

### James Harvey

"When most of us start thinking about building new institutional structures," a former Reagan administration official told us, "we unconsciously think the way a home builder does—with separate functional structures for different needs." But, said Martin Gerry, once deputy secretary of the U.S. Department of Health and Human Services, "When you think about human services, you need to think about building boats, not houses. If you are building a house and you leave a plank out, the house is basically all right. But, if you leave a plank out of a boat, it sinks." Build boats, not houses is Gerry's advice. That is, think comprehensively and systematically about government systems, not narrowly and haphazardly about government programs.

The financial consequences of the walls separating the many government programs are incredible. One consequence of these walls and program silos is that most educators are unaware of other funding possibilities and rarely

> It has been estimated that the United States spends more than $500 billion annually on children's services, nearly one-quarter of which (22 percent) is lost in administration.

know how to take advantage of them. State programs, like most federal programs, are not programs at all but funding streams, administered for the most part outside the state and local education establishment. Most school systems and administrators do not know how to access these monies. Meanwhile, welfare reform in the 1990s and growing numbers of single-parent and two-income families exert increasing demand on resources for early care and education. You need to think about how to help your community deal with these challenges.

At the heart of the conceptual shift discussed at the outset of this section is the idea of thinking and acting systemically. It involves moving from isolated, individual services to comprehensive and coordinated efforts on behalf of families with their many different needs. It requires moving from tightly defined, often rigid, programs and categorical funding to efforts that are much more flexible while offering greater discretion at the local level. It means that leaders consciously think about, and take

> *Build boats, not houses* is really an invitation to the sort of systems thinking advocated by Peter Senge in Part II. Consider the shifting the burden archetype described by Senge. You are struggling to make school work for all students. The problem you define is low achievement. But focusing on school solutions (school curriculum and pedagogy) might easily miss underlying causes of low achievement such as family stress, poor nutrition, lack of medical care, and continuous turnover in housing arrangements.

advantage of, the connections and relationships between and among different systems in order to concentrate public programs for the greatest effect. Finally, it depends on planning and evaluation as effective tools for improving system operations in place of ad hoc efforts put in place with good intentions while hoping for the best.

### Adopt Collaboration as a Way of Life

Collaboration is much more than just cooperation. Collaboration implies shared budgets; joint accountability for results; integrated professional development activities; and the development of new relationships across branches of government, among government agencies, and between state and local units of government. It has both vertical and horizontal dimensions. The most effective collaboration is grounded in this question: "What can we do together for the people we are supposed to serve?"

Collaboration is not a panacea. It is a difficult, often painful and time-consuming process that can delay decision making. Time spent developing trust and cooperation at the outset, however, can be made up many times over later, down the line, in more effective and efficient delivery of services. Still, the potential benefits and savings are impressive. The High/Scope Perry Preschool Study is a major longitudinal study of the benefits of providing early learning opportunities to disadvantaged children (see Section D3: The Need for and Value of Early Learning Programs and Section A3: Picturing a New Way of Thinking). According to this comprehensive cost-benefit evaluation of early learning:

- Preventing low birth weight in babies can be accomplished in one year for almost nothing and is likely to save as much as $100,000 in intensive neonatal services for each low-birth-weight infant.
- It is likely to take five years to reduce community reliance on foster care—but the long-term savings are huge because the correlation between foster care in one's early years and involvement in the criminal justice system later is extremely high.
- It will probably take 10 to 15 years to see the full savings from delaying the arrival of a second child to a young woman who bears her first at the age of 16. But, if the community can help delay that second arrival until the woman becomes 21, it is likely to save as much as $500,000 in public assistance and medical expenses.

The true benefits of these programs to society are like the true costs—they don't appear until years later.

## 2. A New Way of Thinking

### James Harvey

Whatever the cause or causes, over the years, fragmented policy making at the state and local levels has led to fragmented policy and programs. Most states now have many disconnected program and funding streams with a cumulative impact that is far less powerful than it could be. The results are predictable. During a program review some years ago, for example, Florida officials identified one family that, in a single 30-month period, experienced the following:

40 referrals to different community providers

17 separate evaluations

13 different case managers

10 independent treatment plans, including three family support plans, a foster care plan, and a protective services plan

A similar tale was recounted by a Pennsylvania woman. Over several weeks, she had to endure 55 different interviews with social workers from 30 different agencies, all demanding a separate case history that they refused to share with each other because of concerns about confidentiality. Recalling her efforts to maintain a consistent account for each of these caseworkers, the woman commented: "You know, you have to be smart in Philadelphia to be poor."

To change these dynamics, what is required is a new way of thinking about how social systems function. Although the philosophical basis for change is sometimes lost amidst battles about turf and budgets, a clear need exists to develop new mental models for agency collaboration. We need to improve our understanding of what lies beneath the surface of the iceberg of human service delivery failure.

It is increasingly clear that a major reorientation of policy thinking is required to improve the delivery of education and human services. In the

> According to former federal official Martin Gerry, our approach to correcting social problems is off-kilter. Says Gerry, "We believe if we can improve education a bit, things will be a little better. We can reform incrementally, by addition. That is absolutely not true. The system is multiplicative, not additive, so that if any of the factors is zero, the product is zero. No matter how good the education provided to a youngster on crack, that young person will not learn. We can say the same thing about child abuse and neglect. These traumas are so severe they stunt learning."

main, the shift encourages state and local agencies and personnel to become more entrepreneurial, active, and flexible (see Table 7.1). Public policy created this dysfunctional system; public policy can change it.

### 3. Picturing a New Way of Thinking

Beverly Parsons

Sharon Brumbaugh

Table 7.1 maps out how thinking about service delivery is evolving. State officials are being asked to shift from a model that emphasizes crisis intervention, state direction, and the ad hoc delivery of discrete, isolated (and largely undocumented) services to one that focuses on prevention, cooperation, and coordination, while being locally driven, results oriented, and grounded in data.

**Table 7.1** Elements of a New Way of Thinking

| From | To |
| --- | --- |
| Crisis intervention | Preventing, recognizing, and developing the capabilities of youth |
| Little attention to documenting the impact of changes | Documentation of changes in results for children, youth, and families |
| Isolated services | Coordinated services for children and families with multiple needs |
| Public assistance | Emphases on workforce, community, and economic development |
| State decisions | State works with communities as equal partners |
| State directives | Emphasis on empowering communities to identify needs and design systems to meet community-specific needs |
| Defined programs | Broad initiatives designed to provide flexibility at local level |
| Activities detached from results | Results-oriented decision making and budgeting |
| Categorized funds | Decategorization and flexibility of state and federal funds |

## B. ENGAGE THE PUBLIC IN TERMS IT CAN UNDERSTAND

*How do you learn what a community needs and then work with it in ways that the typical member of the community can understand? Program design specialists Beverly Parsons and Sharon Brumbaugh share insights from years of working with state and local groups.*

Beverly Parsons

Sharon Brumbaugh

"I was not always a good mother," a poor, single parent of three children (aged 3, 8, and 12) told a roomful of state legislators a few years ago. With impressive self-possession, she described her family's history to a roomful of strangers. "Once, I lost custody of my children. I lost more than custody; I came to understand I had lost a part of my life."

In the face of such experiences, routine professional and bureaucratic language is woefully inadequate. Phrases that flow effortlessly off the tongue at professional meetings—developmentally appropriate curriculum . . . staff development oriented around learning styles . . . multicultural curriculum . . . monitoring and evaluation . . . collaborative planning teams . . . coordinated services—scarcely begin to connect with this human pain.

Fortunately, this young woman got her life back together with the help of a comprehensive array of programs for child care, transportation, drug abuse treatment, and job counseling and referral. One of the most important parts of that effort was made up of strong, clear communications, both within and across agencies and between government agencies and the public. Engaging the public on its own terms—communications as public engagement—is vital to the service reform agenda. It can become a method of involving the public in designing system change.

### *Engage Communities Around Solutions, Not Needs*

Needs analysis is fine as far as it goes, according to consultants Sharon Edwards and Susan Philliber, who created a new community engagement process (CEP) precisely to address the gap between agency language and public needs. But poor children need everything. As superintendent, you may be committed to closing the achievement gap. The vision sounds wonderful. But traditional needs analysis may be insufficient because it simply tells you what should be there, not what is there or whether the clients are attracted to it or able to take advantage of it.

What developed into the CEP began with that simple insight. Working in Savannah, Georgia, where teenage pregnancy was a huge problem, Edwards and Philliber realized that services were available for young people who did not take advantage of them. "So we started sending youngsters in for services and simply asking them what happened and how they reacted to how they were treated," reports Philliber.

They discovered something fascinating. Most of the time, professionals decide what to do based on what they think will work. Community input?

Who needs it? Philliber concluded that communities are distinct. She and Edwards decided that more needs assessments were not required. What was needed were solution assessments.

### Work With Local People

Community mapping is a distinct process, according to these experts. They actually sit around a table with parents and other residents to define problems. Then, these local people help select local data-collection assistants. Philliber and Edwards train the data collectors to go out and directly administer the questionnaire. The questionnaire is not something developed and administered researcher to researcher—it is a neighbor-to-neighbor proposition.

"Dissemination is a critical result of the process," according to Edwards. "Most people distrust data imposed on them or interpreted for them by experts. But here we have data developed and interpreted by neighbors. That makes it very hard for people to say what they often say to researchers, 'That's not true in my experience.'"

"Many professional researchers and analysts would never do what we are doing," said Philliber without apology. "We involve real people. Some of them abuse drugs. Some may have records. Some aren't able to read. We need both men and women on these teams—and we need diverse interviewers in terms of language and age. We don't just want women talking to women or old men sharing war stories with old men."

> The CEP process consists of three phases: (1) Define the community, (2) map it, and (3) disseminate information. (See Section E for a detailed account of the value of this process in St. Martin Parish, Louisiana.)

Philliber and Edwards deploy their teams first thing in the morning and bring them back in to have lunch and collect their interview sheets. They discovered quickly that food is an important part of the process. Meals help break the ice and cheer local leaders on. "Some interviewers bring in the entire family for breakfast with us!" marvels Edwards.

Despite their modest technical backgrounds, interviewers quickly become worried about the quality of their data. As they collect their information and fret about its adequacy, they begin to bond with each other as a team, reports Edwards. Communities vary, and the strategies have to vary. "In some places, the best time to find people at home is in the evenings or on Saturday or Sunday. In others, we find the exact reverse. Whatever we have to do, we do—and what happens is fascinating," Edwards says. What they have put in place in small areas, perhaps a few city blocks square, are 500 conversations about what the community wants for its children. "The interviewers are seen as advocates, and the interviewees become advocates," notes Edwards.

"It is amazing what people will tell you when they trust you," says Philliber, "even in a highly charged area such as teenage sexuality." There is normally a lot of denial about this topic on the part of parents—and parents become much more concerned about this set of issues when their children pass the age of 10. "But people will tell you anything if they understand who wants to know, why you want it, and whether or not you are trustworthy," says Philliber. To put the last point a different way—respondents unconsciously ask themselves, "What will this cost if you betray me?"

"Whatever the topic—early childhood education, school reform, or teenage pregnancy—we have never encountered a community that did not learn something surprising about itself," notes Philliber. "And the interviewing teams become budding leaders in the community. In one of our communities, the team we left behind set itself up in business to do all interviews and polling in the neighborhood."

Sharon Edwards sums it up with a challenge to ask the right questions. "When this process ends, you will have answers to a lot of questions, but more important, you'll have a better set of questions. Most of the questions we are asking today are the wrong questions. We are trying to assess needs, when we should be assessing what the community thinks the solutions ought to be."

In short, engage your local communities in ways that they will understand, ideally through their own neighbors.

## C. THINK ASSETS, NOT DEFICITS

### James Harvey

For many years, educators have understood that it makes much more sense to concentrate on children's strengths than on their weaknesses. Children can be very resilient. If you as superintendent can help the community tap into the children's assets, you will have much more success.

In recent years, emerging research from the Search Institute in Minneapolis, Minnesota, based on data involving 10,000 students from grades 6 to 12 in some 213 communities across the United States, has developed a much better picture of essential assets. The Institute has identified 40 internal and external assets that are important to young people as they face tremendous challenges outside school. Many have to cope with crumbling local social infrastructures, adults who are disengaged from their lives, parents with little or no time for parenting, and an age-segregated society that denies them access to the wisdom and experience of the elderly.

According to this research, the best predictor of a child's success in later life is whether the child comes from a healthy, strong, supportive family. The second-best predictor is bonding with school. Moreover, a combination of assets is much more important than any individual asset.

Most people can draw on close to 20 assets as they grow up. The more assets they have, the better their chances of avoiding destructive behaviors. The entire list of assets was described earlier, in Part V; here, we want to remind you that the 40 assets come in eight distinct categories:

---

**External Assets**

1. *Support* mostly from adults

2. *Empowerment* from the community

3. *Boundaries and expectations* primarily from family and school

4. *Constructive use of time* including community youth programs

**Internal Assets**

5. *Commitment to learning* including school engagement and motivation

6. *Positive values* such as compassion, integrity, and civic concern

7. *Social competencies* involving planning and interpersonal and cultural competence

8. *Positive identity* in the form of self-esteem and sense of purpose

---

SOURCE: The Search Institute, Minneapolis, Minnesota.

---

Work with your community partners to develop these assets, and you will provide a real service to your community. You will find that empowering youth with more assets will reduce the likelihood of their engaging in high-risk behavior involving alcohol, drugs, violence, and sexual activity.

## D. NEED FOR EARLY CARE AND EDUCATION

*Increasingly, K–12 educators are looking at school readiness as a key issue in helping young children meet higher standards. But the worlds of Head Start, preschools, and fee-based day care are strange and unusual territory for most superintendents. In this section, you are introduced to this new world while learning about the long-term economic benefits of investment in the early years.*

### 1. Orientation

James Harvey

In December 1971, President Nixon vetoed an early childhood education bill passed by Congress. The legislation threatened to undermine the

American family, the president claimed in his veto message. In fact, said syndicated columnist James J. Kilpatrick, it might "Sovietize" American children.

Yet, within 15 years, business groups such as the Committee for Economic Development were calling for early childhood programs as an "investment" in the American future. Within 20 years, President George H. W. Bush and the nation's governors had agreed on a national education goal that children should start school "ready to learn." And within 25 years, Congress and President Clinton had cooperated to enact welfare reform leg-

> In September 2012, the School of Education, Health, and Society and the Farmer School of Business at Miami University, Oxford, Ohio, held a TEDX conference on childhood development, early care, and education. Six outstanding presentations from nationally known experts are available at Tedxtalks.ted.com/search/?search=Miami+university.

islation requiring single parents of infants and children to leave the home for work and expanding early childhood programs to ease the parents' transition to work.

Over one generation, in short, attitudes about the need for preschool programs had been completely transformed. This section of the *Fieldbook* explores what we know about brain development in infants and young children, and it describes the value of a unique seven-year effort to expand early care and education programs funded by the Danforth Foundation in the 1990s.

> A popular paragraph making the rounds of the Internet makes the point that the human brain imposes meaning on what it sees. It turns out that the correct spelling of words isn't that important to people's understanding of written text. What's important is placing the first and last letters in the correct place. Then, human perception corrects for spelling errors. Here's the paragraph:
>
> Aoccdrnig to a rscheearch at an Elingsh uinervtisy, it deosn't mttaer in waht oredr the ltteers in a wrod are, the olny iprmoetnt tihng is taht frist and lsat ltteer is at the rghit pclae. The rset can be a toatl mses and you can sitll raed it wouthit a porbelm. Tihs is bcuseae we do not raed ervey lteter by it slef but the wrod as a wlohe.

## 2. Where Learning Begins: The Remarkable Human Brain

*"The world of education really centers on the human brain and curiosity," asserts John Medina, a molecular biologist associated with the University of Washington. New brain research, he believes, has changed our perception of reality, and it can change our perceptions of how we should understand learning (and hence teaching).*

James Harvey

"The brain is a remarkable instrument," enthuses Medina. Its total power is perhaps six volts; many flashlights have more energy. Yet, it sends messages to each toe about 177,000 times a second and oversees a nervous system that could circle the globe 20,000 times over. The word *remarkable* scarcely begins to do it justice. The brain with its six volts is the raw power behind the prodigious development of individuals and society.

Medina likes to point to research on stroke victims and infants. This work is beginning to unlock the brain's secrets. Because some stroke victims can interpret graphics or perhaps vowels, but not text or consonants, it has become clear that different parts of the brain are responsible for perceiving different things. One part of the brain discerns text, another graphics, and still others pick out vowels and consonants. Scientists who have transferred neurons from quails to chicks have created chicks that trill like quails. All of this is work at the frontiers of human knowledge. Research on artificial intelligence, for example, opens up the possibility of creating a silicon chip capable of human thought because human neurons can be located within it.

> Psychologist Abraham Maslow identified five basic needs that he called a *hierarchy of needs*. The most basic needs are physiological, that is, for food, air, and water. Next, people look for safety and security. Once that need is met, human beings desire affiliation and belonging, and they look for supportive relationships. With those fundamental needs taken care of, people's needs become more complicated. First, they seek what Maslow labeled *esteem*, that is, respect, both from others (i.e., recognition) and from themselves (i.e., confidence and competence). They want to feel their contributions are appreciated. The highest need of human beings is self-actualization. All of us want to feel that our contributions are having a significant impact.

Meanwhile, says Medina, "At the cellular level, we're learning how neurons process and use information and how babies learn." At six months, infants know how to categorize sounds; by eight months, they can learn to categorize some sounds that they won't be able to categorize if the sound is presented to them at 12 months. "The brain can rewire itself around language between birth and age five," he notes.

Science, reports Medina, has completely turned our understanding of reality on its head. Aristotle thought large objects fell to the ground faster than smaller ones. And it used to be thought that men had fewer ribs than women. We now know that neither of those things is true. "Critical, abstract thinking was a luxury before the 20th century," says Medina. "It is now an absolute necessity." It is at the top of Abraham Maslow's pyramid of human needs.

We need to worry about Maslow's basic needs for security, food, shelter, and love and attention, says Medina. Curiosity is fragile, yet critical to human development. Curiosity is fragile in your schools as well. As superintendent, you need to nourish it.

*Early Childhood Learning and Neuroscience*

It doesn't require a brain surgeon to figure out that learning and development in the child's earliest years are important. It's an incredible, spongelike age for children, a period when children are curious about everything.

Katherine Bick, an internationally known neurobiologist, echoes Medina. She compares the development of the human brain to something that earlier generations might recall, transforming Heathkits into working radios. "Our parents received this package of parts in the mail, which they assembled," she recalls. "They put the parts together and didn't know if the radio would work until they turned it on." She argues that "a healthy child is primed to learn, and the brain should work when you switch it on." Citing "spectacular" advances in understanding of the brain in recent decades, Bick offers the following insights:

- **We are born with all the brain cells we'll ever have.** The first great wave of cell creation takes place about 6 weeks after conception; the second, about 10 weeks later.

- **Many more cells are created than survive.** In a critical process known as *pruning* (which we might also think of as cell learning), each of 3 billion brain cells makes an average of 15,000 connections with other brain cells, nerve endings, or muscles. Nature expects brain cells that don't make connections to die—and they do.

- **Remarkably, half of this pruning is already complete by birth.** It proceeds rapidly through age 3; reaches maturity around adolescence; and continues, to some extent, throughout life.

In the past 15 years, we have identified through positron emissions topography (PET) scans involving radioactive material the centers of the brain that govern hearing, seeing, speaking, generating language, and intentional behavior.

Likewise, magnetic resonance imaging (MRI) has helped us understand the brain changes involved with learning mathematics and reading in 4-, 6-, and 10-year-olds as well as the brain centers that govern language, memory, and control of impulsivity in children aged 6 to 10.

Studies indicate, reports Bick, that in solving maze problems over four trials, many parts of the brain are used in the first trial, indicating that the brain is trying to use a lot of different problem-solving strategies. By the fourth trial,

> The significance of emerging neuroscience for education extends well beyond preschool learning. See also Part IV of this *Fieldbook* for a discussion of how new developments in neurobiology have extended our understanding of the neural mechanisms governing attention, emotion, working memory, and motivation, all important elements in the teaching and learning equation.

however, much less of the brain is involved as "improvements in learning efficiency let us become more efficient in using our brains."

What does all of this have to do with educational policy? Everything. We need to pay attention to the ready phases for learning: the periods of greatest learning efficiency, by subject, in babies and children. Babies and children are learning machines. "They learn effortlessly when they're ready," reports Bick. Among the ready phases are the following:

- **Babies can recognize new and old scenes at 4 months old.** They can understand something about numeracy at 10 months, and, everywhere in the world, they appear to start picking up language by 18 months.

- **Children are primed for easy second-language development between the ages of 3 and 5.** Every child born in the world is capable of learning every spoken language. If you're wondering why you're having trouble with those Chinese vowels, it's because you passed up the chance to pick them up effortlessly in childhood.

- **Although neural wiring is fairly complete by age 5, wiring of the prefrontal lobe (the executive function that governs intentionality, planning, and understanding consequences) is not complete until preadolescence.** "If you've ever wondered why your young teenager doesn't worry about tomorrow, that's why," smiles Bick.

- **About 80 percent of preschool children are phonologically aware.** They can recognize phonemes (letters and sounds); about 20 percent can't recognize them and will experience difficulty learning to read—and some of them may never read.

- **Look–say systems of teaching reading rely on brute-force memory and are probably a pretty inefficient and tiring way for most children to learn.** The phoneme approach, on the other hand, is probably pretty efficient. Different interventions are required for different students.

- **Preschool children who have difficulty with rhyming games are likely to have trouble with phonemes later in school and may experience reading difficulty.**

- **Having trouble with music as a child?** You may also experience problems with mathematics later on.

The solutions to early learning challenges, stresses Bick, don't lie in Washington, DC, or state capitals. They lie in local communities and day-care centers and schools. And the solutions aren't high tech. They're much simpler than that. They start with good prenatal care. They continue through high-quality child care. And they require paying attention to individual differences in the early school years. Above all, they involve being "loved, cuddled, played with, and read to." In short, they involve the first four foundations of Maslow's hierarchy.

## 3. The Need for and Value of Early Learning Programs

*If the United States is to meet the promise it makes to every child—that he or she will have a chance to prosper—a powerful preschool experience, either in the home or elsewhere, is absolutely essential, according to Steven Barnett from the Center for Policy Studies at Rutgers University. It's really that simple. In addition, early learning programs provide big-time returns down the line, says Barnett, an expert on the economic benefits of early care and education.*

### James Harvey

Drawing on findings from a number of different studies, Barnett presents data demonstrating startling advantages available to children born to professional and upper-income families in the first 36 months of life (see Table 7.2). At the simplest level of verbal stimulation, a child from a professional family receives twice as much verbal attention as a child from a working-class family. The child from an upper-income home receives four times as much verbal attention as a child in a family on public assistance. Upper-income children also obtain a huge head start over their working-class and public-assistance contemporaries in vocabulary, the basic building block of language and learning. Moreover, says Barnett, "Upper-income children receive many more incidents of encouragement than discouragement within their homes, whereas, for children in welfare families, the reverse is true."

In short, by the age of 3, the child of affluence has mastered a sophisticated and complex vocabulary and has been led to believe that great things lie ahead. The child of poverty, on the other hand, has mastered barely enough words to get by, accompanied by the implicit message that the future is bleak.

Table 7.2   Data on Children's Experiences Through 36 Months

| Indicator at 36 Months | Child From Professional Family | Child From Working-Class Family | Child From Welfare Family |
|---|---|---|---|
| Cumulative Words Addressed to Child | 35,000,000 | 20,000,000 | 10,000,000 |
| Child's Cumulative Vocabulary | 1,100 | 750 | 500 |
| Incidents in Which Adult Encourages Child | 500,000 | 200,000 | 100,000 |
| Incidents in Which Adult Discourages Child | 80,000 | 100,000 | 200,000 |

SOURCE: Hart, B., & Risley, T. R. (1995). *Meaningful Differences in the Everyday Experiences of Young American Children.* Baltimore, MD: Brookes.

From a policy standpoint, the issue is this: Can early childhood education do anything about these disparities? They are apparent, after all, long before the child appears in your classrooms, indeed long before many parents have any idea their child has already fallen behind. Barnett's answer is an unqualified yes. The short-term effects of early childhood education programs are well established, he says. Moreover, "we now have literally dozens of studies demonstrating significant benefits that last through school and are sustained over time in terms of student achievement."

### The Benefits of Early Care and Education

Perhaps the most influential example of these analyses revolved around the famous Perry Preschool Program, funded in Michigan in the 1960s. The study compared 123 African-American children, with 58 randomly assigned to a preschool program and 65 who did not participate. An evaluation of Head Start completed in 1969 by the Westinghouse Learning Corporation and Ohio University shocked advocates of early childhood programs. It concluded that Head Start summer programs were found to have no lasting impact; although full-year programs resulted in cognitive and language gains at the first grade level, they appeared to fade out by second or third grade.

Detailed reports on research conducted on the Perry Preschool Program by the HiScope Foundation can be found at http://www.highscope.org.

The dismaying results, although attacked almost immediately for serious methodological shortcomings, became a rallying cry for opponents of preschool programs and were a serious blow to funding of early childhood education for years.

The Perry Preschool analysis changed all of that. It followed the 123 participants not for three or four years but over four decades. It revealed stunning long-term economic returns on investments in high-quality preschool programs. When these participants, who entered the program at age 3 or 4, were examined at the ages of 27 (and then again at age 40), the results were little less than extraordinary.

Table 7.3 presents the findings at age 40 for those who participated in the program and those who did not. Participants earned more money; they were more likely to have graduated from high school, to be employed, and to own their own homes. They were much less likely to be on public assistance, to use drugs, or to become involved with the juvenile justice or the adult correctional systems. They were also much more likely to own their own car, and to own a savings account. In short, in just about every area where families, society, and policy makers would hope to find positive results, they found positive results. And in just about every area where negative results should be avoided, program participants tended to avoid them.

Analysts have applied this methodology to justify statewide early education programs in New Jersey, Pennsylvania, Ohio, and other states.

Table 7.3    Benefits of Participating in the Perry Preschool Program at Age 40

| Indicator | Program | No Program |
|---|---|---|
| Completed Regular High School | 65% | 45% |
| Employed at Age 40 | 76% | 62% |
| Median Earnings | $20,800 | $15,300 |
| Owned Own Home | 37% | 28% |
| Owned Own Car | 82% | 60% |
| Had Savings Account | 76% | 50% |
| Required Social Services | 71% | 86% |
| Arrested Five or More Times | 36% | 55% |
| Arrested for Violent Crimes | 32% | 48% |
| Arrested for Property Crimes | 36% | 58% |
| Arrested for Drug Crimes | 14% | 34% |
| Males Raising Own Children | 57% | 30% |
| Getting Along Well With Family | 75% | 64% |
| Require Sedatives or Tranquilizers | 17% | 43% |
| Use Marijuana | 48% | 71% |
| Use Heroin | 0% | 9% |

The analysis above is a cost-effectiveness analysis. It evaluated the outcomes over time in terms of educational and social results. But the Perry analysts went beyond cost-effectiveness to add a cost-benefit discussion to the conversation. They emerged with a remarkable figure. They estimated that, for every dollar invested in a preschool effort such as the Perry program, society received an economic return of $17.01 over 40 years. Investing $15,166 per participant returned $258,888 to society per participant, in constant dollars (see Figure 7.1). The return is in the form of reductions on expenditures for education, public assistance, and the criminal justice system and net additions to state and local revenues in the form of higher taxes on participants' earnings. Fully 93 percent of the public return is attributable to more positive outcomes for male participants, due largely to their decreased involvement with the criminal justice system.

Similar analyses in New Jersey, Ohio, Pennsylvania, and other states also indicate promising returns on public investments in preschool programs. In Ohio, for example, it is estimated that expanding preschool

**Figure 7.1**    Every Dollar Invested in the Perry Preschool Program 40 Years Ago Has
Returned More than $17 to Society and the Individuals Involved

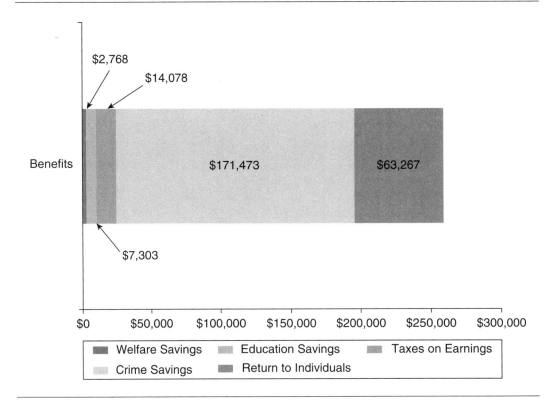

programs would have saved school systems in the state $242 million while
reaping $140 million in tax revenues and ringing up savings of $25 million
in health and public assistance expenditures and $375 million in the crim-
inal justice system.

The Pennsylvania analysis focused solely on school savings. It concluded
that public agencies would get back at least $1.16 for every dollar invested in
preschool programs, with districts recouping more than 75 percent of the
costs almost immediately in reduced expenses for Title I, special education,
school safety, and instructional costs. While the Ohio research looked at
returns in schools and in communities, the Pennsylvania study restricted
itself to potential cost savings in schools. Applying the analysis to eight typical school districts in the state, the report estimates the following results:

- The districts almost immediately recoup 78 cents of every dollar
  invested in preschool programs through savings in special education, compensatory education, school safety costs, and instruction.
- The lowest return, in Dauphin County's Susquehanna Township,
  was 67 cents on the dollar; the highest, in Bucks County's Bristol
  Township, was $1.16 on the dollar.

- Small districts such as Bristol Township, which spend a lot of money on special education, harvested the biggest returns on preschool programs.
- In addition to school returns, surrounding counties benefit from higher tax revenues and reduced expenditures on welfare and the criminal justice system, savings not reflected in the eight-district analysis.

# E. ENGAGING COMMUNITY IN ST. MARTIN PARISH

*Here is a story describing a method for tackling community problems that has worked numerous times in practice. School leaders can use it to help develop an entire community's ability to learn. Parents survey each other, but this is not your typical community survey; it brings people together to learn together. This technique helped St. Martin Parish and its former superintendent, Roland Chevalier, address a pernicious problem with early childhood reading, but it also gave the people of the parish a sense of identity they never had before, with a raft of significant effects.*

## Roland Chevalier

Early on, we identified a serious problem in our district: In some elementary schools, 30 percent of the students were being held back a year. That atrocious record was the good news. The bad news was that many parents, teachers, and principals thought we were doing the right thing, especially for our slow learners in reading, by giving them an extra shot of second- or third-grade medicine. They didn't know that, when children are retained in the early grades even once, their chances of graduating from high school are cut in half. Retain them twice, and you might as well write them off right there; almost none of those students graduate, either in our district or anywhere. By holding back the late developers at the end of second grade, you send the message, "We don't think you can do it," and you disconnect them from their age-group.

> Adapted with permission from Senge et al. (2012). *Schools that learn.* New York: Doubleday.

*Phase I: Defining the Community and Assembling the Core Group*

The first step was to find volunteers from the community in the areas that most needed help. We listed all the kids who had been retained, from grades K through 8, found their home addresses, and stuck pins in a map accordingly. Wherever the pins clustered, we looked

> Step 1: Preliminary meetings are held to define precisely what is meant by *community* and to design a strategy for interviewing individuals most easily.

for key volunteers—people who would join our core group and make long-term commitments to us. Fortunately, I grew up here and knew some parts of the parish very well.

We started with a core committee of six volunteers, all key stakeholders who had credibility and knew the community's needs. It was vital to make sure that not all of them were from the school district administration. Some, like the local director of Head Start and a private day-care center owner, had been traditionally seen as our rivals. (In fact, the Head Start director knew much of the parish I didn't know; his involvement was key to starting off on the right track.) We also had the personnel director from our biggest local employer, someone from social services in Child Protection, some principals of primary schools, and someone from the sheriff's office. This group became our advisory council, and they organized the process.

> Step 2: A discussion is held with a committee of community residents to determine the nature and content of the survey instrument and how best to recruit interviewers.

We needed the community to bare its soul and talk about its needs—which meant talking about shortcomings and weaknesses. That's why it was so critical for community people, not school officials or outside consultants, to create our survey. We brought together about 40 people from every segment of the population, all invited by word of mouth, for a one-day session to create a questionnaire. We included business leaders, elected officials, and people in the sheriff's department.

> Step 3: The researcher or evaluator drafts the survey instrument from committee responses.

We brought them together in a room for several hours and asked, "What do you want to know from the community?" Consultants facilitated the meeting and then took the questions and refined them. They brought the refined questions back to us so the group of 40 could approve the final draft.

> Step 4: The community group reviews the questionnaire and makes recommendations for the final version.

The result was several pages of questions about the things people cared about in their community and in their schools. What kinds of support did they need for their children? What did they think about homework? What did they want for their children's futures? What were they afraid might happen to their kids? What were they afraid their kids would do? We didn't restrict the content to education; we included a page of their questions about safety at home and on the streets, written by the sheriff's department. This ultimately led to a lot of innovations in community policing, including the placement of school resource deputies in our three high schools. Even before we got any answers, the questions themselves were eye-openers for me and other community leaders; we would not have thought to ask many of them.

> Step 5: The community group recruits interviewers and introduces them to the objectives and purposes of the CEP.

### Phase II: Community Mapping

The question design group then suggested another 50 or so people as foot soldiers—to be trained in the interview process and go door-to-door, like the Census Bureau. They would interview their neighbors or conduct coffee get-togethers in their houses. We avoided using teachers or students for this. If a teacher holds the key to your child's future, you will say what you think he or she wants to hear. You're more apt to tell a neighbor how you really feel. Some of our parent-to-parent interviewers had never graduated from high school. Many of them weren't very confident at first until we trained them: "This is how you introduce yourself," and so on. The sheriff, who was getting more and more involved, provided food for the training session.

> Step 6: The researcher/evaluator trains the interviewers and supervises the survey work.

Finally, we conducted a companion survey, with questions on the same themes, for the teachers and administrators. This brought us into dangerous territory. It turned out that teachers and parents disagreed on several key issues. Parents, for example, had much higher expectations for their children than their teachers did. Many teachers believed that parents didn't care much about schools or didn't want to get involved. But 98 to 99 percent of the parents wanted to be involved. They felt shut out.

One question asked: "Do you believe all children can learn?" Most of the parents said yes. Sixty-two teachers said no. That was eye-opening for me; I wouldn't want my own child in the class of a teacher who doesn't believe all kids can learn. That raised some issues in terms of staff development needs for our faculty. The damning part was that parents correctly understood the teachers' attitudes; they knew that the teachers did not expect their children to graduate. In all of our planning sessions, we had never considered this.

Our consultants analyzed the data for us and wrote up a report. We were supposed to hold a focus group for the foot soldiers, and we made it part of a celebration. Once again, the sheriff provided food. We gave them copies of the report because it was their report. We

> Step 7: At the completion of the surveying, a focus group is held with the interviewing team to discuss what they heard.

had awards for the youngest interviewer, the oldest interviewer—a lady in her 70s—and the person with the most interviews. And we talked about what we had found and what we might do about it.

*Phase III: Engaging the Community*

One of the biggest complaints was a lack of quality child care at 5:00 a.m. for people who work factory shifts. People on late shifts had no one to help their kids with homework. Hearing about this, people volunteered solutions. One guy, who was retired, started a homework club in one of the low-income housing projects. All the kids ended up in a common room in the building after school, with older kids helping younger kids, and parents, on a rotating basis, supervising. The school had nothing to do with organizing it; the child care professionals had never imagined it. All of that came out of the residents' sense of efficacy: They could do something significant and make a difference.

> Step 8: The researcher or evaluator prepares a computer database from the questionnaires and develops a report for the community, drawing from the questionnaires and the interviewers' perceptions.
>
> Step 9: The researcher or evaluator reconvenes the group to review the data and report.

> Step 10: The community team plans the dissemination process and the strategies for engaging all stakeholders in dialogue.

The interaction with the community expanded our focus and direction. It made us really take a hard look at what the community expected of us; our task was much more complex than we had realized. We expanded our health services for children to include three school-based health clinics, serving 16 of our 17 schools. We addressed the issue of teenage pregnancy, with a facility where students could have a child, finish their education, find day care, learn parenting and nursing skills, and eventually pay back the costs by working at the center themselves.

Other benefits of community engagement went far beyond our original intent. A group of people living in low-income housing, trained in our method, contracted to conduct surveys for other towns and corporations in the area. They started a tutoring program. We had offered tutoring at school; nobody came. This project was so successful that it needed help from our teachers. Catholic and Baptist ministers who had never been in the same room with each other began to meet with us around monthly lunches. The sheriff's office and mine looked into joint programs and collaborated to build a gymnasium and classrooms in a detention facility. Benefits emerged that we had never expected.

*Making It Work in Your Community*

Can this work in your community? Of course it can. It worked in ours. It was difficult for me at first because I had to learn to listen and not speak. I had to learn to be open to suggestions and prepared for criticism because the community might not necessarily think that my answer was the right answer. And I had to realize that I could not be the one to do everything.

As with the day-care center, which has been successfully managed by Head Start, sometimes I had to learn to support projects that other people were running.

Give it a try. You have nothing to lose. And if you're lucky, you'll hear what I heard from the local personnel director at one of our local plants. At one of the community engagement meetings, she said, "You know, I like these meetings. This is the first group I've worked with that actually gets something done." How often do you hear that in your office!

## F. TOOLS

### 1. First Steps: Getting Started

Luvern L. Cunningham

Getting started can be intimidating. Here are some ideas to keep in mind.

- **Keep it local.** Although the problem is conceptually the same everywhere, whether the district is urban, rural, or suburban, the strategic response probably differs district by district.
- **It's more about mind-set than policy.** New district policies may be required but perhaps not. Policies and legalities intimidate people. The real problem is one of changing views, attitudes, and mind-sets and developing commitment.
- **Bring the board along.** Your board needs to back you. It doesn't need detailed involvement, but you need to brief it, put experts before the board, and draw on the board as a resource and ally when needed. The board also needs to make a commitment to you if you are to succeed.
- **Build on local talent.** Outside experts are nice, but the homegrown variety is always better. Draw on local expertise from Head Start programs, children's hospitals, social service agencies, and universities.
- **Reach beyond the usual suspects.** To get started, make your first calls to local power brokers—business leaders, editorial boards, and professional or business leaders. If you can bring them on board, getting the backing of others within the system will be easier.

### 2. Parental Involvement

Ethel Seiderman

Parents, families, and schools have to work and play together. Here are seven key principles for parental involvement.

1. **Parents are the most important persons to the child.** To ensure the health and well-being of children, assure the well-being of their parents.

2. **Parents are your partners.** Parents are partners in the work on behalf of the child. The relationship with them is predicated on equality and respect. The first priority is to establish and nurture this relationship as a support network that is mutually beneficial to all.

3. **Parents are their own best advocates.** They are decision makers on a collaborative team. Programs should be nonprescriptive so that parents can make their own choices about what services they want.

4. **Parents are assets.** Parents aren't your problem. They're not barriers to be worked around or overcome. They are assets to you. Programs should build on parents' strengths by promoting their excellence and fostering their belief in themselves.

5. **Make programs relevant and community based.** Programs should be grounded in the community and relevant to the ethnic groups in the community. Each community should define its own reality, according to what its members agree is good for them.

6. **Voluntary is good.** Programs and services should be voluntary. Compelling participation accomplishes little. Parents, students, and community members seeking services should be understood as a sign of strength.

7. **Make it fun, not drudgery.** Self-esteem, joy, hopefulness, confidence, and optimism are important elements of strong families. Social support networks are a crucial element in the happiness, health, and productivity of people.

### 3. Parents and Steps to Success for Children

Lynn Beckwith, Jr.

Parental involvement was a hallmark of early learning programs in University City, Missouri. During my time as superintendent, the following 10 steps to success for children were developed by parents for parents and disseminated via refrigerator magnets. They became a sort of child-rearing bible for the parents in our community; they can serve the same role in yours, too.

| TEN STEPS TO PARENTING SUCCESS |
| --- |
| 1. Time. |
| 2. Communication. |
| 3. Reading. |
| 4. Taking your children places. |

5. Plan time for study in a structured environment.

6. Play games with your children.

7. Do not compare or label your children.

8. Set standards for your children's academic success.

9. Seek out support, and expect to get it!

10. Become involved with your children's ongoing learning processes as they prepare for standardized tests.

## 4. Key Elements of Collaboration

Beverly Parsons

Sharon Brumbaugh

Several elements seem to be required to make collaboration work. Here's an action checklist:

*A Checklist of Key Elements*

- **Start with numbers.** You need to build data into your plans to monitor the condition of children and families, and you need to tie data to specific benchmarks of achievement.
- **Think systems, not programs.** Build boats, not houses.
- **Adopt collaboration as a way of life.** Collaboration implies shared budgets, joint accountability, integrated professional development activities, and the creation of new vertical and horizontal relations with other government agencies.
- **Engage the public on its own terms.** Don't give gobbledygook to the public. Develop strong, clear, two-way communications strategies.
- **Develop capacity.** Horizontal linkages with your agency peers are one thing. Vertical linkages up and down your different agencies are something else again, and much harder.
- **Create a critical mass of people who care.** You have to find the right people and invest in them. When you move on, you want this new way of thinking to survive.
- **Beg, borrow, and steal effective ideas.** Everything in public life is in the public domain. You're free to steal it. Do so shamelessly if you see something working.
- **Follow the money.** Talk about system reform is cheap and easy. Make sure that real budget resources are put behind the rhetoric.
- **Insist on results.** This is tough work. If you're going to get into it, you have to be serious. Insist on results, assess progress, and report to the public.

- **Give ownership away.** There's truth to the axiom that, if we don't care who gets the credit, there's no limit to what we can accomplish. Give the credit away, and it will all come back to you.
- **Model the behavior you seek.** You can't expect your people to cooperate with other agencies if you refuse to give the time of day to your peers in local government.
- **Be a practical visionary.** Visionaries have to be practical, too. You have to have your feet on the ground. Develop an effective plan that provides some demonstrable results in a year or two.

---

SOURCE: The Danforth Foundation. (1999). *The Policymakers Program: The First Five Years.* St. Louis, MO: Author.

### 5. Identify Core Community Values

Beverly Parsons

Sharon Brumbaugh

Some localities have found it useful to identify core community values as part of community revitalization work. Here's a 10-part process developed by Seattle consultant Sherry Wong.

| | |
|---|---|
| 1. Identify Stakeholders | Who should participate? List should include formal organizations (e.g., schools, religious groups, businesses) and a diverse group of local residents. |
| 2. Determine Process | How will stakeholder advice be sought? Determine the process for soliciting input on core values, including guidelines for facilitating discussions. |
| 3. Establish Timeline | Process without a schedule is counterproductive and potentially endless. Create a timeline for soliciting stakeholder comments. |
| 4. Locate Responsibility | Who will compile the results? Identify the individual or group responsible for compiling the results. |
| 5. Agree on Process | Who will define the final list and how? Decide on how the final list of core values will be selected (by whom, using which process, and how many core values), and select the final list. |
| 6. Communications Plan | How will the list be communicated to the community? Develop a communications plan to introduce core values into all areas of the community using key stakeholders to carry the message. |
| 7. Encourage Use | Encourage all stakeholders (schools, families, churches, coaches, businesses) to use core values to develop and communicate clear expectations about behavior as well as consistent and appropriate consequences for meeting (or not meeting) expectations. |

| 8. Provide Assistance | Help parents, teachers, coaches, service providers, and others apply behavioral standards through training and support. |
| 9. Identify Barriers | What stands in the way of meeting the values standards? Are things such as neighborhood transience or parental substance abuse blocking progress? Develop and implement plans to overcome barriers. |
| 10. Celebrate Success | Actively seek out and celebrate examples of youth and adults living the standards in all areas of community life. |

SOURCE: The Danforth Foundation. (2002). *Strong Families in Healthy Communities.* St. Louis, MO: Author.

## G. REFLECTIVE PRACTICE

Collaboration—making sure that essential services are delivered effectively and on time—may be a key to your success. Here are some questions you should be exploring.

*Have troubling incidents* of child or spousal abuse received prominent attention in your community? Have you tried to start a conversation about how this relates to school performance?

*Are you routinely involved with local leaders* in thinking through community challenges? Are you a member of Kiwanis or the local chamber of commerce, for example? Could you put issues of collaboration on the table here?

*What kind of data do you have* about patterns of social problems within your district's boundaries? Incidence of substance abuse? Involvement with the criminal or juvenile justice systems? Rates of family poverty? Proportion of adults who have dropped out of high school? What do these imply for your educational mission?

*Who, in your community or state,* is potentially a natural ally on the question of improving service delivery for families and children? Who's going to oppose you? How can you support the former and neutralize the latter?

*Are your elementary principals and teachers* satisfied that the children arriving at their schools are ready to learn? If not, what steps have you taken?

*Can you document early care and learning opportunities* in your community? How many children are enrolled in Head Start–like programs? In proprietary day-care centers? How many are served in home day-care settings? Are day-care providers well credentialed? Can you quantify the number of families seeking day-care or preschool programs who cannot find them?

*Has anyone in your community or state quantified* how an investment in early care and education might return dividends down the line?

*Where is your board* on the question of early learning opportunities? Intrigued? Uninterested? Willing to leave it up to you?

*If you wanted to get started,* who are the first people you would call together to begin the discussion? What's stopping you?

# PART VIII

# *Engaging Your Community*

I t's not clear that there ever really were any "good old days" in American schools, but one of the things that many remember with nostalgia was a sense that school leaders defined the schools' agenda. Those days are over. Today, the public expects to be involved in determining the future of its schools. As superintendent, you need to understand that and learn how to engage your diverse publics.

Rapid national and global change . . . greater racial and ethnic diversity . . . terrorism and the threat of more terrorism . . . violence and rampant abuse of powerful drugs . . . traditional families coming apart at the seams—how are schools to cope? And how, amid demands for better performance, can you as superintendent build and sustain community support for important educational work?

Those two questions frame the concept of public engagement.

The central idea behind public engagement is not public relations but getting the public to own its own schools. You may be tempted to think of the schools as yours. They're not. In the final analysis, they belong to the public. If local citizens don't feel that deep in their bones, you will not be able to count on public support when you need it. It's important, therefore, that you get your local community thoroughly engaged, connected, and deeply committed to its schools.

Here, you will find the people and other resources that can help support this effort. Daniel Yankelovich's work with the Public Agenda Foundation provides a broad framework for understanding the concept of public engagement. Kathleen Hall Jamieson of the Annenberg School for Communication, University of Pennsylvania, teaches you how to negotiate and survive the world of mass media. Will Friedman and Jean Johnson of the Public Agenda Foundation give you a way to think about and do public engagement.

# A. PUBLIC ENGAGEMENT

*Public engagement is really a two-way deal between you and your local community. It's basically a conversation in which the agreement is this: I will listen respectfully to what you have to say as long as you hear me out. Public engagement involves seven distinct stages, and you can use it most effectively if you take advantage of several tools and guidelines outlined in this section.*

### 1. From Public Relations to Public Engagement

*Your challenge in public engagement involves a significant change in mind-set. Experienced urban school administrators Bertha Pendleton and Richard Benjamin remind us that public engagement is not public relations. Ignoring that distinction could cost you community support.*

Bertha Pendleton

Richard Benjamin

True public engagement requires developing strategies that involve all sectors of a community in ongoing deliberations that build common ground for effective solutions. In your district, it will require developing collaboration to sustain the serious work of school reform.

Public engagement is a shift in culture from authoritarian directives to greater self-governance. (We know you don't have to make that shift! But the people reading over your shoulder might.) It is also a shift in perspective from seeing the children solely in schools to seeing them as part of a community committed to the proposition that educating the young is important.

You will find that effective public engagement grows out of several questions: "What do we want for our children? How can we collaborate to help them achieve as students and as citizens? How do we increase student learning and raise student achievement for all the district's children? What do we have to do to sustain American democracy?"

These are not easy questions. If we're honest, most of us will admit we weren't trained to deal with them. In today's environment, however, you and your staff must cope with them. Because the simple truth is that we, as educators, no longer enjoy the luxury of doing things without the public's permission. You and your staff need to develop the skills required to gather and present information about these questions and to listen thoughtfully to what the public has to say.

*Building Capacity and Sustainability*

We understand. Your time is precious. In the face of other priorities, why spend any of it on public engagement? The short answer is that it might help you see around corners. Public engagement won't turn you into a superhero. Yet, it may alert you to changes in the force fields around schools that will permit you to anticipate and respond before you are blindsided by something you didn't expect. So, for you personally and professionally, public engagement has a lot to offer.

The longer answer is equally important. Public engagement is an investment in your district and community. It will provide you and your citizens with huge benefits over the long haul. Despite the behavior of some people, when members of the public ask you to jump, they don't necessarily expect you to say, "How high?" They don't always insist that you do what they ask you to do. What they do expect is that you'll listen to their concerns. Sometimes, that's all they want, a sense that they've been heard. Listening to what people have to say—and helping your citizens have a meaningful conversation about the children of their community—builds local capacity to support and sustain viable schools over time.

You'll find another benefit, too. Properly conducted, public engagement can shield schools from the whims of the market and the shallowness and rancor of much political discourse. You'll be surprised at who will come to your defense once they understand what you're trying to do.

## 2. Listening to Your Public

### James Harvey

The first thing you need to understand about public engagement is that we are living in difficult times, according to internationally known pollster Daniel Yankelovich.

The public is anxious, and educators have to pay attention to that anxiety. This is a period of American life that is "strange, frustrating, and anxious," says Yankelovich. The frustration has been building for years. "Most Americans are deeply troubled. They feel something is wrong, but they don't know what it is." The breadth of the public's discomfort with the rapid rate of change is not restricted to education. "There is a serious decline in levels of confidence in all walks of life," he notes, citing a decline in public confidence in medicine from 70 to 22 percent in the last generation. Large proportions of Americans consider government to

> Interesting insights into public engagement and schools are available in Johnson, J. (2012). *You can't do it alone: A communications and engagement manual for school leaders committed to reform.* New York: Rowman and Littlefield.

be incompetent, he reports, and many more people think American education is getting worse than believe it is getting better.

### *How Americans See the Country Today*

Why has the general public been in such a foul mood in recent years? One reason is that, although news accounts and business leaders hailed the recovery following the 2008 economic collapse, the recovery has been very weak, even for investors. It was nonexistent for the workforce the economy was supposed to support.

According to figures from *Business Insider,* broad measures of joblessness remain at 40-year highs. Manufacturing employment has collapsed since 1980. The number of people completely outside the labor force has exploded. Civilian participation in the workforce has declined. Unemployment among African Americans is sky-high. Progress for women has flatlined. One-fourth of young Americans remain unemployed. The disadvantaged and the ignored—women, young Americans, African Americans, and other minorities—bear the brunt of the economic pain. Still, all is not entirely lost. While government has shed some jobs, public employment is not nearly the disaster of the private sector. And health care jobs continue to grow.

In these difficult circumstances, voters have turned on government and on public service with a fury. From the East Coast to the West and from the North to the South, governors and state legislators have pushed legislative agendas to curtail collective bargaining, impose caps on public servants' salaries, and reduce school funding. A sort of perfect storm has swept over school districts nationwide, washing away recent gains.

Jean Johnson, executive vice president of the Public Agenda Foundation, defines 10 big issues dominating American thought in the second decade of the 21st century, according to opinion polls.

The first thing to understand is that Americans fear the country is moving in the wrong direction, reports Johnson. Tracking polls indicate that the public's sense that the country is moving in the wrong direction shot up to 70 percent after the 2008 collapse of the economy.

Next, says Johnson, Americans feel cynical about government. The poll data is disheartening: 70 percent of Americans feel that people like themselves have little influence on government, 66 percent feel government policies mainly benefit the rich, and 80 percent believe most members of Congress serve interest groups rather than the public.

Third, very few institutions or leaders enjoy the public trust. When asked how they perceive people running various organizations, a majority of the public reports that it has a great deal of confidence in only two institutions—the military (59 percent) and small business (50 percent). Leaders of no other organizations find majority support. Just 35 percent of Americans have "a great deal of confidence" in the leaders of higher education.

Other sectors are even more dismal: medicine (34 percent), the U.S. Supreme Court (31 percent), the White House (27 percent), organized religion (26 percent), major companies (15 percent), organized labor (14 percent), the press and law firms (13 percent), and Congress and Wall Street (8 percent). Public school leaders (with 22 percent of the people reporting "a great deal of confidence") are hardly in a strong position, but their support far exceeds that of the press, the legal profession, Congress, or Wall Street.

In light of the hyper-partisanship of recent years, it is perhaps little surprise that people believe government is broken. However, most believe it can be fixed. While most people also think individuals should do more, the public is genuinely angry at the behavior of banks and financiers, especially around mortgages.

The fifth issue is also unsurprising to anyone who has followed the news for the last decade: Americans are badly divided about the role of government. About half of Americans want government to do more; about half want it to do less.

Next, concern about the economy and jobs dwarfs everything else. While Washington was consumed in the summer of 2011 with the national debt, only 7 percent of respondents thought that was the most important problem facing the country. Concerns about the economy and jobs preoccupied 53 percent of Americans.

Economic fears are personal. Americans' fears are not about headlines, policy, or public debt. Their economic fears are deeply personal as 60 percent of Americans worry about issues such as jobs, health care, and retirement income. Nearly half fret about mortgage payments, financing a child's education, or the possibility of a major wage earner losing a job. For younger Americans, college debt is a brand new anxiety, Johnson reports.

Next, most Americans are searching for ways to regain economic security. They are searching in many different ways. Majorities want higher education made more affordable (63 percent), Social Security and Medicare preserved (58 percent), and expanded job-training programs (54 percent). Nearly half (48 percent) support tax cuts for the middle class.

That the rules have changed is lesson number nine from the polls, says Johnson. This is mostly apparent around perceptions of the need for a college education. Two-thirds of Americans in 2000 believed there were many ways to succeed without a college degree, but today, just 43 percent share that perception.

Finally, Americans are anguished about the culture. The issue, says Johnson, involves the moral rudder of society. Only 17 percent of Americans believe the "overall state of moral values" is good or excellent. Fully 82 percent report it is only fair or poor. More than seven out of ten believe values are getting worse, three-quarters believe people are not as honest as they used to be, and almost eight in ten feel that people's "sense of right and wrong" is not as strong as it used to be.

"Government . . . the economy . . . anguish about the moral culture—those are the big issues," according to Johnson. "There is a craving for leaders who are genuinely willing to listen. The people want problems solved. And they are skeptical about one-way communication from the top."

### 3. A Seven-Stage Model of Engagement

#### Will Friedman

Daniel Yankelovich's seven-stage model provides a powerful tool for you as superintendent. With this tool, you can begin to understand how the citizens in your community behave around public issues. Once you understand these seven stages, you will be in a better position to track how raw, unstable opinion evolves toward stable and responsible public judgment. Ideally, public judgment will mean that your community has deliberated on an issue sufficiently to produce a working consensus that will allow you to move forward.

Take the issue of women in the workplace. At one time, the fact that women pursued careers outside of professions like teaching and nursing was a highly controversial matter. While prejudices remain, the basic idea that a woman has the right to pursue virtually any career she wants is now broadly accepted. Or take school segregation. Within living memory of many is an era when it was inconceivable to white Southerners that their children would attend schools with African Americans. No responsible person takes such views seriously anymore. On issues such as these and others, what had been widely accepted public judgments have been completely transformed.

As a community leader, you cannot make the mistake of thinking you know what your local community thinks about controversial matters. Whether you are conservative, moderate, or liberal in your views, you should not assume that everyone agrees with you. If you are ready to storm the barricades to advance new social, ethical, or environmental views, you should not be surprised to find that some members of your community will object. The point is you need a better understanding of where your community is.

In school reform, the public is wrestling with many important questions. What is the proper role of standardized tests in helping students succeed? Should schools place a greater emphasis on moral education? If so, how? How can we keep our schools safe? Understanding where your community stands on these issues often depends on where it is with regard to Yankelovich's seven stages of public judgment (see box).

---

### SEVEN STAGES OF COMING TO PUBLIC JUDGMENT

#### Consciousness-Raising Stages

1. Awareness
2. Urgency

**Working-Through Stages**

3. Looking for Answers

4. Resistance

5. Choicework

**Integration Stages**

6. Initial, Intellectual Acceptance

7. Moral Commitment

*Awareness and Urgency: The Consciousness-Raising Stages*

The journey toward public judgment begins with a dawning awareness that something is at issue, often as the result of media coverage or the efforts of advocacy groups. But simple awareness isn't enough to drive the hard work of forming public judgment. There must be a sense of urgency that sets it apart from the many issues clamoring for attention. Realistically, your public has room for only a handful of issues at any one time. If your parents are anxious about terrorism, loved ones overseas on military missions, or a local assault on a child, they may have little time to spend worrying about high-stakes testing. In fact, it's conceivable that the worst time to bring up complex issues such as these is when the community is upset and alarmed about life-threatening issues.

*Looking for Answers, Resistance, Obstacles, and Choicework:*
*Working-Through Stages*

During Stage 3, people are looking for answers. Naturally enough, they prefer the easy answers at first. Often, political leaders and advocates for various solutions sense opportunity in the public's growing concern and offer solutions. Just as often, people gravitate to the first attractive solution they encounter. Why struggle with painful trade-offs, giving up $x$ to gain $y$ before it has been established that the pain can't be escaped?

Wishful thinking describes the many types of resistance that mark Stage 4. Premature closure . . . denying the existence of trade-offs ("we won't have to raise taxes or cut programs; we just need to cut waste") . . . excessive cynicism ("there's so much corruption that there's no point in even getting involved") . . . and scapegoating ("if not for them, this wouldn't even be an issue") . . . are all types of wishful thinking and resistance.

*Choicework* (Stage 5) is where people seriously consider alternative solutions, discover how they relate to their values and experience, weigh the trade-offs of different paths, and begin to make hard choices.

*Intellectual Acceptance and Moral Commitment: The Integration Stages*

Finally, the model describes two stages involved in reaching a working consensus and integrating it into the life of the schools. First is accepting an idea or direction in theory, that is, intellectually accepting it. At this point, your people have decided in principle. But they have yet to make a moral commitment to a new position, meaning changing their practices and behavior. So, you may hear, "I don't doubt the high school needs more modern wiring and a new wing, but I can't afford to vote for a levy."

When your community reaches the stage of moral acceptance, it has completed the seven-stage journey to public judgment. And the good news is you can now begin to plan the bond campaign needed to overhaul the high school. Your community is ready to pay for it.

# B. PUBLIC ENGAGEMENT AND EDUCATION

### James Harvey

On PreK–12 education, suggests Jean Johnson, most members of the public aren't sitting around examining test scores or worrying about how to tie assessments to teacher effectiveness. "People have a much broader set of concerns than just test scores or teacher effectiveness. Is my child being bullied? I don't like that. My kid likes drama. Don't cut it. My neighbor's kid likes soccer. Leave sports alone."

Johnson stresses four big issues at the root of public concern about education: the knowledge sweepstakes in a globally competitive workforce, the need for change in public schools, demoralized teachers, and the lack of communication among stakeholders.

**The Knowledge Sweepstakes.** There's been a major shift in recent years regarding the importance of college. Today, 55 percent of Americans think college is essential, compared with just 31 percent in 2000. More than 90 percent of public school parents want their children to go to college, and 95 percent of students say the same thing. But there are serious challenges. Counseling has broken down. Most students give high school counselors a rating of only fair or poor for their college and career counseling; 48 percent of students think high school guidance counselors see them as just a face in the crowd; more students are beginning to worry about whether the costs are worth it—and in fact, recent accounts indicate that 50 percent of recent college graduates are unemployed or underemployed.

Although families are confident that their children are ready for college and schools are better today than when the parents were in school, the consumers of the high school product are not as confident, reports Johnson. The ACT College Readiness Standards indicate that fully 78 percent of entering college students are not adequately prepared in either reading, English, math, or science. And employers and faculty members report broad concerns with readiness also, she says.

Meanwhile, only four in ten teachers strongly agree that all students can go to college with the right support, and 35 percent of adults report they had trouble writing college papers when in college (and 39 percent say they had at least some trouble paying attention in class).

Issues of science, technology, engineering, and mathematics (STEM) attract parents. They understand that more jobs are opening in these fields and would be pleased to see their children enter them. However, parents see STEM as the basics in math and science. Just a quarter of parents see calculus as important in high school, and most parents think things are fine as they are. Low-income parents disagree. Despite these strong feelings, most parents look to schools for leadership on STEM issues and overwhelmingly support the idea of a national math curriculum and requiring students to take four years of math and four years of science.

To most parents, the most pressing problems are around student behavioral issues and social problems, not low standards or outdated curricula. For many parents, social problems and behavioral issues trump academic concerns. Many students would be very unhappy in a career requiring a lot of math and science, reports Johnson.

**Change in Local Schools.** With regard to change in local schools, parents see most solutions as less than satisfying, Johnson notes. Transparency and accountability through data are fine so far as they go, but they are incomplete.

Parents and citizens spend a lot of energy worrying about funding for local schools. They are concerned about federal cutbacks. But education is seen as a quintessentially local issue, and there are concerns about where the money goes. Survey results about people's support for increased funding should be taken with a grain of salt, thinks Johnson.

School closings are big problems for most parents, she notes. In fact, there's a backlash against closing even low-performing schools. "Some parents," stresses Johnson, "compare a school closing to a factory closing in a community." This is not simply around jobs but around an institution that helps hold the community together because "public schools are symbols of community, of the local history, of the local legacy."

**Teachers.** Survey results indicate extreme demoralization among teachers. The numbers are troubling: 76 percent feel they are scapegoats; 70 percent feel they are left out of the loop in district decisions; 80 percent do not feel consulted on what is happening, although they are on the front lines; 80 percent and more see unions as essential protections against poorer working conditions, reduced salaries, unfair complaints from parents or students, and abusive administrators. At the same time, 51 percent of teachers believe that union decisions are made by a small group of deeply engaged teachers and staff, and 66 percent agree that unions sometimes fight to protect teachers who don't belong in the classroom.

About 40 percent of teachers describe themselves as disheartened. Few give their principals excellent ratings; 61 percent say they lack administrative support; 70 percent say testing is a major drawback (a figure that rises to 72 percent when students with behavioral issues are introduced into the discussion). About 37 percent of teachers are contented. They tend to think teaching is "exactly what I wanted," they have enough planning time, and they teach in affluent or middle-income schools. Most have master's degrees and don't overly complain about low pay or lack of prestige. The final 23 percent are described as idealists. By large majorities, they agree that good teachers can lead all students to learn, that effort is mainly determined by what teachers do, and that putting underprivileged kids on the path to success is why they got into teaching. About 6 in 10 idealists see teaching as a lifelong career, with most of the rest planning on leaving for another job in education. More than three-quarters have taught for less than 10 years, and close to half (45 percent) teach in low-income schools.

**Stakeholder Communication.** Johnson also points to serious gaps in communication or attitudes among major stakeholders. Policy makers are focused on college attendance (although what *college* means is less than clear), while many teachers and college students raise questions about the goal. Simultaneously, the "guidance system is failing students and college dropout rates are sky-high."

For their part, business groups are worried about math and science education, but 60 percent of principals and superintendents think this is not a serious problem locally, and parents and students themselves are lukewarm. This may be an opportunity that is not being seized.

In the midst of this great national debate, Johnson's final conclusion is perhaps most troubling: Teachers are alienated and unnerved. "They haven't been invited to the reform table and they believe they are caught between the sword and the wall." Beyond the troubling implication for professional educators is the practical challenge this creates: Teachers are the primary communicators with parents, reports Johnson, with the unstated implication that teacher alienation promises parental concern.

> "Teachers are alienated and unnerved. They haven't been invited to the reform table and they believe they are caught between the sword and the wall."
>
> – Jean Johnson,
> Public Agenda Foundation

So, what are the implications of these attitudes and concerns on the part of the public for you as a school leader? Do you know where your community stands on these issues? How do your teachers feel about their work? What are you doing to stay abreast of these concerns? How can you engage yourself in these community conversations?

## C. WORKING WITH THE PUBLIC ON EDUCATION REFORM

*"Why let the public in to education reform?" asks Will Friedman, president of Public Agenda Foundation. "Because you can improve policy via stakeholder*

*involvement. You can create shared ownership for results. You can inoculate the schools against backlash. You can simultaneously reinforce high expectations in the community and attack the social conditions that obstruct achievement."*

James Harvey

According to Will Friedman, public officials generally and educators specifically need to face the obvious: "For sustainable change, you need buy-in from everyone. Public engagement is a way to promote synergy between the school, the home, and the community."

### Strategies That Backfire

The typical approach to working with the public can backfire, Friedman notes. The public is generally out of the loop in decision making and experts define policy. The decide-and-sell strategy will get superintendents into trouble. People want an authentic chance to have their voices heard. Even well-intended efforts to include the public go awry. "Expert panels confuse glassy-eyed citizens with pie charts. Public hearings typically involve a lot of venting and time wasted. It's a painful theatrical process."

Instead, authentic processes are essential. Here are the signs of authentic engagement, according to Friedman: The community is not seen as the problem but as a partner in defining the problem. Communication is a two-way street. Based on listening and dialogue, communication attempts to clarify challenges and build solutions. Engagement is early and often, not late and cursory. The bias is toward inclusion of as many people as possible. The idea is to go beyond the usual suspects to create the conditions for constructive change.

But engagement is hard to do well, he acknowledges. It has to deal with mistrust and cynicism, bad experiences, and lack of understanding among stakeholders, on one hand, and educators' resistance to open up the discussion on the other.

### Principles of Effective Engagement

"Imagine you have a new initiative aimed at cutting drop-out rates by 25 percent," suggests Friedman. "How do you go about involving the public in this effort?" He offers two comprehensive suggestions.

First, get Communications 101 right. Districts need to do basic communications well. Often, they flunk this basic test. Districts don't have good materials to explain what they're doing. They react to what the media says instead of proactively engaging the media. The people answering phones in the central office give off a sense that the public is wasting their time when they call. "Give people a human being, not a machine. Develop timely, jargon-free information. Reach out to the media and the public. And ensure that you have a solid line of communication from the superintendent down to the teacher's aide."

What this means is that good communication begins by listening. The public likes to put first things first. If bullying, gangs, or school violence are challenges in your district, people won't be able to hear you talk about academic expectations until you've addressed this ground-level concern. Parents want to be sure academic basics are in place before they'll be willing to think about a new program in Mandarin. Parents are happy to talk about a reform agenda but only after you've acknowledged what they see as fundamental—safety, order, and the basics.

It also means you should choose issues ripe for engagement (see the seven-stage model for engagement above). There's little point in seeking moral commitment while people are still wondering if your problem is really worth worrying about.

Obviously, user-friendly information is important. There's no point in giving reams of computer printouts to the public. Everyone in the room needs to be empowered, not just the experts. Most members of the public will not deal with 30-column spreadsheets, so don't use them. Open multiple lines of communication. Think of this as an ongoing process, not "one and done." And create conditions for productive deliberation and dialogue.

Second, community dialogue can be a powerful engagement strategy. Well-designed, face-to-face dialogue works. The keys to success here are to provide local, nonpartisan (or multipartisan) sponsorship; create well-crafted discussion materials to help with choicework; encourage dialogue, not speeches; set up the conditions for diverse participants; employ skilled, neutral, and trained moderators; and develop honest leadership responses and follow-up.

"All of us have to understand," says Friedman, "that many of these issues are our issues, not theirs. You have to make these issues their issues before you ask for money. And you need to talk the local talk. If need be, do focus groups or surveys to learn the community's language."

## 1. Guidelines on Opinion Research

### Will Friedman

Several straightforward questions and commonsense caution should guide you as you consider mounting a public opinion survey.

*First, the Questions*

1. What do you want to know? Generally speaking, it's the job of superintendents and their leadership teams (including, one hopes, local citizens) to decide on the areas of inquiry needing attention. It's the researcher's job to translate those decisions into specific questions.

2. Who do you want to ask? Are you interested in the general population? Parents? Teachers? Students? Homeowners? Older residents? Business leaders? What about religious, racial and ethnic, or income groups? How about all of the above?

3. What's the best way to obtain answers? Do you want to do focus groups, surveys, or both? The main factors coming into play here are purpose and costs. If you want a cost-effective preliminary exploration, focus groups will do the job. More detailed and reliable results probably require a survey and considerable additional time and expense. You need a survey in any of these situations:

   • You want to confirm or expand on your focus group results.
   • You want to go public with the results and stimulate press and public attention.
   • You want to be able to track changing results over time.

*Now, the Cautions*

1. Quality counts. Poor research is not better than nothing. It can steer you in the wrong direction. Do it right the first time because you might not get another chance.

2. The media is a wild card. Public opinion results are natural media hooks. This can be a huge asset. On the other hand, if the press focuses on bad news, you may be on your way out the door.

3. Remember why you are doing it. Many good reasons exist for adding public opinion research into your public engagement efforts. You need to know what your citizens think. But it is a mistake to use this research for political purposes, to manipulate the community, or to look for emotionally charged buzzwords supporting short-term, and illusory, consensus. Don't go there. Remember the seven stages. You can't short-circuit them without engendering cynicism and mistrust.

# D. COMMUNITY CONVERSATIONS IN SAN JOSE

Linda Murray

Thomas S. Poetter

The San Jose described years ago by John Steinbeck bears little resemblance to the image of the capital of Silicon Valley carried around in most people's heads today. Still, the inheritance of the former and the reality of the latter frame the educational task facing schools in San Jose.

San Jose in Brief

Students: *33,000*

Schools: *42*

Geography: *A strip of Silicon Valley measuring 24 miles long and 4 miles wide.*

Demographics: *North, primarily Latino and poor; South, primarily Anglo, Asian, and affluent.*

Steinbeck wrote powerfully about the migrant workers, food processors, and cannery employees who took their living from the fertile fruit fields in the region. Yet, by the 1970s, the demands of burgeoning aerospace and high-tech industries in the area were such that, over the next decades, San Jose's population exploded by 70 percent. With that explosion came a call for a more highly skilled labor force. Clearly, our schools were expected to develop it.

Against the backdrop of those complex economic and social dynamics, we set out to engage the community in a conversation about what it wanted from its schools.

### *Laying the Groundwork*

Before initiating local community conversations, we first held a public forum to get a sense of what was on people's minds. During the meeting, we convened a cross-section of community members to address issues of trust and communication.

The participants in those first sessions identified three primary issues: (1) increasing student achievement, (2) educating parents, and (3) including neighborhoods and communities. The participants felt these issues should be part of any long-range public engagement road map.

Next, we conducted a communications audit that polled principals, teachers, students, parents, and community leaders. Five questions framed a discussion of the data gathered in the communications audit: (1) Which audiences do we need to reach? (2) What do we want these publics to do? (3) What is feasible for them to do (given our resources)? (4) What will success look like? (5) How will we know?

At the conclusion of the audit, analyses of the data yielded a consensus on five broad areas the district should take up: strategic communications planning, focus group research, communicating about standards and assessment, one-on-one group communications training, and parent education and outreach.

The results were fascinating. In all focus groups, people generally agreed that schools in the northern and southern portions of the district were uneven in quality. We were pleased to see broad agreement that something needed to be done about this. There was also widespread agreement across groups on the following:

- Parental and community involvement are important factors that account for uneven quality.
- Academic expectations should be raised.
- Students should receive a broad, balanced education.
- Schools across the district should be equal in quality and in the emphasis placed on different subjects.

Much agreement could be found, therefore, even among our very diverse parent populations in San Jose Unified. What about differences?

A major distinction between groups revolved around support for diversity. Non-English-speaking Latino parents valued diversity in schools. One woman noted, "I like diversity—races, different cultures—because that really nourishes children's souls. Students get to know about everyone."

The English-speaking focus groups, however, voiced little support for policies aimed at increasing diversity. They generally felt that schools should focus on academics and not "social issues beyond their control." Schools should also reinforce social values, they thought, although the core of moral teaching should take place at home through the family.

The members of the non-English-speaking parent focus groups split between those who favored consistent, high academic standards for all students and those who felt that students needed to be treated more individually. The focus groups reached a consensus that higher expectations and clearer, more consistent standards would lead to higher student achievement. Parents asked for very clear and frequent feedback on how their children were doing in school.

> "I like diversity . . . students get to know almost everyone."
>
> —Latina Parent
>
> "Schools should focus on academics and not social issues beyond their control."
>
> —Anglo Parent

Responding to this advice, our school board adopted a policy that increased student graduation requirements to include an additional year of math, science, and foreign language, and it implemented a community service requirement for every entering high school freshman. At about the same time, 74 percent of the district's residents voted to pass a $165 million bond measure. We were making progress.

### Community Task Force

Our community conversation did not stop with focus groups. Working with the Public Agenda Foundation, we launched a task force to plan a community conversation around student achievement, standards, and what students needed in order to succeed. We wanted an open, respectful, and honest discussion.

On a rainy Saturday morning, 140 community members convened in downtown San Jose to discuss standards and expectations. We received a number of recommendations:

- Expand community conversations, and take them into schools.
- Develop an action plan for increasing community involvement.
- Develop strategies to help parents become more effectively engaged in helping their children meet expectations.
- Define and clearly communicate standards and expectations to parents and community.
- Improve articulation and communication between and among levels of schooling and schools.
- Involve parents and community to support teachers in meeting the challenge of helping students achieve.
- Communicate about the community conversation.

*Holding Community Conversations*

We went deeper. The district hosted a series of six community conversations for each of the high school attendance areas. These community conversations involved more than 1,000 people—parents, students, businesses, and community members—from every district school.

---

### THE NUTS AND BOLTS OF COMMUNITY CONVERSATIONS

1. Stress respectful conversations.

2. Provide trained facilitators.

3. Keep school administrators in the background, or else they become the conversation.

4. Start with informed outside observations—academic, community activist, or corporate views of the schools—to get the conversation rolling. Videos can be ideal.

5. Work through a brief, structured list of questions.

6. Make sure everyone participates, paying special attention to the shy and the insecure.

7. Provide visual evidence that comments are being heard by having someone from the community take down key points on poster boards.

Each conversation began with a brief video presentation featuring representatives from local businesses and the community describing their expectations for what district graduates should be able to do to qualify for higher education in Silicon Valley. The video described student-performance data and addressed expectations for student performance.

Facilitators asked participants: "What skills and competencies do students need to perform well on the job," and "What should we be doing in our schools so that our students can meet your expectations?" A breakout session, focused on the needs of individual school communities, addressed the following question: "How can families, schools, and the broader community work together to help students achieve academically?"

### *What We Learned*

The challenge of this effort was to create an internal culture that actively engaged the public around school issues. The old culture was grounded in the belief that, if legal requirements obligated the district to talk to the community, it would, of course, do so. We wanted the public to know that we were interested in changing schools and community expectations of the schools—and we wanted it to know that regardless of our legal obligations.

> Every member of the community cares deeply about children and their educational progress.

We were reminded of something in this process. Too frequently we forget it: Every member of the community cares deeply about children and their educational progress. Parents and community members from all walks of life continue to hold the success of children in school as a central value. Our parents and citizens certainly do—and so do yours.

Trust us: If you can find the courage to listen to your community, you have everything to gain and nothing to lose.

## E. WORKING WITH YOUR NEWS AND MEDIA OUTLETS

*Does your stomach sink when your administrative assistant announces a local reporter is on the phone and holding for you? Are you worried about stepping off the media cliff? What's the first thing you should do on hearing a student was shot outside the high school? How do you handle persistent skepticism during a television or radio interview? Answers to these and other questions are found in this section. Public engagement is proactive; media relations are too frequently reactive. Learn how the pros, from presidential candidates to the best local do-gooders, find their message, stay with it, and work with newspapers and radio and television reporters.*

### 1. Reframe—Inoculate—Communicate

#### James Harvey

"I can give you a framework for a good answer to any question ever put to you in public," says Kathleen Hall Jamieson, an expert on communications who worked in the U.S. House of Representatives before becoming dean of the Annenberg School for Communication at the University of Pennsylvania. "First, you tell them about your own local success." (For example, Johnny, deaf since the age of 4, recently graduated as a Merit Scholar with a physics scholarship to State U. And Mary, a student who's been homeless for the last two years, has been offered voice scholarships from several prestigious universities.) "Then tell them how that fits into the national success." (American public schools are serving more than 4 million students with disabilities and hundreds of thousands who are homeless.) "Then illustrate what that means for real kids." (The career choices of students like Johnny and Mary aren't limited anymore; now, they can pursue their dreams as contributing members of society, as researchers, teachers, managers, and musicians.)

Educators who permit outsiders to put them on the defensive are one of Jamieson's pet peeves. "Don't let them do that to you," she urges. She's right. You shouldn't let journalists define you, you shouldn't let them pigeonhole you, and under no circumstances should you permit them to set the terms of the discussion. To avoid these traps, you always need to know who you're talking to, where they're coming from, and perhaps more important, what you want to get across.

"Remember," admonishes Jamieson, "audiences invest communication with meaning. Communications experts call that an *enthymeme*—the idea that the audience is as responsible for creating meaning as the speaker." Jamieson offers another three-part structure as a scaffolding for understanding communicating with the public. Point 1: Reframe issues—don't let other people define you. You define yourself. Point 2: Inoculate yourself—acknowledge criticisms you know are coming, and define them in your terms. And Point 3: Communicate—don't hide from the public. Get out and tell your story.

> "*Reframe*: don't let other people define you. *Inoculate*: acknowledge criticisms you see coming and define them in your terms. *Communicate*: Don't hide from the public. Get out and tell your story."
>
> —Kathleen Hall Jamieson

**Enthymemes.** In one sense, the Aristotelian concept of enthymemes is like the modern wag's definition of a communications problem: I know you believe you understand what you think I said, but I'm not sure you comprehend that what you heard is not what I meant! People have their own belief structures; you have to work within and around them.

To be aware of enthymemes, says Jamieson, you have to understand the typical critique of schools and be prepared to both acknowledge and attack it. The standard critique might be outlined in several parts: We're spending more and getting less, our teachers aren't very good, teachers are overpaid and underperform, money doesn't make any difference, American students lag behind their peers in other countries, and our schools have too few teachers and too many bureaucrats. (Doesn't that cover most of it?) That's the enthymeme many members of the public carry around in their heads, says Jamieson. As superintendent, you have to be aware of it, but you don't need to confirm any of it.

**Reframe.** When people argue that teachers are overpaid, your question needs to be this: Compared with what? In comparison with other professionals with advanced degrees, teachers are notoriously underpaid. They're certainly underpaid compared with compensation in places like Finland, which leads the Western world on some international student assessments. It's not even unusual for skilled tradespeople to make more than teachers. The point isn't that you want to cut other people's pay; it's that, as Jamieson puts it, "the people who teach our children shouldn't be paid less than computer technicians or plumbers."

Teachers don't work hard? What planet are you on? Who do you think corrects those papers on evenings and weekends? Our teachers average a 50-hour workweek. Money may not make a difference, but tell that to people forking over $50,000 a year or more for private schools. Look at what the wealthy pay on their kids' education. That should be a hint.

**Inoculate.** And, says Jamieson, it's important to inoculate yourself and your profession against many of these criticisms. "It's a very important principle because it means, just as it does in medicine, that you infect yourself with a weaker strain of the virus in order to develop immunity to it." Take up some of the criticisms that you know are out there, even if they're not openly expressed. Don't be afraid, for example, to tackle the issue of bureaucrats. Say openly, "I know some people believe we have too many people on central payroll." Then, says Jamieson, ask, "Surely you don't mean bus drivers, nurses, counselors, and librarians are little more than bureaucrats? These are the people who get your kids to school safely and take care of them when they're ill."

That's how you reframe an issue. Nobody likes bureaucrats. (Deep down in our souls, most of us don't like bureaucrats either.) But you lead a system that's full of nurses, librarians, and teacher's aides, not bureaucrats. And while you're reframing this issue, you're doing one of the essential jobs of leadership: You're defending the institution you lead.

**Communicate.** You need some public relations savvy too, according to Jamieson. One needs to be tactful in telling members of the media, or the public, that they have their facts wrong. But the truth is, often they don't know what they're talking about. Reframing is often a matter of trying to get your audience to pay attention to something that it already knows. In addition, you need to be able to answer Jamieson's 20 Questions (see Section G5). These are basic facts and figures about local schools that any citizen expects the superintendent to have at his or her fingertips. It's often surprising, notes Jamieson, how many professionals in a variety of fields just don't have command of the basic facts. We know your budget people are on top of these numbers. Your assistants (if you have them) can probably come up with most of them or run them down quickly. To communicate effectively, however, you need to be able to toss out these figures effortlessly, on demand, and even when nobody's asking.

### Rules of Engagement for the Media

Your secretary tells you she's not sure what it's all about, but Mr. Making Mountains out of Molehills from the local *Gazette* is on the line. You should pick up right away, correct? Nonsense! You're a busy person. Nobody will be surprised to hear you're tied up in a meeting. Have your secretary get back to Mr. Making Mountains, explaining to him that you're busy, asking what it's about, and telling him you'll be in touch. That way, you'll know if you're dealing with a routine inquiry about a budget number or a hot rumor about your state-championship football coach leaving. (You may also spare yourself the embarrassment of learning from the journalist that the coach is leaving.) You don't want to start answering questions about a serious school brawl without knowing what happened. That's perhaps the most important rule about dealing with the media: You need to scope out the lay of the land ahead of time as much as possible.

Before you give an interview, advises Jamieson, have someone call the newspaper or the television station and find out what it's all about. "You shouldn't be taken by surprise," she says. "You have a right to know what they're interested in. You may, in fact, be the wrong person to talk to about this issue. Besides, you're a busy person; you have other things to do, and you may need time to collect the data they want. You don't have to agree to do an interview immediately unless it's a genuine crisis—then you need to do it right away."

Next, bracket the time for the interview. "Fifteen minutes is normally about the right amount of time. That way you can extend it if it's going well or you can get out of the situation without being defensive—sorry, I told you I had to go."

In interviews or elsewhere, Jamieson recommends being inclusive and being specific. Always talk about *all of our children* and not *these children*. With a pithy checklist (see Section G6: Creating a Newsworthy Statement), Jamieson offers a useful guide for how to communicate with newsworthy statements—ways of saying things that are likely to be covered as opposed to ways of saying things that will elicit a yawn or ridicule.

All professions have their own language, Jamieson notes. But, the public doesn't understand educationese any more than it understands business babble or legal jargon. As she notes, in discussing all of our children, all of our people are "entitled to clear, jargon-free English."

Here's one final point: Pay attention to who's answering your telephone. They can make or break you with journalists. Your assistants need to be your first line of defense, not an excuse for undermining you. You can't afford an administrative assistant who does the following:

- Tells a reporter you'll be right with him or her and puts the call through without a clue about its purpose.
- Responds at 9:45 a.m. that you're not in yet (which is true but overlooks your 7:00 a.m. breakfast with the local chamber and your walkthrough at Jefferson Elementary).
- Gets excited if a journalist calls, conceivably ratcheting up tension in high-pressure situations.

This isn't about blaming your support staff. It's about your obligation to provide the right training to your people so that they don't get you into trouble. It's also about finding the right people for the job. What you want is the unflappable assistant who can respond coolly and smoothly under fire with, "Dr. Smith isn't available right now. Can I tell her what this is about and have her get back to you later today?"

### The District Under Crisis

OK. You've got the main possibilities for problems contained. Your staff is trained and knows how to take a call from a reporter on deadline. You're rarely put in the position of handling a surprise question from a journalist. You can quote facts and figures with the best of them. And, when called on for interviews, you come across with the aplomb and polish of a professional diplomat.

But now, a genuine emergency strikes. We've all seen the headlines. You may be faced with them too. A teacher is shot by a stalking ex-boyfriend outside an elementary school . . . a boiler explodes just after the students arrive at one of your high schools . . . a truly ugly and violent incident of race or gay bashing develops after one of the high school basketball games.

Parents and the public are looking for reassurance here. The metaphor they have in mind (and toward which you might reach) is protector of the community's children. Incidents such as these genuinely frighten people. Parents want to be sure that their children are safe.

Think of Rudy Giuliani, mayor of New York City, in the immediate aftermath of the atrocity of September 11, 2001. Giuliani responded instinctively with precisely the set of attributes any public official should demonstrate amid crisis, says Jamieson. It was a masterful and instinctive performance. Here's what he did (and what you should do with district-size crises):

- He empathized with a shocked community by demonstrating that he shared its sense of horror at the enormity of the great tragedy that had struck the city.

- He communicated clearly about what emergency services were doing in the immediate aftermath of the attacks on the World Trade Center and what the city was doing to prevent further problems.
- He reassured his constituents that New York would emerge stronger and better.
- He gave out information as it came to him, knocked down rumors as nothing more than rumors, and refused to exaggerate the extent of death and destruction until he had a better sense of what was going on.
- He provided phone numbers where anxious citizens could call to learn about fatalities and injuries in the attacks.
- He visited the families of the bereaved, consoling them and sharing their grief.

In short, a man who, on September 10, had been a media laughingstock (because of the collapse of his political ambitions, problems in his personal life that forced him to leave the mayor's mansion, and rumors of an explosive temper) was transformed into a national hero—all this on the basis of an extraordinary public performance on September 11 and the days immediately following.

### 2. Sandy Hook Elementary: Catastrophe Strikes

*Most superintendents don't have to deal with catastrophes as shocking as 9/11, but some do. "Nothing can prepare you for a tragedy like this," says Janet Robinson, Newtown, Connecticut, superintendent, referring to the internationally notorious school killings on December 14, 2012, at Newtown's Sandy Hook Elementary, a K–4 school enrolling about 450 students. "You just have to try to make decisions that focus on helping children and families heal." Before it was over, 20 six- and seven-year-olds and six staff members were dead. Here, Janet Robinson reflects on the experience.*

James Harvey

*When did you become aware that a shooting had occurred at Sandy Hook?*

Shortly after 9:30 a.m., which is when Sandy Hook Elementary doors would be locked according to our security protocols, my assistant told me of a report of a shooting at the school. It was hard to believe. Surely, I thought, this was an incident of domestic violence near the school, but not in the school.

*What was the first thing you did?*

We called the school. No one answered. We called the police. No one answered. We kept calling. Finally, a police officer responded, but he had no information, and then the line went dead. The selectwoman across the hall then told me there had been a shooting at the school. She recommended I stay at the central office. Then, we called the emergency operations center, and they confirmed a shooting and advised me to stay by the phone.

I immediately put every school in the district on lockdown. There were rumors that two gunmen were involved at Sandy Hook. Who knew how many more there might be? Next, we sent an electronic message to all parents in the district alerting them to a rumor of the shooting and informing them of the lockdown. Then, I ignored the advice I had been getting. I couldn't remain in my office worrying; I drove to the school.

*What did you find on the scene?*

It was chaotic. I couldn't get near the school because there were so many emergency vehicles parked around haphazardly—local police, state police, ambulances and fire trucks from all over, and some helicopters. I parked as close as I could and walked to the building.

There is a fire station near Sandy Hook. Teachers had just arrived there with their students. One teacher had her class singing. Others were reading stories to their children. I couldn't see the principal, but a math teacher emerged as a situational leader. She had a clipboard and was going around trying to account for students and teachers. There were reports the principal had been shot. No one had solid information.

*When did you become aware of the full extent of the catastrophe?*

It took a while. The local police, the state police, and the FBI kept on dragging me into a room, asking for information about the school, but they told me nothing. Parents were arriving at the school in hysterics. I got the state troopers to agree to release children to their parents, and it became apparent that many parents were waiting for children for whom we couldn't account.

Finally, the police chief asked me to step outside. "Janet," he said, "this looks like it's going to be really, really bad." I asked: "How bad?" He said: "It looks like there are fatalities." My stomach knotted. "How many fatalities?" I asked. "I'm not sure," he said. "It might be as many as 30."

*How did you respond?*

Well, now I had new responsibilities. There were these teachers looking for leadership, and I feared Dawn Hochsprung, the principal, was among the slain. We sent people to pick up students in homes and daycare centers where they had taken refuge and then concentrated on the remaining parents.

The back room of the firehouse, where these parents were waiting for their children, was just an awful place to be. Parents were frantic with anxiety. Governor Dan Molloy, was on hand. We used school pictures to identify the dead children, but that took a while, and the governor finally said to these parents: "I can't stand to have you sitting here not knowing what is happening. We don't have positive IDs yet, but if you're here, things do not look good." It was a difficult thing to say, but it got the parents prepared to face the worst.

*Can you say something about the emotional impact of all of this?*

It was terrible. The first responders were so devastated by what they came across that they could hardly talk. We had three psychologists in the room with these grieving parents, and the situation overwhelmed even these trained professionals.

We needed to identify these children. Who was going to do that? It would have to be someone like an art or music teacher who saw all the children in the school, but I vetoed that as too traumatic. Then, we realized we had school pictures—but we had to get them out of the school office. The police used the pictures to identify the children.

The state troopers saved an entire section of one classroom wall that had the artwork of the whole class on it. In that classroom, all but one of the children had died. The troopers told me they hoped this legacy would be meaningful for the community because the pictures had had such an emotional impact on them.

> On the day after the Sandy Hook shootings, Newtown Superintendent Janet Robinson spoke of the "incredible acts of heroism" by school staff that helped save many students' lives. The statement is a model for how school leaders can help a traumatized community deal with its grief. You can find video of the statement at http://tinyurl.com/avu99zs.

*What procedures and protocols seemed to work reasonably well?*

We had state-of-the-art security at Sandy Hook. People had criticized me for too much security. They didn't want the schools turned into fortresses. The district has a director of security. Across the district, school doors are locked. We have cameras and buzz-in systems. We have school resource officers on hand at the middle, intermediate, and high school levels. We have lockdown practices regularly. All volunteers are fingerprinted.

If someone has an assault rifle and is determined to get into a school, it's not likely you can stop that person. But I think the fact this man had to shoot his way in is what gave the office time to dial 911 and gave our courageous teachers an opportunity to save many children.

We assigned counselors to teachers and families. That worked well. We assigned a state trooper to every family that lost a child. We think that helped protect their privacy.

*How did you get schools reopened?*

That was a challenge. We decided Sandy Hook could not reopen until after the holidays. And we needed a new building. Jim Agostine, superintendent of neighboring Monroe Schools, put Chalk Hill Middle School at our disposal, and Sandy Hook children started school there on January 3, 2013.

I found myself struggling with the adults in the community, both parents and teachers, about reopening other Newtown schools. We got a lot of push back about opening these schools on the Monday after the shootings. I was told, "We're not ready." But I was determined to reopen these schools before the holidays started and insisted that the children needed the security of their regular routines as soon as possible. We had a delayed opening on Tuesday so that staff could get together before the students arrived. It worked very well. The kids wanted to be back in school.

*Looking back on this terrible incident, what lessons do you think it holds for other superintendents?*

I need time to process this. I think everyone needs emergency protocols in place. With us, it was this terrible gun violence, but it could be hurricanes in New Jersey or the Gulf states or an earthquake in California. You can't make it up on the spot.

First, review your security provisions. You may never have to draw on them, but you will never regret time and attention paid to security. Second, pay particular attention to security protocols at elementary schools. I'm planning on putting in panic buttons in our elementary schools wired directly to the police department. We also need to think about the fact that most of us have fallback leadership in middle and high schools, but in most elementary schools, the principal is the single leader. Third, our schools contracted with individual photographers for school pictures. That had two effects. School IDs for staff all look different. And the pictures of students and staff are in the school. We are going to hire a single, districtwide photographer, require uniform IDs, and keep copies of the photographs in the central office.

Beyond that, you need to put out a statement as soon as you have definitive information to provide. In the process, you need to correct false rumors. The entire world thought for several hours that the gunman's mother worked at Sandy Hook, that school personnel buzzed him in, and that there was a second shooter. None of that was true, but that's what the news accounts said. You have to knock that sort of thing down.

The Sandy Hook parents whose surviving children were out of school over the holidays were desperate for information. We held a meeting for them, where I introduced the former Sandy Hook principal, who would be leading the school when it reopened, and Jim Agostine from Monroe. They got a standing ovation.

Staff and family members also needed emotional support. We've provided abundant mental health resources at our schools. And if we were worried about the emotional needs of particular individuals, we made sure the mental health professionals knew about that.

Of course, you have to maintain your own stability too. My coping style is to go to work. A lot of us are like that. So, that helps. But here was a situation where I couldn't be in two places at once, and I had to be out in the community and helping families cope. So, I accepted help from a retired superintendent who came to the office on a temporary basis. I told my staff: "She is here to make the decisions that I would make if I were on hand. I will stand behind any decisions she makes." That was a hard thing for me to do, but it permitted the district to function while I did what I had to do.

Finally, of course, as a community leader, you have to let the community know you share its grief. We had lost children and staff. We had a community-wide interfaith event that the governor and President Obama attended. During some days in the week following, I attended up to three wakes and funerals. I couldn't get to all of them, but I got to every one I could. This support is very meaningful to traumatized families.

### 3. District Policy on Weapons and Gun Violence

#### Luvern L. Cunningham

There are a lot of firearms in the United States. The Federal Bureau of Investigation (FBI) estimates there are more than 200 million privately owned guns in America. In addition, the U.S. Government Accountability Office (GAO), the investigative arm of Congress, estimates that 8 million people in the United States have permits to carry concealed weapons.

Even with permits, Americans are typically barred from bringing weapons into courts, government buildings, churches and hospitals, elementary and secondary schools, colleges and universities, and interscholastic and intercollegiate competitions. Still, with so many weapons, gun violence develops in all of these locations. As an educational leader, are you confident that your district has satisfactory policies and protocols in place to

- Respond to emergencies, including informing parents and staff throughout the district of reports of gun violence?
- Restrict access to school property?
- Protect against students bringing guns or other weapons to school?
- Restrict district employees and school board members from carrying concealed handguns when in school buildings or engaged in school business outside the schools?
- Protect students and staff in school buildings and central offices?
- Protect school board members, staff, parents, students, and the public during school board meetings?

# F. COMMUNICATIONS PLANNING

*Just as your administrative assistant can leave you open to criticism in dealing with the media, so too can your district's publications. You cannot afford to have the message you are communicating—a dedication to high standards and a commitment to leaving no child behind—contradicted by district publications or surly receptionists. Communications planning is a critical component of public engagement. In this section, you'll learn about internal and external communications, communications planning, and how to use communications audits to improve your district's performance.*

## 1. Communications: Internal and External

### James Harvey

Recently, a former school principal, now a teacher and the father of a middle school boy, discovered that he needed to pay a fee to allow his son to participate in the school band and orchestra. The written instructions were a bit confusing. It was unclear if one fee would be sufficient, or if one was required for the band and another for the orchestra. Eager to get his son signed up, he set out to get some clarification.

Picking up the phone to talk with the school, this experienced school administrator soon discovered himself hopelessly lost in the school's voice mail system. Irritated, he stopped by the school to seek an answer and, following the posted instructions, reported to the school office. There, he found an imposing barrier walling him off from the office itself, behind which a receptionist was talking animatedly on the phone. She glanced at the father fleetingly, before turning her back to continue what seemed to be a private conversation. About five minutes later, she finished her conversation, hung up, and, turning to her visitor, said, without interest, "What do you want?"

Your efforts as a superintendent to create an open, inclusive district that welcomes visitors can be wrecked in five minutes by the receptionist whose attitude says, "Get lost." When you think of communications, you need to think of both external and internal audiences. And you also need to be sure that everyone in your organization is acting on the same set of assumptions. This section of the *Fieldbook* guides you through some of these land mines.

## 2. A Communications Audit

### Adam Kernan-Schloss

### Sylvia Soholt

How do you get started in assessing your communications? A communications audit is one way. You should interview a broad cross-section of the district and its citizens. Interview each group separately. In diverse districts, it is often helpful to subdivide the parent groups by race and ethnicity. A neutral source, not a district employee, should conduct these interviews, using the same questions with each group and guaranteeing confidentiality. The audit report should be divided into findings and recommendations and should include both short- and long-term recommendations. (Short-term recommendations are to be implemented within a month or two as a demonstration that the district acts on the feedback it receives.) Share the report with participants to build trust. Here are the questions you need to begin with.

- What comes to mind when you think of _____ school district?
- How would you describe the district to someone not familiar with it? (Strengths? Weaknesses?)
- What are the most important issues (goals) in your schools?
- *A follow-up to the previous question:* Are you currently receiving information about these issues? *Or:* Do you feel you're being informed about progress on these issues on a regular basis?
- How do you learn about what's going on in the school district? Are the communications activities very effective in your view? Or does the district use tools or activities that don't work very well?
- *For parents and other community members:* What kind of information do you need to be able to talk to your neighbors about what's going on in the district? *For school employees:* What information do you need to be successful in your job?
- *For both:* How would you like to receive this information?
- Do barriers stand in the way of communication in the school district? (What keeps communication from happening?)
- Tell me one thing that would make communications better in _____ schools.
- How does the public judge the success of _____ school district? What measures does the district use? What would you use?
- What would it take for people to know that _____ schools were getting better?
- Is there anything else you would like me to know?

### 3. Vital Signs of Public Engagement

#### Adam Kernan-Schloss

Here are some vital signs of public engagement:

- Are you doing a lot of listening? Do you have a clear idea of the concerns of various segments of the public? Do you have public opinion research about the concerns? Are you regularly surveying staff, parents, students, and the general public?

- Are you responding to what you hear? Do you change policies and practices based on what you're hearing?
- Are you inclusive? Do you communicate clearly with non-English-speaking constituents in your district?
- Is everyone focused on learning? That includes staff, students, parents, and community. Do all policies lead to this goal? Are your communications activities directly linked to this goal?
- Does everyone understand the standards? Are you confident that principals, teachers, and parents could all give a fairly good answer to the question of what students in fourth, seventh, and eleventh grades are expected to know and be able to do?
- Have you taken care of the basics? Do you see welcoming receptionists, clean grounds, sufficient textbooks, timely paychecks, and all the rest of what goes into a respectful environment?
- Are your messages free of jargon? Whether written in English, Spanish, or other languages, can people understand what you're saying?
- Do you have a strategic engagement plan with measurable goals and objectives? "We want to increase public support" is not sufficient. Something like "We want to involve 15 percent more parents in school activities" would be.
- Are you explaining standards clearly to everyone? That includes staff, teachers, students, and parents. Are you reporting results honestly?
- Do you have a calendar of key events and opportunities? This can help you get ahead of the curve to communicate your main messages.
- Do you have a sounding board? Have you formed a group of key communicators as a listening post? Key allies, staff and nonstaff, can serve as a feedback loop and outreach tool.
- Can you point to specific examples of success? What can you identify in terms of student work, classrooms, schools, and the district?

## G. TOOLS

### 1. Tips on the Seven Stages

Will Friedman

Need help? Different stages have different challenges and require different strategies. Table 8.1 offers some general rules of the road.

### 2. Focus Groups and Surveys

Will Friedman

Properly done, focus groups and surveys are an excellent way to improve your understanding of the views, priorities, and concerns of your community.

**Table 8.1**   Tips on the Seven Stages

---

*Consciousness Raising*

---

| | |
|---|---|
| Awareness | Media and traditional public relations strategies help bring issues to public attention. |
| Urgency | Boring and complex issues can be challenging. If a complex issue connects to a strong public concern, that helps (e.g., how does the budget relate to school safety?). |
| Looking for Answers | Remember the first-things-first principle: People must know you understand their priorities if you want them to pay attention to yours. |

---

*Working Through*

---

| | |
|---|---|
| Looking for Answers | Be wary of poll results regarding public preferences before the public has had a chance to deliberate in depth. |
| Resistance | Resistance to the hard work of deliberation and decision making is a natural part of the process. As a leader, your job is to understand resistance and help the public get past it. Sometimes, providing the right piece of information does the trick; sometimes, confronting people's wishful thinking is required. |
| Choicework | Avoid forcing a single solution on people—particularly your preferred one. Help people understand the pros and cons of different approaches. That provides opportunities to develop mature views. |
| | Nonpartisan, user-friendly issue guides can help people deliberate effectively, as can public journalism strategies that provide nonpartisan, in-depth, user-friendly treatments of issues. |
| | Community conversations are an excellent strategy for helping significant cross-sections of the community work through their thinking (see Sections G3 and G4 on community conversations). |

---

*Integration*

---

| | |
|---|---|
| Intellectual Acceptance | People need time to really integrate new ideas and solutions. Don't mistake initial acceptance as wholehearted commitment. |
| Moral Commitment | Give people opportunities to play an active role as solutions develop. Include the community in implementing and devising solutions. This deepens the sense of ownership and helps ensure success as all community assets are brought to bear on the problem. |

---

What do people with "If You Have to Ask, You Can't Afford It" estates think about the new tax levy? What about the folks in the trailer park across the tracks? You probably have many different publics in your community. You need to understand what each group thinks.

Focus groups are a qualitative way for you to explore views in depth. They help you probe the motivations underlying people's responses. Focus group interviews are especially useful in exploring issues that people haven't really given much thought to because time can be taken during the interview to present background information. Focus groups are often the essential first step in survey design.

Opinion surveys, conducted by telephone or mail (and occasionally in person), expand on focus group research. They provide a more detailed and quantitative look at public attitudes. Obviously, they have to be properly done. Loaded questions will provide loaded answers. To the extent possible, questions should be neutral and nonjudgmental. How you ask the question has a lot to do with the answers you get.

There is no doubt about the following: If you launch a well-conceived survey, you will receive extremely valuable information. It will be information to which you will return again and again. And it will help you plumb the thinking of your community. You will also gain something else: There is nothing like the results of a survey to concentrate media attention on the issues that concern you.

The terms *focus groups* and *focus group interviews* mean the same thing. The technique was developed decades ago at the University of Minnesota and was called, at the time, *focused interviews.* The interview aspect of the focus group is important. If you employ this technique, what you want to know is what your focus group participants think. You want to interview them. You are not conducting this exercise to persuade them of your views but to discover theirs.

A questionnaire directed at employers might ask: "When I employ the graduates of Anytown High, I find them (1) well equipped to begin work immediately, (2) moderately well equipped to begin work, with some training, or (3) poorly equipped to begin work no matter what we do." On balance, that's a fairly neutral question and the choices seem reasonable. But the question might begin with a variation of the following: "In light of recent newspaper reports indicating that the graduates of Anytown High are incapable of brushing their own teeth, would you say that, when they come to work in your community they are . . ." Even if offered the same three choices, there's no doubt that respondents are being asked to check off (3).

### The Limits and Uses of Opinion Research

We want to stress that you need to understand that focus groups and surveys are tools, not public engagement itself. Both tools can be powerful assets in a public engagement effort, but they are not a substitute for the effort, much less public engagement. You shouldn't mistake the tools for the process.

These tools provide a reading of what's on your people's minds, but these tools do not, by themselves, help your citizens develop their thinking. They illuminate confusion but do not provide the communication to fix it. They distinguish issues your constituents are willing to delegate to professionals from those issues they want a voice in, but they do not necessarily give your people much of a say. They can clarify differences in priorities among various stakeholders, but they will not help your community work through those differences. In brief, they are the beginning, not the end.

As part of a larger engagement effort, focus groups and surveys can be useful tools for steering you and other local leaders in productive directions. Prior to community conversations, media campaigns, or the production of informational materials, public opinion research can help answer questions such as these:

- What are the main concerns and priorities of the people in our community? Which issues emerge spontaneously and provoke lively debate? How do people view the importance of this particular issue in comparison with that one?
- On which issues do our people especially want a voice? On which are they comfortable relying on the direction of our elected and appointed officials? Do they insist on addressing aspects of particular issues?
- Where does our community start out on particular issues (e.g., closing the achievement gap or consolidating schools)? Is a problem that is high on the leaders' agenda even on the public's radar screen? Are our people aware of a range of potential solutions? Or are they stuck on a single train of thought?
- Have people given much thought to the issue, or is it pretty new to them? If the former, is there much common ground? Or do people see powerful divisions in the community? If the latter, how willing are people to engage the issue, and what kinds of information do they need? In other words, where do you locate our public (and its various subpublics) on the seven stages of public judgment?
- What language do people in our community typically use when talking about a particular issue? What are people's first questions and concerns? What is the most useful way to frame issues so that we can have a productive public conversation?
- Are these topics easy to explain? Or do they invite confusion? How much contextual information do our people need to engage effectively with these issues? What other hurdles are likely to come up? Are there, for example, misperceptions, hot-button issues, or alienated groups that need addressing?

As your public engagement campaign unfolds, focus groups and surveys can help assess how well things are going and help you fine-tune your efforts.

### 3. Community Conversations: A Tool for Public Engagement

#### Will Friedman

*Sponsorship Should Be Nonpartisan and Broad Based*

When districts are the lone organizers and hosts of community conversations, they attract the usual suspects—those already active in school affairs. A broad-based leadership coalition is more likely to draw fresh faces, both because it includes leaders that more people relate to and because it communicates openness to new views.

*Who Should Attend?*

Anyone who wants to should attend. Beyond that, open the conversation to anyone with interesting perspectives on kids and schooling. Ask yourself this: Who do we rarely hear from? You want them. Among important participants are the following:

- Parents of students in public and private schools
- Students (especially juniors and seniors) and recent graduates
- Nonparent taxpayers from the community and employers of young people
- Educators (but their participation should be limited, so they do not dominate)
- Representatives from higher education, such as admissions officers and freshman professors
- Community leaders including public officials, activists, and religious and law-enforcement leaders
- Experts on specific topics on the agenda, for example, law enforcement if the topic is school safety

Participants should reflect the community's diversity.

*How Do We Get Them There?*

People have a lot of ways to spend their time. Here are ways to encourage participation:

- Personal outreach is best. Senior citizens will generally have more success recruiting peers, business leaders more success recruiting employers, and so on.
- Hold the conversations in safe, accessible, and neutral sites. A community center or library may be better than a school (more neutral).
- Recruit those who don't think of themselves as parts of the school community, such as senior citizens. Address the needs of more marginalized segments of the community by considering language, transportation, and child-care needs.

- Community conversations should be more engaging and meaningful than typical public meetings. They should expect a lively, participative session, where hearing from regular folks is the heart of the effort. This is a forum where everyone needs to work together if the right decision is to be reached.
- Just as important, people should know there will be a social dimension. Food is always a good idea. Perhaps you can persuade the local school jazz band to give a brief performance. You should advertise these elements to draw a robust and diverse participation. (Free food, music, and the chance to give the superintendent an earful! What more could anyone want?)
- Finally, it is crucial that the specific topic of conversation be one that most people care strongly about and want to weigh in on.

> Community conversations must be real, not empty gestures creating an illusion of participation.

### Choose the Issue to Be Discussed With Care

People's time and energy for public engagement is limited. It shouldn't be wasted. Here are some guiding principles:

- An issue is likely to be seen as relevant and legitimate if it is chosen by a broad steering committee.
- In selecting an issue, separate the educational priorities of the district from those of the community. Those that overlap will be ripe for discussion.
- The topic must be one you and the public care about and about which you are open. If your mind is made up, or legal issues drive your options, this isn't the place for a community conversation. Community conversations must be real, not empty gestures creating an illusion of participation.
- Also, highly technical issues, or highly technical dimensions of issues, aren't appropriate. Questions about basic values and general directions are. The role of standardized tests in schooling is a question in which the public can engage. Detail about question design and format is best left to experts.
- It is usually a good idea to tackle truly important but not nearly intractable issues. You might want to discuss bullying and discipline or testing for graduation, for example, but you may want to hold off on race relations in our schools until you've had more practice.

> Visit Public Agenda Foundation's website at www.publicagenda.org for a range of print and video materials (often in English and Spanish) to help guide you in your efforts to engage your community.

## 4. Framing Community Conversations

### Will Friedman

Issues must be carefully framed in a community conversation, as shown in Table 8.2.

**Table 8.2**   Framing Community Conversations

| Don't Ask People to: | Instead: |
|---|---|
| • Brainstorm solutions out of thin air. | • Provide people with choices to weigh. |
| • Critique a single approach, which deprives them of leverage. | • Reflect a spectrum of credible and competing views. |
| • Present material in an antagonistic cross-fire style. | • Spell out pros and cons. |
| • Use hype-charged buzzwords. | • Make the connection to people's deeply felt values and concerns. |
| • Use professional jargon and stiff, formal language. | • Use plain, straightforward language and visuals that everyone can understand. |
| • Work in large groups. | • Break large groups down to working groups of about 12 participants. |
| • Imagine anyone can lead this work. | • Understand you need well-trained, nonpartisan moderators and recorders. |
| • Go home and forget the conversation. | • Take suggestions seriously and follow up. |

## 5. Twenty Questions

### Kathleen Hall Jamieson

All superintendents should have answers to the following 20 questions at their fingertips.

**DISTRICT PROFILE: INFORMATION EVERY SUPERINTENDENT NEEDS TO KNOW**

1. What is the expenditure per pupil in your district?

2. How much has that figure increased or decreased in the last decade?

3. What is the average teacher salary?

*(Continued)*

(Continued)

4. How much has the average teacher salary increased or decreased in the last decade?

5. What is the district graduation rate?

6. How much has the graduation rate increased or decreased in the last decade?

7. What proportion of students go on to college?

8. What proportion of students are classified as special-needs students?

9. What proportion of students use English as a second language?

10. What proportion of students qualify for help under the Americans With Disabilities Act?

11. What are district test scores (local and in comparison with national data)? What are five-year comparisons with national and local scores?

12. What is the total district budget? How much has the budget increased or decreased in the last decade? Compare that with the city budget? The county budget?

13. What proportion of students come from homes defined as in poverty?

14. What is the ethnic and minority composition of the student body?

15. What proportion do not speak English at home?

16. What proportion of students are mainstreamed? Have a serious disability?

17. What is the average salary of workers in your community? What has been their proportionate salary increase over the last five years?

18. List members of your state legislature who have public school educations. What proportion was educated in public versus private schools?

19. Are any legislators alumni of your district or schools?

20. List members of the press who have public school educations. Are any of them alumni of your district or schools?

## 6. Creating a Newsworthy Statement

### Kathleen Hall Jamieson

Want the press to pay attention to your news? Make it easy for them by following the easy checklist in Table 8.3.

Table 8.3    A Checklist for Creating Newsworthy Statements Likely to Be Covered and Published

| *To Be* | *Or . . . Not to Be* |
| --- | --- |
| A coherent statement clearly summarizing the issue in jargon-free English | A rambling statement skirting the issue in gobbledygook |
| Available before deadline at a convenient place for news gatherers | Available at midnight near the North Pole |
| Requiring no additional information | Requiring at least five appendices to clarify the point |
| Written to be understood on first hearing | Written for cryptographers |
| Which can be delivered clearly and dramatically in less than 15 seconds | Which could not be delivered by Olivier in less than 35 minutes |
| Delivered in a symbolic setting | Delivered in a setting with no apparent relationship to the statement |
| By a person who dramatizes the issue | By a mumbler |
| In a manner not subject to parody | In a manner that brings joy to the hearts of comedians everywhere, who encourage the speaker to run for office |

## 7. Tackling the Media Interview

### Kathleen Hall Jamieson

So, a journalist wants to interview you? You need to come across as professional and competent. Table 8.4 shows some guidelines for making a good impression and staying on message.

Table 8.4    Tackling the Media Interview

| *Interviewer Takes Seriously Someone Who:* | *Interviewer Takes With a Grain of Salt Someone Who:* |
| --- | --- |
| Is professionally dressed (decent tie and coat for men; jacket for women) | Is inappropriately dressed (in work jeans or sweaty golf shirts) |
| Is professionally groomed | Is unshaven or tattooed |
| Understands what the interview is about | Is curious about what the interviewer wants |
| Is on top of district facts | Is at sea on critical points |
| Reframes, inoculates, and communicates | Wanders all over the map |
| Hands you a district fact sheet (knows the interviewer just reported on rising car prices) | Expects interviewer to understand the district, its population, and geographic boundaries |
| Offers a business card with clearly spelled name and title | Trusts the producer will spell your name and the district's properly |
| Follows up on promised information | Forgets the interview the minute it ends |

## H. REFLECTIVE PRACTICE

Public engagement, sending messages through the media, making sure you're communicating effectively . . . it's a big challenge. Here are some questions that may hold the key to your success.

*How would you define* the difference between public engagement and public relations? Do key staff members, including those in public affairs, share your understanding?

*How many different kinds of publics* do you serve in your district? Do they all share the same perceptions, or do variations exist? What, if any, differences exist between how you and the other elites in your community view the world and the perceptions of your publics?

*Where do you and your key people* stand on the seven-stage continuum of coming to public judgment? Where do the leaders of your community stand? What about citizens and parents?

*Define the issues* that might frame a community conversation in your district. Think about how you could hold such a conversation. How would you start? Where would you hold the meetings? Who would you invite? How could you ensure expert and neutral facilitation?

*Are you confident* that your administrative assistants possess the poise and savvy to act in your best interests when the phones light up during a crisis?

*Are emergency procedures available in your schools* to cover unexpected events and disasters? Does everyone understand them? Are you confident of that?

*Can you answer Kathleen Hall Jamieson's* 20 questions? If not, why not? How do you know what's going on in your district?

*Can your board members answer the same questions?* If not, why not? How do they know what's going on in their district?

*Are you relaxed and confident during media interviews?* Don't worry if you are not. These situations are stressful for everyone. Can you find some coaching to improve your performance and reduce the level of stress?

*How user-friendly are your schools?* Is there a welcoming atmosphere? Are communications clear and in jargon-free English? Are clear, jargon-free communications available in any second languages spoken in your community?

*Have you thought about a communications audit* to improve communication with your publics?

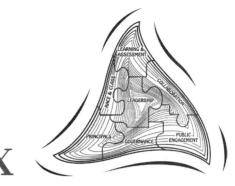

# PART IX

# *So, What Does All This Mean?*

James Harvey

Nelda Cambron-McCabe

We can't blame you if your head is spinning. We've asked you to keep your eye on several moving targets (the seven "commonplaces") from a platform that moves from one image or metaphor to another. We've presented you with a lot of information on how the policy direction of the nation is shifting in terms of standards, accountability, and assessment (often in tension with expert advice on leadership and organizational development) and what this means for you at the local level. And we've provided you with a lot of tools throughout the *Fieldbook* to help you work through some of the challenges you face.

This concluding part pulls these disparate strands together. First, it asks how each of the "commonplaces" would play itself out in your district depending on which metaphor of the district you (and your colleagues) have in mind. How would you expect your district to behave if driven by an image of the district as a political entity? What would it look like if the image were a brain or a learning organization? And what does each of these images mean for each of the "commonplaces"?

Then, we suggest a conception that reconciles the tension between the advice of organizational development experts (which tends to emphasize systems thinking and the importance of the element of trust in organizational improvement) and the technocratic, top-down policy direction of federal and state directives (which increasingly emphasize assessment, accountability, and punitive consequences). That conception emphasizes the need to understand education as a classic "wicked" problem. This description is not a moral judgment but a simple recognition of the difficulty and complexity of improving school performance in a large, diverse, democratic, free-market society with surprisingly large numbers of children from low-income families. We support the conception that reform of American schools, especially in urban areas, is a complex and time-consuming business that does not yield to quick and easy solutions, as can be seen from a review of 15 years of research on Chicago school reform.

We then turn to one of the questions asked at the outset of this *Fieldbook*: How do you respond to critics who assert that educational standards have collapsed and public schools are failing the nation? This is a difficult leadership challenge. You are facing a story line over the last 30 years in which oracular reasoning has met incestuous amplification. Communications theorists describe a phenomenon of *oracular reasoning*. When the oracle speaks, primitive people take what they're told at face value. All evidence contrary to the oracle's prediction is ignored or explained away. This is due to a phenomenon that military strategists describe as *incestuous amplification. Jane's Defense Weekly*, the bible of military analysts, describes incestuous amplification as "a condition . . . where one only listens to those who are already in lock-step agreement, reinforcing set beliefs and creating a situation ripe for miscalculation."

So, you're facing a situation in which a lot of people think they understand the problem better than you do. We try to lay out a defense against this oracular reasoning. Such a defense exists, and although much of the generalized criticism of public schools in the United States has a point, a lot of it is misplaced and leading the country in counterproductive directions.

Finally, we try to illustrate the leadership challenge you (and state superintendents and federal and foundation officials) face by working around a graphic that ties together much of the discussion of images, adaptive work, and learning organizations. This helps leaders revisit their leadership role against a straightforward template. This template asks two questions. How complicated is the challenge you are addressing? And how confident are you that you know how to respond? We suggest four leadership styles you might adopt, depending on your answers to these questions.

## A. RECONCILING "COMMONPLACES" AND IMAGES

Nelda Cambron-McCabe

Theory's fine. It's as true in this part as it was when we mentioned it in Part II: There's nothing as practical as a good theory.

But, amid all the data and theory presented here, how are you as a superintendent or aspiring district leader to make sense out of what's happening around you? We don't pretend that's easy. We've covered a lot of ground with you. Let's review it. First, recall each of the "commonplaces" of leadership explored in this *Fieldbook*: leadership, governance, learning and assessment, race and class, school principals, collaboration, and community engagement. Now, try to imagine how each of these "commonplaces" might play itself out in districts functioning under different images. To keep this as straightforward as possible, we've laid out many of the possibilities you'd expect in Table 9.1.

We're going to lead you through the table, but first, just take a look at it. Anything jump out at you? What seems clear is that as different images interact with the "commonplaces" within your district, they are likely to elicit different behaviors, on either your part or the part of others. A district functioning under the machine image, for example, is likely to react to issues of race and class by insisting that everyone should be treated alike. But the political image may well involve selective advocacy around race and class—on behalf of either minority or majority groups. Glance at the table again. The interrelationship between the images and the "commonplaces" potentially explains a lot of the behavior you see in your district.

The second thing that stands out in the table is that most of the behavior elicited by the old images is tough and hardnosed, whichever image is involved. This is Mars talking. And Mars speaks single-loop language (see p. 330), appealing to the status quo or the status quo ante. The images encourage behaviors that strengthen current structures, continuing to narrow our aspirations for human possibilities. Most of these images are likely to take for granted that the problems you encounter are technical in nature. The expectation is that you should be able to fix them with technical approaches, tinkering around the edges without disturbing the organization you inherited. These images emphasize playing by the rules, following bureaucratic norms, reinforcing tradition, manipulating data and interest groups, and expecting schools to sort children into winners and losers. If you see unattractive behavior in your district, examine the images people use when speaking and writing to you. You can count on it: Most of these will be older, inherited images of the world.

Conversely, the emerging images elicit behaviors that are much more nuanced in their appreciation for the challenges the "commonplaces" pose. Here, Venus enters the picture. And Venus is a double-loop thinker. These metaphors demonstrate considerably more skepticism about the status quo and much more respect for the possibilities of human growth. Emerging images also are more likely to acknowledge the complexity of what you're facing, to consider emerging challenges to be adaptive in nature, and to require the entire range of skills and talents in the community for their resolution. These images emphasize that all children can learn, that collaboration is important, that feedback is essential, and that organizations have meaning and purpose that we shape every day. If you see kinder and gentler behavior in your district or portions of it, you may be sure that what is driving this behavior are images of the district as more of a culture or organism than a machine or political system.

**Table 9.1**   How Images Drive the "Commonplaces" of Leadership

| *The Commonplaces* | *Inherited Images* | | | |
| --- | --- | --- | --- | --- |
| | *Machine* | *Political* | *Psychic* | *Domination* |
| Leadership | Hierarchical and rule driven | Balance group demands | Protect status quo | Autocratic |
| Governance | Focused on control | Interest driven | Focus on ends | Winners and losers |
| Standards/ Assessment | Ensuring uniform outcomes | Data manipulation | Selective data usage | Expect bell curve |
| Race and Class | Treat everyone alike | Selective advocacy | Tracking | Blame the victim |
| Developing Principals | Technical skills | Emphasis on loyalty | Groupthink | Demand party line |
| Collaboration | Limited by rules | Shifting alliances | Narrow and limited | Polarize groups |
| Engagement | Mechanical | Building coalitions | Reinforce tradition | With selected elites |

| *The Commonplaces* | *Emerging Images* | | | |
| --- | --- | --- | --- | --- |
| | *Culture* | *Organism* | *Brain* | *Flux and Transformation* |
| Leadership | Symbolic | Nurturing | Distributed | Transformative |
| Governance | Focused on values, norms, rituals | Survival | Self-organizing systems | Evolving |
| Standards/ Assessment | Ethnography—story, symbol | Feedback | Integrated information web | Data as attractor |
| Race and Class | All children can learn | Nourishing | Formative and summative | Massive system and social change |
| Developing Principals | Shape school culture | Emphasize adaptation | Learning to learn | Leaders of chaos |
| Collaboration | Affirm cooperation | Stress cohesion | Systems perspective | Around meaning and purpose |
| Engagement | Develop shared meaning | Symbiotic | Authentic and continuous | Relational |

Work your way through these images and "commonplaces." Explore them with your staff and members of the board. Bringing into focus the underlying tensions involved in the interaction of these images with the "commonplaces" might go a long way toward illuminating some of the problems keeping you awake at night. This exercise is unlikely to do much harm. If it does, you shouldn't be in that district anyway. But potentially, it can do you and the children in your district a lot of good. It can do so by bringing greater clarity to what is going on in the district, spotlighting the motivations underlying the behavior you see, and surfacing potential double-loop responses in place of attractive but deceptive quick fixes.

## 1. Inherited Images

Clearly, in the terms of Peter Senge, Ron Heifetz, and others, the inherited images presented here do not encourage a learning organization focused on difficult, adaptive work. These are images emphasizing power. Most of them assume the answers are out there. As such, why waste time on questions? We already have the answers. You, and the obdurate people on your payroll, are probably part of the problem. And why should we adapt to the environment around us? The environment should bend to our will.

### District as a Machine

This appears to be one of the more benign of the inherited images. Unlike several of the others, it has the attraction of apparent neutrality. Its drawback, of course, is its technocratic (and therefore unrealistic) approach to resolving complicated human problems. The district as machine is a district committed to alignment to such a degree that everybody will be marching to the same drummer, conceivably creating oppressive conditions for the most challenged children. This is a metaphor in which district leadership will be driven by rules and governed by hierarchy. The governance system of which you are (or will be) a part will be organized around maintaining control. Standards and assessment will be central to your district's functioning here (and the state's and the nation's) and oriented around attempting to ensure uniform results for all children. This mode of thinking has crystal-clear implications for race and class as district officials insist on treating everyone alike. What this metaphor implies for developing principals, collaboration, and public engagement is not promising. Principal development will emphasize mastery of technical skills (because we know what we're doing). Collaboration will be grudging and rule driven, while community engagement, to the extent it exists at all, will be perfunctory, mechanical, and oriented around confirming where the district is already headed.

As superintendent, you will be a mechanic in charge of a bureaucracy, greasing and lubricating the gears that keep the machine functioning, while periodically replacing parts and personnel during routine inspections.

### District as Political System

This metaphor describes many school systems, large and small. It might describe yours. On the surface, of course, few acknowledge the politics of district leadership, but behind the scenes, many districts are all about who is in charge and how the money is spent and jobs allocated.

If you find yourself worrying more about procurement and hiring than learning, you're probably in a highly politicized district. This is a district that is driven by the imperative to balance the demands of competing interests. To achieve those ends, it will not hesitate to advocate selectively on the part of key groups (advantaged or disadvantaged) and to manipulate data to make itself look as good as possible. It emphasizes principal loyalty; collaboration and public engagement will be seen as coalition building and system maintenance.

As superintendent, you will be a political operative, more attuned to constituency demands than student needs.

### District as Psychic Prison

This powerful image describes the people within the district perhaps more than the district itself. This could very easily be the mind-set of the inhabitants of any of the eight images presented here. People create their own psychic prisons, whether in a district dominated by a power-driven autocrat in the mayor's office or a flower child leading the board. But, in general, if this is your district, it will be one that sees governance as something oriented around protecting the status quo. It will selectively use data to serve its purposes; it will also be surprised that anyone would think of questioning tracking (or expanding programs for the gifted and talented) as a sound educational strategy. Seeking convergent thinking (groupthink) will drive principal selection and collaboration, while engagement will be narrow, limited, and oriented around reinforcing tradition.

Where do you stand in this district, as superintendent or potential superintendent? The expectation of your role will be clear: You will be there to tend the flame and keep it alive.

### District as Instrument of Domination

Practically all of us can recall a boss at some point who was an intimidating autocrat, a bully. But what if an entire district behaves that way? Impossible, you say? How would you describe the existence of "separate but equal" schools in the South until a few generations ago if not as instruments of domination? Vestiges of such behavior undoubtedly remain in some districts. Here, leadership will be autocratic. It's not likely to be your leadership style, but it could be. It could also be the board chair's, or the mayor's, or the local county commissioner's. It will be all about control. Governance will nod approvingly as winners and losers are defined in the classroom because the bell curve will be taken for granted and failure will be blamed on the students. The ability to hew to the party line will be the major selection criterion for principals. Collaboration will be more akin to polarization and demonizing of weaker groups, while public engagement will be limited largely to local elites.

There's no nice way to say it: As superintendent, you will be a flunkey. If you sense these dynamics at work in your next interview, don't take the job. If you're already there, get out.

## 2. Emerging Images

The emerging images described here are much more suited to working through adaptive challenges. These are images of organizations that don't assume leaders and other influential figures have all the answers. Leaders in these organizations don't believe they're smarter than everyone else. People in these districts are likely to be far more modest about their own certainties and more respectful of the knowledge and experience brought to the organization by employees and people outside the district. Districts found in the emerging-images cluster will heed the wisdom of the great journalist H. L. Mencken to the effect that "For every problem, no matter how difficult or complicated, there is a solution that is simple, direct, and wrong."

### District as Culture

Individual public school districts in the United States follow this model, but it is likely to be much more common in associations of like-minded school leaders (e.g., The Coalition for Essential Schools) or in private (frequently religious) school coalitions. This is a system in which leadership often emphasizes symbolism because symbols carry so much meaning within the community. Governance focuses also on shared values, norms, and rituals. Standards and assessment are as likely to rely on stories and symbols as on tests and data, because universal meanings can be read into individual experience. Districts emphasizing shared culture will always insist that all children can learn and will encourage cooperation and the development of shared meaning because collaboration and engagement are at the heart of the culture.

As superintendent, you will be a very lucky man or woman. You will preside over a district that shares your norms and values. It will also be a district that is much more likely to seek to explain failure by looking for faults within itself than by highlighting your shortcomings or those of your students.

### District as an Organism

This district will be another one with a remarkably open environment. If this district is seriously threatened, however, it will, like most organisms, concentrate on survival. And then, things might get sticky for you as superintendent. Here, leadership will emphasize nurturing staff, teachers, and students. It will rarely be coercive except, perhaps, when the need to emphasize survival emerges, and balancing relationships between the schools and the community comes to the fore. Standards and assessment will be directed at feedback for students, teachers, and parents, not high-stakes decisions or punishment. The district as organism will emphasize nurturing all students as a strategy for closing the achievement gap. And it will also concentrate on encouraging principals who can adapt, while emphasizing community cohesion and close bonding with the community (symbiosis) as strategies for collaboration and engagement.

As superintendent, you will be a gardener, expected to lovingly tend to the needs of the organism for which you're responsible.

### District as a Brain

Here, we find one of the most complex images. It is also an image that, while appearing highly technocratic, works at creating conscious looping and feedback systems to encourage innovation and growth. It routinely engages in double-loop learning in the process questioning the appropriateness of its norms and practices. Here, district leadership is distributed. The board is likely to delegate to you a great deal of author-ity, which you, in turn, are expected to pass on to school teams. Governance will not be hierarchical, but more self-organizing, with groups and committees springing up to deal with issues as they arrive. Standards and assessment will go far beyond mindless "truth and conse-quences" to set out to build a truly integrated web of information. Are children in your seventh grade classroom doing poorly on math tests? This district will be able to point to assessments on these specific chil-dren indicating that the blockage lies in order of operations, not convert-ing fractions to decimals. The brain will emphasize formative and summative evaluations to deal with challenges of race, class, and the achievement gap. In fact, it will consider the existence of the achieve-ment gap to be a challenge to the system's intelligence. Principals? They must become learners who model learning for others. And collaboration and community engagement will be genuine, authentic, and continuous, both because the brain continuously senses its environment and because it is committed to a systems approach to everything.

As superintendent, you will be a combination of field scientist (presiding over data) and systems designer (ever alert to how changes in one part of the district's nervous system vibrate elsewhere in this complex organism).

### District as a Site of Flux and Transformation

Leading this district will provide you with the ultimate experience in dealing with adaptive challenges and developing a learning organiza-tion. Educational organizations have been described as loosely organized anarchies, and the district as a site of flux and transformation is likely to exhibit those tendencies. Leadership here will require you to be transformative. All leaders today say that's what they're interested in, but in this district, that is what you'd better be.

Governance in this district will evolve as the district changes. Data will not so much drive change as attract attention around which change can be explored. Issues of race and class will call for similar transformation—in this case, reaching far beyond the school to encourage massive social transformations. Principals will be developed as people who are comfortable with the ambiguity (or even chaos) of the district. Collaboration and engagement will be important but only to the extent that they serve the district's interest in evolving. Collaboration will be around meaning and purpose, while public engagement will emphasize relationships that assist the change the district pursues.

What about you? As superintendent, you are likely to be a philosopher, attuned to the Zen of change. Even if you're not a philosopher, you'll need to be comfortable with the central contradiction of flux and transformation, the reality that the district might shift direction tomorrow.

### 3. Mutually Exclusive?

These metaphors resonate powerfully with much of the current discussion about organizational life in school districts. Are these images and their implications for organizational behavior around the "commonplaces" mutually exclusive? Of course not. That's the value of the images. You are almost certain to find several of these images (and their associated behaviors) simultaneously at work in your district.

In many ways, each of these metaphors describes a genuine reality in your organizational life. At different times, you will draw on different metaphors to describe what is happening before you—and others within your district will also. Doing justice to the complexity of a school district requires multiple images.

Our argument (and Gareth Morgan's) is not that a single metaphor exists to best explain your district but that you must become adept at developing a story line to read and shape your organization. What is the dominant metaphor that applies in a particular situation (e.g., the machine)? What other images support and shape that dominant metaphor (e.g., organizations as cultures or political systems)? How do different people within your district (for example, the board and the union) read what's happening? And what are the implications of what both you and they believe in terms of the seven "commonplaces"? Your challenge is to move beyond the conflicts that appear in your office with predictable regularity every morning to understand the mind-sets and mental models contributing to them. Here, nuance and a subtle touch will be your allies.

### 4. The New Governance Paradigm

#### James Harvey

How well do current national and state efforts fit into these images? Do these images make sense in terms of No Child Left Behind (NCLB), Race to the Top (RTTT), Common Core State Standards, and large-scale state assessments and data bases? Actually, they do. These are all clearly initiatives that see a governance structure directed from on high, in which states and districts are viewed largely as political systems and machines that can be manipulated, indeed dominated, with enormous amounts of federal cash.

"I do not believe the president and secretary of education can improve education in America with what they are doing now," said Pasi Sahlberg, the Finnish ministry official responsible for international education cooperation during a Roundtable visit to Finland in June 2012. Finland leads the Western world on Program for International Student Assessment (PISA) assessments of 15-year-olds in reading, math, and science.

It's entirely possible, of course, that these approaches will produce the desired results. But, given the disappointments of prior federal efforts to reshape education that a number of contributors to this *Fieldbook* noted, it is not beyond the realm of possibility that a punitive, accountability-based approach that encourages the firing of principals and staff, no matter how satisfying it seems to be on paper, will fail to bear fruit. There is, of course, almost no research or field studies justifying the school turnaround strategies embedded in the $3.5 billion School Improvement Grants strategy.

What is compelling in reviewing the literature on organizational change is how little respect the RTTT and School Improvement Grant turnaround strategies pay to current thinking about how to improve organizational effectiveness. Jim Collins's *Good to Great* pays a lot of attention to the importance of getting the right people on the bus. Much of the turnaround strategy, with its emphasis on firing principals and replacing school staff, seems to be predicated on Collins's advice. But even Collins has acknowledged in a separate monograph that principles of *Good to Great* that make sense in the profit-making sector are inapplicable in public service.

Barely concealed within the approaches supported by the new governance paradigm is Douglas McGregor's long-discredited Theory X: the belief that management needs to lead through threats, coercion, and punishment. The extent to which the turnaround strategy contradicts today's organizational development theorists is striking. Argyris insists that prevailing management practices (in the private sector) encourage chronic absenteeism, psychological withdrawal, and the formation of unions. Leaders in a learning culture, reports Schein, assume the good intentions of the workforce and incorporate positive assumptions about human nature into human resource practices. (What should a school be if not a learning culture?) Fullan calls for cultivating relationships and creating a shared vision of the future. In fact, he asks for respect for *slow knowing*, that is to say, craft knowledge that is accumulated and developed over long and painful experience. Like Block, who warned against accepting the plans of self-styled experts, Fullan sounds the alarm against "leaders who are always sure of themselves."

What comes across in all of these expert observations about how organizations of any kind grow, develop, and thrive is the sense that values are at the core of organizational development, and they depend, in Haneberg's words, on human engagement, relationships, inclusion, respect, and empowerment.

At root, school transformation is adaptive work, not technical. It consists, in Heifetz's words, in diminishing "the gap between the values people stand for and the reality they face." By their very nature, situations requiring adaptive leadership (such as turning around low-performing schools in low-income communities) may not be susceptible to technical fixes of the sort contemplated by NCLB, RTTT, or the School Improvement Grants program, which seems to be grounded in a coercive management theory from the 1920s (Theory X).

A better approach might be to bet on William Ouchi's Theory Z. Ouchi called for greater job security, consensual decision making, and individual responsibility within the context of the group because he understood that involved workers are the key to increased productivity. That certainly seems to be the approach adopted in Finland (which espouses light steering from the center coupled with massive trust in the capabilities of educators at the school level). In Finland's high-performance public school system, public leaders understand that it is no less true for principals and teachers than it is for supervisors and assembly-line workers that the key to turning around lagging productivity lies in involving people on the front lines in the development of solutions.

> References to most authors noted here can be found throughout the book. For the work of Argyris, Ouchi, and Schein, see: Argyris, C. (1964). *Integrating the individual and the organization*. New York: Wiley; Ouchi, W.G. (1982). *Theory Z: How American businesses can meet the Japanese challenge*. Reading, MA: Addison-Wesley Press; and Schein, E. H. (2010). *Organizational culture and leadership*. (4th ed.). San Francisco, CA: Jossey-Bass.

## B. SCHOOL REFORM: A "WICKED" PROBLEM

### James Harvey

"Some problems are so complex that you have to be highly intelligent and well informed just to be undecided about them," said Laurence J. Peter, best known for revealing his Peter Principle: that people rise to meet their level of incompetence. That quote headlines Jeff Conklin's *Wicked Problems and Social Complexity*.

To hear the mainstream discussion, it seems clear that public education in the United States is a failed enterprise that can be reformed only through test-based accountability, charter schools, and the wholesale replacement of school staff. Research suggests, however, according to New York University historian Diane Ravitch, that charter schools are typically no improvement over traditional schools, that value-added assessment is beset with technical and practical challenges, and that turning schools around depends on a complex interplay, often over years, of several essential supports. See a summary of Ravitch's presentation to the Roundtable in 2010 at www.superintendentsforum.org.

Ravitch (2010) discusses these ideas at length in her bestselling book, *The Death and Life of the Great American School System*. New York: Basic Books.

The concept of *wicked problems* was developed by Horst Rittel in the 1970s. Rittel, a theorist and professor of design and social planning at Berkeley, was concerned about ill-conceived design solutions proposed for messy and difficult problems. He tagged such problems *wicked* to contrast them with relatively straightforward problems in mathematics and chess.

Unlike the challenge of calculating return on investment or making sense of a lot of numbers on a spreadsheet, "wicked" problems have incomplete, contradictory, and changing requirements, according to Rittel. They involve complex interdependencies. Solving one aspect of the problem reveals or creates other, sometime even more complex, problems. (In Senge's terms, they would be susceptible to quick-fix or shifting-the-burden archetypes discussed in Part II and later in this chapter.)

Jeff Conklin, a computer scientist at the Microelectronics and Computing Consortium (MCC) in Austin, Texas, produced a paper further describing and defining "wicked" problems and their characteristics in 2006. (MCC is a research consortium established in the 1980s, led at one time by Admiral Bobby Ray Inman, former head of, in succession, the Naval Intelligence Agency, the Defense Intelligence Agency, and the National Security Agency. MCC employees tend to be expert, focused, and very practical.)

For a complete picture of "wicked" problems, see Conklin, Jeff. (2006). "Wicked" problems & social complexity. In *Dialogue mapping: Building shared understanding of wicked problems* (chap. 1). Hoboken, NJ: Wiley. Additional information is available at the CogNexus Institute at http://cognexus.org.

One of the characteristics defining a "wicked" problem, according to Conklin, is that solving it requires large numbers of people to change their attitudes and behaviors (e.g., environmental issues). Another is that competing stakeholders have different views of what needs to be done (e.g., transportation issues). Does any of this sound familiar?

According to Conklin's paper, "wicked" problems exhibit the following characteristics:

- Fragmented understandings of what needs to be done arise because stakeholders are all convinced that their solution to the problem is correct. Fragmentation equals "wickedness" (i.e., difficulty and complexity) multiplied by social complexity. Remember those multiple facets on the diamond?
- You don't understand the problem until you have developed a solution. Indeed, there is no definitive statement of *The Problem.*
- "Wicked" problems have no stopping rule. Because there is no definitive *The Problem,* there is also no definitive *The Solution.*
- Solutions to "wicked" problems are not right or wrong. They are simply better, worse, good enough, or not good enough. With "wicked" problems, the determination of solution quality is not objective and cannot come from a formula.
- Every "wicked" problem is essentially unique and novel. There are so many factors and conditions, all embedded in a dynamic context, that no two "wicked" problems are alike, and the solutions to them will always be custom designed.
- Every solution to a "wicked" problem is a one-shot operation. Every attempt has consequences. The Catch 22 of "wicked" problems is that you can't learn about the problem without trying solutions, but every solution is expensive and has lasting, unintended consequences, which may well spawn new "wicked" problems.
- "Wicked" problems have no obvious solutions. There may be no solutions. Or there may be a host of potential solutions that can be imagined, and another host that are never even thought of.

Conklin offers these as examples of "wicked" problems: whether to route highways through cities or around them, how to deal with crime and violence in communities, and what to do when the world's supply of carbon-based fuels runs out. He does not include how to reform American schools as an example of a "wicked" problem, but the problem seems to classically match his definition. "Fixing" American schools will require large numbers of people to change their attitudes. Diverse stakeholders will have to come to agreement on how to proceed. It is clear from the failed efforts of the last 30 to 50 years that we don't fully understand the nature of the problem, although some attempts at solutions (e.g., focusing funds and the best teachers on students with greater need) may be better or good enough, while others (e.g., imposing curriculum solutions on local schools or judging teachers on student outcomes on the basis of tests designed for other purposes) may be worse or not good enough. And the Catch-22 of school reform is that solutions need to be tried in the hope they make a difference, but they may create more problems than they solve (e.g., adequate yearly progress requirements).

Indeed, as with most "wicked" problems, we may not so much invent an acceptable educational solution as stumble across it. At least three implications follow from this understanding of the challenge we face. First, continued experimentation at the school site and district levels should be thoughtfully pursued. The same is true of experimental or model efforts at the state and federal levels with regard to policy. Second, the positive and negative effects of these experiments need to be continually monitored. After 20 years of experimentation with charters and a decade of experiments with vouchers of various kinds, the evidence of their failure to address the achievement challenge they were designed to resolve seems indisputable. Third, because we are dealing with a "wicked" problem, experiments with both top-down imposition of standards, assessments, and accountability systems and bottom-up efforts to build local capacity for problem solving at the school and district levels are warranted. The opening lines of Conklin's monograph are instructive.

This is what Conklin has to say: "This book is about collective intelligence: the creativity and resourcefulness that a group or team can bring to a collaborative problem." Those words could just as easily be the opening lines of a book about systems thinking, organizational development, or the value of professional learning communities (PLCs). The fact that the appeal to collective intelligence embedded in theories of organizational development or PLCs runs counter to the certitudes embedded in NCLB or RTTT is no reason to abandon these appeals. On the contrary, the fact that we won't fully understand the nature of education's "wicked" problem until we have solved it argues for intensifying them.

## C. A 15-YEAR URBAN CASE STUDY IN THE UNITED STATES

James Harvey

Fifteen years of first-rate research on school improvement in Chicago confirms the "wicked" nature of the challenge of improving urban schools. Penny Bender Sebring is a senior research associate at the University of Chicago and founding codirector of the Consortium on Chicago School Research (CCSR). She was a major figure in a 15-year effort to examine Chicago school reform movements, an effort that culminated in *Organizing Schools for Improvement,* a striking intellectual accomplishment by five authors (including Bender Sebring) in 2010 that documented the complexity of school reform in urban areas. The book has been described as the "counter narrative" to the current reform discussion.

For a history of 15 years of school reform in the Windy City, see Bryk, Anthony S., Bender Sebring, Penny, Allensworth, Elaine, Luppescu, Stuart, & Easton, John Q. (2010). *Organizing schools for improvement: Lessons from Chicago.* Chicago: University of Chicago Press.

**The Good News.** Based on this research, Bender Sebring told the Roundtable: "I am convinced a comprehensive approach is required. It doesn't have much to do with merit pay, charter schools, or teacher compensation systems." Citing an analogy frequently mentioned in the consortium, she reported that genuine and deep-rooted reform is complex: "It is like baking a cake. If one of the ingredients is missing, the cake is ruined." Schools, she maintained, are complex organisms, with multiple interacting subsystems, each involving a mix of human and social factors that shape what is going on. Effective urban schools, she reported, require five major supports:

1. **School Leadership That Is Strategic and Focused on Instruction.** This requires district leadership to be the driver for change and, more specifically, school principals to serve as catalysts for systemic improvement. The principal builds "agency" for change at the school and community level, encouraging element number two.

2. **Parent and Community Ties.** It is essential to build new relations with local communities and parents to repair the "long-standing disconnect between urban schools and the children and families" they serve. Active outreach is critical.

3. **Professional Capacity.** This involves strengthening the processes supporting faculty learning while enhancing the faculty's professional capabilities through deliberate focus on the quality of new staff.

4. **A Student-Centered Learning Climate.** An environment needs to be nurtured in which students feel safe while being supported to engage and succeed in more ambitious intellectual activity.

5. **Instructional Guidance.** Cultivate schoolwide supports around curriculum and instruction to promote ambitious goals of academic achievement for every child.

If Chicago schools adhered to these five principles, for the most part, they'd improve over time. The real value of these supports rested on their combined strength. Schools that were strong in three to five of the supports were 10 times more likely to improve in reading and math than the other schools. Conversely, a persistent weakness in one of the supports undermined the school's efforts.

**The Bad News.** That's for the most part. What about the remaining part? Bender Sebring acknowledges that success was not always guaranteed. "We could find improving schools throughout Chicago," she reports. But "stagnating schools far more often than not were found in low-income communities." In truly disadvantaged Chicago communities, 70 percent of families were below the poverty level, compared with just 7 percent in integrated schools. In schools serving high proportions of truly disadvantaged students, 46 percent of these schools made little or no progress. "Just 15 percent of truly disadvantaged schools improved substantially over the life of the study, compared to 42 percent of racially integrated schools."

Looking beyond race and ethnicity, the study explored *bonding social capital* (a collective sense of efficacy in the community, religious participation, and crime statistics), *bridging social capital* (contacts with people outside the community), and the percentage of students living in extraordinarily difficult circumstances with histories of abuse or neglect. The results were troubling. Only 5 to 8 percent of individuals in communities with stagnating schools reported contacts outside the community, regular church attendance, or a sense that their destiny was in their own hands. By contrast, 33 to 39 percent of individuals in communities with improving schools felt a stronger sense of bonding and bridging social capital. Similar ranges could be determined with respect to crime rates (4 percent versus 36 percent) and the incidence of abuse and neglect (2 percent versus 40 percent).

> "When the density of problems walking through the front door is so palpable every day, it virtually consumes all your time and energy and detracts from efforts to improve teaching and learning."
>
> —Anthony S. Bryk, cofounder of the Consortium on Chicago School Research and president of the Carnegie Foundation for the Advancement of Teaching

"There are almost no good schools for children suffering abuse and neglect," said Bender Sebring. "These are children suffering terribly traumatic lives." One of Bender Sebring's coauthors, Anthony Bryk, was quoted in *Education Week* (January 25, 2010): "When the density of problems walking through the front door is so palpable every day, it virtually consumes all your time and energy and detracts from efforts to improve teaching and learning."

Bender Sebring concluded that disadvantaged communities need robust essential supports. Communities can respond to this need, she suggested, by investing in strengthening the capacity of schools and their ability to work together, adopting the five essential supports as the tasks around which schools should plan, encouraging professional development around the five essential supports, and bolstering partnerships with other agencies serving students.

## D. ARE YOU AND EDUCATORS LIKE YOU THE PROBLEM?

James Harvey

*Still, you have to deal with that activist cited in Part I who shows up at a board meeting or on local television to complain that Americans are spending more on schooling and getting less, while results on assessments are an international embarrassment. This is all part of the powerful new school zeitgeist described by Jennings, Rogers, and Josefsberg earlier in this volume. Here are some facts and figures you should have at your fingertips.*

## 1. Spending More and Getting Less?

This is a complete fabrication. It's a view that only the ignorant or malicious would put forward seriously. This myth comes in two parts—first, that spending is completely out of control and, second, that we are getting less for our money. Let's examine those in order.

Spending is out of control? That's a hard case to make when school spending is considered historically and in the context of the nation's ability to educate the next generation. Critics have liked to make the case by looking at per-pupil expenditures in isolation since 1920. Look at Figure 9.1, which examines national expenditures per pupil in the context of income per member of the labor force and national income per pupil since 1920. All figures are in constant 2009 dollars. It is crystal clear that national income per pupil and income per member of the labor force have risen dramatically faster than per-pupil

Dean of the Graduate School of Education and Human Development at George Washington University Michael J. Feuer served as executive director of the Division of Behavioral and Social Sciences and Education in the National Research Council (NRC) of the National Academies. He was the founding director of NRC's Board on Testing and Assessment.

Delivering the prestigious Angoff Lecture at the Educational Testing Service in 2012, Feuer warned that, although international assessment data can be helpful, policy makers should exercise caution in three areas: inferring trends from snapshots, linking educational measures to national economic outcomes, and overrelying on international assessments for high-stakes policy decisions. A link to Feuer's lecture, "No Country Left Behind," is available at http://tinyurl.com/beco72y.

**Figure 9.1**   Per-Pupil Expenditures in Broader Context, 1920–2008

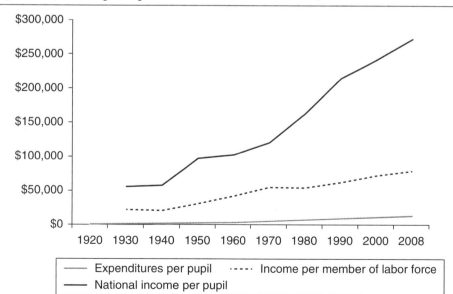

SOURCE: National Center for Education Statistics (NCES), Digest of Education Statistics, 2011, Table 35.

Much of the "research" undergirding criticisms of American public schools is quite weak. See Wainer, H. (2011). *Uneducated guesses: Using evidence to uncover misguided education policies.* Princeton, NJ: Princeton University Press.

expenditures. Both of these measures tell us something about the nation's ability to support its schools. Schools are nowhere near straining the nation's capacity to support the education of the next generation.

Less for our money? That's simply a preposterous claim. Again, if the 1920s are taken as an Augustan Age to which the nation should return, we would cut the proportion of high school graduates at age 17 from 76.7 percent in 2010 to 16.8 percent. Do we really want to go there? But that's not all.

- Status drop-out rates among those aged 16 to 24 would triple, just going back to 1960, when those rates first began to be calculated (jumping from 8 percent today to 27 percent).
- Enrollment of students with disabilities has nearly doubled since those data were first collected in 1976 (from 3,694,000 in 1976 to 6,483,000).
- The number of students with limited ability to speak English has nearly tripled in our schools since 1980 (from 4,691,000 to 11,204,000).
- And the number of girls participating in high school sports has increased tenfold since Title IX was enacted (jumping from 294,015 in 1972 to 3,057,266 in 2008).

Critics who argue we are getting less for our money forget that turning back the clock to a simpler and less-expensive era would require public schools to turn their backs on the educational and extracurricular needs of students with disabilities, those with limited ability to speak English, and of course, young women. But the most grievous consequence of following that advice would require American schools to once again pursue legalized discrimination against African-American students.

For a penetrating discussion of *de jure* and *de facto* segregation in the United States from the Jim Crow era to the present, see Clotfelter, Charles T. (2004). *After Brown: The rise and retreat of school desegregation.* Princeton, NJ: Princeton University Press.

In eight states in the old South, per-pupil expenditures on African-American students averaged only about 33 percent of expenditures on white students in the 1940s, according to Charles Clotfelter. In Mississippi, the figure was just 17 percent. Even in the 1950s, as the historic *Brown* decision made its way through federal courts, per-pupil spending on African-American students averaged about 66 percent of expenditures on white students in these eight states (with Mississippi again taking up the rear with a figure of 30 percent). One-room schoolhouses were the norm for African-American students throughout the South, many of them unheated wooden shacks without running water or bathrooms, much less libraries or gymnasiums. Surely, the people who complain about increased educational expenditures are not holding that discredited system up as the model to which we should return?

Expenditures per pupil have risen. But they have done so in order to ensure that all American children, black and white, men and women, English-speaking and English language learners, and those with and without disabilities enjoy equal access to publicly funded schools.

## 2. Student Achievement Declining?

Then, there's the assertion that student achievement is declining. Given the changing demographics in American schools, and the growth in the proportion of students living in poverty or enrolling with special needs, it might be understandable if such a decline had taken place. But, in fact, there has been no decline. On the contrary, data from the National Assessment of Educational Progress (NAEP), which is the only longitudinal data on the performance of American students, reveals encouraging progress in student learning (see Table 9.2).

> For a quick look at improvements in American student achievement, see "Statement on the Nation's Report Card: 2011 NAEP Mathematics and Reading," from David Driscoll, Chairman, National Assessment Governing Board at http://tinyurl.com/any2wmd.

Commenting on these results, former *New York Times* columnist Richard Rothstein noted:

> We can see that in 4th grade math, black students now have higher average achievement than white students had when the assessments began. Average black students' gains have been a full standard deviation, a rate of progress that would be considered extraordinary in any area of social policy. The black–white score gap has narrowed some, but not very much, because white students have also shown improvement.

It should be noted that analysts typically consider a gain of 10 to 15 points on NAEP to be the equivalent of a gain of one full grade level. Improvements in the raw NAEP numbers may look unexceptional, but they have powerful consequences. Even a four-point gain represents improvement of about half a grade level. Remarkably, as Table 9.2 indicates, American students

> Improvements in the raw NAEP numbers may look small, but they have powerful consequences. American students have climbed almost three full grade levels in fourth grade mathematics performance in the last two decades. Eighth graders have climbed about two grade levels.

Table 9.2    Long-Term Changes in NAEP Achievement Results

| Indicator | 1990 or 1992 NAEP | 2011 NAEP | Gain |
|---|---|---|---|
| **Fourth Grade** | | | |
| Proficient in reading | 29% | 34% | +5% |
| Proficient in math | 13% | 40% | +27% |
| **Eighth Grade** | | | |
| Proficient in reading | 29% | 34% | +5% |
| Proficient in math | 15% | 35% | +20% |
| **Fourth Grade** | | | |
| Average in reading | 217 | 221 | +4 |
| Average in math | 213 | 241 | +28 |
| **Eighth Grade** | | | |
| Average in reading | 260 | 265 | +5 |
| Average in math | 263 | 284 | +21 |

have climbed almost three full grade levels in fourth grade mathematics performance in the last two decades. Eighth graders have climbed about two grade levels.

None of this is meant to imply that additional improvements cannot be made. But it is to insist that the claim that student achievement has declined is false.

> The dissertation prospectus began with this claim: "Every year since 1950, the number of American children gunned down has doubled." But if that were true, even if only one child was shot dead in 1950, the number of American children gunned down would have been one billion by 1980, many times the size of the total U.S. population. "Most of the time," said Joel Best in 2001, "people accept statistics without question. . . . They accept even the most implausible claims without question." Best argued for casting a critical gaze on statistical reports because, although "most are pretty good, they are never perfect." See Best, Joel. (2001, May 4). Telling the truth about damned lies and statistics. *Chronicle of Higher Education.*

## 3. Threat to American International Competitiveness?

So, too, is the claim that international assessments demonstrate that American public schools put at risk the nation's economic competitiveness. This claim has been taken for granted for so long by so many that hardly anyone questions it anymore. But it is based on flimsy evidence, at best, and on a determined focus on numbers that help make the case, while ignoring evidence to the contrary.

Let's take the flimsy evidence first. Iris C. Rotberg, research professor of education policy at George Washington University and editor of *Balancing Change and Tradition in Global Education*

*Reform*, put the issue succinctly in an opinion column in *Education Week*: International test scores, she concludes, lead to irrelevant policies.

This is what Rotberg had to report:

> First, our rhetoric has assumed that test-score rankings are linked to a country's economic competitiveness, yet the data for industrialized countries consistently show this assumption to be unwarranted. For example, the World Economic Forum's 2010–2011 global-competitiveness report ranks the United States fourth, exceeded only by Switzerland, Sweden, and Singapore. Many of the countries that ranked high on test scores rank lower than the United States on competitiveness—for example, South Korea, No. 22, and Finland, No. 7.

> Although we cannot predict future economic trends, we do know that test-score rankings are a poor basis upon which to understand these trends or to know what to do about them. The reason is clear: Other variables, such as outsourcing to gain access to lower-wage employees, the climate and incentives for innovation, tax rates, health-care and retirement costs, the extent of government subsidies or partnerships, protectionism, intellectual-property enforcement, natural resources, and exchange rates overwhelm mathematics and science scores in predicting economic competitiveness.

Following Best's advice to cast "a critical gaze on most statistics," George Washington University's Iris Rotberg did so in a critical review of the value of most international assessments. See http://tinyurl.com/b9jwlay.

The Brookings Institution's Tom Loveless did also in examining whether there was any real statistical significance to the league tables reporting international means on the Trends in International Mathematics and Science Study (TIMSS).

There is also the issue that *league tables* of average student performance that place the United States around the midway point in global rankings may be relatively unimportant. What practical or statistical difference is there between one score and another? According to a recent Brookings Institution analysis of mathematics rankings produced by the Trends in International Mathematics and Science Study (TIMSS), although American fourth graders ranked 11th in the world, the scores were so close for so many nations that the United States was essentially tied for fifth place.

Or take the evidence to the contrary that is ignored. Much is made of the relatively mediocre performance in terms of average scores on the Program for International Student Assessment (PISA) assessment. Presidential candidates comment on these results. Business leaders complain that American competitiveness is at risk. Global energy companies mount expensive television advertising campaigns to raise alarm about the situation. But another piece of evidence from PISA is largely ignored and practically unknown. As Figure 9.2 indicates, as measured by PISA, American schools produce 25 percent of all high-achieving 15-year-old science students in the world. No one else is even close. Japan, which ranks second by this metric, produces just 13 percent of all high-achieving students.

**Figure 9.2**   Proportion of Science High Achievers

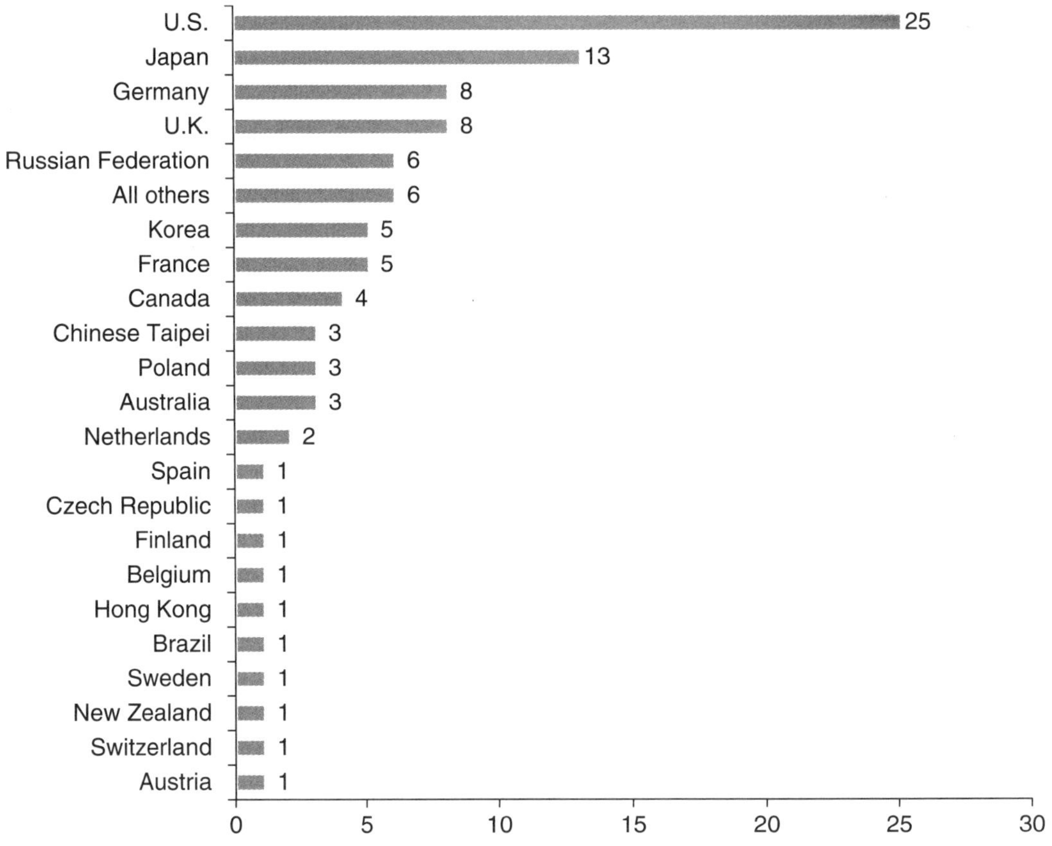

SOURCE: OECD, Top of the Class, 2009 (p. 21).

Let's be clear. U.S. average scores in science for 15-year-olds on PISA are not impressive. But that is because the United States also produces a lot of low-scoring students. The value of PISA to the United States is not that it points to a competitiveness issue but that it confirms the achievement gap.

## EDUCATION IN SINGAPORE

Preliminary observations based on a three-day 2011 visit

*Alan Burke*

### Competition

- This is fundamental to Singaporean education.
- Smartest students, identified by test scores, go to the best schools.
- Clear task is maximizing performance on test scores.
- Teachers are highly motivated to help students in test preparation.
- Educators and government officials believe strongly in ability grouping.

### Hard Work

- This is the norm in Singapore schools. Teachers work from 7:00 a.m. to 5:30 p.m. Some principals are responsible for two shifts of students.
- Culture is unforgiving for students who don't perform well. Although a sixth-grade education is maximum requirement, 98 percent of students graduate from high school.
- Math and science are not required high school subjects, but almost all students elect to take them.
- Singapore officials support a culture of meritocracy because a small nation with few natural resources must maximize its human potential.

### Respect for Teachers

- Teachers are highly regarded in Singaporean culture.
- Teaching candidates come from the top one-third of college graduates, and entrance to college is tightly controlled.
- As in Finland, competition for teacher training places is fierce. About 15,000 candidates compete for 3,000 places in teacher training institutions.
- As in Finland, once admitted, tuition is free (and living stipends are provided).
- Primary teachers may teach without a bachelor's degree, but observed quality of teaching was uniformly high.

### Centralized Control

- The central government is responsible for just about all facets of national life.
- A sign adjacent to a pedestrian and bicycle underpass indicated that failure to walk the bike through the underpass involved a potential $600 fine (U.S.).
- Citizens wishing to purchase a car must pay $48,000 (U.S.) queue fee before paying the full price of the car. The government can use this fee to limit traffic congestion without apparent resentment from citizens.

### Conclusions

- Comparing Singaporean and American education is a comparison of apples and oranges.
- We can't and shouldn't emulate Singapore, but we can learn from them, especially around the issue of well-prepared and -compensated teachers.

That said, one should view with considerable skepticism the claim that a national school system responsible for about 5 percent of all students in the world, which produces 25 percent of the highest-achieving 15-year-olds in science in the world, is putting the nation's competitiveness at risk.

Finally, it should be noted that, when PISA data for American schools is disaggregated by poverty level of the schools and performance of these "mini-American nations" is compared to performance in other nations with similar poverty rates, American average performance always leads the world. Table 9.3 provides the relevant data. It simply compares U.S. performance with the top two nations following it by poverty level.

Table 9.3    PISA Reading Results Disaggregated by Poverty

In the category of schools with poverty levels of 10% or less, the U.S. average of 551 placed  first out of nine nations.

| Country | Poverty Rate | PISA Score |
| --- | --- | --- |
| United States | <10% | 551 |
| Netherlands | 9.0% | 508 |
| France | 7.3% | 496 |
| Czech Republic | 7.2% | 478 |
| Switzerland | 6.8% | 501 |
| Belgium | 6.7% | 506 |
| Norway | 3.6% | 503 |
| Finland | 3.4% | 536 |
| Denmark | 2.4% | 495 |

In the next category (10–24.9%) the U.S. average of 527 placed first out of the ten comparable nations.

| Country | Poverty Rate | PISA Score |
| --- | --- | --- |
| United States | 10–24.9% | 527 |
| New Zealand | 16.3% | 521 |
| United Kingdom | 16.2% | 494 |
| Ireland | 15.7% | 496 |
| Italy | 15.7% | 486 |
| Portugal | 15.6% | 489 |
| Poland | 14.5% | 500 |
| Japan | 14.3% | 520 |
| Canada | 13.6% | 524 |
| Austria | 13.3% | 471 |
| Hungary | 13.1% | 494 |
| Greece | 12.4% | 483 |
| Australia | 11.6% | 515 |
| Germany | 10.9% | 497 |

For the remaining U.S. schools, their poverty rates over 25% far exceed any other country tested.

The differences are frequently small. But Table 9.3 provides striking confirmation of (1) the downward pressure on average American performance of the remarkably high levels of childhood poverty in the United States and (2) the capacity of American schools to outperform other school systems when poverty is taken into account.

**The Real Challenge.** The very real problem that American schools must face (and that most of the current crop of reformers should acknowledge) is the remarkably high levels of childhood poverty in the United States. This reality came home with startling clarity to Roundtable members during a 2012 study mission to Europe to obtain a better understanding of PISA by means of a briefing on the assessment at the Organization for Economic Cooperation and Development (OECD), which administers PISA, and to examine schools in Finland, France, and England. Table 9.4 illustrates some of the main differences in the four national school systems.

Several features stand out in this comparative chart. The United States is a very large country and remains the wealthiest nation in the world. It spends a lot of money on education. And although it ranks just 22nd in the world in science by average scores, it produces 25 percent of all high-performing PISA students. But the most startling statistic is the indicator of childhood poverty. In a world in which the Great Recession hit Europe every bit as hard as it hit the United States, nearly 22 percent of American children are in families living on half of the national median income or less. That figure falls to 16 percent for England, 7 percent for France, and just 3 percent for Finland. When one wonders why Finland leads the Western world on average PISA scores, one perhaps need look no further than Table 9.4 for a significant part of the explanation. This is the elephant in the room that most current reformers ignore at their peril.

Table 9.4   Education in an International Perspective

|  | Finland | France | England | United States |
| --- | --- | --- | --- | --- |
| Population | 5.4 million | 65 million | 53 million | 312 million |
| Per-Capita GDP | $36,236 | $35,156 | $35,090 | $48,387 |
| PISA Science Mean | 554 (2nd) | 498 (25th) | 514 (15th) | 502 (22nd) |
| Proportion of world's high-performing PISA students in science | 1% (tied for 14th) | 5% (6th) | 8% (3rd) | 25% (1st) |
| Children below 50% of median income | 3.4% | 7.3% | 16.2% (Britain) | 21.7% |

## 4. OBSERVATIONS ON EDUCATION ABROAD

Between 2008 and 2012, delegations of Roundtable superintendents participated in five 10-day study missions to China, visiting schools and meeting with government officials in Beijing, Harbin, Zhangjiakou, Nanjing, and Guanxi and Hebei provinces, and in an 11-day study mission to Europe, visiting schools and receiving briefings from government and OECD officials in Helsinki, Paris, and London. Based on these investigations, the Roundtable drew the following conclusions.

*James Harvey*

### China

- Education in China has made giant leaps in the last two generations, moving literacy from perhaps 10 percent of the population when Mao Zedong took control to near universal literacy today.
- The Chinese system is centrally controlled, with five-year plans for improvement regularly approved by the Politburo of the Communist Party of China.
- In the last decade, Chinese policy has aimed to provide universal access to schooling through what Americans would consider junior high school.
- The system is highly competitive, with only about 50 percent of students gaining admission to the equivalent of an American high school.

### Finland

- Finnish national policy emphasizes quality, efficiency, equity, and internationalism.
- A basic right to "education and culture" is embedded in the Finnish constitution.
- About 13 percent of the national budget is devoted to education.
- Universities typically have 7,000 applicants for 900 places.
- Finnish officials explain high performance on international assessments as based on trust and professionalism. The national model is described as one of "gentle steering built on the principle of trust."
- Inspection, ranking of schools, or national tests do not exist in Finland until the final examination for high school graduation.

### France

- The French system has been highly centralized since the time of Napoleon.
- Every teacher in France is a civil servant, and teachers represent about 60 percent of all government employees.
- Teachers are paid by the national government, but capital expenditures are covered by localities.

- France is cautiously piloting devolution and decentralization approaches, along with efforts to apply performance assessment to public policies but not personnel.

## England

- Full-time education has been compulsory up to the age of 16 and the school-leaving age was raised to 18 in 2008.
- The English system reflects many of the characteristics of the American reform movement—assessment, accountability, and the establishment of charter-like schools.
- In the last decade, 50 percent of all secondary schools in England have become privatized as either academies, trust schools, or "free" schools (free of government regulation).
- A university degree in England typically takes three years. A proposal under consideration is to add an additional year for teachers, devoted to theory and practice.
- The secretary of education is on public record as favoring free schools run for profit and staffed by teachers without certificates.

## 5. China Is Not "Eating Our Lunch"

*Kam Wing Chan, a native of Guandong Province, China, is a professor of geography at the University of Washington. His research focuses on China's migrant labor and urbanization. He describes the Shanghai students assessed by PISA as such a highly selected group in the wealthiest city in China that they can be considered "an extract of China's extract."*

### Kam Wing Chan

The lackluster performance of our 15-year-olds in math, science, and reading in a standardized test, compared with Shanghai's students scoring first in all three subjects, have stirred some interesting and somewhat self-deprecating comments. President Obama declared it a *Sputnik moment,* and syndicated columnist Esther Cepeda opined alarmingly about China "eating our lunch."

To be sure, our 14th to 25th ranking in PISA is no cause for complacency. Neither is China eating our lunch or any meal—at least not yet.

Following the first of five Roundtable visits to Chinese schools, Roundtable members Gerald Kohn and James Harvey concluded that only about 50 percent of Chinese students enter what Americans would consider a four-year high school. See Kohn, G. W., & Harvey, J. (2009, March). Acting decisively: China's story. *The School Administrator, 6*(3) (http://tinyurl.com/a3wwzx8).

We know that China is a master of turning out sparkling economic statistics. Some of those are real and deserve congratulations—China's economy is indeed on a meteoric rise. But many others are not so real, gamed by bureaucrats whose careers are tied to certain short-term statistical yardsticks or as a result of our ignorance of how China functions.

Cepeda is right in pointing out that the contrast of the U.S. scores with Shanghai's is not totally appropriate: It is comparing the entire U.S. population—including many who are on free or reduced-price lunches—with China's cream of the crop, the Shanghai kids.

Even more important, but far less known, is that, in Shanghai, as in most other Chinese cities, the rural migrant workers who are the true urban working poor (totaling about 150 million in the country) are not allowed to send their kids to public high schools in the city. This is engineered by the discriminatory *hukou*, or household registration system, which classifies them as outsiders. Those teenagers will have to go back home to continue education or drop out of school altogether.

In other words, the city has 3 to 4 million working poor, but its high school system conveniently does not need to provide for the kids of that segment. In essence, the poor kids are purged from Shanghai's sample of 5,100 students taking the tests. The Shanghai sample is the extract of China's extract. A fairer play would be to ask kids at Seattle's private Lakeside School to race against Shanghai's kids.

> The rhetoric of decline in American schools parallels a larger rhetoric of looming disaster in the United States itself. "Through the entirety of my conscious life, America has been on the brink of ruination, or so we have heard, from the launch of Sputnik through whatever is the latest indication of national falling apart or falling behind," wrote James Fallows in *The Atlantic* early in 2010. See http://tinyurl.com/9hlagsw.

More fundamentally, I would argue, the winner of the next true Sputnik race will not be called by PISA test scores.

It will be decided, instead, by other strengths the U.S. still has over China. We have a more open and receptive social system. For example, Washington State, like many other states, accepts undocumented immigrant children in their public schools and universities. Whereas in China, children of migrant workers—and these kids are Chinese nationals, not foreigners—are barred from attending high schools in cities where their parents work.

Moreover, U.S. education is generally far broader than simply getting good test scores, while top Chinese schools fixate on those. Kids in many American schools are exposed to a wider, sometimes open-ended, learning experience and are encouraged to explore beyond the conventional.

It is the openness and creativity of the American system and the opportunities it brings—the crucial factors that unleash the Bill Gateses of the world—that not only determine who eats the lunch but even what's on the menu.

After all, just a mere 20 years ago, the menu did not have anything to do with American inventions like iPods, Google, Twitter, and Facebook.

## E. SINGLE-LOOP OR DOUBLE-LOOP THINKING?

Nelda Cambron-McCabe

Decision making in government and our organizations moves between reflection and action. Ideally, we observe what has been happening; reflect on what we or others have done; compare this observation with our established norms; and then use the data to decide on our next course of action. Argyris and Schön described this process as *single-loop learning*, which may be effective in bringing about change in the short run.

> Argyris, Chris, & Schön, Donald. (1974). *Theory in practice: Increasing professional effectiveness.* San Francisco: Jossey-Bass.

As national, state, and local systems become more complex, however, this type of learning creates barriers to making necessary changes because single-loop learning fails to question the assumptions and norms of the system.

Suppose, for example, that the behaviors and norms you're attempting to improve are ineffective or inappropriate for dealing with the changes you face (whether you are the U.S. secretary of education or a local superintendent)? How do you know what's appropriate? Suppose the problem is not how well you do what you do but what you choose to do in the first place? The challenge isn't to do something properly; it's to figure out the proper thing to do.

Gareth Morgan, whom we met in Part II, highlighted the limitations of single-loop thinking with the example of a household thermostat. The thermostat represents a simple system that moves through the single-loop cycle of monitoring the environment for deviation from the set temperature (or norm) and correcting it. The thermostat, using its single loop, cannot determine if the preset temperature is right for the number of the people in the room and thus adjust it accordingly. In other words, because the thermostat cannot question the established norm, it cannot change its behavior and learn to do its job more effectively. This act requires engaging in a second learning cycle (in communication with the first), often referred to as *double-loop learning*.

According to Morgan and others in organization research, organizations rarely engage in double-loop learning. In fact, the bureaucracies of our organizations actually impede the learning process. Yet, it is this self-questioning ability that enables individuals and organizations to learn.

> Bureaucracies not only impede the learning process; they also frequently behave as though individuals who question established procedures or the status quo are somehow disloyal to the organization's larger mission. This is a surefire recipe for guaranteeing single-loop thinking.

These questions engage reflection about standards and assessment. You can modify the list to reflect on any issue in any organization.

When you feel you are pushing against the system and your actions are not generating meaningful changes in your schools, slow down and take up the questions in the following exercise. They may be able to lead you into double-loop learning and meaningful transformation.

*Questions for Double-Loop Reflection About Standards and Assessments*

- What are we doing now to measure student progress? Why are we using this approach? What assumptions drive it?
- Do our current actions make sense educationally?
- Are we measuring what we think we are measuring?
- Are we measuring the appropriate things?
- Who benefits under this approach? Who loses?
- What beliefs, attitudes, and values prevent us from creating other alternatives?
- What are our aspirations for student learning?
- What aspect of my thinking must change to promote transformation of our present practices?

## 1. Are We "Shifting the Burden" in Schools?

*In systems archetypes (see Part II), a "shifting the burden" story usually begins with an urgent problem or symptom followed by demands to fix it. A quick fix is often obvious and immediate; it has the illusion of certainty and the reward of short-term efficiency. But it diverts attention away from the real source of the problem and ultimately does not sustain itself. A better solution is more fundamental, but it takes longer and is much more uncertain. Building support for it is more difficult. Torn between these two approaches, we are naturally drawn to the quick fix. The example that follows traces potential effects of more standardized tests in schools, but it could just as easily be applied to starting more charter schools, implementing vouchers, or evaluating teachers on the basis of their students' assessment results.*

Michael Goodman

Janis Dutton

Art Kleiner

Schools have felt increasing pressure from federal and state leaders and their communities to "prove" their competence by improving scores on standardized tests. But standards have nothing to say about the fundamental reasons why performance in some schools might be worse than others or about how to close the gap in any sustainable way. So, the quick fix plays out: Typically from January through March, teachers convert their classrooms into preparatory courses for test-taking skills, and the initial results are indeed higher. The quick fix works!

Once the test is over, however, most students forget the material acquired through the intensive drills. (Confess. Can you still remember how to solve a quadratic equation? Do you even remember what a quadratic equation is?) Students who have difficulty with tests, whatever the reason, see fewer opportunities to excel. They may see no reason to try. The result? Failure and drop-out rates increase. In effect, the students who are not attuned to test taking are punished. This situation affects overall skill levels, which leads to lower overall performance. With the symptom reappearing, there is a renewed demand for another quick fix—raising the bar again for even tougher standards and tests.

> This section was adapted with permission from Senge, Peter, Cambron-McCabe, Nelda, Lucas, Timothy, Smith, Bryan, Dutton, Janis, & Kleiner, Art. (2012). *Schools that learn: A fifth discipline fieldbook for educators, parents, and everyone who cares about education.* New York: Doubleday, pp. 375–380. This book can be consulted for an overview of archetypes and causal-loop diagrams.

The causal-loop diagram in Figure 9.3 portrays this "shifting the burden" story. Faced with pressures to improve performance (in the center of the diagram), educators can either focus on improving test results (upper loop) or concentrate on the fundamental solution (bottom loop).

Everyone in the school system understands the dangers of the standardized test "quick fix." Yet, everyone feels forced into the pattern. Why? Because the fundamental solutions require investment, time, and care. They require attentiveness to varied learning styles, in-depth staff development, curriculum revisions, nutrition, and much more, including perhaps many things in the community. Most of all, fundamental solutions are slower to produce results, and we cannot be certain of them. It is very difficult to endure the delay before results improve.

The loop on the right side maps the negative side effects of diverting attention and resources to quick fixes, such as eliminating learning activities or professional development not specific to the tests and short-circuiting teachable moments. When well-intentioned, quick-fix efforts themselves become the problem, it is harder to seek and apply fundamental solutions. Often, the availability of quick fixes reduces the perceived need for fundamental solutions.

This archetype can assist you as you reflect on other pressing issues. Follow these steps to gain insight into whether you are relying on quick fixes (or as Ron Heifetz would say, technical responses) or taking steps to develop fundamental solutions.

- What problem is creating a sense of urgency for you?
- What quick fixes are tempting you?

Remember several points as you use this archetype for reflection. First, various groups within the district may see different fundamental solutions. This offers an opportunity to engage all constituencies in conversations to develop a shared understanding of the problem and options. Second, some problems must be addressed immediately with a quick fix. Using a quick fix buys time to pursue a fundamental solution as long as you do not lose sight of the fact that the quick fix is not the fundamental solution.

- What could be the unexpected results of these short-term fixes?
- What alternative approaches could you try if the quick-fix avenue were not available?
- Do any of these alternatives represent a more fundamental response to the problem?
- What kinds of investment would you need to really make them work?
- What time frame would be required?
- How can you sustain an approach involving substantial delays with your various publics?

**Figure 9.3**   Causal-Loop Diagram

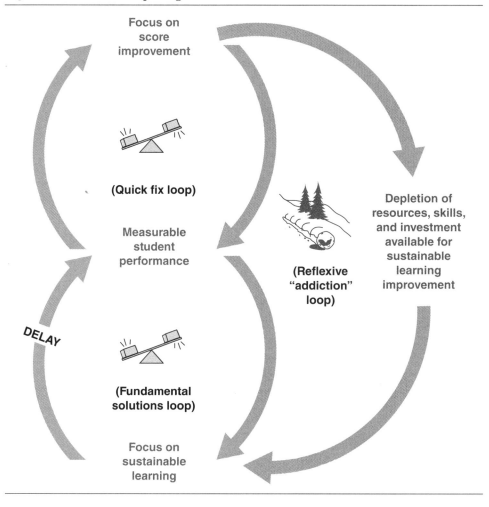

# F. FOUR LEADERSHIP STYLES

In the end, of course, your success as superintendent will come down to leadership. It always does. The same is true for the success of federal, state, and foundation officials. What does all the detail and complexity we've nearly overwhelmed you with in this book imply for your actions as a leader?

Marc Roberts of the School of Public Health at Harvard University has a take on this that you may find helpful. It pulls together in a useful way a lot of the material presented here. Are you intrigued by the distinctions between adaptive and technical work? Are you trying to use double-loop learning? You can find a way to think about both here. Do the organizational images interest you? You will be able to see them here and find new images to guide your own behavior. What about leading a learning organization? Are you relying too frequently on quick fixes? Roberts's intuition can help you with all of these leadership challenges.

What is a learning organization? And how do we create one? The answer to these questions, suggests Roberts, cannot be found in particular models. You need to get your district to understand that its sense of mastery is embedded not in specific technologies or procedures but in its capacity to adapt and change, that is, its capacity to learn. Progress depends on a state of mind that's willing to say "farewell."

## 1. Leader as Poet, Prophet, Coach, or Therapist

Metaphors are a form of knowledge, agrees Roberts, an important way for us to understand the realities we experience. There is no ideal leadership model, he argues. Different situations require different ways of looking at leadership. Sometimes, it's reasonable to issue ultimatums and orders (if a hurricane is bearing down on the district, for example, you don't want principals wondering whether to close schools). In other situations, exhortation may be the leadership style required (for example, encouraging the local child protective services agency to visit a home one more time).

One way to think of this is to envision a two-part continuum, suggests Roberts (see Figure 9.4). Along the vertical continuum, we find changes ranging from the very big to the relatively modest. That continuum intersects with a horizontal one, where leaders' confidence in what they know about the challenge varies from almost complete ignorance to total mastery. The leadership style appropriate for each of the quadrants this figure creates is quite different.

The leadership style called for in Quadrant A (the change required is major, and you are confident you know what to do) is that of a prophet. You are determined to close the achievement gap. You are

Figure 9.4   Leader as Poet, Prophet, Coach, and Therapist

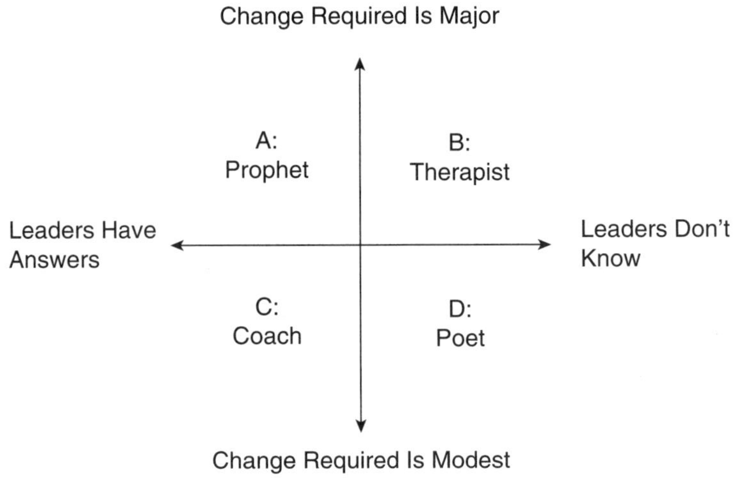

Change Required Is Major

A:
Prophet

B:
Therapist

Leaders Have
Answers

Leaders Don't
Know

C:
Coach

D:
Poet

Change Required Is Modest

convinced that the way to accomplish that is through standards and assessment, harnessed to powerful consequences for failure. You cannot blow an uncertain trumpet in such a situation. Only Moses will do. To succeed as a leader here, you have to show people the Promised Land while guaranteeing them a road map through the desert. In this role, if you need the seas to part and the sun to stand still to permit you to finish your work, you must assure the public you're up to the task.

Being a prophet is a big job. It's a very satisfying role. The public will stand in awe of you. But make sure you deliver on the prophecy. People very quickly get testy with prophets who disappoint them.

Quadrant B presents a different leadership challenge. Here the required change is massive, but you're not sure what to do. This is the classic adaptive challenge. The leadership style required is that of a therapist. Think of Bob Newhart dealing with the impossible demands of a neurotic on the phone. When things start falling apart, everyone tends to become a bit neurotic, particularly when faced with the loss of something precious.

When a judge hands down a decision about integration that requires substantial realignment of attendance boundaries, your community will tighten up. People in the district will also get excited when population shifts require you to close schools in the south end while building new ones in the north. (Beware of false prophets showing up in this quadrant, promising easy solutions to these challenging problems. Neurotics are likely to be attracted to them.) When it comes to shutting down schools, citizens are going to look around for someone to blame. You could very easily wind up in the firing line. In these situations, you have to do a lot of hand-holding, keeping the community together and listening to its problems as it works them out. This is precisely the role Ron Heifetz suggests you adopt in working through adaptive challenges. In addition to hand-holding, make sure you gather some critical friends around you and find some way to get to the balcony. This is very difficult work, requiring double-loop learning. It's not a question of doing things properly but of doing the proper thing.

Life is much simpler when the changes required are minimal (Quadrant C) and you are confident you know what to do. This is technical and single-loop work. You know how to handle it. It's a breeze. Ideally, you could turn the problem over to an assistant and head for the beach. If it's a little more challenging, you can coach your people through what needs to be done. The changes required are probably fairly minor. You don't have to be a prophet or a therapist. People can see what's required and probably won't be angry about it. Here, you can visualize yourself as a coach.

A therapist may be required when the changes are enormous and you are unsure, but when relatively modest change is in the air and you are uncertain (Quadrant D), you might want to think of yourself as a poet. Here, it's important to remind the community of what it stands for, what its "song" is. This can be challenging, too, especially if you are new in town and still trying to learn the lyrics yourself.

Even though, in your mind, the change is a relatively modest administrative matter (closing High School A for 12 months to refurbish it while enrolling School A's students in School B), it may loom as enormous and life shattering for many students and parents. You have to help people through this, too. A little hand-holding is probably in order while reminding the community of its values—passing on excellence in education to the next generation. So, you need to be a bit of a bard here. Bards and poets, after all, remind the community of its history and songs; they help preserve the vision and emotions that make the community a community.

The challenge, of course, is knowing when to apply which leadership style to which challenge. On one level, that might require another fieldbook. But, for now, revisit the images and "commonplaces" outlined in this one. They cover a lot of ground and promise to give shape and meaning to your superintendency and your leadership. Good luck.

## G. REFLECTIVE PRACTICE

Think about leadership, your style, and your district. Where are you, your colleagues, and your district on these issues?

*What images of organization do you hold* about your district? Think about this carefully. What's the dominant story line in your mind? What images support that story?

*Track recent developments in the district against your images.* Do the images still hold up? Or are you kidding yourself about how the district functions?

*What images of organization do major players* in your district hold? Board members? Unions? Business and community leadership? Are they similar or different?

*What are the implications of those images* for your work?

*How do the images of the various stakeholders affect the "commonplaces"?* Are you fairly comfortable with the cross-indexed table presented in this section? If not, how would you change it?

*Are you more attracted to the emerging images? Or do the inherited images seem more real to you?* Each of these metaphors has some strengths and weaknesses. Can you work through an exercise in which, individually, your board, unions, and central office lay out the pros and cons? Could you then bring the three groups together to compare their perceptions?

*Identify three to five issues in your community,* and relate these issues or developments to the images and "commonplaces" described in this section. Does your district lean toward quick fixes or toward laying the groundwork to pursue fundamental solutions?

*If you had to define your job from the many metaphors* presented in this part (ranging from prophet to flunky), what would it be?

*Can you describe situations in which you have exercised leadership in a different way* depending on your level of knowledge and the complexity of the challenge? When have you been a prophet? When have you felt more like a therapist?

*Where is your board* on these leadership questions? What about the union and the central office?

*How would you defend American education?* One defense was laid out above. Are you comfortable with that? Or would you offer a different defense?

*What criticisms would you make of American schools?* A conventional wisdom about school failure exists. Do you accept it? Or would you make a different set of criticisms?

*Are you open to the idea that the solution to the "wicked" problem of school reform will require constant effort and experimentation?* Or do you see that as a cop-out?

*What about your community and your board?* Are they open to hearing that defining the problem, much less the solution, is likely to be difficult and time-consuming, calling for rethinking on the part of everyone?

*What do you stand for?* Name the one thing on which you'd be willing to stake your career.

# *Appendices*

The four of us have spent the two decades since 1992 working with fascinating leaders in American education, first in the Danforth Forum for the American School Superintendent and then with its successor, the National Superintendents Roundtable. Our experiences with some 300 superintendents in these organizations provided the backbone of this *Fieldbook*. Here, in these appendices, we provide a short description of the Forum and the Roundtable and as complete a listing of the membership over the years in both as we can reconstruct.

Clearly, we relied on a lot of help, both within and outside the Forum and the Roundtable, to put this volume together. We want to acknowledge the huge debt we owe to our contributors. These appendices also tell you who they are.

# *Appendix A*

## *The National Superintendents Roundtable and the Forum for the American School Superintendent*

James Harvey

**A**s a school leader, do you smile grimly if someone reminds you that, when you're up to your knees in alligators, it's hard to remember you started out to drain the swamp? You're not alone. That's why the Danforth Foundation set out in 1992 to create a 10-year effort to help practicing school superintendents deal with the leadership challenges they face. When foundation support ended, the superintendents decided they wanted to continue this professional learning community (PLC), renaming it the National Superintendents Roundtable and financing it with membership fees drawn from their professional development budgets.

Throughout this work, these superintendents challenged themselves to improve learning opportunities for their students. In semiannual meetings, working groups known as *initiatives,* study missions to China and to Europe, and in hotel meeting rooms, public gatherings, and school board meetings, the questions they put to themselves were always the same: How can we make sure all children learn? What do we have to do to help young children make the transition from home to school? How can we work with our communities to create schools that are vibrant and strong? Can we lead when difficult problems have no easy answers? Where can we find new ways to strengthen the front line of school administration, the school principal? And, as the number of "minority" Americans becomes a majority, how does this society make good on its forgotten promises of equal opportunity?

The people who made up the Roundtable and the Forum harbored no illusions that the task of improving American schools was easy. Turnover among superintendents is endemic. Part of the turnover relates to the maturity of people who become school superintendents; within 5 to 10 years of assuming their positions, many reach retirement age. But chaos within individual members' districts is hardly unknown. Signs of turnover are easy to see. Forty-one superintendents gathered at the inaugural Forum meeting in 1992. Ten years later, just one of them held the same position. When the Roundtable first met in 2007, 40 members participated. Five years later, just 7 were in the same position. The rest had retired or moved on, voluntarily or involuntarily, and several members served in more than one superintendency. In both the Roundtable and the Forum, it was not unusual to see districts with several different superintendents in just a few years. Sustaining leadership amid turmoil of this sort is beyond being a challenge; it's well-nigh impossible.

Several considerations dominated the structure and functions of both organizations:

- The Roundtable and the Forum were for superintendents. These were not activities about superintendents or to study them. These were for them, and superintendents themselves determined the agenda.
- Both provided a safe harbor, a place where superintendents could feel secure discussing the challenges they faced while reflecting on their successes and disappointments.
- Third, both organizations encouraged a diverse membership base, both in terms of gender and ethnicity and in terms of representation of small, medium, and large school districts.

And so was created, in both organizations, a diverse group harnessed to a diverse agenda—men and women, white superintendents and super-intendents from minority backgrounds, superintendents committed to examining education in the United States and abroad, big districts, small districts, and everything in between. Something greater than the sum of its parts developed in both the Roundtable and the Forum. These superintendents realized that what they shared in common was much more powerful than what seemed to set them apart.

Like most people in the world today, educators rarely have the opportunity to stick to one thing for many years in a row. The Roundtable and the Forum were gifts to their participants. The great value of both was the extended support they provided to help superintendents cope with the challenges they faced. The great benefit was delivered to the children and families in these superintendents' districts. And their great glory consisted of the men and women in them. This *Fieldbook* is dedicated to them.

# Appendix B

## Members of the Danforth Forum for the American School Superintendent

Our records haven't been perfect, and the list below may miss a few people, but it includes most of the superintendents who were members of the Forum. Because several participants moved among positions, the affiliation listed is the last position held during the Forum's lifetime. The list includes members of the Forum's advisory committee.

| | |
|---|---|
| Antony Amato | Hartford, Connecticut |
| Raymond Armstrong | Normandy Public Schools, Missouri |
| Lynn Beckwith, Jr. | University City, Missouri |
| Alan Beitman | Manchester Public Schools, Connecticut |
| Arnold Bell | Chaffee R-2 Public Schools, Missouri |
| Richard Benjamin | Cobb County Schools, Georgia |
| Stuart D. Berger | Baltimore, Maryland |
| Cloyde "Mac" Bernd | Arlington Public Schools, Texas |
| Thomas C. Boysen | Commissioner of Education, Kentucky |
| Hugh Burkett | Clover Park Schools, Washington |
| Paula Butterfield | Mercer Island, Washington |
| Nelda Cambron-McCabe | Miami University, Oxford, Ohio |
| Benjamin Canada | Portland, Oregon |
| Gene R. Carter | ASCD, Alexandria, Virginia |
| Rudy M. Castruita | San Diego County, California |

*(Continued)*

(Continued)

| | |
|---|---|
| Cile Chavez | Littleton, Colorado |
| Roland Chevalier | St. Martin Parish School District, Louisiana |
| Carol B. Choye | Scotch Plains–Fanwood Public Schools, New Jersey |
| Pendery Clark | San Mateo, California |
| Audrey Clarke | Lynwood, California |
| Constance Clayton | Philadelphia, Pennsylvania |
| Dan Colgan | St. Joseph, Missouri |
| Paul Copes | Bloomfield, Connecticut |
| Joe Coto | East Side Union High School District, California |
| Rudolph F. Crew | New York, New York |
| Luvern L. Cunningham | (Retired) The Ohio State University, Columbus, Ohio |
| Beatriz Reyna-Curry | San Elizario, Texas |
| Patricia Daniel | Hartford, Connecticut |
| Ray Daniels | Kansas City Public Schools, Kansas |
| Daniel Daste | Anderson County, Tennessee |
| Eddie Davis | Manchester, Connecticut |
| John E. Deasy | Santa Monica–Malibu Unified School District |
| Ronald Epps | Richland County Schools, Columbia, South Carolina |
| Howard Fuller | Marquette University, Wisconsin |
| Barbara Gates | Crossett School District, Arkansas |
| Shirl Gilbert | Indianapolis, Indiana |
| T. Josiha Haig | East Orange School District, New Jersey |
| James Hager | Washoe County, Nevada |
| Beverly Hall | Atlanta, Georgia |
| Cleveland Hammonds | St. Louis, Missouri |
| Geraldine Harge | Nye County School District, Nevada |
| E. Jean Harper | Elyria City Schools, Ohio |
| Lois Harrison-Jones | Boston, Massachusetts |
| James Harvey | University of Washington, Seattle, Washington |
| Robert Henley | University of Missouri, Kansas City, Missouri |
| Paul T. Hill | University of Washington, Seattle, Washington |

| | |
|---|---|
| N. Gerry House | Memphis, Tennessee |
| Peter Hutchinson | Minneapolis, Minnesota |
| Clifford Janey | Rochester City Schools, New York |
| Robert H. Koff | The Danforth Foundation, St. Louis, Missouri |
| Joan P. Kowal | Hayward Unified School District, California |
| Diana Lam | Providence Public Schools, Rhode Island |
| Mary Leiker | Kentwood Public Schools, Kentwood, Michigan |
| Wayne Lett | Newport News Public Schools, Newport News, Virginia |
| David Mahan | St. Louis, Missouri |
| Mark A. Manchin | Webster County, West Virginia |
| Floretta McKenzie | The McKenzie Group, Washington, DC |
| Patsy Menefee | Kendleton, Texas |
| Richard "Pete" Mesa | Oakland, California |
| Iris Metts | Christina Schools, Newark, Delaware |
| Vern Moore | University City, Missouri |
| Linda Murray | San Jose Unified School District, California |
| Mary Nebgen | Washoe County, Nevada |
| Peter Negroni | Springfield Public Schools, Massachusetts |
| Margaret E. Nichols | Eugene School District 4-J, Oregon |
| Steven C. Norton | Cache County School District, North Logan, Utah |
| Les Omotani | West Des Moines Community Schools, Iowa |
| Sammi Campbell Parrish | Cleveland, Ohio |
| Bertha Pendleton | (Retired) San Diego Public Schools, California |
| Robert Peterkin | Harvard University, Cambridge, Massachusetts |
| Frank Petruzielo | Broward County, Florida |
| Michael Redburn | Bozeman Public Schools, Montana |
| Waldemar Rojas | San Francisco, California |
| George Russell | Eugene School District 4-J, Oregon |
| Abelardo Saavedra | Corpus Christi, Texas |
| Howard Sanders | Hollandale, Mississippi |
| Neal Schmidt | Santa Monica–Malibu Unified School District, California |

*(Continued)*

(Continued)

| | |
|---|---|
| Janice Sheets | Tahlequah, Oklahoma |
| Patricia Sholar | Binger-Oney School District, Oklahoma |
| Bruce Smith | Normandy Schools, St. Louis, Missouri |
| Franklin Smith | Washington, DC |
| Rosa Smith | Columbus Public Schools, Ohio |
| Ronald Stanfield | Coalville, Utah |
| William Symons | Charlottesville City Schools, Virginia |
| Charles Terrett | Fulton County, Kentucky |
| John Thompson | Pittsburgh Public Schools, Pennsylvania |
| J. Herbert Torres | Silver Consolidated Schools, Las Cruces, New Mexico |
| Frank Tota | Dobbs Ferry, New York |
| Doris Walker | Clover Park Schools, Washington |
| Richard C. Wallace, Jr. | (Retired) Pittsburgh Public Schools, Pennsylvania |
| Gary Wegenke | Des Moines, Iowa |
| Ron White | Cameron, Missouri |
| Cheryl Wilhoyte | Madison, Wisconsin |
| James Williams | Dayton, Ohio |
| Henry P. Williams | Kansas City, Missouri |
| Ron Williams | Webster County, West Virginia |
| Charlotte Wright | Weiner, Arkansas |
| Gary Wright | Cooperating School Districts, St. Louis, Missouri |
| Saul Yanofsky | White Plains City School District, New York |
| Arthur Zarrella | Providence, Rhode Island |

# Appendix C

## Members of the National Superintendents Roundtable

This list includes most of the superintendents who were members of the National Superintendents Roundtable between 2007 and 2012. Because several participants moved among positions, the affiliation listed is the last position held during their membership in the Roundtable. The list also includes members of the Roundtable's steering and advisory committees.

| | |
|---|---|
| Anthony Annunziato | Smithtown Central Schools, New York |
| Peter Ansingh | West Des Moines Community Schools, Iowa |
| Paul Ash | Lexington Public Schools, Massachusetts |
| James Baker | Middlesex Borough Public Schools, New Jersey |
| Twyla Barnes | Vancouver Public Schools, Washington |
| Marianne Bartley | Lebanon Public Schools, Pennsylvania |
| Donald Beaudette | Norwell Public Schools, Massachusetts |
| Louise Berry | Brooklyn Schools, Connecticut |
| David Bickford | Orange-Windsor Supervisory Union, Vermont |
| Joyce Bisso | Hewlett–Woodmere Public Schools, New York |
| Bruce Borchers | Rockwood School District, Missouri |
| Diana Bourisaw | St. Louis Public Schools, Missouri |

*(Continued)*

(Continued)

| | |
|---|---|
| Martha Bruckner | Council Bluffs Community Schools, Iowa |
| Carl Bruner | Mount Vernon School District, Washington |
| J. Kamala Buckner | Thornton Township High School District 205, Illinois |
| Nelda Cambron-McCabe | Miami University, Oxford, Ohio |
| Carol Choye | Scotch Plains–Fanwood Public Schools, New Jersey |
| Constance Clark-Snead | Westbury Schools, New York |
| Pendery Clark | San Mateo–Foster City Schools, California |
| Kathleen Cooke | Hamilton Public Schools, Wisconsin |
| Harriet Copel | Shoreham–Wading Schools, New York |
| Bernard Creeden | Tri-Town School Union, Massachusetts |
| Luvern L. Cunningham | Leadership Development, New Albany, Ohio |
| Yvonne Curtis | Forest Grove School District, Oregon |
| Suzanne Cusick | Longview School District #22, Washington |
| Gloria Davis | Decatur District 61 Public Schools, Illinois |
| John E. Deasy | Prince George's County Public Schools, Maryland |
| Juli Di Chiro | Ashland Public Schools, Oregon |
| Margaret Dolan | Westfield Public Schools, New Jersey |
| Janie Edmonds | Mendham Borough Schools, New Jersey |
| James Egan | Southwestern Wisconsin Schools, Wisconsin |
| Eric Eversley | Freeport Public Schools, New York |
| Daniel Fishbein | Ridgewood Public Schools, New Jersey |
| Charles Fowler | School Leadership LLC, New Hampshire |
| Mark Freeman | Shaker Heights Public Schools, Ohio |
| David Gentile | Millville Public Schools, New Jersey |
| Michael Gorman | Pemberton Township Schools, New Jersey |
| Timothy Grieves | Northwest Area Education Agency, Iowa |
| Frank Hackett | Pembroke Public Schools, Massachusetts |
| James Harvey | National Superintendents Roundtable, Washington |
| Margaret Hayes | Scotch Plains–Fanwood Public Schools, New Jersey |

| | |
|---|---|
| Douglas Hesbol | Laraway Community Schools, Illinois |
| Joseph Hochreiter | Elmira City School District, New York |
| Mary Ellen Johnson | Johnson & Associates, Massachusetts |
| Mark Jones | Pennsville Township Schools, New Jersey |
| Bernard Josefsberg | Easton–Redding Region 9 District, Connecticut |
| Kelly Kalinich | Kenilworth School District 38, Illinois |
| Richard Katz | Clinton–Glen Gardner Schools, New Jersey |
| Matthew Keegan | Norwell Public Schools, Massachusetts |
| Susan King | Rockport Public Schools, Massachusetts |
| Scott Kizner | Harrisonburg City Schools, Virginia |
| Robert Koff | Washington University of St. Louis, Missouri |
| Gerald Kohn | Harrisburg Public Schools, Pennsylvania |
| Kevin Konarska | Kent Intermediate School District, Michigan |
| Michael Kuchar | Bergenfield Public Schools, New Jersey |
| Steven Ladd | Elk Grove Unified School District, California |
| William Lahmann | Olympia School District, Washington |
| Mary Leiker | Kentwood Public Schools, Kentwood, Michigan |
| Michael Liechty | Cache County School District, Utah |
| Darrell Lockwood | Masconomet Regional Schools, Massachusetts |
| Marilyn Loushin-Miller | Hillsborough City School District, California |
| Betheny Lyke | Thornton Township High School District 205, Illinois |
| Christine Mahoney | East Granby Public Schools, Connecticut |
| Ralph Marino, Jr. | Horseheads Central School District, New York |
| Gerri Martin | McDowell County Public Schools, North Carolina |
| Mike Maryanski | Tahoma School District, Washington |
| Art McCoy | Ferguson–Florissant Schools, Missouri |
| Michael McGill | Scarsdale Public Schools, New York |
| C. Kent McGuire | Southern Education Foundation, Georgia |
| Paul Mohr, Jr. | Murphy Public Schools, Phoenix, Arizona |

*(Continued)*

(Continued)

| | |
|---|---|
| Beverly Mortimer | Concordia Public Schools, Kansas |
| Peter Negroni | The College Board, New York |
| Daniel Nerad | Birmingham Public Schools, Michigan |
| Richard Noonan | Wallingford–Swarthmore School District, Pennsylvania |
| Steven Norton | Cache County School District, Utah |
| Susan O'Brien | Torrington Public Schools, Connecticut |
| Les Omotani | Hewlett–Woodmere Public Schools, New York |
| Scott Palczewski | Kentwood Public Schools, Michigan |
| Thomas Perkins | Northern Local School District, Ohio |
| Valerie Pitts | Larkspur–Corte Madera Schools, California |
| Gary Plano | Mercer Island School District, Washington |
| Phillip Price | Mayfield Public Schools, Ohio |
| Steve Price | Hazelwood School District, Missouri |
| Joylynn Pruitt | University City Schools, Missouri |
| Steve Rasmussen | Issaquah School District, Washington |
| Gregory Riccio | Nadaburg Unified School District, Arizona |
| James Rickabaugh | School District of Whitefish Bay, Wisconsin |
| Gary Richardson | MOC–Floyd Valley Community Schools, Iowa |
| Janet Robinson | Newtown Public Schools, Connecticut |
| Thomas Rogers | Nassau Board of Cooperative Education Services, New York |
| Theresa Rouse | King City Union School District, California |
| George Russell | Eugene School District 4-J, Oregon |
| Kathleen Semergieff | Alpine Public Schools, New Jersey |
| Edward Seto | Franklin Township Public Schools, New Jersey |
| Claire Sheff Kohn | Masconomet Regional Schools, Massachusetts |
| Morton Sherman | Alexandria City Public Schools, Virginia |
| Richard Silverman | Randolph Public Schools, Massachusetts |
| Robert Slaby | Storey County School District, Nevada |

| | |
|---|---|
| Jemry Small | West Shore School District, Pennsylvania |
| Jeffrey Smith | Balsz Elementary School District, Arizona |
| David Snead | Waterbury Public Schools, Connecticut |
| Patricia Sullivan-Kriss | Hauppauge School District, New York |
| Bernard Taylor, Jr. | East Baton Rouge Parish Schools, Louisiana |
| Ira Trollinger | McDowell County Schools, North Carolina |
| Debra Van Gorp | Saydel Community Schools, Iowa |
| Lane Weiss | Saratoga Union School District, California |
| Don White | Troy Community Consolidated Schools, Illinois |
| Colleen Wilcox | Santa Clara County Schools, California |
| Preston Williams | Urbana School District 116, Illinois |
| Kathleen Willis | North Reading MEC, Massachusetts |
| Gerry Wilson | Poudre School District, Colorado |
| Phyllis Wilson | Joliet School District 86, Illinois |

# *Appendix D*

## *Contributors*

The experience of the contributors to this volume amounts to several hundred years' background in education. The affiliations listed here are the last held by the contributors in relation to their contributions to the *Fieldbook*.

| | |
|---|---|
| Pamela J. Ansingh | Seattle University, Seattle, Washington |
| Lynne Beckwith | University City Schools, University City, Missouri |
| John Brademas | New York University, New York, New York |
| Sharon Brumbaugh | State Department of Education, Harrisburg, Pennsylvania |
| Jonathan Budd | Joel Barlow High School, Easton, Connecticut |
| Alan Burke | Deputy Superintendent of Public Instruction, Olympia, Washington |
| Nelda Cambron-McCabe | Miami University, Oxford, Ohio |
| Mary Beth Celio | University of Washington, Seattle, Washington |
| Roland Chevalier | Senior Associate, Schlechty Center |
| Luvern L. Cunningham | The Ohio State University, Columbus, Ohio |
| Janis Dutton | Freelance writer, Oxford, Ohio |
| Janie Edmonds | Mendham Borough Schools, Mendham, New Jersey |
| Jim Ellsberry | Dewitt Institute for Professional Development |
| Will Friedman | Public Agenda Foundation, New York, New York |

*(Continued)*

(Continued)

| | |
|---|---|
| Ed Fuller | Pennsylvania State University, State College, Pennsylvania |
| Howard Fuller | Marquette University, Milwaukee, Wisconsin |
| Otto Graf | University of Pittsburgh, Pennsylvania |
| Gene Hall | University of Nevada, Las Vegas |
| James Harvey | National Superintendents Roundtable, Seattle, Washington |
| Constance Iervolino | White Plains City School District, New York |
| Kathleen Hall Jamieson | University of Pennsylvania, Philadelphia, Pennsylvania |
| Jack Jennings | Center on Education Policy, Washington, District of Columbia |
| Brent Johnson | Miami University, Oxford, Ohio |
| Bernard Josefsberg | Easton–Redding District 9, Easton, Connecticut |
| Adam Kernan-Schloss | A+ Communications, Arlington, Virginia |
| Art Kleiner | *Strategy+Business* magazine, New York |
| Robert H. Koff | Washington University, St. Louis, Missouri |
| Diana Lam | New York City Public Schools, New York |
| Mary Leiker | Kentwood Public Schools, Kentwood, Michigan |
| Gene Medina | North Kitsap Public Schools, North Kitsap, Washington |
| Linda Murray | Education Trust West, California |
| Peter Negroni | The College Board, New York, New York |
| Steven Norton | Cache County School District, North Logan, Utah |
| Barbara Omotani | Heartland Area Education Agency, Johnston, Iowa |
| Les Omotani | Hewlett–Woodmere Public Schools, New York |
| Beverly Parsons | InSites, Fort Collins, Colorado |
| Lee Pasquarella | Cascade Consulting, Bellevue, Washington |
| Bertha Pendleton | San Diego Public Schools, San Diego, California |
| Thomas Poetter | Miami University, Oxford, Ohio |
| Brad Portin | University of Washington, Seattle, Washington |
| Linda Powell Pruitt | New York University, New York, New York |
| Steve Price | Hazelwood Public Schools, Hazelwood, Missouri |
| Thomas Rogers | Nassau BOCES, Garden City, New York |

| | |
|---|---|
| Ethel Seiderman | Parent Services Project, San Rafael, California |
| Claire Sheff Kohn | Masconomet Public Schools, Masconomet, Massachusetts |
| Sylvia Soholt | A+ Communications, Arlington, Virginia |
| Circe Stumbo | West Wind Education Policy, Inc., Iowa City, Iowa |
| Richard C. Wallace, Jr. | Pittsburgh Public Schools, Pittsburgh, Pennsylvania |
| Gary Wegenke | Western Michigan University, Kalamazoo, Michigan |
| Emily White | Bank Street College of Education, New York |
| Saul Yanofsky | White Plains City School District, New York |
| Stephen Zsiray, Jr. | Cache County School District, North Logan, Utah |

# *Index*

**CORWIN**

A SAGE Company

The Corwin logo—a raven striding across an open book—represents the union of courage and learning. Corwin is committed to improving education for all learners by publishing books and other professional development resources for those serving the field of PreK–12 education. By providing practical, hands-on materials, Corwin continues to carry out the promise of its motto: **"Helping Educators Do Their Work Better."**

NATIONAL SUPERINTENDENTS ROUNDTABLE

The Roundtable, often called a think tank for superintendents, is a learning community that hones the leadership skills of its members by conducting intense analysis, expanding their professional horizons, and providing hands-on tools and new perspectives that draw on the wisdom and experience of prominent national and international leaders from a variety of fields.